# 16th International Conference e-Learning (EL2022)



Held at the 16th Multi-Conference on Computer Science and Information Systems (MCCSIS 2022)

Lisbon, Portugal
19-22 July 2022

**Editors:**

**Miguel Baptista Nunes**
**Pedro Isaias**
**Piet Kommers**
**Luís Rodrigues**

ISBN: 978-1-7138-6088-4

# INTERNATIONAL CONFERENCE

# E-LEARNING 2022

**part of the**

**MULTI CONFERENCE ON COMPUTER SCIENCE**

**AND INFORMATION SYSTEMS 2022**

# PROCEEDINGS
# OF THE
# INTERNATIONAL CONFERENCE

# E-LEARNING 2022

## JULY 19 - 21, 2022

Organised by

iadis

international association for development of the information society

As a member of Crossref (a non-profit membership organization for scholarly publishing working with the purpose to make content easy to find, link, cite and assess) each published paper in this book of proceedings will be allocated a DOI (Digital Object Identifier) number for its fast and easy citation and indexation.

Volume Editors:
Miguel Baptista Nunes and Pedro Isaias

Computer Science and Information Systems Series Editors:
Piet Kommers and Pedro Isaias

Associate Editor: Luís Rodrigues

# FOREWORD

These proceedings contain the papers of the 16th International Conference on e-Learning (EL 2022), which was organised by the International Association for Development of the Information Society, 19-21 July, 2022. This conference is part of the 16th Multi Conference on Computer Science and Information Systems 2022, 19-22 July, which had a total of 608 submissions.

The e-Learning (EL) 2022 conference aims to address the main issues of concern within e-Learning. This conference covers both technical as well as the non-technical aspects of e-Learning.

The conference accepted submissions in the following seven main areas: Organisational Strategy and Management Issues; Technological Issues; e-Learning Curriculum Development Issues; Instructional Design Issues; e-Learning Delivery Issues; e-Learning Research Methods and Approaches; e-Skills and Information Literacy for Learning.

The above referred main submission's areas are detailed below:

**Organisational Strategy and Management Issues**
- Higher and Further Education
- Primary and Secondary Education
- Workplace Learning
- Vocational Training
- Home Schooling
- Distance Learning
- Blended Learning
- Change Management
- Educational Management
- Continuous Professional Development (CPD) for Educational and Training Staff
- Return on e-Learning Investments (ROI)

**Technological Issues**
- Learning Management Systems (LMS)
- Managed Learning Environments (MLEs)
- Virtual Learning Environments (VLEs)
- Computer-Mediated Communication (CMC) Tools
- Social Support Software
- Architecture of Educational Information Systems Infrastructure
- Security and Data Protection
- Learning Objects
- XML Schemas and the Semantic Web
- Web 2.0 Applications

**e-Learning Curriculum Development Issues**
- Philosophies and Epistemologies for e-learning
- Learning Theories and Approaches for e-learning
- e-Learning Models
- Conceptual Representations
- Pedagogical Models
- e-Learning Pedagogical Strategies
- e-Learning Tactics
- Developing e-Learning for Specific Subject Domains

**Instructional Design Issues**
- Designing e-Learning Settings
- Developing e-Learning Pilots and Prototypes
- Creating e-Learning Courses
    - Collaborative learning
    - Problem-based learning
    - Inquiry-based learning
    - Blended Learning
    - Distance Learning
- Designing e-Learning Tasks
    - E-learning activities
    - Online Groupwork
    - Experiential Learning
    - Simulations and Modelling
    - Gaming and Edutainment
    - Creativity and Design Activities
    - Exploratory Programming

**e-Learning Delivery Issues**
- e-Delivery in different contexts
    - Higher and Further Education
    - Primary and Secondary Schools
    - Workplace Learning
    - Vocational Training
    - Distance Learning
- Online Assessment
- Innovations in e-Assessment
- e-Moderating
- e-Tutoring
- e-Facilitating
- Leadership in e-Learning Delivery
- Networked Information and Communication Literacy Skills
- Participation and Motivation in e-Learning

**e-Learning Research Methods and Approaches**
- Action Research
- Design Research
- Course and Programme Evaluations
- Systematic Literature Reviews
- Historical Analysis

- Case Studies
- Meta-analysis of Case Studies
- Effectiveness and Impact Studies
- Evaluation of e-Learning Technologies
- Evaluation of Student and Tutor Satisfaction
- Learning and Cognitive Styles
- Ethical Issues in e-Learning

**e-Skills and Information Literacy for Learning**
- Teaching Information Literacy
- Electronic Library and Information Search Skills
- ICT Skills Education
  - in schools and colleges
  - for business, industry and the public sector
  - in adult, community, home and prison education
  - informal methods (peer groups, family)
- Education for Computer-mediated Communication Skills
  - Netiquette
  - Online safety for children and vulnerable users
  - Cybercrime awareness and personal prevention
- Student Production of Online Media
  - Web design
  - Digital storytelling
  - Web 2.0 tools
  - etc.
- Digital Media Studies

The e-Learning 2022 conference received 112 submissions from more than 21 countries. Each submission has been anonymously reviewed by an average of four independent reviewers, to ensure that accepted submissions were of a high standard. Consequently, only 17 full papers were approved, which meant an acceptance rate of 15%. A few more papers were accepted as short and reflection papers. An extended version of the best papers will be selected for publishing in the Interactive Technology and Smart Education (ITSE) journal (ISSN:1741-5659) and also in the IADIS International Journal on WWW/Internet (ISSN: 1645 7641). Other outlets may also receive extended versions of the best papers.

Besides the papers' presentations, the conference also included one keynote presentation from an internationally distinguished researcher. We would therefore like to express our gratitude to Professor Piet Kommers, UNESCO Professor of Learning Technologies, The Netherlands, for being the e-Learning 2022 keynote speaker. The conference also featured one special talk by Professors: Cathie Norris, Regents Professor, University of North Texas, USA, Elliot Soloway, Arthur F. Thurnau Professor, University of Michigan, USA, and Anne Tapp, Professor, Dept. of Teacher Education, College of Education, Saginaw Valley State University, USA, and a talk by Dr Yaping Gao, EDD, Senior Academic Director, Member Services & Partnerships Quality Matters, USA.

A successful conference requires the effort of many individuals. We would like to thank the members of the Program Committee for their hard work in reviewing and selecting the papers that appear in this book. We are especially grateful to the authors who submitted their papers to this conference and to the presenters who provided the substance of the meeting. We wish to thank all members of our organizing committee.

Last but not least, we hope that everybody enjoyed the presentations, and we invite all participants for next year's edition of the International Conference on e-Learning.

Miguel Baptista Nunes, School of Information Management, Sun Yat-sen University, Guangzhou, China
Pedro Isaias, The University of New South Wales (UNSW – Sydney), Australia
*e-Learning 2022 Conference Program Co-Chairs*

Piet Kommers, University of Twente, The Netherlands
*MCCSIS 2022 General Conference Co-Chair*

July 2022

# PROGRAM COMMITTEE

### E-LEARNING 2022CONFERENCE PROGRAM CO-CHAIRS

Miguel Baptista Nunes, School of Information Management, Sun Yat-Sen University, Guangzhou, China
Pedro Isaias, The University of New South Wales (UNSW – Sydney), Australia

### MCCSIS 2022 GENERAL CONFERENCE CO-CHAIRS

Piet Kommers, University of Twente, The Netherlands
Pedro Isaias, The University of New South Wales (UNSW – Sydney), Australia

### E-LEARNING 2022 CONFERENCE COMMITTEE MEMBERS

Adamantios Koumpis, RWTH Aachen, Germany
Alex Voychenko, International Research and Training Center for ITS, Ukraine
Alexandru Vulpe, University Politehnica of Bucharest, Romania
Ana Barata, ISEP-GILT, Portugal
Andreas Bollin, Klagenfurt University, Austria
Andreas Papasalouros, University of the Aegean, Greece
Angélica De Antonio, Universidad Politecnica de Madrid, Spain
Ania Lian, Australian Catholic University, Australia
Antoanela Naaji, Vasile Goldis West University of Arad, Romania
Antonio Hervás-Jorge, Universidad Politécnica de Valencia, Spain
Antonio Navarro, Universidad Complutense de Madrid, Spain
Apostolos Gkamas, University Ecclesiastical Academy of Vella of Ioan, Greece
Bertil P. Marques, Instituto Superior de Engenharia do Porto (ISEP) -, Portugal
Charalampos Karagiannidis, University of Thessaly, Greece
Christos Bouras, University of Patras, Greece
Christos Troussas, University of West Attica, Greece
Claudia Steinberger, Klagenfurt University, Austria
David Guralnick, Kaleidoscope Learning, United States
Demetrios Sampson, University of Piraeus, Greece
Dessislava Vassileva, Sofia University "St. Kliment Ohridski", Bulgaria
Dimitra Pappa, National Center for Scientific Research - Demokritos, Greece
Eliza Stefanova, Sofia University, Bulgaria
Elliot Soloway, University of Michigan, USA
Erick Araya, University Austral of Chile, Chile
Esteban Vázquez Cano, Spanish National University of Distance Education, Spain
Eugenia Kovatcheva, University of Library Studies and Information Technologies, Bulgaria
Eva Jereb, University of Maribor, Slovenia
Francesca Pozzi, Instituto Tecnologie Didattiche – CNR, Italy
Gabriela Grosseck, West University of Timisoara, Romania
George Tsihrintzis, University of Piraeus, Greece
Giovanni Bonaiuti, University of Cagliari, Italy
Giuliano Vivanet, University of Cagliari, Italy
Ibrahim Ahmed, University of Bahrain, Bahrain
Isidoros Perikos, University of Patras, Greece
Jennifer-Carmen Frey, European Academy of Bozen/Bolzano, Italy
Jose Bidarra, Open University, Portugal

# KEYNOTE LECTURE

## NEEDS AND TOOLS FOR ARTIFICIAL INTELLIGENCE IN 21$^{ST}$ CENTURY SOCIETY

**Professor Piet Kommers, UNESCO Professor of Learning Technologies, The Netherlands**

## ABSTRACT

The Covid-19 era unexpectedly made all sectors dependent from remote communication, virtual- and vicarious learning.

This lecture is based upon the new book: "Sources for a Better Education: Lessons from Research and Best Practices".

It signals parallels in society, technology, and demonstrates the risk for biased information; not just lacking knowledge or naïve misconceptions. Starting from abundant information access we now see tempting options for learners to restructure and even reconceive existing information. From the perspective of cognitive growth, the last four decades let learners 're-construct meaning' to stimulate highly individualized understanding: Simulations, modelling, concept mapping, and lately the cultivation of storytelling; they have been promoted as an extra to just absorbing new knowledge. So far, education still underestimated the flip side of constructivist learning practices: Critical thinking seemed to be a good candidate for a more active learning attitude; It may create more authentic students who build upon existential drive: "What do I need to 'make a difference' in life. Problem- and challenge-based learning are the keywords. The book appetizer "Sources for a better Education" exposes the landscape of learning theories and how teachers can benefit from the larger spectrum of A.I. tools: big data, data mining, deep learning, machine learning, learning analytics and multi-variate inductive reasoning? This lecture will guide you to the main questions: What didactic measures allow teachers to make students resilient to fake news? What scenarios for thematic- rather than mono-disciplinary courses need to be developed? For instance, in the attempts to implement and disseminate STEAM (Science, Technology, Engineering, Arts and Mathematics)? What social media mechanisms lead to web-based communities? And: What are valid ways to assess the quality of learning outcomes? I hope to meet you and your counter questions imaginary Lisbon.

# SPECIAL TALK

## USING DEEPLY-DIGITAL CURRICULA TO SUPPORT ALPHA GENERATION LEARNERS: FINDINGS FROM A THREE-YEAR STUDY

**Cathie Norris, Regents Professor, University of North Texas, USA**

**Elliot Soloway, Arthur F. Thurnau Professor, University of Michigan, USA**

**&**

**Anne Tapp, Professor, Dept. of Teacher Education, College of Education, Saginaw Valley State University, USA**

## ABSTRACT

Research suggests that current curricula and pedagogy need to change to effectively support Alpha Generation children in elementary and middle school. Born after 2010, Alphas, truly the "digital-first" generation, have grown up tapping on screens, not watching TV or sitting with paper-based books. Towards addressing the learning needs of Alphas in K-5, we have been conducting a study of how deeply-digital, highly-interactive curricula plus digitally-motivated, pedagogical practices can increase their engagement and achievement. Over the past three years, 10,000+ children, from low socio-economic-status (SES), K-5 schools in Michigan, have been using deeply-digital, standards-aligned, "Roadmap" curricula developed by the University of Michigan's Center for Digital Curricula (UM.CDC). The year-long, free to schools, curricula in English, social studies, math and science employ a social-constructivist learning framework.

Hosting those deeply-digital Roadmap lessons is the Collabrify Roadmap Platform, also developed by the UM.CDC. Device-independent and browser-based, the Platform supports a range of Alpha-aligned learning practices. For example, the Platform makes it easy for students to synchronously collaborate, e.g., a student, quarantined at home, can talk through the computer to a student in the classroom, as they work in the same document.

Deeply-digital Roadmap lessons are expressed as visual lesson plans. On a Roadmap, a learner can literally see where learning starts, where it ends, and all the learning activities along the way. Learning activities are encapsulated in nodes; click a node and the hyperlink takes the student to a learning activity. Learning activities can point to OER or they can point to licensed, commercial materials. Roadmaps are open – any URL can be included in Roadmap lesson.

Learning activities can also employ a suite of productivity tools expressly designed by UM.CDC to support Alphas. For example, as video and audio are primary media for Alphas – like text is for other generations – the productivity tools make manipulating audio, video, and drawings as easy as manipulating text. Emotionally-impaired students, who are silent in class, become hyper-engaged when video-recording themselves telling their stories using MediaWriter. As Roadmap lessons visually provide students with a start to finish learning pathway, teachers employ pedagogical moves to better support students engaging in self-regulated learning.

In the school year 2020-21, during the height of the COVID disruption, at one school where the focus was on science and K-5 students used the Platform with deeply-digital, NGSS-aligned science curricula, the Assistant Principal commented on the children exhibiting a dramatic improvement on a standardized-test in science: "... despite periods of extended school shut down and COVID-related absences ... Having the learning tools and content on the Roadmap platform has been a game changer." In an urban school, the Director of Curriculum and Instruction noted: "Our teachers and students find the Roadmap curricula engaging ... We are seeing more students progressing quicker towards their growth goals than we did prior to implementing Roadmaps."

In our presentation, then, we will describe more fully our findings and lay out our plans to continue expanding the reach of the Platform + curricula, and expanding Platform's library of deeply-digital curricula for other subjects and other grades to reach all the Alphas!

# TALK

## ENSURING ACADEMIC QUALITY AND STUDENT SUCCESS IN ELEARNING: EVERYONE HAS A ROLE!

**Dr Yaping Gao, EDD**
**Senior Academic Director, Member Services & Partnerships Quality Matters, USA**

## ABSTRACT

One of the most important lessons that institutions all over the world have learned from the disruptive impact of the COVID pandemic is that we need to be more resilient and better prepared for an unpredictable future. As a result, institutions are making big investments in digital transformation in order to offer online/blended/digital learning in different formats to meet the needs of an increasingly diverse student population. However, among the disconnections and silos taking place at institutions are the lack of common understanding of institutional goals and coordinated efforts from all internal stakeholders. As institutions continue to face tightening budget, it becomes increasingly important to examine and realign resources needed to ensure academic quality and help all students succeed.

Participates in this session will be engaged to examine and reflect on 1) what digital transformation entails at an academic institution, 2) how to ensure quality in teaching and learning at course, program and institutional level during digital transformation, and 3) how each of us contribute to ensure academic quality and student success regardless the role we play at the institution.

Learning Outcomes / Take-aways for Participants

- Define digital transformation and the components/shifts needed
- Articulate the relationship between digital transformation and quality teaching and learning
- Describe the importance of ensuring quality at course, program and institutional levels
- Reflect on the role each of us plays in the process

Participant Benefits:

Participants will gain a big picture of why digital transformation is necessary for their institution, reflect on how each of us contribute to the process, and appreciate how important it is for all stakeholders to work together to ensure quality for teaching and learning in the new digital environment.

Targeting Participants:

- Faculty and support staff such as instructional designer or technologists who support faculty with course design, development and delivery
- Middle or senior-level administrators, deans or directors or managers responsible for offering online/ blended programs
- IT professionals who are responsible for providing infrastructure and technology tools to teaching and learning
- Executive directors or officers responsible for e-learning initiatives and/or digital transformation

**KEYWORDS**

Academic Quality, Quality Assurance, Student Success, Digital Transformation, Engage Stakeholders.

# FULL PAPERS

# SHINE A LIGHT – E-LEARNING INITIATIVES FROM TWO EU PROJECTS

Vladan Devedžić[1], Sonja D. Radenković[2] and Mirjana Devedžić[3]
*[1]University of Belgrade, Faculty of Organizational Sciences, Jove Ilića 154, 11000 Belgrade, Serbia*
*[2]Union University, Belgrade Banking Academy – Faculty of Banking, Insurance and Finance, Zmaj Jovina 12, 11000 Belgrade, Serbia*
*[3]University of Belgrade, Faculty of Geography, Studentski trg 3, 11000 Belgrade, Serbia*

**ABSTRACT**

The paper presents ideas and initiatives from two ongoing Erasmus+ projects funded by the European Commission. Both projects use e-Learning as an enabler for communicating interesting and important learning contents that are believed to increase and improve employability prospects for the targeted groups of learners. The WINnovators project targets young women with reduced opportunities for quality education in different areas of STEM/STEAM and intends to demonstrate how their entrepreneurial skills can gradually grow by providing them with e-Learning incentives in such areas. The YNSPEED project intends to offer free MOOC courses addressing hot topics of modern society – artificial intelligence, sustainable development, and fake news. In the YNSPEED project, the target group of learners are young people (aged 16-29). It is believed that their interest in such important topics can be boosted by communicating the corresponding relevant learning content in a carefully designed way. The *Shine a light* metaphor is a common point and a common approach in both projects – e-Learning technology is used to facilitate informal education for the targeted learners and to indicate directions that often get either omitted or misunderstood in traditional schools.

**KEYWORDS**

Informal Education, Disadvantaged Learners, Youth, MOOC, Artificial Intelligence, Entrepreneurial Skills

## 1. INTRODUCTION

According to IGI Global (2022), disadvantaged learners are those who face specific challenges compared to their peers. This category of learners does not include only learners with disabilities. The challenges of such learners can take many other forms, like poverty, family issues, little or no family support, many school moves, pregnancy, the necessity to earn a living in addition to attending classes and studying, etc. In addition, the recent Covid-19 pandemic has shown that in low-income societies, as well as in societies where online learning faces difficulties related to low bandwidth and instable Internet connection, many students have less chances to get appropriate education.

Still, as many post-pandemic analyses indicate – e.g., (Horváth et al. 2022) – the world of education is shifting more and more towards online education. Many analysts agree that hybrid/blended education arrangements, i.e., appropriate mixtures of online and offline activities supporting the study process best reflect the current needs of education at different levels.

On the other hand, informal education by means of e-Learning often provides some "missing links" that schools usually omit in the teaching they provide (Eshach 2006). To disadvantaged learners, these might fulfill some of the educational needs that bring such learners closer to their peers who do not suffer from disadvantages in their education. Although this typically does not provide an absolute leveling of opportunities, it certainly opens new avenues for disadvantaged groups to better employability.

It is also important to note that young people, defined by Eurostat (2022) as people with age between 15 and 29 years, often lack appropriate information on important topics underlying the driving forces of modern society. This creates another "missing link" in school education, most frequently for those young people who do not go to college. Consequently, a considerable proportion of youth still remain rather ignorant of essential processes in industry, economy, business, and technology.

To address these issues, the European Commission funds different projects in the area of education with the common objective of narrowing the gap between disadvantaged groups of learners and those with better access to education, as well as projects focusing specifically on education of youth.

This paper presents ideas and initiatives taken by two such projects funded by the Erasmus+ program. It also discusses common points of these two projects, albeit they are of a different nature, are being developed and implemented by different consortia, and target somewhat different groups of learners.

## 2. THE WINNOVATORS PROJECT

The WINnovators project (Boosting young women entrepreneurial spirit and skills to become the women innovators of the future, https://www.winnovators.eu/) focuses on using e-Learning technology to help young women from rural areas build and develop their digital, entrepreneurial, and STEM/STEAM skills. Of course, STEM/STEAM refers to the creation of innovative educational materials, which encourage innovation, critical thinking and problem-solving using knowledge from science (S), technology (T), engineering (E), art (A) and mathematics (M) (White 2014).

By targeting young women from rural areas, the WINnovators project aims at promoting gender equality and create educational opportunities for those young women who are disadvantaged to this end when compared to women living in cities and other more developed regions where education is more accessible. Examples of disadvantages of such young women include:

- *Lower income*. Life in rural areas is often correlated with lower income compared to life in urban centers. Access to quality education typically means high costs, and these are not easily affordable for people in rural areas.
- *Lifestyle*. In many countries, women in rural areas are expected to work in agriculture and simultaneously take care of the household they live in (Belingheri et al. 2021). The time they can allocate for education is limited and can be the key factor for giving up education (AFA Network 2022).
- *Family duties*. Patriarchal lifestyle, still prevailing in rural areas in many countries, means that it is women who take care of children the most. Pregnancy often only increases these duties. As a consequence, young women in rural areas stay at home more than men.
- *Mindset*. The lifestyle in rural areas has already created a mindset that in many cases holds back young women who want to get better education.
- *Lack of computer literacy*. Women make up a higher percentage of the illiterate and computer illiterate population compared to men in all age groups, and the differences are even more pronounced between urban and rural areas (AFA Network 2022).

In order to address these issues and offer better educational opportunities for such young women in rural areas, the WINnovators project has started from the following ideas:

- There *are* points and assets in lifestyles of young women in rural areas that can be used as a good starting ground for furthering their education. For example, selling agricultural products on green markets can be augmented with selling them online as well, simultaneously leaving more time for home duties. Likewise, rural tourism (agrotourism) can bring additional income to many families and can be a great opportunity for young women in villages to develop their entrepreneurship. Still, both these activities require additional education in entrepreneurship, digital marketing, Web development, and the like. Informal education by means of e-Learning can help to this end. This is perfectly in line with the observations of Eshach (2006), who has noticed that the potential of out-of-school learning is not fully exploited. Back in 2006, it was probably even less exploited than it is today, but new underexploited opportunities continue to arise.
- Technology helps, although it is not a panacea. Mobile phones and Internet access are often sufficient prerequisites for basic e-Learning. The bandwidth problem remains in some cases.
- It is the networking with target learners, appropriate content (the learning material) and a carefully designed pedagogical approach that can start off some changes – changes in attitudes, in mindset, and in lifestyles, reducing eventually the disadvantages of living in rural areas.

Figure 1 illustrates the approach taken by the WINnovators project in order to develop these ideas in practice. Once the project is completed, the expected results will include:

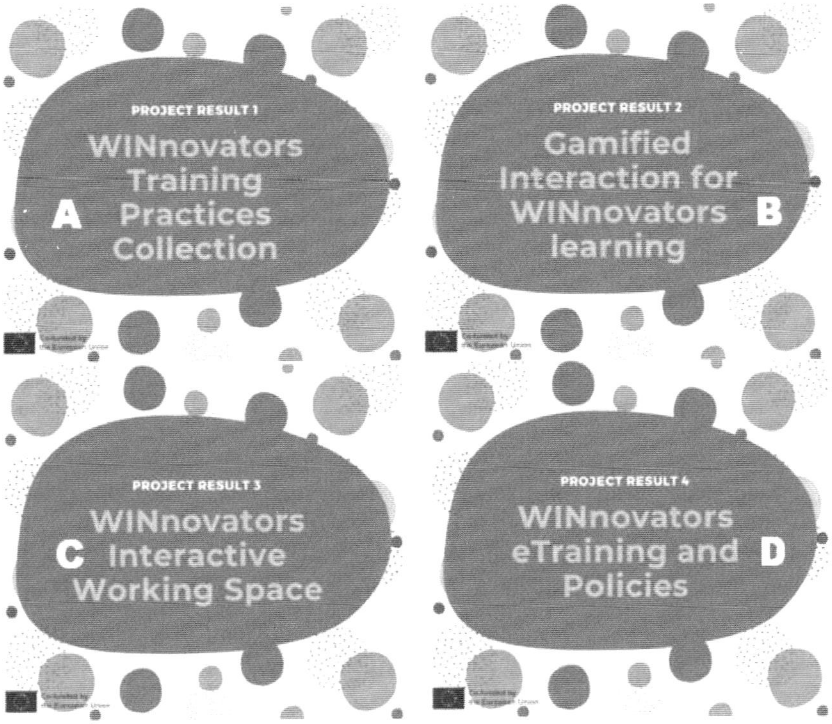


Figure 1. The WINnovators project results

- The collection of training practices (Figure 1A) that involve college students in providing training to the targeted young women. The idea is to have both university teachers and students run online training sessions with young women in selected STEM/STEAM, entrepreneurship, sustainability, and other relevant disciplines. The students can act as capacity developing agents for young women in their communities, thus adding value to the process in the form of their college learning practices. It is believed that similar age and energy that university students acting as teachers bring to the training sessions can benefit the learners. All the experiences and best practices from these sessions will be collected and published.
- Specific capacity building actions run by the WINnovators project through the development of an educational Open Innovative Ecosystem (OIE) based on gamification (Figure 1B). The gamification principles can contribute to the creation of entrepreneurial, STEM/STEAM digital skills of young women at risk of marginalization in rural and outskirts communities.
- The interactive working space (Figure 1C) as the main tangible result of the WINnovators project. It is essentially an e-Learning platform and a collection of valuable learning resources for both the teachers and learners. The interaction between the learners and the teachers by means of a gamified approach promotes STEM/STEAM, innovation, and entrepreneurship among the targeted young women, supported by higher education students.
- The WINnovators project will eventually suggest valuable measures to policy makers in order to tackle the lack of cooperation and capacity building activities between disadvantaged students and businesses (Figure 1D). This will help improve and update different teaching approaches in terms of supporting sustainability, entrepreneurship, and innovation.

There is also an important general question here: *who exactly* are the women that the WINnovators project targets, and *how to reach them*? To this end, the WINnovators project maintains contacts with different women associations in the countries of origin of the project partners. Through these associations, information about the project and relevant questionnaires are distributed among women in rural areas and suitable candidates are recruited for free e-Learning sessions with university teachers and students who train the candidates in local languages in STEM/STEAM, entrepreneurship, and sustainability topics and provide guidance in using online learning resources developed by the project participants.

## 3. THE YNSPEED PROJECT

The focus of the YNSPEED project (Youth new personal & employable skills development, https://ynspeed.mystrikingly.com/) is on youth education. The objective is to provide more information to young learners about important topics and themes of today's society, those that often do not fit in school programs but are essential in understanding technology and practices underlying industry, businesses, economy, education, mind-shaping societal changes, and generally in getting oriented and understanding real-life situations. The topics and themes covered include artificial intelligence (AI), sustainable development, fake news, and learning English with the help of technology.

The major project results are four different massive open online courses (MOOCs), one for each of the four broad topics, developed by the YNSPEED project consortium and offered to youth learners through a MOOC platform in English and in the local languages spoken in the YNSPEED project partner countries.

A "pedagogical sugar" added in development of all four MOOCs is the participation of skilled young people. In other words, parts of the courses are developed by young people, not only by experts with years of experience in the related topics. This is considered motivating for young learners – they are more likely to interact and to resonate better with people of their age than with senior teachers, resulting in more interest in MOOC videos and other learning materials featuring young people.

Who are these skilled young people, specifically? The term adopted in the YNSPEED project is *youth workers*. Wikipedia (2022) defines a youth worker as "a person that works with young people to facilitate their personal, social, and educational development through informal education, care (e.g., preventive), or leisure approaches. Youth workers can work in many contexts and according to the roles they are known as enablers, facilitators, emancipators, animators, or could be known by the set of activities they use to reach out to youth. The validity of youth work approaches is based on whether they are educational, participative, empowering, promote equality of opportunities, etc. The basic principles of youth work are respecting young people, providing accessible and value-oriented opportunities (genuinely useful) for voluntary participation, accountability, being anti-oppressive (e.g., social model of disability, unconscious bias training) in processes, confidentiality, reliability, trustworthiness, and being ethical in keeping boundaries." Most youth workers participating in the YNSPEED project are university students, young teaching assistants, and PhD candidates, who are already sufficiently skilled and knowledgeable in the topics covered by the YNSPEED project MOOCs. Also, some young people employed by relevant companies and institutions or running relevant startups are part of the MOOCs as well.

In order to illustrate the approach and the essentials of the MOOCs developed by the YNSPEED project, one of the MOOCS is presented here in more detail. It is the AI MOOC, called AIM4YOU (AI for Young People). AIM4YOU is developed by 7 university teachers and 8 youth workers. They work in 5 different countries, spanning different cultural backgrounds and contexts.

The topics covered in the AIM4YOU MOOC are hot topics in AI nowadays – robotics, machine learning, neural networks, natural-language processing, self-driving cars, AI ethics, etc. – as well as some foundational topics like knowledge representation, reasoning, rule-based systems, and the like. The topics are presented in 80+ short videos, developed in English (with subtitles), and include a number of examples carefully designed to bring the presented topics closer to young learners' minds. For each major topic, there are always introductory videos, quizzes, and further readings to select from the menu. Figure 2 gives an idea of learners' interaction with AIM4YOU.

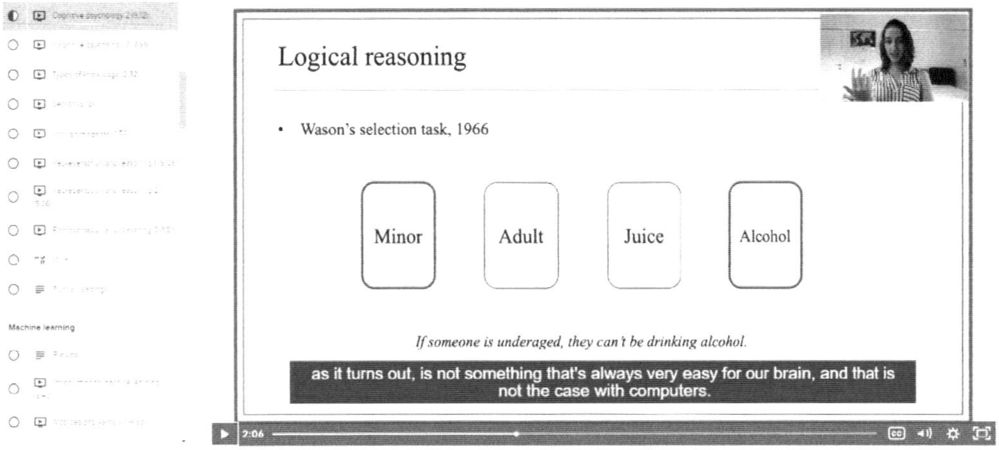


Figure 2. A screenshot from an AIM4YOU MOOC

To reach potential learners, the YNSPEED project promotes its MOOCs extensively, both online and through special events organized for young people. The events feature presentations given by the project participants and youth workers, networking activities, as well as Q&A sessions intended to motivate young learners to take the four MOOCs free of charge. In addition, several promotional videos have been developed in order to increase the number of visits to the platform running the four MOOCs (e.g., https://cdn.fs.teachablecdn.com/h4m6YN3TPCQlyCQSTKlR).

## 4. DISCUSSION

The motivation of both the WINnovators an YNSPEED project development teams in running these projects is to bring interesting and important learning contents closer to learners who need them. To this end, both projects have common points:

- Providing critical skills related to using the Internet to specific groups of learners who might not be aware of them (such as disadvantaged young women and youth). Many Internet users from these populations are not using the Internet for education to its full capacity (Eshach 2006). Thus, the WINnovators and YNSPEED projects are driven by the same Shine a Light metaphor, meaning that opening different educational avenues through e-Learning tools can benefit the targeted groups.
- The skills taught in the WINnovators and YNSPEED projects are nowadays compulsory for an active and responsible digital citizen. Such skills will be useful not only for a brief period of time, but also for lifelong learning and employability – all of them are listed among the required skills that employers are looking for and will be looking for in the forthcoming years (World Economic Forum 2020).
- Both projects also want to develop and increase entrepreneurial spirit with the targeted learners. In some cases, the innate feeling for entrepreneurship can be enough, but training young people in sustainability, finance, digital marketing, and modern AI technologies can raise their entrepreneurship to a much higher level.
- Informal learning through MOOCs and other e-Learning technology can be an eye-opener for many young people. Both the WINnovators and YNSPEED projects intend to introduce certification of the efforts of learners who complete the training courses developed by the project teams. Gamification elements (e.g., badges) introduce digital certificates and micro credentials that nowadays more and more employers informally recognize as evidence of informally acquired competences fostering employability.

- Both projects implicitly prepare young people and disadvantaged learners for lifelong learning by involving them in a process of operationalizing the newly acquired skills in sustainable ways.
- From the pedagogical and methodological points of view, both projects rely on active participation of youth workers. In the results achieved by the projects so far, this decision has proven to be beneficial for both the youth workers and the targeted learners.
- Likewise, both projects have similar tangible outputs – e-Learning platforms used for storing learning materials and for enabling active learning through educational social networking activities (collaboration, group work, discussions, and the like).
- Last but not least, both projects offer training in skills that are not just career skills but can positively affect other aspects of life like communication, healthcare, social aspects, everyday activities, etc.

## 5. CONCLUSION

The two projects described in this paper target somewhat different groups of learners and allow to assess somewhat different pedagogical contexts but share similar learning scenarios and experiences. The most important among them are related to increasing young people's employability prospects through learning informally about topics of importance for their careers and for living in modern society in general, as well as raising awareness of different kinds of knowledge, tools, technologies, and lifelong learning approaches underlying distinct aspects of living in the real world.

Note, however, that neither of these projects guarantees employment to young people who attend the training and complete the courses developed by the project teams. Employment, entrepreneurship, and career building are still on the learners themselves. The two projects act as enablers in developing critical skills that come useful in career building for the targeted young learners.

An important feature of both projects is the active participation of youth workers in training courses that the projects run, in preparation of learning materials, in networking activities, in dissemination of the project results, and in policy-development activities related to the targeted groups of learners. Involving youth workers in all the project activities is an advantage, since, truly, there are many similar courses on the Web that anyone can take.

Both projects are still ongoing, and there are no statistics yet related to running the training courses and the MOOCs developed. However, initial reactions from young learners who have received the news about the projects, as well as the informal pilot tests organized by the project teams are very encouraging.

## ACKNOWLEDGEMENT

This paper results from the authors' work on the WINnovators and YNSPEED projects, both funded by the Erasmus+ program of the European Commission. The European Commission support for the production of this publication does not constitute an endorsement of the contents which reflects the views only of the authors, and the Commission cannot be held responsi-ble for any use which may be made of the information contained therein.

## REFERENCES

AFA Network 2022, *The position of rural women in Serbia*, viewed 22 April 2022, < https://www.afa.co.rs/post/polo%C5%BEaj-%C5%BEena-na-selu-u-srbiji> (in Serbian).

Belingheri, P. et al., 2021, Twenty Years of Gender Equality Research: A scoping review based on a new semantic indicator, *PLOS ONE*, 16(9), viewed 22 April 2022, < https://journals.plos.org/plosone/article?id=10.1371/journal.pone.0256474 >.

Eshach, H., 2006, Bridging in-school and out-of-school learning: Formal, non-formal, and informal education. *Journal of Science Education and Technology*, 16(2), pp.171–190.

Eurostat 2022, *Overview - Youth*, viewed 22 April 2022, <https://ec.europa.eu/eurostat/web/youth>.

Horváth, D. et al., 2022, Online only: Future outlooks of post-pandemic education based on student experiences of the Virtual University, *Society and Economy*, 44(1), pp.2–21.

IGI Global 2022, *What is disadvantaged students*, viewed 22 April 2022, <https://www.igi-global.com/dictionary/inclusive-universities/57684>.

White, D., 2014, What is STEM education and why is it important? *Florida Association of Teacher Educators Journal*, 14(1), pp. 1-9, viewed 22 May 2022, < http://www.fate1.org/journals/2014/white.pdf>

Wikipedia 2022, *Youth worker*, viewed 22 April 2022, < https://en.wikipedia.org/wiki/Youth_worker>.

World Economic Forum 2020, *The Future of Jobs Report 2020*, viewed 22 April 2022, <https://www.weforum.org/reports/the-future-of-jobs-report-2020>.

# UNIVERSITY STUDENTS GRADING BEFORE AND DURING COVID-19 CRISIS

Nello Scarabottolo
*Università degli Studi di Milano, Milan, Italy*

**ABSTRACT**

The paper analyses the grades assigned by the professors of the University of Milan to their students at the end of written exams, comparing what happened in academic year 2018-19 and in academic year 2020-21, i.e., before and during the crisis caused by the Covid-19 pandemic.
In March 2020, the lockdown closed the classrooms, stopping face-to-face interactions among professors and students: it became then necessary to identify possible scenarios for carrying on written exams online, suitably monitoring student behaviors, and to propose them to the University professors.
Main purpose of the analysis reported in this paper is a preliminary evaluation of the effectiveness of these scenarios, through comparison of the grades the professors assigned to their students.

**KEYWORDS**

Written Exams, Online Student Monitoring, Exam Sessions, Grades Assigned to Students.

## 1. INTRODUCTION

As already presented in recent e-learning conferences (Haus et al. 2020, Haus et al. 2021, Scarabottolo 2022) the lockdown imposed by the Covid-19 pandemic around the end of February 2020 forced the Italian Universities to transfer suddenly online all the teaching activities normally carried on with students physically present in classrooms.

To understand better the context and the dimensions of the problem, it is worth noticing the presence at the University of Milan of 67 bachelor degrees (3 years, 180 ECTS – European Credit Transfer System – credits) 64 master degrees (2 years after bachelor, 120 ECTS credits) and 9 single-cycle master degrees (5 or 6 years, 300 or 360 ECTS credits). According to the rules of the Italian University system, these degrees are allocated to different groups of professors, belonging to entities called (for historical reasons) faculties or schools.

In our University, we have eight faculties: Agricultural and Food Sciences, Humanities, Law, Medicine, Pharmacy, Political, Economic and Social Sciences, Science and Technology, Veterinary Medicine, and two schools: Exercise and Sport Sciences, Language Mediation & Intercultural Communication. They group 2179 staff professors and almost 2000 contract professors (supported by 1960 technical and administrative staff units) teach every year more than 3000 courses.

Despite the dimensions of the University, classroom lectures were transferred online without dramatic effort, by asking professor to adopt streaming and recording in equipped rooms as well as using their own personal computers. The support offered by the university personnel mainly consisted in a set of instructions published on the web portal, helping professors in using streaming and recording facilities and in publishing didactical materials on the proprietary LMS (Learning Management System). Similar approach has been followed to allow the thesis discussion of graduating students: the web conference platforms used for lectures have been adopted also to connect these students from home with the committee of professors evaluating their final exam.

Exams at the end of single courses were initially converted in oral form, allowing interaction between professors and single students by web conferencing supports (e.g., Teams, Zoom, Skype). However, several courses in our university are followed by huge numbers of students, making impractical to examine in oral form each of them. Moreover, in an oral exam, it is hard to ask students to solve problems requiring (even a short) autonomous work, and it is not easy to find a set of equally difficult questions to pose to several students.

To overcome the above limits, a group of experts (including the author of this paper) was asked to identify monitoring scenarios and tools allowing remote control of student behavior (to avoid usage of unauthorized supports and cheating) during written exams performed at home. After several tests and analyses of tools offered by the market, we proposed two scenarios for online student monitoring during written exams to the professors of the University of Milan, depending on the number of students registered to the same exam session. In particular, it has been decided the threshold of 100 students as the discrimination between SMALL and LARGE exam session. In fact, it is proper considering that:

- a reasonable student number that can be monitored by a single person is in the range 20-30;
- it is not worth to ask professors to split students in more than 4 to 5 groups, to be monitored in parallel (with the help of some collaborators) or one after each other.

Figure 1. Direct monitoring of student during a written exam

## 1.1 Direct Monitoring

For SMALL exam sessions, the envisioned exam scenario, deeply described in (Haus et al. 2020) requires that each group of 20÷30 students is monitored using a web conference platform (e.g., Microsoft Teams, Zoom, etc.) established between the computer of the professor and the smartphone of each student, placed behind her/him to allow a very effective proctoring. In fact, the professor can control that no forbidden material (e.g., books, written notes, etc.) is used by the student during the exam; moreover, by zooming on each student window in the web conference, the professor can look at the desktop and see if the student is operating correctly (i.e., using only the allowed applications). Figure 1 gives an example of such a monitoring scenario.

For open answer tests, the exam is carried on using the exam.net platform (Exam.net 2020) implemented by the Swedish company Teachiq AB, characterized by:

- the adoption of SEB – Secure Exam Browser (SEB 2020) – that turns any computer temporarily into a secure workstation, forbidding usage of other programs and resources during an exam;

- a very easy professor interface, greatly facilitating creation and test of exams;
- real time monitoring of student work, since the professor can browse among students and see what each of them already wrote;
- a chat support, allowing the professor to interact with every student without disturbing the overall group.

An example of what this platform allows is given in Figure 2: on the left information regarding the exam, on the right real time monitoring of the exam of a single student.

For closed answer quizzes, not easy to implement with exam.net, direct integration of SEB with the Moodle LMS hosting the quizzes has been adopted.

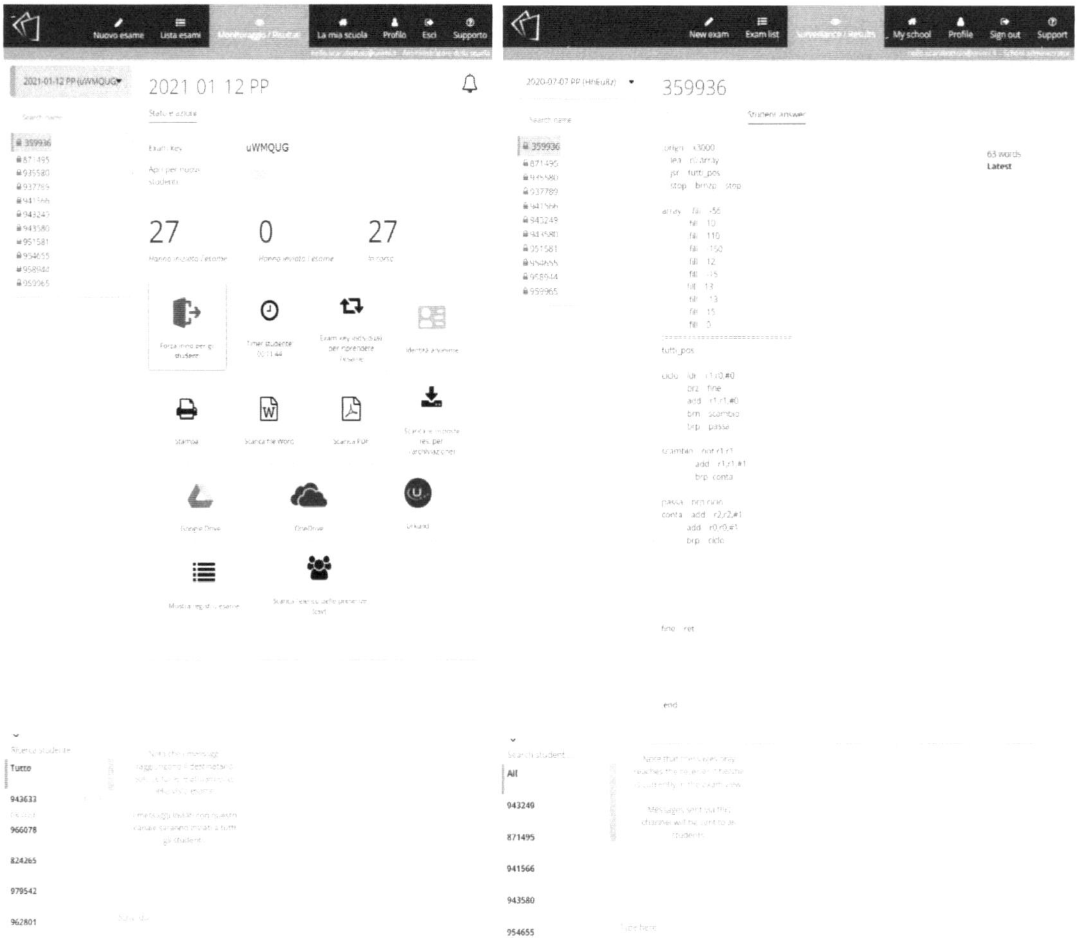


Figure 2. Characteristics of the exam.net platform

## 1.2 Software Supported Proctoring

For LARGE sessions, where direct monitoring would require too many professors/collaborators, we decided to use a proctoring tool available on the market, designed to record the behaviour of each student during the exam through the webcam of her/his computer. After the end of the exam, all recordings are processed by suitable Artificial Intelligence algorithms, that mark "suspect" behaviours of each student (e.g., eyes or head movements, noises, appearance of other people, etc.) to allow the professor to analyse them and decide accordingly how to manage student evaluation.

After some tests, we adopted Proctorio (Proctorio 2020) mainly for these reasons:

- Proctorio uses a simple add-on for browsers like Chrome that creates a secure exam environment by restricting internet navigation and computer functionality, thus facilitating student computer setup;
- student behaviour monitoring is very accurate, since Proctorio records the webcam stream and also the desktop of the student computer;
- the browser add-on sends only some video frames instead of a continuous streaming, thus significantly reducing the network bandwidth requirements (and facilitating monitoring of students with poor internet connections);
- the final AI algorithm can be tuned by the professor in terms of sensitivity to the different kinds of suspected behaviours after receiving the recorded exams; this allows the professor to emphasize the aspects considered most dangerous and/or more common.

## 2. EXAM SESSIONS BEFORE AND DURING PANDEMIC

A first analysis is the comparison between a normal academic year (2018-19, before Covid-19 pandemic) and the academic year 2020-21, when all exams have been carried on online due to the various limitations imposed by the lockdown rules.

Table 1 shows the numbers of SMALL and LARGE written exam sessions per month in 2018-19 and 2020-21 (August has been omitted, since almost no exams take place during the traditional Italian vacation month).

It is interesting to note that almost in every month the number of SMALL sessions decreased during pandemic, with the exception of May. The most likely explanation for that is the delay in defining the scenarios recalled above, that forced professors to postpone exams during the first pandemic months (March-April 2020).

Table 1. SMALL and LARGE exam sessions in 2018-19 and 2020-21 per month

| **Month** | **SMALL exam sessions** | | | **LARGE exam sessions** | | |
|---|---|---|---|---|---|---|
| | **2018-19** | **2020-21** | ***delta*** | **2018-19** | **2020-21** | ***delta*** |
| January | 1'150 | 992 | *-158* | 51 | 29 | *-22* |
| February | 1'238 | 1'232 | *-6* | 32 | 35 | *3* |
| March | 306 | 319 | *13* | 10 | 21 | *11* |
| April | 516 | 433 | *-83* | 18 | 7 | *-11* |
| May | 534 | 650 | *116* | 11 | 16 | *5* |
| June | 1'323 | 1'111 | *-212* | 51 | 30 | *-21* |
| July | 1'780 | 1'461 | *-319* | 27 | 39 | *12* |
| September | 1'537 | 1'357 | *-180* | 16 | 7 | *-9* |
| October | 284 | 252 | *-32* | 1 | 0 | *-1* |
| November | 529 | 411 | *-118* | 4 | 8 | *4* |
| December | 506 | 461 | *-45* | 39 | 31 | *-8* |
| **Total** | **9'703** | **8'679** | ***-1'024*** | **260** | **223** | ***-37*** |

Table 2 shows the same data of Table 1 over the various faculties. The numbers of written exam sessions decrease everywhere with the exception of the Humanities faculty. A possible explanation for that is the huge numbers of enrolled students (14'878 in 2018-19, almost twice the 8'450 students enrolled in the second faculty, Science and Technology) suggesting adoption of software supported proctoring for managing the largest exam sessions.

Table 2. SMALL and LARGE exam sessions in 2018-19 and 2020-21 per faculty

| Faculty/School | SMALL exam sessions | | | LARGE exam sessions | | |
|---|---|---|---|---|---|---|
| | 2018-19 | 2020-21 | *delta* | 2018-19 | 2020-21 | *delta* |
| Agricultural and Food Sciences | 893 | 613 | *-280* | 7 | 2 | *-5* |
| Exercise and Sport Sciences | 168 | 69 | *-99* | 14 | 9 | *-5* |
| Humanities | 532 | 687 | *155* | 53 | 40 | *-13* |
| Language Mediation & Intercultural Communication | 590 | 416 | *-174* | 32 | 25 | *-7* |
| Law | 147 | 124 | *-23* | 7 | 3 | *-4* |
| Medicine | 1'814 | 1'489 | *-325* | 2 | 1 | *-1* |
| Pharmacy | 701 | 622 | *-79* | 8 | 3 | *-5* |
| Political, Economic and Social Sciences | 2'003 | 1'869 | *-134* | 84 | 89 | *5* |
| Science and Technology | 2'372 | 2'295 | *-77* | 42 | 47 | *5* |
| Veterinary Medicine | 483 | 495 | *12* | 11 | 4 | *-7* |
| **Total** | **9'703** | **8'679** | ***-1'024*** | **260** | **223** | ***-37*** |

# 3. GRADES OBTAINED BY STUDENTS

In (Weiner & Hurtz 2017) a comparison between online and onsite proctored exams is reported, showing that there are no significant differences in final grades: this allows authors of that paper to state that the effectiveness of student proctoring can be satisfactory both online and onsite.

To evaluate what happened at the University of Milan, Table 3 reports the average grades (ranging from 18/30 to 30/30) obtained by students of the various faculties in written exams after and during pandemic, for SMALL and for LARGE exam sessions. It is easy to see that data confirm the correctness of the (Weiner & Hurtz 2017) conclusions: the largest difference between the two years is the 0.6/30 increase in grades obtained in LARGE sessions by students of the Political, Economic and Social Sciences faculty.

Table 3. Average grades obtained by students in 2018-19 and 2020-21 per faculty

| Faculty/School | SMALL exam sessions | | | LARGE exam sessions | | |
|---|---|---|---|---|---|---|
| | 2018-19 | 2020-21 | *delta* | 2018-19 | 2020-21 | *delta* |
| Agricultural and Food Sciences | 24.4 | 24.3 | *-0.1* | 23.9 | 23.4 | *-0.4* |
| Exercise and Sport Sciences | 26.0 | 25.7 | *-0.3* | 26.9 | 26.4 | *-0.5* |
| Humanities | 25.7 | 25.5 | *-0.2* | 24.5 | 24.9 | *0.4* |
| Language Mediation & Intercultural Communication | 25.0 | 25.2 | *0.3* | 25.4 | 25.3 | *-0.1* |
| Law | 24.2 | 24.6 | *0.4* | 26.8 | na | *na* |
| Medicine | 25.6 | 25.7 | *0.1* | 28.5 | 26.9 | *-1.6* |
| Pharmacy | 24.3 | 24.6 | *0.3* | 24.3 | 23.9 | *-0.4* |
| Political, Economic and Social Sciences | 24.8 | 25.2 | *0.5* | 24.9 | 25.5 | *0.6* |
| Science and Technology | 25.2 | 25.4 | *0.2* | 25.0 | 23.6 | *-1.5* |
| Veterinary Medicine | 24.9 | 25.2 | *0.3* | 24.5 | 24.4 | *-0.1* |
| **Total** | **25.0** | **25.3** | ***0.2*** | **25.2** | **25.2** | ***0.0*** |

Table 4. Standard deviations of grades obtained by students in 2018-19 and 2020-21 per faculty

| Faculty/School | SMALL exam sessions | | | LARGE exam sessions | | |
|---|---|---|---|---|---|---|
| | 2018-19 | 2020-21 | *delta* | 2018-19 | 2020-21 | *delta* |
| Agricultural and Food Sciences | 3.9 | 4.1 | 0.2 | 3.7 | 3.3 | -0.3 |
| Exercise and Sport Sciences | 3.5 | 3.6 | 0.1 | 3.1 | 3.3 | 0.2 |
| Humanities | 3.8 | 3.9 | 0.1 | 4.1 | 4.3 | 0.2 |
| Language Mediation & Intercultural Communication | 3.9 | 4.0 | 0.1 | 3.9 | 3.4 | -0.4 |
| Law | 4.6 | 4.4 | -0.2 | 3.7 | na | *na* |
| Medicine | 3.5 | 3.6 | 0.2 | 3.4 | 1.6 | -1.8 |
| Pharmacy | 4.1 | 4.5 | 0.4 | 3.8 | 6.5 | 2.7 |
| Political. Economic and Social Sciences | 4.1 | 4.1 | 0.0 | 4.0 | 4.1 | 0.1 |
| Science and Technology | 4.0 | 4.4 | 0.4 | 4.3 | 5.5 | 1.3 |
| Veterinary Medicine | 3.7 | 3.6 | -0.1 | 3.5 | 3.6 | 0.1 |
| **Total** | **3.9** | **4.1** | **0.2** | **4.0** | **4.2** | **0.2** |

Even if considering the standard deviations of grades obtained, the picture – reported in Table 4 – does not indicate significant differences after and during pandemic. The highest differences for SMALL sessions – both equal to 0.4 – regard the two faculties of Pharmacy and Science and Technology, whose professors evidently used materials produced in online exams to better differentiate final grades. Definitely higher differences are present for LARGE sessions, but they refer to faculties (Medicine and Pharmacy) where the very limited numbers of this kind of sessions does not allow significant statistical evaluations.

Another interesting analysis is the behavior of students in the different types of university degrees, namely: bachelor degree (BD: 3 years) master degree (MD: 2 years after bachelor) single cycle master degree (SC: 5 or 6 year). As shown in Table 5, grades reported in master degree are always higher than in bachelor degrees, since master students already obtained a bachelor, they decided to continue studying, they are for sure well acquainted with university exams.

Even the single cycle master degree of the Medicine faculty (Medicine and Surgery) shows an average grade in line with the other master degrees of the same faculty, since less than one fourth of perspective students can enroll to this single cycle degree, after passing a very hard admission test. On the contrary, then single cycle master degrees of the Pharmacy faculty (Pharmacy and Pharmaceutical Chemistry and Technology) show average grades in line with the bachelor degrees of that faculty, probably because the admission tests to these single cycle degrees are far less crowded.

Note that two faculties – Law and Veterinary Medicine – are not present in Table 5. This is because both bachelor and master students of these faculties can follow the same courses. Thus, no distinction in final grades is possible.

Again, standard deviations – given in Table 6 – do not show significant differences after and during pandemic.

Table 5. Average grades obtained by students in the various types of degrees per faculty

| **Faculty/School** | | **2018-19** | | | **2020-21** | |
|---|---|---|---|---|---|---|
| **Type of degree** | **BD** | **MD** | **SC** | **BD** | **MD** | **SC** |
| Agricultural and Food Sciences | 24.0 | 26.2 | | 24.2 | 27.3 | |
| Exercise and Sport Sciences | 26.1 | 26.6 | | 26.1 | 26.0 | |
| Humanities | 25.2 | 26.1 | | 25.2 | 27.1 | |
| Language Mediation & Intercultural Communication | 25.1 | 25.8 | | 24.9 | 26.6 | |
| Medicine | 25.0 | 26.6 | 27.0 | 25.3 | 27.0 | 27.0 |
| Pharmacy | 23.6 | 28.3 | 24.3 | 23.3 | 27.2 | 24.5 |
| Political, Economic and Social Sciences | 24.5 | 26.1 | | 25.0 | 26.4 | |
| Science and Technology | 24.9 | 26.7 | | 24.9 | 27.2 | |
| **Total** | **24.8** | **26.3** | **25.8** | **25.0** | **26.8** | **25.7** |

Table 6. Standard deviations of grades obtained by students in the various types of degrees per faculty

| **Faculty/School** | | **2018-19** | | | **2020-21** | |
|---|---|---|---|---|---|---|
| **Type of degree** | **BD** | **MD** | **SC** | **BD** | **MD** | **SC** |
| Agricultural and Food Sciences | 3.9 | 3.4 | | 4.1 | 3.4 | |
| Exercise and Sport Sciences | 3.4 | 3.3 | | 3.4 | 3.5 | |
| Humanities | 4.0 | 3.6 | | 4.1 | 3.3 | |
| Language Mediation & Intercultural Communication | 3.9 | 3.7 | | 3.6 | 3.7 | |
| Medicine | 3.5 | 3.3 | 3.5 | 3.6 | 3.1 | 3.6 |
| Pharmacy | 4.0 | 3.9 | 4.0 | 4.3 | 3.6 | 4.6 |
| Political, Economic and Social Sciences | 4.1 | 3.9 | | 4.1 | 3.8 | |
| Science and Technology | 4.0 | 3.6 | | 4.5 | 3.6 | |
| **Total** | **3.9** | **3.7** | **4.0** | **4.1** | **3.7** | **4.3** |

Similar considerations can be made by examining average grades obtained by students in the various years of their curricula, whenever such information is available (again, some faculties leave to students the freedom to follow a course in different years). Tables 7 and 8 show these average grades, for academic year 2028-19 and 2020-21 respectively. As it can be easily noted, grades usually increase when passing from each study year to the following one, since students become more and more acquainted with university studies.

Standard deviations – given in Tables 9 and 10 – confirm the above.

Table 7. Average grades obtained in 2018-19 by students in the various study years per faculty

| Faculty/School | 2018-19 | | | | | |
|---|---|---|---|---|---|---|
| Course year | 1 | 2 | 3 | 4 | 5 | 6 |
| Agricultural and Food Sciences | 23.6 | 24.2 | 24.5 | 26.1 | 26.5 | |
| Exercise and Sport Sciences | 26.3 | | 25.3 | 26.3 | 28.2 | |
| Humanities | | 28.2 | | 28.4 | | |
| Language Mediation & Intercultural Communication | 24.5 | 25.7 | 25.0 | 25.5 | 26.7 | |
| Medicine | 24.7 | 25.7 | 26.0 | 26.9 | 27.4 | 29.5 |
| Pharmacy | 23.3 | 24.7 | 24.0 | 25.2 | 24.2 | |
| Political, Economic and Social Sciences | 24.2 | 24.5 | 25.0 | 26.0 | 26.4 | |
| Science and Technology | 24.7 | 24.8 | 25.2 | 26.9 | 26.9 | |
| **Total** | **24.4** | **24.9** | **25.2** | **26.2** | **26.8** | **29.5** |

Table 8. Average grades obtained in 2020-21 by students in the various study years per faculty

| Faculty/School | 2020-21 | | | | | |
|---|---|---|---|---|---|---|
| Course year | 1 | 2 | 3 | 4 | 5 | 6 |
| Agricultural and Food Sciences | 23.6 | 24.6 | 24.9 | 27.3 | 26.9 | |
| Exercise and Sport Sciences | 27.0 | 25.5 | 25.5 | 26.0 | | |
| Humanities | 26.2 | 24.7 | | | | |
| Language Mediation & Intercultural Communication | 24.6 | 25.7 | 24.9 | 26.5 | 27.0 | |
| Medicine | 25.2 | 26.4 | 26.1 | 26.7 | 28.1 | 27.7 |
| Pharmacy | 23.8 | 24.4 | 26.0 | 25.3 | 25.0 | |
| Political, Economic and Social Sciences | 24.9 | 24.5 | 26.0 | 26.2 | 26.8 | |
| Science and Technology | 24.8 | 24.9 | 25.7 | 27.4 | 28.4 | |
| **Total** | **24.8** | **25.0** | **25.8** | **26.5** | **27.1** | **27.7** |

Table 9. Standard deviation of grades obtained in 2018-19 by students in the various study years per faculty

| Faculty/School | 2018-19 | | | | | |
|---|---|---|---|---|---|---|
| Course year | 1 | 2 | 3 | 4 | 5 | 6 |
| Agricultural and Food Sciences | 4.1 | 3.9 | 3.7 | 3.6 | 3.0 | |
| Exercise and Sport Sciences | 3.4 | | 3.4 | 3.1 | 3.5 | |
| Humanities | | 3.0 | | 5.2 | | |
| Language Mediation & Intercultural Communication | 3.8 | 4.0 | 3.6 | 3.8 | 3.2 | |
| Medicine | 3.7 | 3.4 | 3.6 | 3.2 | 3.3 | 2.6 |
| Pharmacy | 4.3 | 3.6 | 3.9 | 4.1 | 4.0 | |
| Political, Economic and Social Sciences | 4.1 | 4.0 | 4.0 | 3.9 | 3.8 | |
| Science and Technology | 4.1 | 3.9 | 3.8 | 3.2 | 3.1 | |
| **Total** | **4.0** | **3.9** | **3.8** | **3.7** | **3.6** | **2.6** |

Table 10. Standard deviation of grades obtained in 2020-21 by students in the various study years per faculty

| Faculty/School | 2020-21 | | | | | |
|---|---|---|---|---|---|---|
| Course year | 1 | 2 | 3 | 4 | 5 | 6 |
| Agricultural and Food Sciences | 4.2 | 4.0 | 3.9 | 3.5 | 3.2 | |
| Exercise and Sport Sciences | 2.6 | 3.8 | 2.9 | 3.5 | | |
| Humanities | 3.3 | 3.4 | | | | |
| Language Mediation & Intercultural Communication | 3.5 | 3.7 | 3.9 | 3.9 | 3.0 | |
| Medicine | 3.7 | 3.5 | 3.5 | 3.4 | 3.0 | 3.6 |
| Pharmacy | 4.8 | 4.9 | 4.1 | 4.2 | 4.0 | |
| Political, Economic and Social Sciences | 4.1 | 4.1 | 4.0 | 3.9 | 3.5 | |
| Science and Technology | 4.6 | 4.2 | 3.9 | 3.4 | 2.9 | |
| **Total** | **4.2** | **4.1** | **3.9** | **3.8** | **3.5** | **3.6** |

# 4. CONCLUDING REMARKS

In this paper, some preliminary analyses on written exam sessions at the University of Milan have been performed, to assess the efficacy of the monitoring scenarios for online written exams identified during the first lockdown phase of the pandemic.

The results of that analysis are definitely satisfactory. Even during pandemic, lot of written exams have been smoothly carried on thanks to the different scenarios proposed to professors for conducting them. Moreover, grades obtained by students before and during pandemic show very limited differences, confirming what stated in (Weiner & Hurtz 2017) about the significance of online proctored exams. It should be emphasized that up to now we did not receive any complaint about the necessity of reducing the exam difficulties when going online. On the contrary, some problems arose in collecting handwritten diagrams or drawings, requiring a scan and send procedure not so easy to manage.

Another interesting result of the analysis is the progressive increase in grades obtained by students as soon as they proceed in their university careers, becoming more and more acquainted with university studies and exams.

Future work will address in more detail the behavior of each professor, even if this requires surveys and questionnaires whose return rate are usually limited. However, it is already possible to conclude that carrying on online written exams is feasible and satisfactory: this is why we will still use online exams even when our University will reopen, e.g. for particular courses or degrees reserved to older, full-time employed students, definitely preferring online exams to avoid necessity of vacation days to undergo exams.

# ACKNOWLEDGEMENT

Sincere thanks to Dr. Tiziano Traversi, of the ICT Division of our University, for his invaluable support in extracting all the data necessary to perform the evaluations discussed so far.

# REFERENCES

Exam.net 2020, A robust, easy-to-use and secure exam platform, viewed June 10th 2020, < https://exam.net/>.

Haus, G, Pasquinelli, YB, Scaccia, D & Scarabottolo, N 2020, 'Online Written Exams during Covid-19 Crisis', Proceeding of the Intl. Conf. e-Learning 2020, pp. 79-86.

Haus, G, Pasquinelli, YB, Scaccia, D & Scarabottolo, N 2021, 'Online Written Exams during Covid-19 Crisis: an Update after One Year', Proceeding of the Intl. Conf. e-Learning 2021, pp. 115-119.

Proctorio 2020, A Comprehensive Learning Integrity Platform, viewed June 10th 2020, < https://web.proctorio.com/>.

SEB 2020, Safe Exam Browser, viewed June 10th 2020, < https://safeexambrowser.org/>.

Scarabottolo, N 2022, 'University Written Exams before and during the Covid-19 Pandemic', Proceeding of the 16th annual International Technology, Education and Development Conference, INTED 2022.

Weiner, JA & Hurtz, GM 2017, 'A Comparative Study of Online Remote Proctored versus Onsite Proctored High-Stakes Exams', Journal of Applied Testing Technology, vol. 18, no. 1, pp. 13-20.

# VIRTUALIZATION PROCESS OF LEARNING IN A DEVELOPING COUNTRY

Mary Ann Barbour El Rassi
*Saint Joseph University, Beyrouth, Lebanon*

**ABSTRACT**

In some low-resource settings, there are several challenges such as financial crisis, inadequate infrastructure facilities, personal skills efficiency and motivation that contribute or hinder the success of virtualization in an industry. This study investigates the factors that could influence the success of virtualization requirement in the learning industry during and after the COVID phase on students' perceived usefulness and their intention to continue using electronic learning. A qualitative research was conducted among university students through several focus groups and one to one interviews. Several factors that are expected to influence students' perceived usefulness and intentions to continue using online learning were identified and a trifold model was proposed based on three different theories to be empirically tested on a larger scale in the future. This study provides input to improving knowledge of e-learning for educational institutions in developing countries.

**KEYWORDS**

Virtualization, e-Learning, Developing Countries, Online Learning.

## 1. INTRODUCTION

The outbreak of the COVID-19 epidemic has irrevocably changed education forever (Dhawan, 2020). While people all over the world were forced to shift from physical classrooms to virtual classrooms due to the burst of the pandemic, one might wonder if this new trend of e-learning would be successful and efficient enough for schools and universities in developing countries to continue using it despite the economic and infrastructure challenges they might face.

Throughout the COVID-19 lockdown period, academic institutions were obliged to adopt the online learning to fill the gap as it was the only alternative and a vital solution to ensure delivering learning process (Dhawan, 2020; Mseleku, 2020). As a matter of fact, e-learning was considered as an innovative and collaborating method to study. But how do students today, and after such an experience, perceive the usefulness of the online learning is still debatable somehow.

While many studies have investigated the perspectives of online learning during and after the pandemic rise (Barnes, 2020), not many of them have investigated the factors that could influence students' intention to continue using the online platforms for learning in developing countries. Cheng (2021) had argued that the online learning success depends on the students' readiness and intentions to continue using the online platform which is usually a good indicator that influences the successfulness and effectiveness of the online experience and the students' learning quality. Thus, it is very crucial to investigate the factors that could affect student's intention to continuously use the online platforms for education as it is an indicator that could lead us to better understand if this new trend could be a successful tool in the future especially that the Covid risk had somehow diminished and most of the students are back to their campuses. This could somehow, help us to better understand if the use of the online platforms for education could satisfy students' needs (Huang, 2019). During the last decade, and with the introduction of the online learning, may studies have focused on examining the students' intentions to continue using the online platforms for education and have used many technology adoption theories and models (Valverde-Berrocoso et al., 2020). This could lead one to assume that the online learning, methods are fully acceptable among users and in any conditions. Nevertheless, there aren't any studies, and not to our knowledge that investigated the virtualizability of the learning process in a developing country. The virtualizability in terms of the suitability and the responsiveness of the online learning process in an adequate manner especially that in countries where there are low resource settings, there are several socioeconomic challenges such as inadequate facilities, cultural barriers, access to the internet and other reasons that could hinder the use of the online platforms for education. In other examples, an obvious gap in the online learning could be related to practical understandings of the virtualize ability of such a process. Overbry (2008; 2012) proposed a process virtualization theory (PVT) that is grounded on the fact that some processes could be more suitable for being conducted virtually than any others. For example, buying books online showed to be well-suited to virtualization, while the online groceries process has demonstrated to be less efficient.

Nonetheless, and regardless of the variation of existing literature on online learning adoption, none of the current studies in the literature had so far gone further in investigating the process of visualization factors to determine personal factors that affect the user 's perception while using the online platform as a fit for his expectations and continues using it. Thus, and in order to fill this gap in knowledge, this research offers several main objectives:

(1) what are the main requirements for the learning process that could predict the students' perceived usefulness for using the online platform for learning as a result of the covid-19 pandemic in low resource settings?_(2) what are the main requirements for the learning process that impact students' intentions to continue using OL after the COVID experience? (3) Identify a model that could predict the virtualization process in e-learning in developing countries._This study was mainly done in Lebanon, which, according to the Ministry of Economy and Trade Report, (2017), is considered as a developing country. The Lebanese experience with the online learning adoption is expected to inspire other regional countries as Lebanon is looked upon as a leader in information and communication development and in the academic that it offers. For hundreds of years, the geographical location of this country and since the Phoenicians has served as a commercial platform for services and commerce exchange between the Mediterranean coasts, East Asia and India. Lebanon is considered as a role model in business and has a high level of education (Gordon, 2016). Therefore, the Lebanese case in this domain could offer an inspiring example for the e-learning diffusion in other developing countries, especially that it had encountered many difficulties recently after the 2019 revolution that was a result of a deterioration in its economy, infrastructure facilities (electricity which is a must for online use, internet availability etc...) the difficulties which makes it a practical choice for evaluating e-learning in developing countries and particularly in the Middle East ( El Rassi, 2018; El Rassi, 2019; El Rassi ,2020).

To accomplish the study's main objective outlined in this introduction, we proceed by presenting a literature review concerning the e-learning and the exploited theories in the literature.

# 2. LITERATURE REVIEW

## 2.1 E- Learning

E-learning has recently become more crucial for educational institutions especially in a world where the fierce competition has become global. The introduction and adoption of new methods and tools in educational institutions, such as delivery and support systems had a great effect on their performance (Broadfoot, 2016). Before proceeding further, we aim at briefly defining e-learning. E-learning could be related to any learning mean that is enabled electronically or empowered by the use of digital technologies. Other scholars have defined it as a concept that refers to the use of applications, learning methodologies or processes. Thus, it is not easy to agree on a definition that could be adopted but we may summarize it as the employment of online technologies to facilitate the access to educational materials such as online courses or online exams. Several schools and higher educational institutions have realized what e-learning could bring to them in terms of added value as it could shape people's knowledge and enhance their skills. E-learning could take different shapes and types and could also be employed with different techniques. Nevertheless, several authors believe that e-learning could be considered as an interesting alternative for teaching students (Lam, Williams & Chua, 2007).

## 2.2 Theoretical Frameworks

There have been many research studies that focused on the e-learning perspective in the literature. While most of them have examined the factors that could possibly influence students' acceptance, others have investigated the adoption and the e-learning use. Some of them have verified how to predict the use of theoretical knowledge of causal connections such as Davis and Venkatesh (2004). These authors used the Technology acceptance model (TAM) to study the use and acceptance of a new system based on the perceived usefulness variable while Bhattacherjee and Premkumar (2004) provided an empirical evidence on predicting the user's approach when testing the users' acceptance. In more recent studies, there has been more focus on the students' continuous intention to use the online learning system (Valverde-Berrocoso et al., 2020). Nevertheless, after going through several research studies in this field, we notice that the IS theory has been used with many other theories to explain the e-learning adoption and predict students' intention to continue or not to continue using the online learning system. Theories such as TAM and others perceive the e-learning from a limited usefulness perspective. While the TAM, UTAUT and DOI theories measure the usefulness of a certain system by investigating how the users evaluate it, the Process of Virtualization Theory for example explicates the usefulness based on the process characteristics and the system's abilities which allows for more significant explanations.

The Process virtualization which is almost new in the IS discipline (Overby, 2012), comprises four major constructs (sensory requirements, relationship requirements, synchronism requirements, and identification and control requirements) that are usually expected to influence a process and detect whether it is responsive or resistant to being piloted virtually.

### 2.2.1 Motivation

Contextual characteristics, according to Farid and Lamb (2020), have a significant impact on motivation. Prior studies had proven that perceived utility was a significant influence in shaping the formation of motivation and feelings, if this viewpoint was accepted. Perceived usefulness, for example, enhanced learners' motivation in the computer-assisted language learning environment, according to Hsu's and Li (2017) research. Increased learners' perceived usefulness, according to Chan and Norlizah (2017), could boost their learning motivation. Similarly, Kong and Wang (2021) observed that students' motivation to study is boosted by perceived usefulness. According to Kim and Shin (2021), integrative motivation mediates the link between learners' self-efficacy and their actual learning capacity, meaning that integrative motivation is a reaction to subjective traits such as perceived self-efficacy.

### 2.2.2 Self-Efficacy Theory

Self-efficacy refers to a person's belief in his or her capacity to carry out the actions necessary to meet specific performance objectives (Bandura, 1997). A person's conviction in his ability to regulate his own motivation, behavior, and social environment is referred to as self-efficacy.

Self-efficacy was developed as a predictive variable using the Technology Acceptance Model (TAM) and Computer Self-Efficacy (CSE) (Davis 1989). The variable is used to determine a person's ability to use technology to obtain access to healthcare information and services. This predictor was used in particular to evaluate people's ability to use mobile phones to get prenatal care and information in distant regions.

### 2.2.3 Attitude (Theory of Planned Behavior)

Prior behavioral science research has revealed that one's attitude influences one's evaluation of a certain behavior, issue, or action (Hagger et al, 2002). As a result, past experiences and empirical findings from studies based on the Theory of Planned Behavior (TPB) prompted the addition of attitude as a predictor variable (Ajzen, 1999; Hagger et al, 2002). In the TIPFit approach, attitude is critical in determining how patients and caregivers perceive an intervention before and after exposure. We expected that when the advantages of an intervention become more realistic as a result of sustained usage, attitudes alter.

# 3. METHODOLOGY

## 3.1 Research Methodology

In order to answer our research questions and based on the above stated literature review that had allowed us to develop a basic idea, we opted to continue our study with a qualitative technique in order to answer the above questions. According to Benbasat et al (1987), a qualitative study allows us to explore "a phenomenon in its natural surroundings, using multiple data collection methods to gather information from one or a few entities". Individual interviews and focus groups are, indeed, the most appropriate qualitative methods for our study, and this is for a variety of reasons. Firstly, they can be considered as a primary data method for gathering information from expert people. Secondly, they allow us to better understand the human behavior while collecting data on opinions, perceptions and attitudes in order to explain the factors that impact a certain behavior in a new setting. These two approaches focus on the "how" and "why" of a decision-making rather than the "what," "where," and "when" (Kendall, (2008).

## 3.2 Field of Choice, Data Collecting Source and Method

Fort the purpose of our study, we chose our data sample from university students because the majority of e-learners are young. Typically, at this age, also known as the "Z" generation, they are internet savvy users and most of them do not have any problem using the internet. Not like the older age that are more reluctant and find difficulties in using new technologies and internet (Jariah et al, 2004). We pursued the study by performing planned discussions and interviews with a small group of people that was managed by a moderator and that is by relying on the literature. We started with three focus groups, each group consisted of 8 students and we also did 12 semi-structured interviews. Each interview was scheduled for about an average of 50 minutes. The collection of the data took almost 75 days and the information gathered during the interviews started to reflect a saturation as of the $12^{th}$ interview which allowed us to conclude that the collected information represents a good understanding of the phenomenon we aim to study. Thus, we have created an interview guide based on the related literature which major objective was to answer our major research questions. Therefore, and based on the data that was collected during this study, we had identified relevant categories and that is by using the open coding. This had allowed us to identify the interesting elements for our study in the data. Then, we opted for the axial coding that had allowed us to link the existing data to the literature. By applying this method, we have conducted an analysis of the interviews, while going over the main themes of our research study.

# 4. RESULTS

In this section we will start by presenting the results of the interviews and focus groups that we have conducted. Our major objective is to iterate between the literature and the results as follows:

-Personal attributes: Personal attributes could be related to self-efficacy and motivation. Self-efficacy is based on an individual's conviction in their own ability to achieve a goal, which is required to create particular performance attainments (Bandura, 1997), whereas motivation is based on an individual's desire to achieve a certain goal. Motivation is what explains why people keep doing something or cease doing it at a certain point in time. Internal elements that lead an agent to wish to engage in goal-directed behavior are sometimes referred to as motivational moods. Different mental states are said to compete with one another, with only the most powerful mood determining behavior. Based on the conducted interviews, major factors that could influence person's attitude towards e-learning are self-efficacy and learning motivation.

The below table represents some of the quotes that were expressed by the focus group members and the interviewers.

Table 1. Personal attributes: Technology Self-Efficacy and Learning motivation

| Verbatims | Axial coding | Theoretical concepts | Respondents out of 36 students |
|---|---|---|---|
| -"It is ok for me to use the internet for e- learning even if there is no one around to show me how to do it." -"It is not an issue, I can manage. I always did" | Self confidence in achieving a task through technology | **Technology Self-Efficacy (TSE)** Kim and Shin, 2021; Kong & Wang, 2021; Farid & Lamb,2020; Li, 2014. | 31 students (86%) |
| -"I like to continue using it. It is useful and efficient. But it is not my first choice. I still prefer to come and take my courses on campus". | Desire to achieve certain goals | **Learning Motivation (LM)** Hsu and Li, 2017; Kim and Shin, 2021; Kong & Wang, 2021; Farid & Lamb,2020; | 32 students (89%) |

- Practice: Strong relationships with instructors, students, and peers may drastically improve students' motivation and hence boost learning in practice. Students that have more solid relationships have shown higher academic engagement, better social skills, and exhibit more good conduct. For many, these ties were severed when schools shuttered their doors in April 2020. Building trusted connections, on the other hand, will be crucial in dealing with the months of stress and missing or incomplete academic lessons that have followed. The below table represents some of the quotes that were expressed by the focus group members and the interviewers.

Table 2. Practices

| Verbatims | Axial coding | Theoretical concepts | Respondents out of 36 students |
|---|---|---|---|
| -" I honestly enjoy walking and looking around the campus life. That is why I prefer being physically present". | Feeling people and physical aspects of the campus around | **Sensory requirements** (SR) Kim and Shin, 2021; Farid & Lamb,2020; Overby, 2008; Overby, 2010. | 29 students (80.5%) |
| -"what I like when I am on campus is that I can be in direct contact with my friends, peers, meet new people and build strong ties with them. Which is not an option when I am online". | Maintaining bonds and good relationships with people around | **Relationship requirements** (RQ) Hsu and Li, 2017; Kim and Shin, 2021; Kong & Wang, 2021; Farid & Lamb,2020; Li ,2014; Overby, 2008; Overby, 2010. | 33 students (92%) |
| -"it is crucial for me to know which one of my friends or colleagues could be attending the university classes with me." -"I feel more comfortable when I know which other colleagues are attending the course with me ." | Personal identification around | **Identification and control requirements** (IR) Hsu and Li, 2017; Kim and Shin, 2021; Kong & Wang, 2021; Farid & Lamb,2020; Li ,2014; Overby, 2008; Overby, 2010. | 32 students (89%) |

-Representation relationship: Representation relationship refers to the technology capacity to mimic or replace the physical learning process. This variable was developed from PVT-IT (Overby, 2008; Overby, 2010) and Task Technology-Fit (TTF) (Goodhue and Thompson, 1995). In telemedicine, for example, mobile phones may be combined with wireless sensors and multimedia technologies to allow patients and physicians to consult remotely. However, in low-resource environments, such services are difficult to supply due to insufficient connection (Overbru, 2010).

Table 3a. Technology

| Verbatims | Axial coding | Theoretical concepts | Respondents out of 36 students |
|---|---|---|---|
| -" when I am on campus, I enjoy my classmates presence which I miss online. Especially that the online connection is not available sometimes" | Enjoying a closer relationship with others on campus | **Representation relationship** Agrawal et al, 2020; Mburu & Oboko, 2018; Mbuthia et al, 2021; Mechael et al, 2010; Overby, 2008; Overby, 2010; | 29 students (80.5%) |

-Reach: Reach is a measure of technology's capacity to give adequate access to e-learning at a lower cost, in a shorter amount of time and at a person's convenience sometimes. Due to extensive distances, economic issues, infrastructure failing sometimes, limited e-learning and cultural obstacles, most of m-Health programs for example in developing economies programs fail to offer enough access to maternity care services and information, according to evaluated research (Agrawal et al, 2020; Mburu & Oboko, 2018 Mbuthia et al, 2021; Mechael et al, 2010). As a result, we investigated how online learning may provide sufficient reach for e-learning.

Table 3b. Technology

| **Verbatims** | **Axial coding** | **Theoretical concepts** | **Respondents out of 36 students** |
|---|---|---|---|
| -" easy for me to attend classes online as long as I have internet".<br>-" taking courses online is convenient. No need to relocate especially with the financial crisis and the increase in fuel price. It is really convenient" | Reachable anytime, anywhere | **Reach.**<br>Agrawal et al, 2020; Mburu & Oboko, 2018; Mbuthia et al, 2021; Mechael et al, 2010; Overby, 2008; Overby, 2010. | 27 students (75%) |

-Perceived usefulness and intention to use: According to Davis (1986)'s Technology Acceptance Model, perceived utility is the most crucial component in user acceptance of a technology, ahead of perceived ease (TAM). Perceived utility and perceived ease of use both influence behavioral intention to use, which is defined as a person's conscious decision to do or not undertake a future activity. "The degree to which a person believes that employing a given system would enhance their job performance," Fred Davis defined perceived usefulness (PU) as "the degree to which a person thinks that implementing a certain system would improve their work performance." It relates to whether or not a piece of technology is considered useful for the task at hand.

Table 4. Perceives usefulness and intention to use

| **Verbatims** | **Axial coding** | **Theoretical concepts** | **Respondents out of 36 students** |
|---|---|---|---|
| -" it could be if you can offer me internet and electricity. Know those are things that are hard to reach these days. Despite all that, I still intend to use it again if available." | Learning affects the decision of usefulness and intention to use and is related to self-efficacy. | **Perceived usefulness; intention to continue use; Learning.**<br>Davis 1989; Mbuthia et al, 2021; Rahmi et al, 2018; Overby, 2008; Overby, 2010. | 27 students |

# 5. DISCUSSION

After identifying the problematic related with online learning, we conceptualized the construct. A construct is defined by Edwards and Bagozzi (2002) as "a conceptual term used to describe a phenomenon of theoretical interest".

## 5.1 Conceptualization of Constructs

In the first phase, we expressed our problematic as the need to understand the "process requirements that predict students' perceived usefulness and intention to reuse the online learning after Covid 19". Thus, we defined several factors that influence students' perception and intention to use. Subsequently, a list of personal, practices and technological attributes that are related with the online learning behavior have been developed throughout an inclusive search in the literature.

In a second phase, the qualitative study aimed at emphasizing any attitude that could be related to personal, practices and technological attributes that our interviews may correlate with the literature review related to online learning.

Also we tried to relate these attributes to any possible additional dimensions that were not mentioned or found in the literature review (Hudson et al, 1998). We had also screened the list of interviews to make sure that our sample would include interviews with different perspectives and backgrounds (for example, gender, cultural background, region, etc…). The answers were then checked by a coding team that consisted of two researchers who attempted to identify the key themes and illustrative quotes.

Based on the findings, we were able to identify two potential dimensions for personal attributes, three potential dimensions for the processes in addition to two potential dimensions for technology characteristics. The latent dimensions identified in table.1 for personal attributes are self-efficiency (Hagger et al, 2002; Kong & Wang, 2021; Kim and Shin ,2021) and motivation (Kim and Shin, 2021; Kong & Wang, 2021; Farid and Lamb,2020; Li ,2014). The latent dimensions identified in table 2 processes included sensory requirements, relationship requirements, identification and control requirements. The potential dimensions initially identified in table 3.a and 3.b representation relationship and reach (Kim and Shin, 2021; Kong & Wang, 2021; Farid and Lamb,2020). In addition, as our sample consisted in general of 3 focus groups (8 participants in each group) and 12 individual semi structured interviews, most of them were university undergraduate students that had experience the online learning at least during COVID if not before. They perceived that the technology self-efficacy is a major attribute that could influence their perception about online learning (86%) and that learning motivation could have a weight and influence on the online perceived usefulness and their intention to reuse the system after covid. (89%) (Ajzen, 1999; Bandura, 1997; Kong & Wang, 2021; Kim and Shin ,2021). Furthermore, we have identified a second construct that could influence their opinion about perceived usefulness and related to processes and it includes "Sensory requirements" ( 80.5%), "relationship requirements (92%) and Identification and control requirements (89%). This has been related in the literature to many research papers that have discussed the virtualization process theory among others (Overby, 2008; Overby, 2010).

A third construct that we call technology has been identified while iterating back between the literature and the students' opinions and it is composed of "Representation relationship" (80.5%) and "Reach" (75%), (Mbuthia et al, 2021; Mechael et al, 2010; Overby, 2008; Overby, 2010).

Based on our preliminary findings, we conclude that those attributes represent the major components that could influence students' perceived usefulness for the online learning and their intention to continue using the same system and that learning motivation could be considered as a mediator variable between self-efficacy and perceived usefulness and between perceived usefulness and intention to continue using the online platform or education. Therefore, the analysis of the qualitative study leads us to propose the following model to answer our research questions:

Based on this model, the following hypotheses are proposed and are recommended to be tested with a larger sample with quantitative data if possible:

H1-a. The higher the students' SE is, the more positive the impact on their learning motivation (LM) is.

H1-b. The higher the students' learning motivation (LM) is, the more positive the impact on their perceived usefulness of e-learning is.

H2. The higher the students' SR is, the lower the impact on their perceived usefulness of e-learning is.

H3. The higher the students' RQ is, the lower the impact on their perceived usefulness of e-learning is.

H4. The higher the students' ICR is, the lower the impact on their perceived usefulness of e-learning is.

H5. The higher the students' RR for the learning process are, the more positive the impact on their perceived usefulness of e-learning is.

H6. The higher the students' Rc for the learning process are, the more positive the impact on their perceived usefulness of e-learning is.

H7. The higher the students' PU for the learning process are, the more positive the impact on their ICU of e-learning is.

# 6. CONCLUSION, LIMITATIONS AND FUTURE RECOMMENDATIONS

This study, without exception, contains a number of shortcomings. Participants were depicted as homogeneous entities apart from their gender in our study environment and owing to time constraints. Additional study might be conducted to look at additional factors, such as the influence of the Lebanese culture's cultural background and the impact of the second language on online learning intention and attitude.

Furthermore, it is strongly advised that we test this model on a bigger sample size, as this would provide us with more reliable findings. Both genders should be represented in the sample, which should be drawn from different institutions (one from the French system and the other from the American system) or areas. For this reason, and after gathering a vast amount of data, the use of structural equation modeling to test the suggested model is recommended. Structural Equation Modeling (SEM) technique is high recommended in IS and is very efficient to test a complex model with several variables (Chin et al., 1995).

## REFERENCES


Agrawal, K. P., Pani, A. K., & Sharma, R. (2020). Pandemic Pandemonium and Remote Working: An Investigation of Determinants and their Contextual Behavior in Virtualization of Work-from-home (WFH) Process. In *International Working Conference on Transfer and Diffusion of IT*.pp. 261-273. Springer, Cham.

Ajzen I. (1999). The theory of Planned Behavior. *Organ Behav Hum Decis Process*. Vol. 50, pp.179–211.

Bandura, A. (1987). Self-efficacy: The exercise of control. New York: Freeman.

Barnes, S.J. (2020). Information Management Research and Practice in the Post-COVID-19 World. *International COMP Journal of Information Management*, Vol. 55.

Benbasat, I., Goldstein, D.K., & Mead, M. (1987). The Case Research Strategy in Studies of Information Systems Case Research. *MIS Quarterly*, Vol.11, No.3, pp. 369-386

Broadfoot, P. (2016). Assessment for Twenty-First-Century Learning: The Challenges Ahead. *Learning, Design, and Technology, Springer*, pp. 1-23.

Chan, Y. L., & Norlizah, C. H. (2017). Students' Motivation Towards Science Learning and Students' Science Achievement. *International Journal of Academic Research in Progressive Education and Development*, Vol. 6, No. 4, pp.174-189.

Cheng, Y.-M. (2021). Investigating Medical Professionals' Continuance Intention of the Cloud-based e-Learning System: An Extension of Expectation–Confirmation Model with Flow Theory. *Journal of Enterprise Information Management*, Vol. 34 No. 4, pp. 1169-1202.

Dhawan, S. (2020). Online Learning: A Panacea in the Time of COVID-19 Crisis. *Journal of Educational Technology Systems,* Vol. 49 No. 1, pp. 5-22.

Davis FD. (1989). Perceived Usefulness, Perceived Ease of Use, and User Acceptance of Information Technology. *MIS Q*. Vol.13. pp.319–40.

Davis, F. D., & Venkatesh, V. (2004). Toward Preprototype User Acceptance Testing of New Information Systems: Implications for Software Project Management. *IEEE Transactions on Engineering management*, Vol. 51, No. 1, pp. 31-46.

Edwards, J.R., & Bagozzi, R.P. (2000). On the Nature and Direction of Relationships between Constructs and Measures. *Journal of Personality and Social Psychology*, Vol. 5, No.2, pp. 155-174.

El Rassi, M. (2018). Firm's Size Effect in the E-Service Industry: The Case of a Developing Country. *AIS electronic library (AISeL)*.https://aisel.aisnet.org/cgi/viewcontent.cgi?article=1013&context=ecis2018_rp

El Rassi, M. A. B. (2019). Assessing Open-book-open-web Exam in High Schools: The Case of a Developing Country. In *part of the multi conference on computer science and information systems*. p. 33.

El Rassi, M. A. B. (2020). Why One e-Business Adoption Model Won't Fit All Firm Sizes: The Case of Lebanon's e-Service Industry. *The Electronic Journal of Information Systems in Developing Countries,* Vol. 86, No. 5.

Farid, A., & Lamb, M. (2020). English for Da'wah? L2 Motivation in Indonesian Pesantren Schools. *System*, Vol. 94, 102310.

Gordon, D.C. (2016). The Republic of Lebanon: Nation in Jeopardy. *Routledge*.

Hagger MS, Chatzisarantis NLD, Biddle SJH. (2002). A Meta-Analytic Review of Theories of Reasoned Action and Planned Behavior in Physical Activity: Predictive Validity and Contribution of Additional Variables. *J Sport Exerc Psychol*. Vol.24, pp.3–32.

Huang, Y.M. (2019). Examining Students' Continued Use of Desktop Services: Perspectives from Expectation-Confirmation and Social Influence. *Computers in Human Behavior,* Vol. 96, pp. 23-31.

Hudson, L.A., & Ozanne, J.L. (1998). Alternative Ways of Seeking Knowledge in Consumer Research. *Journal of Consumer Research,* Vol. 14, No.4, pp. 508.

Hsu, C. H., & Li, M. (2017). Development of a Cruise Motivation Scale for Emerging Markets in Asia. *International Journal of Tourism Research, Vol,* 19, No. 6, pp. 682-692.

Jariah, M., Husniyah, A. R., Laily, P., & Britt, S. (2004). Financial Behavior and Problems among University Students: Need for Financial Education. *Journal of Personal Finance*, Vol.3, pp. 8296.

Kendall, L. (2008). The Conduct of Qualitative Interviews: Research Questions, Methodological Issues, and Researching Online. *Handbook of Research on New Literacies New York: Lawrence Erlbaum*, pp.133-150.

Kong, S. C., & Wang, Y. Q. (2021). The Influence of Parental Support and Perceived Usefulness on Students' Learning Motivation and Flow Experience in Visual Programming: Investigation from a Parent Perspective. *British Journal of Educational Technology*, Vol. *52*, No. 4, pp. 1749-1770.

Kim, S. H., & Shin, H. W. (2021). Second Language Learners' Self-efficacy and English Achievement: The Mediating Role of Integrative Motivation. *English Teaching & Learning*, Vol. *45*, No. 3, pp.325-338.

Mbuthia, F., Reid, M., & Fichardt, A. (2021). Development and Validation of a Mobile Health Communication Framework for Postnatal Care in Rural Kenya. *International Journal of Africa Nursing Sciences*, Vol.14, 100304.

Mburu, S., & Oboko, R. (2018). A Model forPpredicting Utilization of mHealth Interventions in Low-Resource Settings: Case of Maternal and Newborn Care in Kenya. *BMC medical informatics and decision making*, Vol. 18, No. 1, pp. 1-16.

Mechael P, et al. (2010). Barriers and Gaps Affecting mHealth in Low and Middle Income Countries: Policy White Paper. Columbia: Academic: *Center for Global Health and economic development earth institute*.

Mseleku, Z. (2020). A Literature Review of e-Learning and e-Teaching in the Era of Covid-19 Pandemic. *International Journal of Innovative Science and Research Technology*, Vol. 5 No. 10, pp. 588-579.

Overby EM. (2008). Process Virtualization Theory and the Impact of Information Technology. *Organ Sci.* 19, pp.277–91

Overby EN, Slaughter SA, Konsynski B. (2010). The Design, Use, and Consequences of Virtual Processes. *Information Systems Research, INFORMS*. Vol.21:700–10.

Rahmi, B. A. K. I., Birgoren, B., & Aktepe, A. (2018). A Meta Analysis of Factors Affecting Perceived Usefulness and Perceived Ease of Use in the Adoption of E-learning Systems. *Turkish Online Journal of Distance Education*, Vol.*19*, No.4, pp. 4-42.

Valverde-Berrocoso, J., Garrido-Arroyo, M.D.C., Burgos-Videla, C. and Morales-Cevallos, M.B. (2020). Trends in Educational Research about e-Learning: a Systematic Literature Review (2009-2018). *Sustainability,* Vol. 12 No. 12, p. 5153.

# PREREQUISITES FOR STEM CLASSES USING AN EXAMPLE OF LINEAR ALGEBRA FOR A COURSE IN MACHINE LEARNING: INTERACTIVE ONLINE VS TRADITIONAL CLASSES

Genady Grabarnik[1], Luiza Kim-Tyan[2] and Serge Yaskolko[3]
[1]*Department of Math & CS, St. John's University, Queens, NY, USA*
[2]*Department of Mathematics, NUST MISIS, Moscow, Russia*
[3]*AD&D, College Board, Pittsburgh, PA, USA*

**ABSTRACT**

Any advanced class in Science, Technology, Engineering, and Mathematics fields requires prerequisite knowledge. Typically, different students will have different levels of knowledge in these prerequisite areas. A prerequisite (Linear Algebra for Machine Learning course) was implemented as an interactive online course using Jupyter Notebooks and nbgrader and compared with traditional classroom mode. Post-assessment test shows that traditional class provides a better level of understanding. However, a survey shows a preference by students and instructors for interactive implementation compared to traditional class.

**KEYWORDS**

Prerequisites, Machine Learning, Linear Algebra, Interactive Self-Study Course, Traditional Course Delivery, Jupyter Notebooks

## 1. INTRODUCTION

One of the characteristics of Engineering, as well as advanced Science and Mathematics, classes is that they are based on a wide spectrum of knowledge, study of which is usually spread among different subjects and fields. While a deep level of knowledge of each subject is highly beneficial, in many cases we lean to "understanding main concepts" level of knowledge as sufficient for the foundational or pre-requisite subjects.

For example, while studying in depth the main mathematical facts; mathematical classes targeting Engineering and Science students have a tendency to skip on methodology of proof, etc.

Similar situation exists for all major vs applied courses. The standard approaches, dealing with addressing such content dependencies, are either creating specialized applied courses coupled with proper rigid class schedule addressing these dependencies or creating highly specialized list of pre-requisite facts in the form of either self-study mini-courses or required material, which is covered in the recitations.

Some of the courses, so called "buzz" courses, have tendency to be taken by students of many specializations and levels. One of such courses in our university is a course in Machine Learning (ML), due to ML applicability in almost any current science and engineering major.

Our previous paper describes and analyzes the Interactive Online Concept Inventory (IOCI) system, see (Grabarnik, Kim-Tyan, & Yaskolko, 2020)

An ML course relies on knowledge of linear algebra, multi-dimensional calculus and probability. Another approach to handling pre-requisites, in addition to the above-mentioned two, is to provide material for student self-study on top of the refresher material and/or crash course material given during the course. The advantage here is that students get at least the minimum amount of the required material, with an option for additional self-learning if desired. We encounter multiple disadvantages, however, with such an approach. For one, time needed for the main subject is spent on prerequisites. Review time for prerequisites should be limited as it is very challenging to cover necessary material at a sufficiently high level. While students have the option to self-study, learning with an instructor is significantly more effective and efficient. Another disadvantage:

neither students nor instructors could verify whether the necessary level of understanding and ability to apply the prerequisite material had been achieved. This may be remedied with quizzes or tests, which in turn require additional precious instruction time.

We implemented the IOCI (Interactive Online Concept Inventory) course using iPython Notebook (Perez & Granger, 2007) software with additional course management support provided by the nbgrader plugin (Jupyter Notebooks, 2020). The course was developed on Amazon's c9 cloud and is available to students online. The course works in an automated or semi-automated way, allowing the instructor to see test results by topic and, if necessary, intervene and comment on student answers.

During COVID time it was difficult to overestimate the timing and usefulness of such IOCI course, however, as we return to normal classes, we pay more attention to the quality of instructions outcomes, and as our initial estimation shows, there is an instruction quality gap in the self-study vs traditional classes.

Due to finally ending COVID restrictions, we thought that it is important to return to this topic and spend more time on comparison of the traditional classes vs IOCI classes. This paper is devoted to describing our system(s) and courses, steps taken to make sure that we compare as close systems as possible, and the result of our initial analysis, that confirmed our previous, very restricted, observations.

This paper proceeds as follows. In section 2, we describe existing CIs and state-of-the-art Interactive Online Systems and work on a comparison of the traditional vs online classes. In subsection 3.1, we proceed to a description of LA (Linear Algebra) as a prerequisite material for the Machine Learning course. We show how CI addresses the requirement of the specific prerequisite material. In subsection 3.2, we describe the cloud system used for the initial implementation of the course as well as hardware requirements for running a test experiment of about 200 software simulated test students. In section 4, we provide a preliminary (proof of concept) evaluation of our approach. We end our paper with a conclusion and discussion of future work.

# 2. INTERACTIVE ONLINE CLASSES: STATE OF THE ART

## 2.1 Overview

The purpose of a prerequisite class differs from a "normal" class. It prepares a student for another class, not directly for a future career. Hence, it is often perceived as something less necessary. As observed in (Sato & et al., 2017), (Grabarnik, Kim-Tyan, & Yaskolko, 2018) students often see prerequisites as a waste of time and avoidable. If handled appropriately, a prerequisite course would solve motivational issues. One way to minimize time and resources spent is to make it self-paced so that a student goes through it at a comfortable pace and when time is available.

The first part of the outlined program – teaching only the material needed - is course specific and should be addressed on case-by-case basis.

The second part about level and form of material taught, however, can be answered in general, at least for Science, Technology, Engineering, and Mathematics (STEM) classes.

## 2.2 Notion of Concept Inventory

While teaching STEM classes, as we observed in most cases, a conceptual understanding and an ability to apply the prerequisite material are sufficient. Students are not expected to know details, such as proofs, etc. The CI is the best existing approach to assessing conceptual understanding rather than memorization of a set of facts. CI, as a form of an assessment, is based on checking if a student understands basic concepts of a given subject as opposed to reciting a number of subject specific facts, equations, etc. As David Hestenes states in his paper, *Force Concept Inventory*, (Hestenes, 1992) CI Assessment is "not a test of intelligence" but rather, "it is a probe of belief systems".

An immediate advantage of CI is that it can be used for any student. That is, it does not matter what the subject specific background of the student is, since, as stated above, CIs do not test formal knowledge but rather understanding of basic concepts. For example, as was demonstrated in (Epstein, 2013), there is no significant difference observed between the test results even if the class time, class readiness, or type of class are different. That includes even classes that lack traditional lectures, such as Mathematica-based classes.

Typically, CIs are created and delivered as multiple-choice tests. However, as opposed to standard tests CIs are not comparison tests but norm-referenced tests.

The main goal of CIs, as stated above, is to test the students' understanding of basic concepts. However, a typical CI test also checks for typical misconceptions.

The first CI was developed and published by David Hestenes in 1992 (Hestenes, 1992). It is known now as the Force Concept Inventory, or FCI and covers Newtonian Mechanics concepts. It was an immediate success and was recognized and accepted by thousands of educators.

Hestenes coined the term "modeling" to describe the conceptual approach to teaching – as opposed to the traditional factual approach. By now "modeling" approach covers well over 100,000 students each year.

As a result of CI's popularity, the American Modeling Teachers Association (AMTA) was created and grew into a nationwide community. Moreover, CIs began in various fields of engineering, science and mathematics.

CI assessment in introductory and prerequisite classes was studied, in (Grabarnik, Guysinsky, & Yaskolko, 2014), (Grabarnik & Yaskolko, 2013), (Sands, Parker, Hedgeland, Jordan, & Galloway, 2018), (Madsen, McKagan, & Sayre, 2017) (ALEKS), and (Krause, Decker, & Griffin, 2003). With CI the subject specific background of a given student is not significant as stated above because CIs do not test formal knowledge but rather test the student's understanding of related concepts, that is the student's working knowledge.

An understanding of related concepts is exactly what is needed in prerequisite classes: Mastering prerequisite material at a working knowledge level to apply it to the upcoming class.

Another advantage of using CIs: they are already developed for a wide variety of subjects in such areas as Natural Sciences, Engineering, Life Sciences, Mathematics & Statistics.

Therefore, there already exist large depositories of test problems for many subjects in case a need to create a prerequisite class for one of such subjects.

The last aspect – the interactive, self-paced form of the class – can be addressed only using technology.

## 2.3 Existing Interactive Online Systems

Interactive Online Systems are now widely used in both purely online and mixed-mode programs. The most popular ones are ALEKS™ (ALEKS), Cengage WebAssign (WebAssign), Knewton (Knewton), Pearson MyMathLab Study Plan (MyMathLab), Acrobatiq (Acrobatiq), Adapt (Adapt), etc. All these systems offer self-paced automatically graded classes for various subjects. Typically, each such class offers an Initial Assessment and then, based on the output each student gets, activities and learning material to work on with regular re-assessments to check on progress. Such re-assessment outputs in turn are again used to adjust the assigned activities and learning material.

As stated in (Lockee, 2021) the flexibility and learning possibilities that have emerged from necessity are likely to shift the expectations of students and educators, fading more away the line between classroom-based instruction and virtual learning.

The largest summary of online vs. classroom comparison research (Means & et al., 2010) concludes that students in online conditions perform modestly better, on average, than those learning the same material through traditional instruction. Learning outcomes for "students in online learning exceeded those of students in traditional classrooms, with an average effect size of +0.20 favoring online conditions."

However, "mixed-mode approach had a larger advantage relative to purely face-to-face instruction than did purely online instruction." The mean effect size in studies comparing mixed mode with traditional instruction was +0.35, $p < .001$. The existing systems, however, all emulate traditional classes in terms of curricula and syllabi. The only difference is the form in which the material and assessment are presented.

On one hand it makes the comparison quoted above reliable since there is an objective expected output for each curriculum – and the only difference is the form of presenting the material. Indeed, according to the study itself "analysts examined the characteristics of the studies in the meta-analysis to ascertain whether features of the studies' methodologies could account for obtained effects. Six methodological variables were tested as potential moderators: (a) sample size, (b) type of knowledge tested, (c) strength of study design, (d) unit of assignment to condition, (e) instructor equivalence across conditions, and (f) equivalence of curriculum and instructional approach across conditions. Only equivalence of curriculum and instruction emerged as a significant moderator variable ($Q = 6.85$, $p < .01$)."

On the other hand, simply emulating the existing traditional classes does not allow the online interactive form to use completely its intrinsic advantages. We do believe that prerequisite classes can benefit more from advantages than the online interactive form offers.

Using these three aspects together facilitates the creation of prerequisite classes that cover only the material really needed and taught in a conceptual form, assessed using the CI approach and put in a form of a self-paced interactive online class using Jupyter Notebook, or a similar platform.

## 2.4 Comparison of IOCI and Traditional Courses

The key aspects of IOCI classes are use of CI, asynchronous access and self-paced learning. While traditional classes can use, and many do use CI, two other aspects are of inherently online nature. Therefore, these two are mostly responsible for the differences in performance between the two learning modes.

The number of online classes has grown fast in recent years and will continue growing, and that creates multiple access issues, both technical and on a personal level (Lockee, 2021). Asynchronous self-paced classes obviously greatly alleviate the access issues and therefore make IOCI classes useful and valid solutions for post-COVID era.

There is a lot of research of online classes vs traditional classes based on learner characteristics and engagement, while influence of course design and development was examined to lesser degree (Martin, Sun, & Westine). That makes it important to compare learner perspective and actual performance in a close conjunction with the specific classes' designs.

E-learning is effective in increasing knowledge and is highly accepted. However, it is important not to focus only on increasing knowledge, but also on a field specific and social skills. E-learning should not only be based on the delivery of content, but students should be able to work with the materials and receive feedback. Successfully implementing online learning into the curriculum requires a well-thought-out strategy and a more active approach (Bączek & et al.). IOCI classes do offer both the field specific material to learn and constant proactive feedback, allowing to make the learning process more effective emulating traditional classes in that aspect, while keeping all online learning advantages listed above.

# 3. IOCI LINEAR ALGEBRA (LA) VS TRADITIONAL LA AS PREREQUISITE COURSES FOR ML

## 3.1 Required LA and IOCI content

The LA prerequisite class for Machine Learning class is an interactive online self-paced class built on the Jupyter Notebook platform.

The lectures are based on "Linear Algebra Review and Reference" by Zico Kolter and consist of four chapters:

1. Basic Concepts and Notation
   1.1. Matrix Multiplication
   1.2. Operations and Properties
   1.3. Matrix Calculus

The material presents basic definitions and concepts of LA necessary for studying Machine Learning.

Each chapter is divided into smaller sections. For example, the "2 Matrix Multiplication" chapter is divided as follows:

2.1 Vector-Vector Products
2.2 Matrix-Vector Products
2.3 Matrix-Matrix Products

Each section is supplemented by an auto-graded assessment based on CI principles.

A typical problem for Basic Concepts would be:

*Find the dimensions of the matrix*

$$A = \begin{bmatrix} 1 & 2 & 3 \\ 4 & 5 & 6 \end{bmatrix}$$

1. *2x3 (*)*
2. *3x2*
3. *1x6*
4. *6x1*

Option A is a key since the matrix has two rows and three columns.

Option B is a distractor that checks for a misconception that mixes rows with columns.

Option C is a distractor that checks for a misconception that considers a matrix as one long row with six elements.

Option D is a distractor that checks for a misconception that considers a matrix as one long column with six elements.

Another typical example would be

*Matrix*

$$\begin{bmatrix} -1 & 0 \\ 0 & 2 \end{bmatrix}$$

*has eigenvalues:*
*A. -1 and 0*
*B. -1 and 2 (*)*
*C. 0 and 2*
*D. It has no eigenvalues*

Option B is a key since (-1-x)(2-x)-0*0=0 has two roots, -1 and 2.

Option A is a distractor that checks for a misconception of the eigenvalues being the values of first row elements.

Option C is a distractor that checks for a misconception of the eigenvalues being the values of second row elements.

Option D is a distractor that checks for a misconception of considering a characteristics polynomial being -1*2-(0-x)(0-x).

IOCI assessments are based on a sufficiently large pool of problems and are randomly generated for each student and for each attempt. IOCI course provides final assessment after completion of the course material.

A student is able to take this class any time before taking the Machine Learning class, at a pace that fits her or his schedule and degree of prior knowledge. In addition to the lectures, we include the option of having students ask the instructor questions or discussing any aspect of the class with other classmates. Each assessment is auto graded but also can be graded by the instructor in case a student challenges the grade.

Traditional LA class covers material of the regular LA class, which, in turn covers all required pre-requisites and content of the IOCI course.

Pre-ML course evaluation for the students taking ML course after traditional LA course is taken from the final evaluation for the IOCI LA course. Comparison results of the Pre-ML evaluation and IOCI final are given in section IV. It shows a small but statistically significant advantage of the traditional course.

## 3.2 Organization of Classes and System Implementation

The system supporting IOCI was implemented on AWS Cloud 9 virtual machines with 20 Gb. hard-drive and 2 Gb RAM running Ubuntu v. 14, with Python 3.6, miniconda and installation of JupyterHub with nbgrader.

The system had some performance issues. To deal with performance the system was moved to a Lenovo P-520C workstation with Intel Xeon 6 core W-2133 Processor with vPro, 32 Gb. of RAM with dual hard-drive 512 Gb SSD and 2 Tb. HDD and 2 GB Nvidia P2000. This PC configuration proved to be sufficient to run up to 200 test students. We run IOCI on that workstation now.

The IOCI system was heavily used during COVID years 2020-21. Starting with Fall of 2021, we are in a process of returning to normal schedule and running regular pre-requisite classes. It is interesting to compare students' performance and satisfaction from regular classes and IOCI system. For that we had classes taught by the same faculty, using a similar style and methodology that were used in IOCI. Students were offered pre-course tests similar to the IOCI tests.

# 4. EVALUATION OF THE APPROACH

We evaluated traditional classroom and IOCI approaches by running two classes in parallel. for about 20 graduate students each taking the Machine Learning course. Half of the students studied the LA prerequisite material in the form of traditional class. Another half used the IOCI class we created. For both groups regular CI based assessments were used to compare the objective output. These assessments included pre- and post- preparation CI-based tests that check the quality of the required comprehension of the LA material. We also offered one-question survey for both instructors and students. The survey seeks to discover if the student/instructor prefers traditional classroom form or an IOCI form. An outline of the measurements approach may be found in (Means & et al., 2010), (Sands, Parker, Hedgeland, Jordan, & Galloway, 2018), (Evans, Howson, & Forsythe), (Gossman & Powell, 2019).

Both classes offered a sample that shows prerequisite materials used by their counterparts. Both the tests and the survey showed a statistically significant preference by the students of IOCI class over traditional class with 5% significance level.

Test results analysis is summarized in Table 1 below and uses standard t – test with a different standard deviation for testing if one of the means is larger than the other. The value of the test t shows statistical significance with a confidence level of $\alpha = 5\%$. Here the value *df* is degree of freedom, *d* is value of statistics, *t* is value of t-test corresponding values *d* and *df*.

Survey preference is analyzed in Table 2 using small samples t-test for population proportion (see D'Agostino et. Al., 1988, Upton 1982). A summary of analysis is offered below in Table 2. Here, the value of *N-2* is the degree of freedom, the value *d* is calculated (see D'Agostino et. Al., 1988, Upton 1982) as

$$d = (ae - bc)\left(\frac{N-2}{N(nac+mbe)}\right)^{\frac{1}{2}} \quad (1)$$

and values of the variables *a, e, b, c, N, n, m* used in the formula are corresponding ones in the numerical data below.

Table 1. One sided two means T-test for grades IOCI vs Traditional

| | IOCI | Traditional |
|---|---|---|
| N | 20 | 19 |
| mean | 82 | 88 |
| std | 6.3 | 6.6 |

| | |
|---|---|
| df (degree of freedom) | 29.0407 |
| d (see formula (1)) | 1.738422 |
| t | 0.046237 |

Figure 1. One sided two means T-test for grades IOCI vs Traditional (for data see Table 1)

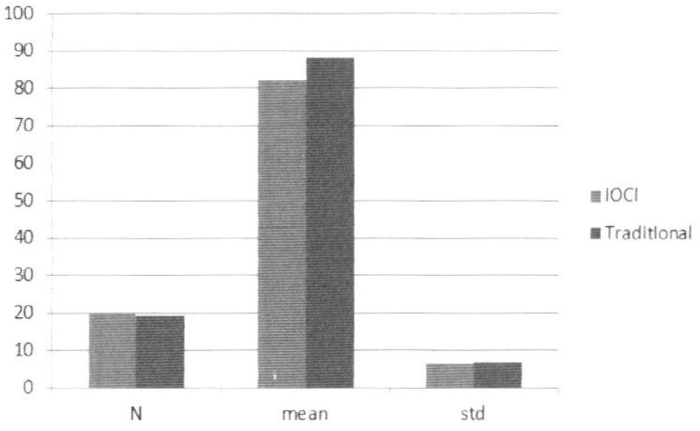

Table 2. Small samples T- test for population proportion comparison

| | IOCI Users | Traditional Users | Total |
|---|---|---|---|
| Prefer IOCI | a = 17 | b = 10 | s = 27 |
| Prefer Traditional | c = 3 | e = 9 | f = 12 |
| Total | m = 20 | n = 19 | N = 39 |

| N-2 | 37 |
|---|---|
| d | 2.196271215 |
| t | 0.018612316 |

Table 1 confirms our intuition that the average tests results for traditional classes is greater than the average tests results for IOCI classes – by about 6%. The difference is significant with 5% confidence level.

Table 2 shows that benefits and convenience of the IOCI classes are still preferred by users by vast majority of IOCI classes' users and by marginal majority of Traditional classes' users. This result is also statistically significant with 5% confidence level.

# 5. CONCLUSION

In our previous paper on the topic of prerequisites for the STEM courses, in particular, courses in Machine Learning, we analyzed option of providing prerequisites in the form of suggested reading only or, as an alternative, interactive online concept inventory (IOCI) form. Due to the new, COVID, reality we encountered the situation when regular scheduling of the courses was disturbed, and we had to rely only on IOCI for prerequisites. We observed that the general level of understanding as well as pre-course grades were lower than usual. We compared pre-COVID, normal scheduling pre-course assessment and COVID time assessment involving IOCI approach. Our limited in size study showed that while students show better satisfaction with IOCI approach, assessment shows statistically significantly better results for regularly scheduled courses.

We plan to run the LA prerequisite course with larger numbers of instructors and students and incorporate comments and suggestions from all participants. In a future we intend to offer the IOCI course as open source available to anyone.

# REFERENCES


Acrobatiq. (n.d.). acrobatiq.com.

Adapt. (n.d.). https://www.adaptlearning.org/.

ALEKS. (n.d.). www.aleks.com.

Bączek, M., et al. (n.d.). Students' perception of online learning during the COVID-19 pandemic. Medicine: February 19, 2021 - Volume 100 - Issue 7.

Epstein, J. (2013). The Calculus Concept Inventory - Measurement of the Effect of Teaching Methodology in Mathematics. Notices of the AMS Volume 60, N. 8, 1018.

Evans, C., Howson, K., Forsythe, A. (n.d.). Making sense of learning gain in higher education. Higher Education Pedagogies. 2018 Jan 1;3(1), 1-45.

Gossman, P., Powell, S. (2019). Learning Gain: Can It Be Measured? InEmployability via Higher Education: Sustainability as Scholarship, Springer, Cham., 37-51.

Grabarnik, G. Y., Guysinsky, M., & Yaskolko, S. (2014). An integrated approach to using statistics concept inventories in instruction. Integrated STEM Education Conference (ISEC). IEEE.

Grabarnik, G. Y., Kim-Tyan, L., Yaskolko, S. (2020). Addressing Prerequisites for STEM Classes Using an Example of Linear Algebra for a Course in Machine Learning. Mobile, Hybrid, and On-line Learning, eLmL, 29.

Grabarnik, G., & Yaskolko, S. (2013). Teaching statistics to non-mathematics majors: Interdisciplinary integration with R and EDA. 2013 IEEE Integrated STEM Education Conference. IEEE.

Grabarnik, G., Kim-Tyan, L., & Yaskolko, S. (2018). Improving STEM's Calculus education using cross-countries best teaching practices. 2018 IEEE Frontiers in Education Conference (FIE). IEEE.

Hestenes, D. (1992). Force concept inventory. The Physics Teacher, 30(3), 141.

Jupyter Notebooks. (2020). A system for assigning and grading Jupyter Notebooks. https://github.com/jupyter/nbgrader.

Knewton. (n.d.). www.knewton.com.

Krause, S., Decker, J., & Griffin, R. (2003). Using a materials concept inventory to assess conceptual gain in introductory materials engineering courses. Frontiers in Education, 2003. FIE 2003 33rd Annual, Volume 1, 7-11.

Lockee, B. (2021). Online education in the post-COVID era. Nature Electronics volume 4, 5-6.

Madsen, A., McKagan, S., & Sayre, E. (2017). Best practices for administering concept inventories. The Physics Teacher. Dec. 55(9), 530-536.

Martin, F., Sun, T., & Westine, C. (n.d.). A systematic review of research on online teaching and learning from 2009 to 2018. Comput Educ. 2020 Dec; 159.

Means, B., et al. (2010). U.S. Department of Education, Office of Planning, Evaluation, and Policy Development, Evaluation of Evidence-Based Practices in Online Learning: A Meta-Analysis and Review of Online Learning Studies. Washington, D.C.

MyMathLab. (n.d.). Pearsonwww.pearsonmylabandmastering.com.

Perez, F., & Granger, B. (2007). IPython: A System for Interactive Scientific Computing. Computing in Science & Engineering, vol. 9, no. 3, 21-29.

Sands, D., et al. (2018). Using concept inventories to measure understanding. Higher Education Pedagogies, 3(1), 173-182.

Sato, B., et al. (2017). What's in a Prerequisite? A Mixed-Methods Approach to Identifying the Impact of a Prerequisite Course. CBE Life Sci Educ, 16(1).

WebAssign. (n.d.). WebAssign.net.

# AN APPROACH TO SEMANTIC EDUCATIONAL CONTENT MINING USING NLP

Aisha Abdulmohsin Al Abdulqader[1], Amenah Ahmed Al Mulla[1], Gaida Abdalaziz Al Moheish[1], Michael Jovellanos Pinero[2], Conrado Vizcarra[1], Abdulelah Al Gosaibi[1] and Abdulaziz Saad Albarrak[2]
*[1]Computer Science Department*
*[2]Information Systems Department*
*College of Computer Sciences and Information Technology, King Faisal University, P.O. Box 400, Al-Ahsa 31982, Saudi Arabia*

**ABSTRACT**

The COVID-19 epidemic had caused one of the most significant disruptions to the global education system. Many educational institutions faced sudden pressure to switch from face-to-face to online delivery of courses. The conventional classes are no longer the primary means of delivery; instead, online education and resources have become the prominent approach. With the increasing demand for supplementary course materials to fulfill the needs of each area of study, students began to use search engines and online resources that contain discussions, practical demonstrations, and tutorial videos to aid students in their studies and course work. This study addresses the underlying challenges of retrieving relevant online educational materials by introducing an intelligent agent for semantic data mining. It works as middleware infrastructure that allow context-aware data processing and mining. YouTube was used to assess the consistency of the proposed model since it returns a large number of results in its search pool. The results showed that using the extraction of topics method, the similarities scores with the proposed model provided favorable results. Furthermore, an improvement in video ranking and sorting was realized. According to the findings, using this method provided users with a more productive and reliable study experience.

**KEYWORDS**

Information Retrieval, E-Learning, Natural Language Processing, Intelligent Agent, Semantic Data Mining

## 1. INTRODUCTION

On January 30, 2020, the World Health Organization declared the COVID-19 outbreak a global health emergency that caused a massive shift world wide's education system (Oyedotun, 2020). This crisis created an immense disruption of the education system that affected the teaching pedagogy. Educational institutions worldwide have seen a dramatic change in the educational system and faced a sudden pressure to switch from face-to-face to online delivery of courses (Kedraka & Kaltsidis, 2020). Due to the closure of educational institutions caused by COVID-19, conventional classes are no longer the primary means of delivery. Instead, online education has become the prominent approach where learning becomes virtual, practical, and smart (Raja & Nagasubramani, 2018). Closures of educational institutions will continue to substantially affect education, opening a path to exploring innovative teaching strategies to ensure learning continuity during pandemics. Alternately, the closures of educational institutions hinder the provision of essential services to students, specifically in accessing learning facilities such as the library and laboratory rooms where learning resources can be found to aid students in their studies. This poses a challenge in the current educational system to provide students with relevant online resources to support online learning besides course slides, handouts, and manuals to fulfill the needs of each area of study.

Students have unlimited learning resources which can easily be accessed online to help them in their assignments, projects, and learning (Yılmaz & Orhan, 2010). According to Li and Lalani, students can retain an average of 25% to 60% of materials when learning online (Li & Lalani, 2020). Similarly, existing research on the use of online learning resources reveals that it improves students' achievements and positively impacts students' academic self-confidence because they provide them with extra information that is required (Alshahrani et al., 2017). Although abundant materials are accessible online, there is a challenge finding suitable materials online. Retrieving relevant online materials is critical for online education as students rely heavily on it in researching their homework and assignments, which are the standard assessment methods in online education. Searching online for relevant materials can be a burden as different resources are within the search pool. Students may consume much time browsing all search results and, later on, find that these results are irrelevant (Biaz et al., 2014).

This research seeks to address these issues by introducing a data-driven approach to improve the retrieval of relevant educational materials online. The proposed approach extracts topics from the course syllabus and uses it to retrieve the most relevant and valuable materials online, reduces the time consumed in searching, and improves the search results to aid students in studying and course work. Additionally, the approach is based on two factors to determine the relevance of online materials. The first factor depends on retrieving information or the materials from websites and other online educational resources. The second factor is the ranking strategy to determine the most relevant resources online among the search pool. These factors will help us achieve our objectives to provide relevant educational materials to aid students in their studies and course work and lessen the time spent searching educational materials online.

The remainder of the paper is organized as follows: Section II presents the overview of previous studies related to online learning and discusses the different ways to cope with the COVID-19 pandemic in education. Section III presents a detailed discussion of the proposed model. Section IV describes the methodology to be used in this study. Section V provides the results, and the discussion will be in Section VI. In Section VII, the conclusion of the study is presented.

## 2. LITERATURE REVIEW

Several studies have shown the importance of online learning during the COVID-19 pandemic. One of these studies is "Freedom of learning in the 'elementary arts and culture' subject the character-based COVID-19 pandemic". The purpose of this study is to find the ability of students in the academic field to study online during the Covid-19 pandemic from February 2020 and to find out the advantages of online. The study results show that Covid-19 has a significant impact on education at the University of Muhammadyah Malang. Home teaching and learning processes utilize Edmodo, Google classroom, etc. The study also presented that employing educational YouTube videos can improve teaching, communication, and motivation for students to learn (Restian, 2020).

The school's readiness and response to COVID-19 in terms of pedagogy, curriculum, and assessment were investigated in a recent study (Gonzales, 2020). The researchers gathered data from the school's teachers to have a clear understanding of the main issues and listen to some proposed solutions. Finally, the researchers proposed a model focusing on six factors that are believed to be the most critical factors, which are, ICT Literacy Training, Stakeholder's Educational Equity, and Re-engineering of Teacher's Mindset, Pedagogical Innovation, Re-designing of the Curriculum, and Re-evaluation of Assessments and Grading System. Moreover, researchers in Georgia aimed to study the country's capacity to continue the education process in the online form of distance learning. This is done by making a case study where online learning using the Google Meet platform was implemented in a private school. The statistics of this case study showed that the quick transition to online education went successful. The experience of this study can be helpful for other countries that have not found the proper ways of change (Basilaia & Kvavadze, 2020).

Another study has been conducted to analyze the reliability and quality of YouTube educational content in the healthcare field. The overall result of the study shows that educationally useful videos are higher than non-educationally helpful videos with a 55.7% score (Lim et al., 2018). Although YouTube is known as an entertainment medium, it has become one of the popular learning platforms. Kohler and Dietrich (2020) recognize that YouTube has evolved into a complementary learning platform that promotes on-demand learning with instructional films and that educational videos are viewed as a successful method for improving a user's knowledge. However, the authors feel that it is important to distinguish educational films used in classrooms from educational videos found on YouTube. Also, a study was made to evaluate the quality of some areas related to medical information about COVID-19 on YouTube as educational resources for dental practitioners. YouTube was used to search for the phrases COVID-19 and dental practice, which yielded 1102 videos. Ultimately, the study results show that YouTube can provide relevant educational information (Yüce et al., 2020).

On the other hand, an evaluation has been conducted over the usefulness of YouTube videos as a health education tool for diabetes self-management. According to the article, the result of the evaluation shows that the probability of getting false information is high compared to finding useful information (Gimenez-Perez, 2018). Despite the availability of these professional education channels, YouTube is nevertheless filled with unpleasant and deceptive information that casual learners are forced to filter through when doing searches (Maynard, 2021). Anyone can use YouTube to post their own User Generated Content (UGC) by creating a personal YouTube channel and then uploading videos in his channel. Additionally, other users can subscribe to channels that they are interested in so they can follow the newly uploaded videos. Although YouTube is famous as an entertainment medium that is a non-educational platform, it became a valuable learning resource for many users and is considered an alternative to written text (Chintalapati & Daruri, 2017).

Information Retrieval offers more advanced tools in learning community and the mobile devices expands the educational activities thru collaboration and sharing of information (Parmigiani et al., 2016 & Meisalo et al., 2004). A video retrieval system in early 2000s (Milrad et al., 2004) was designed and implemented to enable semantic search for specific portions of a video clip in a library of educational digital movies. Gil et al., (2011), developed models and strategies for information retrieval that addressed by distributed information retrieval, often known as federated search. Finding the relevant materials in rich content resources could be a difficult task and time-consuming because of the enormous amount of search results that are generated. For example, the YouTube search ranking system looks through hundreds of pieces of content (Southern, 2020). Hence, it is essential to identify the right search keys when retrieving materials. Natural language processing (NLP) techniques were used by (Guitart et al., 2016) to extract information from the syllabus and to assess course materials. In information retrieval, it is important to evaluate the relevance of each result. The most prevalent measures for evaluating retrieval performance are recall and precision ratios. It was used by Guo & Zhang (2013) to assess the effectiveness of their semantic retrieval technique.

In this study, a semantic-based middleware model was proposed that applies NLP to extract topics from the course syllabus/outline and utilize them as a search key. Since a given rich content online resources will yield a large number of results in its search pool, another layer was proposed using a semantic text similarity analysis and ranked these results to get the most relevant materials based on the extracted topic.

## 3. PROPOSED MODEL

The proposed approach presents the architectural design of the semantic-based middleware model. It is divided into two main stages: topics extraction and topics enhancement. Figure 1 shows the proposed process model.

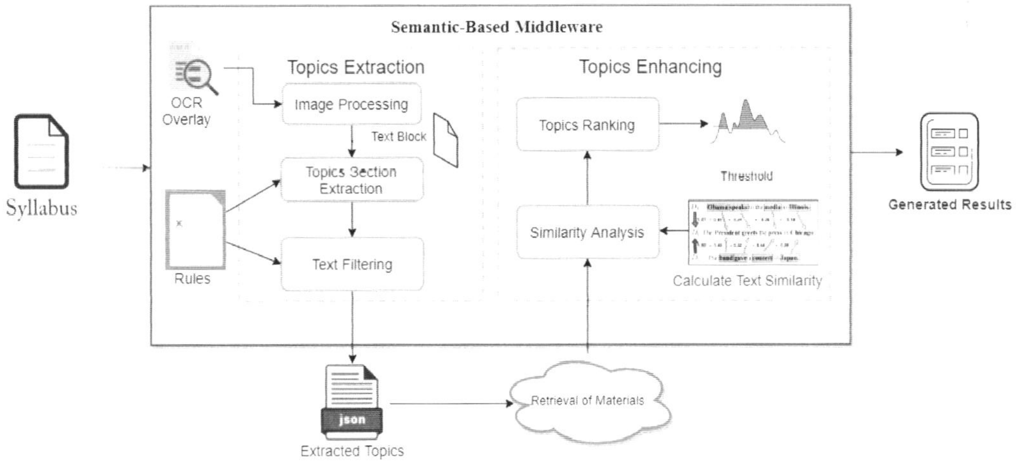


Figure 1. Semantic-Based Middleware Model

## 3.1 Topics Extraction

Extraction and recognition of text are principal stages in building efficient indexing and retrieving data (Misra et al., 2012). The approach utilizes topics either by uploading as text or captured from the syllabus. In this study, it is assumed that topics in the syllabus are properly sorted out. Extraction of topics will employ Optical Character Recognition (OCR) to highlight and extract the content of the syllabus. The processed syllabus image returned only as a text block in JSON format. The extracted text will be used to filter all course topics from a course syllabus at one time. In order to have a cleaner result, common keywords, e.g., "topics," "weeks," "lecture," "assessment," "project," "assignment" from the syllabus, are excluded from the extraction as shown in Figure 2.


```
["Introduction to Object Oriented
Programming", "Introduction to
Java","OOP main concepts: Objects
vs Classes Identifying", "Objects",
"UML class diagrams", "Modularity
& Encapsulation", "Inheritance &
Polymorphism"]
```


Figure 2. Sample extracted topics

## 3.2 Topics Enhancing

Once materials are retrieved, each extracted topic from the text extraction process will be queued for semantic text analysis. This study uses the term-based text similarity measures. Cosine similarity as shown in Eq. (1), a known technique of NLP, to find the closeness of two texts which operate on string sequences and character composition (Gomaa & Fahmy, 2013). The approach investigates the distance between two texts (A, B) for comparison and matches our requirement in comparing the title of retrieved materials and the topic titles. Then, the score results of all processed text similarities are stored and used for the ranking process.

$$similarity = \cos(\theta) = \frac{A.B}{|A||B|} = \frac{\sum_{x=1}^{n} A_i\, B_i}{\sqrt{\sum_{x=1}^{n} A_i^2}\,\sqrt{\sum_{x=1}^{n} B_i^2}} \quad (1)$$

After calculating text similarities, a novel ranking strategy will be applied to the retrieved materials to sort and rank the results. Behnert & Lewandowski (2015) discussed that presenting the result in a manner where the most relevant topic comes first before the less relevant topics is a way for us to assist every user in determining the significance of every search result. The proposed approach ranks the materials based on the score from text similarity analysis and sorts them out where the highest similarity scores will be at the top. This stage also includes a threshold, meaning any retrieved material scores less than the threshold value will be skipped, and the ones within the threshold range will be used. Sorted and ranked materials are then displayed on the application with the helped of WebView.

Algorithm 1 shows the topics ranking algorithm.

**Algorithm 1**

**Input:** Course Syllabus (Si)
**Output:** Sorted and Ranked Supporting Materials (Vi)

```
Ti ← Course Syllabus
foreach ti at Ti do
    SupMat-ti ← retrieve materials for each topic
  end for
foreach ti at SupMat-ti do
    tiScore ← calculate Semantic Similarity of the extracted topic and
      SupMat − ti

    if (SupMat − tiScore > th) then
        SupMat-tiScore ← tiScore
    end for
Sort SupMat-ti descendingly
```

# 4. RESEARCH METHODOLOGY

In order to evaluate this approach, YouTube was used, which is an online platform that includes enormous learning materials. To execute a simulation, five syllabuses were retrieved from online resources coming from different areas and levels of education (higher education, K to 12, and online courseware); Introduction to Algorithms (MIT OpenCourseWare), Data Science (University of Cambridge), Object-Oriented Programming 1 (King Faisal University), Grade 7 Science (K to 12 Curriculum from the Philippines), and Grade 6 Math (International Schools Group – Dammam) are used on this experiment. To process and extract topics from the syllabuses, Space OCR (Free OCR API, n.d.) and Optical Character Recognition API (Application Programming Interface) were used, which allows a simple way of parsing images and getting the extracted text results returned in a JSON format.

Extracted course descriptions and a list of topics are then fed to the search API. YouTube provides a data API that enables other platforms to retrieve YouTube videos to their applications. Based on the user interaction, YouTube will suggest videos. YouTube Data API (API reference, n.d.) was used, and the result is a simulated search on behalf of the user that supplies a limited result (Malik & Tian, 2017). The materials used in the ranking process started after retrieving all the videos and their data. Retrieved materials are stored and queued for text similarity analysis. The application uses TwinWord's Text Similarity API (Natural language processing APIs, n.d.) to compare each result to the topic title. The end result is sorted in a descending manner, in which materials with the highest similarity result will be on the top of the list.

# 5. RESULTS

The model's performance was assessed after executing the simulation using five syllabuses retrieved from online resources as discussed in the experimental setup, one topic per syllabus was used, which includes "Introduction to Object-Oriented Programming" (experiment 1), "Characteristics of Waves" (experiment 2), "The Number System" (experiment 3), "Binary Search Trees" (experiment 4), and "Linear Modelling" (experiment 5).

In identifying the best criteria for retrieving the relevant materials, two methods were tested. The first method was searching the relevant materials using the extracted course description and calculating the text similarity between the titles of the retrieved materials and the course description. The second method was searching relevant materials using the extracted topics and calculated the text similarity between the titles of the retrieved materials and the extracted topic titles. The Custom Search JSON API was used to dynamically retrieve the materials (Custom Search JSON API, n.d.). For simplification, Table 1, shows one of the experiments that shows the course description and title of the retrieved materials and the corresponding text similarity scores, and Table 2, shows the sample retrieved materials and their corresponding text similarity scores from the extracted topic title. Figure 4 to Figure 8 shows the graphical representation of results for text similarity scores of retrieved materials titles with course description from the syllabus.

Table 1. Sample retrieved materials using course description

| Course Description | Title | Similarity Score |
|---|---|---|
| The purpose of this course is t | JS. Drawing & Animation \| Computer programming \| Khan ..." | 0.412 |
| provide students with | "Planning a programming project (article) \| Khan Academy" | 0.226 |
| fundamental knowledge of | "Teaching guide: Intro to JS - Object-oriented design (article)." | 0.323 |
| Object-Oriented Programming | "Welcome to SQL (video) \| SQL basics \| Khan Academy" | 0.348 |
| (OOP). | "Random walks (article) \| Randomness \| Khan Academy" | 0.651 |

Table 2. Sample retrieved materials using extracted topics

| Course Description | Title | Similarity Score |
|---|---|---|
| Introduction to Object-Oriente | "Introduction of Object-Oriented Programming - GeeksforGeeks" | 1.00 |
| Programming. | "Object Oriented Programming in C++ - GeeksforGeeks" | 0.744 |
| | "Object Types \| Object-Oriented Design \| Intro to JS - Khan " | 0.857 |
| | "Java Tutorial: Introduction to Object-Oriented Programming" | 0.838 |
| | "Intro to Objects - Computer programming - Khan Academy" | 0.506 |

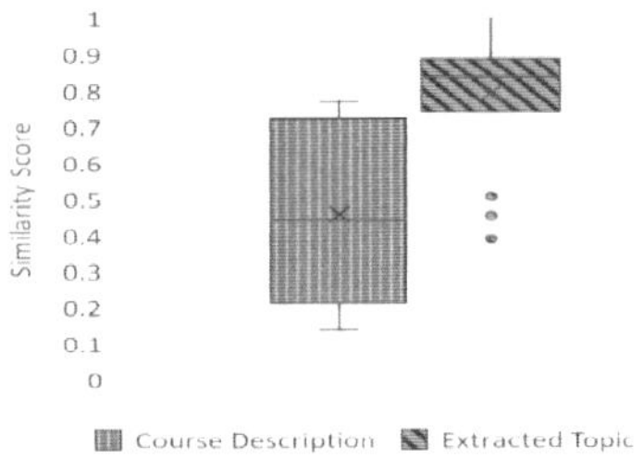


Figure 3. Scores of similarities in experiment 1

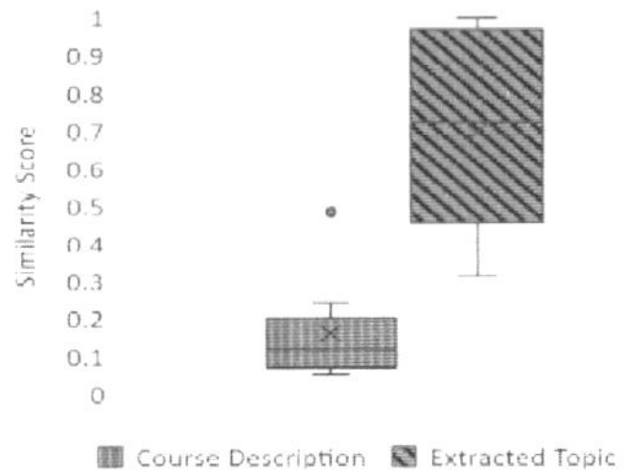


Figure 4. Scores of similarities in experiment 2

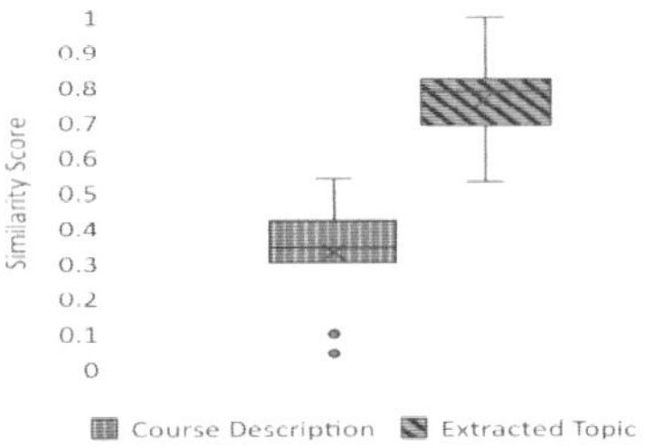


Figure 5. Scores of similarities in experiment 3

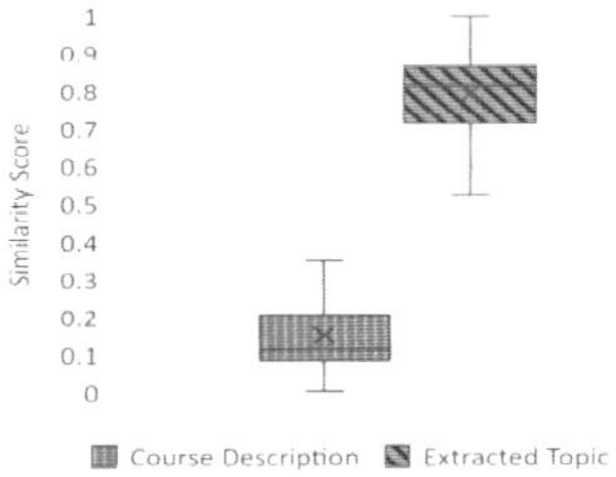


Figure 6. Scores of similarities in experiment 4

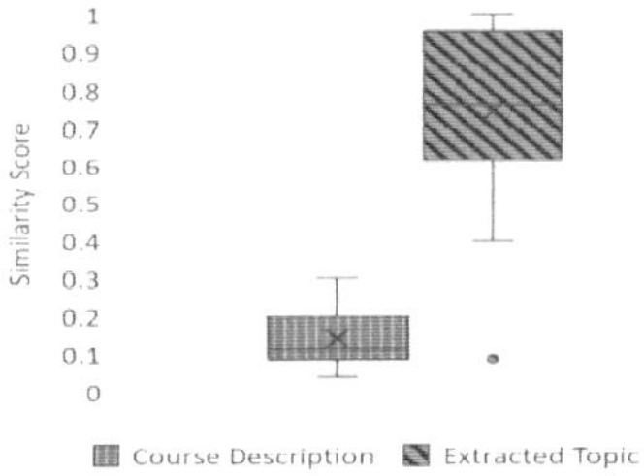


Figure 7. Scores of similarities in experiment 5

From Figure 3 to Figure 7, it is observed that the average scores of the retrieved materials using course description from five experiments ranges between 0.05 (low score average) to 0.49 (high score average), which is relatively low. Searching using the course description gives a large area of results which produces a low score in text similarity analysis between course descriptions and the result titles.

This also shows the results of the proposed approach, which calculates the similarity between the titles of the retrieved materials and the extracted topics. To simplify the discussion, one extracted topic per syllabus was selected from the experiments. It was observed that the result gave a much higher average score and ranged between 0.09 (low score average) to 0.80 (high score average), which is better compared to the similarity score with the course description. This happened as the search result was narrowed to a specific topic from the syllabus hence giving a higher similarity score.

Considering the results, the second method in the model was applied, which uses extracted topics from the syllabus in searching relevant topics on YouTube as it shows a much higher efficiency in similarity tests.

After retrieving the top twenty materials per topic, the similarity score between the retrieved video's titles and the extracted topics used in searching were calculated. Figure 8, shows the five experiments results and with average scores ranging between 0.36 (low score average) to 1 (high score average).

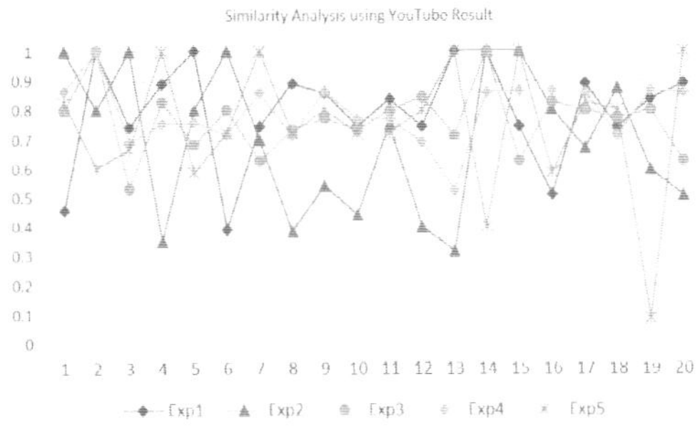


Figure 8. Similarity scores of unranked YouTube results from five experiments

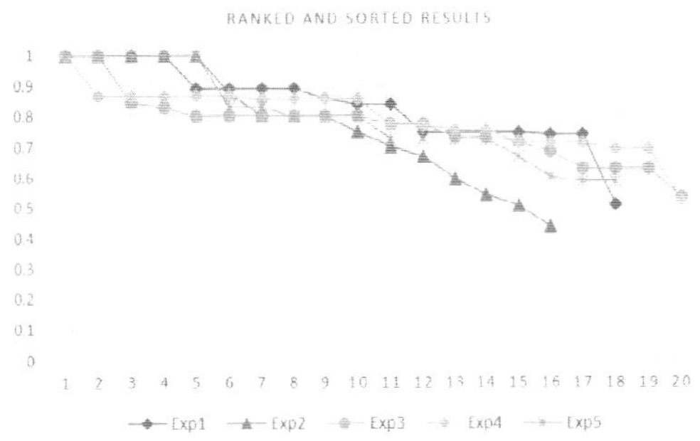


Figure 9. Ranked and Sorted Results

It can be observed that the videos can now be ranked and sorted based on the relevance to the topic according to the text-similarity scores and discard some results that are below the 0.4 thresholds, as shown in Figure 9.

## 6. DISCUSSION

This study used NLP to introduce a semantic-based middleware approach to address the underlying issues of accessing suitable online educational content. Filtering the list of topics was challenging, especially when the syllabus and course outline were using different layout formats. The best criteria for retrieving materials were also identified, and the two tested methods: searching using the course description and using the extracted title of each topic. Each method used five different syllabi with a total of 100 test samples per method. Table 3, shows the comparisons of the result of this experiment.

Table 3. Comparison between text similarity scores result from five experiments

| | Low Score (Ave) | High Score (Ave) |
|---|---|---|
| Scores of similarities with the course description | 0.05 | 0.49 |
| Scores of similarities with the extracted topics | 0.09 | 0.80 |
| Scores of similarities with the YouTube Result | 0.36 | 1.00 |

Searching using the course description method gave a large area of results which produced a low score in text similarity analysis between course descriptions and the titles of the retrieved materials. On the other hand, the result of the proposed approach using extracted topics title on the syllabus produced a higher average score (0.80), which gave an edge in retrieving many relevant materials from external sources and contributed to the high average score (1.00) in similarity scores with YouTube results from the five experiments conducted. One-Sample T-Test (One sample T test, 2021) with a Confidence Interval of 95% was run to assess if the similarity scores from extracted topics differ significantly in comparison with the similarity scores using the course description method. The descriptive statistics showed a mean of 0.4706 from similarity scores of the proposed approach with a 0.2680 standard deviation. Table 4, shows the result ($t(99)=7.936$, $p < .001$) and reveals a significant difference in score similarities of extracted topics.

Table 4. One Sample Test result

| | Similarities Scores of Extracted Topics |
|---|---|
| **Mean** | 0.4706 |
| **Std. Deviation** | 0.2680 |
| **t** | 7.936 |
| **df** | 99 |
| **Sig (p)** | < .001 |
| **Mean Differenc** | 0.2127 |

*Note: Test Value =0.257862(Mean similarity score of Course Description method)*

Even though the five experiments came from different levels of education, it can be observed that the area of concern does not affect the retrieval of data on YouTube. To evaluate the relevance of the retrieved materials, recall and precision were used, as discussed in (Arora et al., 2016). In the conducted experiments, 100 materials were retrieved from YouTube using the extracted topics and filtered 93 relevant materials using a threshold of 0.4 in the text similarities scores. This resulted in a recall of 93% using Eq. (2) and a precision of 100% using Eq. (3).

$$Recall = \frac{Relevant\ Materials}{Total\ Retrieved\ Materials} \quad (2)$$

$$\text{Precision} = \frac{Relevant\ Materials}{Actual\ Relevant\ Materials} \quad (3)$$

The result also shows that retrieved materials from YouTube are not ranked and not sorted for the user. Figure 9 presented the ranked and sorted result using the similarity scores of each material from highest to lowest. This helped in serving many relevant videos to be on the top of the list.

## 7. CONCLUSION

COVID-19 pandemic changed the way education is delivered. Number of governments moved to the online platform to overcome the virus outbreak and to keep social distancing. The study incorporates the Artificial Intelligence as an attempt to improve the results of information retrieval. It employs natural language processing (NLP) techniques to ensure data relevancy. The proposed approach utilizes an intelligent agent for semantic data mining and works as middleware infrastructure that allow context-aware data processing and mining. With the condition right now, it is crucial for learners to study from relevant educational materials to their courses from reliable online resources. Upon further reflection, the proposed system revealed some limitations that can be avoided in future work. One of the limitations is, the proposed system only supports the English language. Finally, it is identified that the initial results are auspicious. With proper authorizations, YouTube search API allows us to manipulate the feeds, and based on the test and observations conducted, the model improved the information retrieval quality in a rich content online resource. However, this framework was only applied to the YouTube platform. The content quality of the retrieved video materials is not assessed on this study. Future study may include the different factors in assuring the content quality by including the video category which to date is not used by YouTube in its search functions and the number of likes, dislikes, and views. This experiment concludes that using this approach gives the users a better study experience efficiently and effectively.

## REFERENCES

Alshahrani, S., Ahmed, E., & Ward, R. (2017). The influence of online resources on student–lecturer relationship in higher education: A comparison study. Journal of Computers in Education, 4(2), 87-106. https://doi.org/10.1007/s40692-017-0083-8

API reference. (n.d.). Google Developers. https://developers.google.com/youtube/v3/docs

Arora, M., Kanjilal, U., & Varshney, D. (2016). Evaluation of information retrieval: Precision and recall. International Journal of Indian Culture and Business Management, 12(2), 224. https://doi.org/10.1504/ijicbm.2016.074482

Basilaia, G., & Kvavadze, D. (2020). Transition to online education in schools during a SARS-Cov-2 coronavirus (COVID-19) pandemic in Georgia. Pedagogical Research, 5(4). https://doi.org/10.29333/pr/7937

Behnert, C., & Lewandowski, D. (2015). Ranking search results in library information systems — Considering ranking approaches adapted from web search engines. The Journal of Academic Librarianship, 41(6), 725-735. https://doi.org/10.1016/j.acalib.2015.07.010

Biaz, A., Bennamara, A., Khyati, A., & Talbi, M. (2014). Informational strategies and the use of information systems by doctoral students: A case study at the University of Hassan II Mohammedia, Casablanca. Procedia - Social and Behavioral Sciences, 116, 3598-3604. https://doi.org/10.1016/j.sbspro.2014.01.809

Chintalapati, N., & Daruri, V. S. (2017). Examining the use of YouTube as a learning resource in higher education: Scale development and validation of TAM model. Telematics and Informatics, 34(6), 853-860. https://doi.org/10.1016/j.tele.2016.08.008

Custom Search JSON API | Google Developers. (n.d.). Retrieved from https://developers.google.com/custom-search/v1/overview

Free OCR API (n.d.). Best Free OCR API, Online OCR, Searchable PDF - Fresh 2022 On-Premise OCR Software. https://ocr.space/ocrapi

Gil, A., De la Prieta, F., Rodriguez, S., & Martin, B. (2011). Educational content retrieval based on Semantic Web services. 2011 7th International Conference on Next Generation Web Services Practices. https://doi.org/10.1109/nwesp.2011.6088166

Gimenez-Perez, G., Robert-Vila, N., Tomé-Guerreiro, M., Castells, I., & Mauricio, D. (2018). Are YouTube videos useful for patient self-education in type 2 diabetes?. Health Informatics Journal, 26(1), 45-55. https://doi.org/10.1177/1460458218813632

Gomaa, W., & Fahmy, A. (2013). A survey of text similarity approaches. International Journal of Computer Applications, 68(13), 13-18. https://doi.org/10.5120/11638-7118

Gonzales, KP. J. (2020). Rising from COVID – 19: Private Schools' Readiness and Response Amidst a Global Pandemic, International Multidisciplinary Research Journal 2(2) 2020:81-90. DOI: 10.5281/zenodo.3918577

Guitart, I., Conesa, J., Baneres, D., Moré, J., Duran, J., & Gañan, D. (2016). Extraction of relevant terms and learning outcomes from online courses. International Journal of Emerging Technologies in Learning (iJET), 11(10), 22. https://doi.org/10.3991/ijet.v11i10.5928

Guo, K., & Zhang, S. (2013). A semantic medical multimedia retrieval approach using ontology information hiding. Computational and Mathematical Methods in Medicine, 2013, 1-7. https://doi.org/10.1155/2013/407917

Kedraka, K., & Kaltsidis, C. (2020). Effects of the COVID-19 pandemic on university pedagogy: Students' experiences and considerations. European Journal of Education Studies, 7(8). https://doi.org/10.46827/ejes.v7i8.3176

Kohler, S., & Dietrich, T. C. (2020). Potentials and limitations of educational videos on YouTube for science communication. https://doi.org/10.31235/osf.io/w4d9c

Li, C., & Lalani, F. (2020). The COVID-19 pandemic has changed education forever. This is how. World Economic Forum. https://www.weforum.org/agenda/2020/04/coronavirus-education-global-covid19-online-digital-learning

Lim, K., Kilpatrick, C., Storr, J., & Seale, H. (2018). Exploring the use of entertainment-education YouTube videos focused on infection prevention and control. American Journal of Infection Control, 46(11), 1218-1223. https://doi.org/10.1016/j.ajic.2018.05.002

Malik, H., & Tian, Z. (2017). A framework for collecting YouTube meta-data. Procedia Computer Science, 113, 194-201. https://doi.org/10.1016/j.procs.2017.08.347

Maynard, A. D. (2021). How to succeed as an academic on YouTube. Frontiers in Communication, 5. https://doi.org/10.3389/fcomm.2020.572181

Meisalo, V., Sutinen, E., & Tarhio, J. (2004). The possibilities of information retrieval in education. In Current research on mathematics and science education, Proc. The XXI annual symposium of The Finnish Association of Mathematics and Science Education Research (eds. A. Laine et al.) (pp. 528-549).

Milrad, M., Rossmanith, P., & Scholz, M. (2004). A web-based video retrieval system of educational films: Design, architecture and implementation aspects. IEEE International Conference on Advanced Learning Technologies, 2004. Proceedings. https://doi.org/10.1109/icalt.2004.1357385

Misra, C., K. Swain, P., & K. Mantri, J. (2012). Text extraction and recognition from image using neural network. International Journal of Computer Applications, 40(2), 13-19. https://doi.org/10.5120/4927-7156

Natural language processing APIs - Twinword API. (n.d.). Twinword. https://www.twinword.com/api/

One sample T test: SPSS, by hand, step by step. (2021, September 12). Statistics How To. https://www.statisticshowto.com/probability-and-statistics/hypothesis-testing/one-sample-t-test

Oyedotun, T. D. (2020). Sudden change of pedagogy in education driven by COVID-19: Perspectives and evaluation from a developing country. Research in Globalization, 2, 100029. https://doi.org/10.1016/j.resglo.2020.100029

Parmigiani, Davide & Giusto, Marta. (2016). Using smartphones and tablets in higher education contexts: an exploratory study within a teacher education programme. Research on Education and Media. 8. 10.1515/rem-2016-0002.

Raja, R., & Nagasubramani, P. C. (2018). Impact of modern technology in education. Journal of Applied and Advanced Research, S33-S35. https://doi.org/10.21839/jaar.2018.v3is1.165

Restian, A. (2020). Freedom of learning in the "elementary arts and culture" subject the character-based COVID-19 pandemic. Journal for the Interdisciplinary Art and Education, 1(1), 57-64. https://doi.org/10.29228/jiae.5

Southern, M. (2020). Google explains how YouTube search works. Search Engine Journal. https://www.searchenginejournal.com/google-explains-how-youtube-search-works/373189/#close

Yılmaz, M. B., & Orhan, F. (2010). The use of internet by high school students for educational purposes in respect to their learning approaches. Procedia - Social and Behavioral Sciences, 2(2), 2143-2150. https://doi.org/10.1016/j.sbspro.2010.03.296

Yüce, M. Ö., Adalı, E., & Kanmaz, B. (2020). An analysis of YouTube videos as educational resources for dental practitioners to prevent the spread of COVID-19. Irish Journal of Medical Science (1971 -), 190(1), 19-26. https://doi.org/10.1007/s11845-020-02312-5

# USING VIRTUAL REALITY SIMULATION TO REDUCE STAGE FRIGHT DURING PUBLIC APPEARANCES

Roger Seiler and Roberto Coviello
*Zurich University of Applied Science*
*St.-Georgen-Platz 2, P.O. Box, CH-8401 Winterthur, Switzerland*

**ABSTRACT**

Past applications of virtual reality (VR) and related research have provided evidence that VR technology is helpful for educational and training purposes and that it can be used as a therapeutic measure. Virtual reality exposure therapy (VRET) may, therefore, be beneficial in reducing public speaking anxiety (PSA), which is a very common phenomenon. In this preliminary study, we conducted an experiment to investigate the psychological and physiological response to stressors experienced when speaking in public by creating a virtual audience displaying worst-case-scenario behavior (gossiping, shaking their heads, pointing at the speaker, standing up, and even leaving the room). In addition, other potential stressors were introduced (standing on an elevated platform, jumping off the platform, blocking someone's path, approaching a door that opens automatically, and throwing objects). To measure the responses of participants to these stimuli, we asked them to complete a questionnaire and monitored their heart rate. Our findings suggest that people's anxiety increases when they interact with other people in a virtual world, and when they are exposed to certain stimuli, which may be reduced with the repeated application of VRET.

**KEYWORDS**

VR, Public Speaking, Stage Fright, Simulation, Education, VRET.

## 1. INTRODUCTION

Virtual reality (VR) has been used to reduce anxiety, traumata, and phobias (e.g., acrophobia, the fear of heights, or arachnophobia, the fear of spiders) for twenty years (Puscher, 2019). One form of anxiety, public speaking anxiety (PSA), affects the majority of the population. More than 70% of US citizens feel uncomfortable about appearing in public (Montopoli, 2017). As Asher et al. (2017) found, this problem can have a negative effect on the income, career, and quality of life of those affected. Virtual reality exposure therapy (VRET) can, therefore, be a useful resource in this context.

This paper adds to the existing knowledge on the topic of VR in healthcare. The experiment we conducted on the stressors of public speaking using a virtual world provides empirical evidence on factors affecting anxiety in VR by conducting a VR experiment in the context of public speaking.

## 2. LITERATURE REVIEW

Stress is omni-present and, according to Fink (2017), unavoidable as it is a unspecific response of the body to any external stimuli. Even basic bodily functions such as breathing or the consumption of energy (Selye and Selye, 1982). The concept of stress was investigated by Gebel (2012) who distinguished models of stress based on situation (stimuli), reaction, and transaction. The situational approach is linked to stressors such as noise, pain, and situations requiring performance (Seiffge-Krenke, 2007). Reaction-based models date back to Selye (1936), who further differentiated between "eustress" (negative stress) and "distress" (positive stress) (Selye and Selye, 1982). Lazarus (1966) expanded on this earlier work by creating a transactional model, in which the interpretation of the stressor and an analysis of the resources enable individuals to cope with stress, which leads to adaptation and learning.

A common form of anxiety is stage fright, also known as public speaking anxiety (PSA), which can, incidentally, also be present when videoconferencing (Pelletier, 2002). According to Reeves et al., "PSA is a prevalent condition with disabling occupational, educational, and social consequences" (2021a, p. 1). This fear is believed to have a prevalence ranging from 20 % (Leary and Kowalski, 1995) up to 85 % (Motley, 1995). Individuals suffering from PSA may even develop social anxiety disorder (SAD) (Blöte et al., 2009).

Symptoms of stage fright include nausea, dizziness, and heart palpitations (Abromeit, 2014). While these symptoms may not be noticeable to others, others such as sweating, or a trembling voice are. According to a study on the topic (Bippus and Daly, 1999), the top three factors contributing to feeling anxiety during public speaking are fear of making mistakes (M=7.04, S.D.=1.26), the unfamiliar role (M=6.61, S.D.=1.25), and fear of humiliation (M=6.6, S.D.=1.49) on a 9-point Likert scale. An overview of all factors is presented in Table 1.

Past research has shown that 360° videos (Reeves et al., 2021b) as well as training in virtual worlds can reduce anxiety (Wallach et al., 2009). Acoustic and physiological reactivity during a VR simulation can even predict the effectiveness of mitigating PSA (von Ebers et al., 2020).

Empirical evidence leans towards positive effects of VR training on PSA (Nazligul et al., 2017; Sakib et al., 2019; Yadav et al., 2020, 2019). Meta-analysis (Reeves et al., 2021a) and systematic literature reviews (Daniels et al., 2020) support these findings. Cognitive behavior therapy (CBT) and virtual reality exposure therapy (VRET) help treat PSA (Daniels et al., 2020). Daniels et al. (2020) even highly recommended the use of VR to treat PSA and reported reduction of PSA levels ranging from 7.8 % up to 54.7 %. This finding is backed by the meta-analysis conducted by Reeves et al. (2021a), who found significant effects for in-vivo exposure therapy (IVET) and VRET in marginal favor of IVET compared to VRET. In this context, self-led exposure seems to be as efficient as therapist-led exposure (Lindner et al., 2019).

Table 1. Ranking of factors based on averaged item ratings (Bippus and Daly, 1999)

| Factor | *M* | *SD* | *N* |
|---|---|---|---|
| 1. Mistakes | 7.04 | 1.26 | 192 |
| 2. Unfamiliar Role | 6.61 | 1.25 | 192 |
| 3. Humiliation | 6.60 | 1.49 | 189 |
| 4. Negative Results | 6.59 | 1.63 | 192 |
| 5. Rigid Rules | 6.08 | 1.40 | 192 |
| 6. Personality Traits | 6.07 | 1.74 | 192 |
| 7. Preparation | 5.50 | 1.65 | 192 |
| 8. Audience Interest | 4.86 | 1.78 | 192 |
| 9. Physical Appearance | 4.75 | 2.05 | 192 |

*Note.* Ratings are based on a 9-point scale, with 1 representing "not very likely" and 9 representing "very likely" as a cause of stage fright.

VR training in medical education has been proven to have a positive effect on learning outcomes (Cohen et al., 2005). This finding is backed by meta-analysis concluding that VR and AR (augmented reality) can have a positive effect on motivation and learning success (Garzón et al., 2019; Tekedere and Göke, 2016) and can be applied in continuous education, for instance, in the form of edutainment (Fritz, 1997). Furthermore, VR training can be used to deliver speech training to children, who readily accept this form of training and been shown to benefit as a result (Liu et al., 2017, 2013).

The concepts also have limitations, however. Health and safety issues (Hicks, 2016), such as the risk of cybersickness (Meeri, 2019), are a possible obstacle in VR simulation and training.

Because prior research has shown positive effects of VR on PSA, we conducted a preliminary, initial study to implement a prototype incorporating not only a traditional setting of public speaking but also measuring the physiological responses and comparing them to self-reported measures. This study compares different stimuli or stressors and sheds light on physical and psychological responses. The contribution of this research is, therefore, initial exploratory insights.

## 3. METHOD

This study uses an exploratory approach to gain first insights into how people respond to different stressors in a virtual environment in the context of public speaking. The virtual environment was generated by an HTC Vive HMD (2160x1200 px) and a VR system running Windows 10, an AMD Ryzen 5 2600 CPU, and an AMD Radeon RX580 GPU.

The virtual scenario was modelled with 50 virtual people in a lecture hall (see Figure 3). Some sat and listened, others talked to each other, stood up or even left the room to distract the person speaking.

The degree of realism was high (see Figure 1, Figure 2, and Figure 3). Unity was used as software to implement the immersive and realistic environment. The scene was built on a Unity asset, and objects such as laptops, books, pens, and bottles were imported from Unity's asset store. Noises were used To add further to the degree of realism since, according to Beqiri and Barnard (2019), this fosters immersion. In addition to a high degree of realism, haptic feedback (vibration of the controllers) was introduced because, according to Gutiérrez et al. (2008), this can also foster the degree of immersion experienced by participants.

Stressors were introduced to the scenario to exacerbate the speaker's stage fright in a scenario that could potentially be used to train participants and reduce their anxiety. According to Abromeit (2014), humiliation as the most common fear was also used. Stressors such as laughter (sound) and people shaking their heads (gesture) were added to contribute to the feeling of humiliation (Bippus and Daly, 1999). Distractions can lead to stress when holding a speech as they shift the mind from the current task (Priem and Solomon, 2009). The ringing of mobile phones, individuals talking to each other in the audience, and laughter are common stressors (Sherman, 2013). Furthermore, the size of the audience can contribute to anxiety (McKinney et al., 1983). In our experiment, therefore, we used people talking as well as laughing, shaking their heads, and pointing at the speaker as stressors. Some individuals even got up and left the room. Furthermore, a platform which was able to ascend and descend was another distraction. A real lecture hall environment was simulated with the sounds of people laughing, typing, and gossiping, and a school bell. Finally, objects such as cubes and balls were placed in reach of the speaker to further distract him or her.

In other words, to expose the speaker to stressors, five actions were part of their experience:

1. Using the platform to ride up and down
2. Jumping off the elevated platform
3. Blocking the path of the person leaving the room
4. Approaching the door to activate the opening of the door animation
5. Throwing a cube and a ball into the room

The levels of stress were measured using a questionnaire as well as monitoring the subjects' heart rate with a Polar H10 heart rate sensor. The completed questionnaire was compared to the heart rate recorded.

The questionnaire consisted of two parts. The first part contained questions regarding quality perception and the second part to self-reported degree of stress experience (see Table 2).

Table 2. Items contained in the questionnaire

| **Quality aspect (5-point Likert scale)** | **Perceived stress level aspect (5-point Likert scale)** |
|---|---|
| Quality 1 (Degree of realism) | Perceived Stress Level 1 (Riding the platform) |
| Quality 2 (Image quality) | Perceived Stress Level 2 (Jumping from platform) |
| Quality 3 (Usability) | Perceived Stress Level 3 (Opening door) |
| Quality 4 (Degree of concentration needed) | Perceived Stress Level 4 (Blocking person leaving) |
| Quality 5 (Degree of interaction) | Perceived Stress Level 5 (Throwing an object) |

Figure 1. Screenshot of environment

Figure 2. Screenshot of first-person view

Figure 3. Screenshot of scene (lecture hall) in Unity

# 4. RESULTS, DISCUSSION, IMPLICATIONS, AND LIMITATIONS

An abrupt increase in the heart rate indicate stress, negative feelings (Van Deusen, 2021), and is a reaction to a stimulus (Schubert et al., 2009), while a medium-range, stable heart rate can be a sign of health and wellbeing (Kim et al., 2018).

In our experiment, the data logged by the heart rate sensor indicated where an interaction took place in the virtual world (see Figure 4 and Figure 5). A raised heart rate was, therefore, used to identify the stimuli used (riding the platform, jumping off the elevated platform, approaching a door opening automatically, blocking people, and throwing objects) as stressors. As a result, we propose that the scenario we developed can be used to train public speakers and, eventually, reduce their anxiety levels.

Jumping from the platform showed the largest self-reported responses, followed by riding the platform, approaching the door that then opened automatically as well as blocking someone's way ('door' and 'blocking' showed the same levels), and throwing objects.

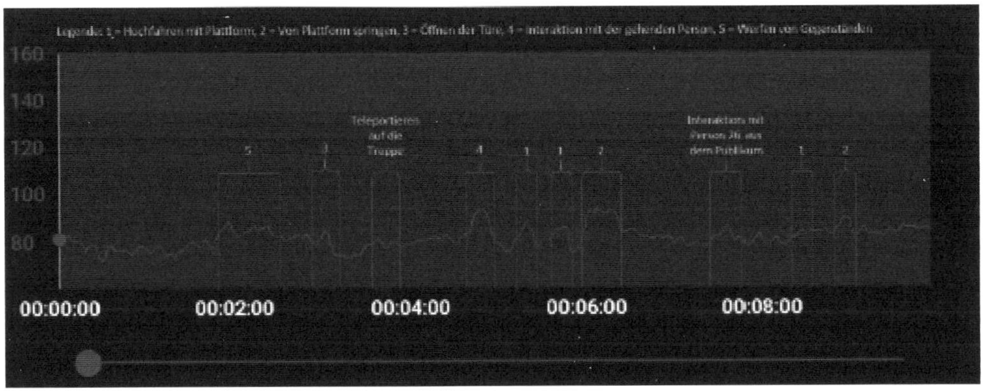


Figure 4. Heart rate analysis for Subject 1
(1 = ride platform, 2 = jump from platform, 3 = open door, 4 = interaction with person, and 5 = throwing an object)

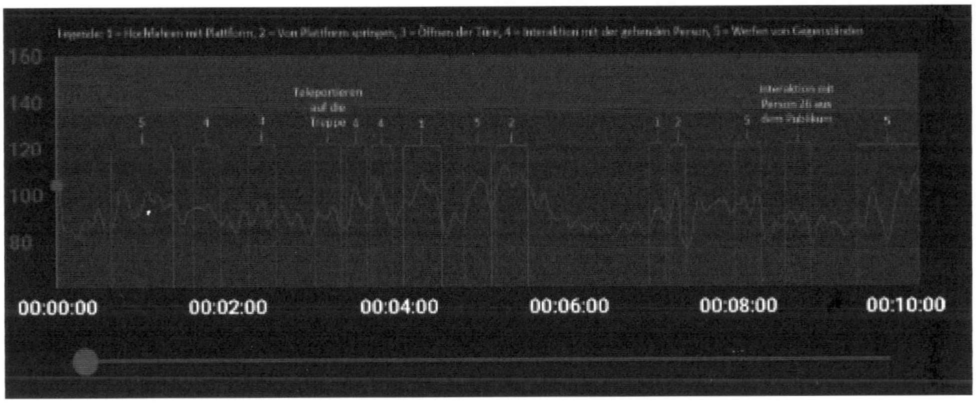


Figure 5. Heart rate analysis for Subject 2
(1 = ride platform, 2 = jump from platform, 3 = open door, 4 = interaction with person, and 5 = throwing an object)

The experiment was conducted using only six subjects and must, therefore, be considered early-stage, initial, and preliminary research. Nevertheless, the results show that responses can be observed as an impact on the heart rate of individuals exposed to public-speaking-related stimuli. Further research with a larger sample size needs to be conducted to confirm and expand on the findings of our study.

## 5. CONCLUDING REMARKS

The results presented in this paper indicate that anxiety levels can be deliberately manipulated in virtual environments and that these virtual events have an impact in the real world. The heart rate data collected indicates that responses to the stimuli provided have an effect (e.g., they cause stress and add to anxiety). This result contributes to the work of Pelletier (2002) finding PSA present in videoconferencing. Furthermore, this extends the work of Fink (2017) stating that stress is omni-present and an unavoidable unspecific response of the body conducted offline as the results in this paper suggest that this holds true in a virtual environment too.

Further, work on situational approaches (Seiffge-Krenke, 2007) or reaction based models differentiating between "eustress" and "distress" (Selye and Selye, 1982) are confirmed as well as extended as the results of this experiment suggest that they too, hold true in VR settings.

Symptoms of PSA (e.g., heart rate) found by Abromeit (2014) can be confirmed in the virtual world too. This knowledge may be helpful in training public speakers as symptoms of PSA can be triggered by VR training and thus, enabling public speaking simulation. Furthermore, according to Wallach et al. (2009) or Daniels et al. (2020), VR can help reduce this anxiety too and thus we imply that virtual worlds are used to reduce PSA by using the stimuli identified in this study.

Additionally, events and activities that involve a change of elevation and blocking people have the strongest impact. As described in the previous sections, the stressors presented in this paper can be used to raise anxiety levels for training purposes (VRET) (see Reeves et al., 2021b; Wallach et al., 2009) and subsequently reduce them permanently. This is rather relevant in the light of previous research into PSA (Leary and Kowalski, 1995;Motley, 1995). Consequently, our research can be considered as a contribution towards reducing PSA prevalence by providing stimuli for reducing PSA by VR training.

## REFERENCES


Abromeit, J., 2014. Lampenfieber und Prüfungsangst besiegen, 1. Aufl. ed, TaschenGuide. Haufe-Lexware, Freiburg.

Asher, M., Asnaani, A., Aderka, I.M., 2017. Gender differences in social anxiety disorder: A review. Clinical Psychology Review 56, 1–12. https://doi.org/10.1016/j.cpr.2017.05.004

Beqiri, G., Barnard, D., 2019. VR for Soft Skills Training. VirtualSpeech, London.

Bippus, A.M., Daly, J.A., 1999. What do people think causes stage fright?:Naïve attributions about the reasons for public speaking anxiety. Communication Education 48, 63–72. https://doi.org/10.1080/03634529909379153

Blöte, A.W., Kint, M.J.W., Miers, A.C., Westenberg, P.M., 2009. The relation between public speaking anxiety and social anxiety: A review. Journal of Anxiety Disorders 23, 305–313. https://doi.org/10.1016/j.janxdis.2008.11.007

Cohen, C.J., Hay, R., Urquhart, A., Gauger, P., Andreatta, P., 2005. A Modular Interactive Virtual Surgical Training Environment, in: Interservice/Industry Training, Simulation, and Education Conference (I/ITSEC). pp. 2074–2086.

Daniels, M., Palaoag, T., Daniels, M., 2020. Efficacy of virtual reality in reducing fear of public speaking: A systematic review. https://doi.org/10.1088/1757-899x/803/1/012003

Fink, G., 2017. Stress Neuroendocrinology, in: Stress: Neuroendocrinology and Neurobiology. Elsevier, pp. 3–15. https://doi.org/10.1016/B978-0-12-802175-0.00001-2

Fritz, J., 1997. Edutainment - Neue Formen des Spielens und Lernens?

Garzón, J., Pavón, J., Baldiris, S., 2019. Systematic review and meta-analysis of augmented reality in educational settings. Virtual Reality 23, 447–459. https://doi.org/10.1007/s10055-019-00379-9

Gebel, M., 2012. Stress und Motivation im Job - ein Zusammenspiel? Diplomica Verl, Hamburg.

Gutiérrez, M.A.A., Vexo, F., Thalmann, D., 2008. Stepping into Virtual Reality. Springer London, London. https://doi.org/10.1007/978-1-84800-117-6

Hicks, P., 2016. The Pros and Cons Of Using Virtual Reality In The Classroom [WWW Document]. eLearning Industry. URL https://elearningindustry.com/pros-cons-using-virtual-reality-in-the-classroom (accessed 11.28.21).

Kim, H.-G., Cheon, E.-J., Bai, D.-S., Lee, Y.H., Koo, B.-H., 2018. Stress and Heart Rate Variability: A Meta-Analysis and Review of the Literature. Psychiatry Investig 15, 235–245. https://doi.org/10.30773/pi.2017.08.17

Lazarus, R.S., 1966. Psychological stress and the coping process., Psychological stress and the coping process. McGraw-Hill, New York, NY, US.

Leary, M.R., Kowalski, R.M., 1995. Social anxiety. Guilford Press, New York.

Lindner, P., Miloff, A., Fagernäs, S., Andersen, J., Sigeman, M., Andersson, G., Furmark, T., Carlbring, P., 2019. Therapist-led and self-led one-session virtual reality exposure therapy for public speaking anxiety with consumer hardware and software: A randomized controlled trial. Journal of Anxiety Disorders, Virtual reality applications for the anxiety disorders 61, 45–54. https://doi.org/10.1016/j.janxdis.2018.07.003

Liu, D., Bhagat, K.K., Gao, Y., Chang, T.-W., Huang, R., 2017. The Potentials and Trends of Virtual Reality in Education, in: Liu, D., Dede, C., Huang, R., Richards, J. (Eds.), Virtual, Augmented, and Mixed Realities in Education. Springer Singapore, Singapore, pp. 105–130. https://doi.org/10.1007/978-981-10-5490-7_7

Liu, X., Yan, N., Wang, L., Wu, X., Ng, M.L., 2013. An interactive speech training system with virtual reality articulation for Mandarin-speaking hearing impaired children, in: 2013 IEEE International Conference on Information and Automation (ICIA). Presented at the 2013 IEEE International Conference on Information and Automation (ICIA), pp. 191–196. https://doi.org/10.1109/ICInfA.2013.6720294

McKinney, M.E., Gatchel, R.J., Paulus, P.B., 1983. The Effects of Audience Size on High and Low Speech-Anxious Subjects During an Actual Speaking Task. Basic and Applied Social Psychology 4, 73–87. https://doi.org/10.1207/s15324834basp0401_6

Meeri, K., 2019. Cybersickness: Why People Experience Motion Sickness During Virtual Reality [WWW Document]. Inside Science. URL https://www.insidescience.org/news/cybersickness-why-people-experience-motion-sickness-during-virtual-reality (accessed 11.28.21).

Montopoli, J., 2017. PUBLIC SPEAKING ANXIETY AND FEAR OF BRAIN FREEZES. National Social Anxiety Center. URL https://nationalsocialanxietycenter.com/2017/02/20/public-speaking-and-fear-of-brain-freezes/ (accessed 11.28.21).

Motley, M.T., 1995. Overcoming your fear of public speaking: a proven method. McGraw-Hill, New York, N.Y.

Nazligul, M.D., Yilmaz, M., Gulec, U., Gozcu, M.A., O'Connor, R.V., Clarke, P.M., 2017. Overcoming public speaking anxiety of software engineers using virtual reality exposure therapy, in: European Conference on Software Process Improvement. Springer, pp. 191–202.

Pelletier, M.-H., 2002. Cognitive-behavioral therapy efficacy via videoconferencing for social (public speaking) anxiety disorder : a single case design. University of British Columbia. https://doi.org/10.14288/1.0054529

Priem, J.S., Solomon, D.H., 2009. Comforting Apprehensive Communicators: The Effects of Reappraisal and Distraction on Cortisol Levels Among Students in a Public Speaking Class. Communication Quarterly 57, 259–281. https://doi.org/10.1080/01463370903107253

Puscher, F., 2019. Mit Virtual Reality gegen das Lampenfieber [WWW Document]. t3n Magazin. URL https://t3n.de/news/virtual-reality-gegen-1213866/ (accessed 11.28.21).

Reeves, R., Curran, D., Gleeson, A., Hanna, D., 2021a. A Meta-Analysis of the Efficacy of Virtual Reality and in Vivo Exposure Therapy as Psychological Interventions for Public Speaking Anxiety. Behav Modif 014544552199l102. https://doi.org/10.1177/0145445521991102

Reeves, R., Elliott, A., Curran, D., Dyer, K., Hanna, D., 2021b. 360° Video virtual reality exposure therapy for public speaking anxiety: A randomized controlled trial. Journal of Anxiety Disorders 83, 102451. https://doi.org/10.1016/j.janxdis.2021.102451

Sakib, M.N., Yadav, M., Chaspari, T., Behzadan, A.H., 2019. Coupling virtual reality and physiological markers to improve public speaking performance, in: 19th International Conference on Construction Applications of Virtual Reality (CONVR2019), Bangkok, Thailand. pp. 171–180.

Schubert, C., Lambertz, M., Nelesen, R.A., Bardwell, W., Choi, J.-B., Dimsdale, J.E., 2009. Effects of stress on heart rate complexity—A comparison between short-term and chronic stress. Biological Psychology 80, 325–332. https://doi.org/10.1016/j.biopsycho.2008.11.005

Seiffge-Krenke, I., 2007. Stress und Stressbewältigung im Kindes- und Jugendalter. Hogrefe, G??ttingen.

Selye, H., 1936. A Syndrome produced by Diverse Nocuous Agents. Nature 138, 32–32. https://doi.org/10.1038/138032a0

Selye, H., Selye, H., 1982. Stress: Bewältigung und Lebensgewinn. Piper, München Zürich.

Sherman, R., 2013. How to Deal with Distractions During Your Presentation. Patricia Fripp. URL https://www.fripp.com/how-to-deal-with-distractions-during-your-presentation/ (accessed 12.3.21).

Tekedere, H., Göke, H., 2016. Examining the Effectiveness of Augmented Reality Applications in Education: A Meta-Analysis. International Journal of Environmental and Science Education 11, 9469–9481.

Van Deusen, M., 2021. Everything You Need to Know About Heart Rate Variability (HRV) [WWW Document]. WHOOP. URL https://www.whoop.com/de/thelocker/heart-rate-variability-hrv/ (accessed 12.3.21).

von Ebers, M., Nirjhar, E.H., Behzadan, A.H., Chaspari, T., 2020. Predicting the Effectiveness of Systematic Desensitization Through Virtual Reality for Mitigating Public Speaking Anxiety, in: Proceedings of the 2020 International Conference on Multimodal Interaction. Presented at the ICMI '20: INTERNATIONAL CONFERENCE ON MULTIMODAL INTERACTION, ACM, Virtual Event Netherlands, pp. 670–674. https://doi.org/10.1145/3382507.3418883

Wallach, H.S., Safir, M.P., Bar-Zvi, M., 2009. Virtual Reality Cognitive Behavior Therapy for Public Speaking Anxiety: A Randomized Clinical Trial. Behav Modif 33, 314–338. https://doi.org/10.1177/0145445509331926

Yadav, M., Sakib, M.N., Feng, K., Chaspari, T., Behzadan, A., 2019. Virtual reality interfaces and population-specific models to mitigate public speaking anxiety, in: 2019 8th International Conference on Affective Computing and Intelligent Interaction (ACII). Presented at the 2019 8th International Conference on Affective Computing and Intelligent Interaction (ACII), pp. 1–7. https://doi.org/10.1109/ACII.2019.8925509

Yadav, M., Sakib, M.N., Nirjhar, E.H., Feng, K., Behzadan, A., Chaspari, T., 2020. Exploring individual differences of public speaking anxiety in real-life and virtual presentations. IEEE Transactions on Affective Computing 1–1. https://doi.org/10.1109/TAFFC.2020.3048299

# AN INCLUSIVE EDUCATIONAL TOOL

Paula Escudeiro[1], Márcia Campos Gouveia[2] and Nuno Escudeiro[3]
*Games, Interaction and Learning Technologies R&D Center, Instituto Superior de Engenharia do Porto,*
*Rua Dr. António Bernardino de Almeida, 431, Porto, Portugal*

**ABSTRACT**

Communicating in languages other than one's mother language is a demanding task. Even when mastering basic skills in a foreign language, communication is challenging unless you are a frequent user. The vocabulary and grammar rules tend naturally to be forgotten over time. This is even more critical when distinct channels are used by one's mother language and a given foreign language; this is the current setting when communication among deaf and non-deaf users is undergoing, even in the same country. We expect that the use of technology may assist users in such cases, notably through the Figure Out application. Figure Out is a mobile application designed to translate text, automatically captured by the mobile camera, to a given language. This application will allow translation from and to any language, including sign languages. The aim is to enable everyday users like, students, and all individuals to access information in their first language or the one they choose. By simplifying access to information, the application will improve accessibility, inclusion, and communication, namely between the deaf and non-deaf communities. With Figure Out it is possible to enhance the access of, students, tourists, and the deaf population to education, culture, and international mobility while reducing communication barriers.

**KEYWORDS**

Educational Communication, Inclusive Technology, Automatic Translation, Accessibility, Inclusion.

## 1. INTRODUCTION

In this paper, the authors suggest an alternative for the already known translators. The aim is to overcome limitations these may have with other precise solution, which enables translation in real-time through an image containing small parts of the text. This innovative, full-developed and tested technology not only allows individuals to read or hear the translation in the default language but also allows deaf individuals to understand the message through visual capture. No application on the market meets the features of Figure Out gathering optical text recognition from a captured image and converting it to text, audio, or sign language (Escudeiro, et al., 2017).

This application is designed to help everyone interested in communicating autonomously and in their first language, since communication between people who do not share the same language can be a challenge, whether their spoken language users or sign language ones.

Sign language faces low diffusion among the hearing community, making this assistive technology helpful for the deaf community when using services and infrastructures, visiting cultural venues, or reading text information, and even for deaf students by allowing them to use the same educational written material as their classmates. The same happens with Erasmus students, that can be certain that access to information will not be an obstacle by relying on this application.

## 2. ACCESSIBILITY AND INCLUSION

Foreigner environment "is not always accessible or inclusive (...) due to its barrier-laden and socially exclusive nature" (Gillovic & McIntosh, 2020). When talking about an inclusive foreigner environment we cope with

[1]*pmo@isep.ipp.pt*
[2]*magia@isep.ipp.pt*
[3]*nfe@isep.ipp.pt*

the need to reduce uncertainty for everyone who comes to visit us, ensuring that they are welcomed and supported, even if the host does not know sign language (Santa, 2020).

This will ensure that everyone can take advantage of learning and education, using services and infrastructures, visiting cultural sites, or accessing information independently and without the need for adaptation (Gillovic & McIntosh, 2020).

By promoting social inclusion and accessibility, communication between the deaf community and others will be improved (Escudeiro, et al., 2015). That is the aim of Figure Out.

## 2.1 The importance of Translation

Figure Out is not limited to users that travel outside their own country; the mobile application is helpful to every deaf who cannot easily access information, since it is designed to be multilingual and allow translation to Portuguese Sign Language.

By enabling translation to Portuguese Sign Language, this tool mediates communication, creating a relation of equivalence between two different languages thus overcoming communication barriers (House, 2016).

To do so, the Figure Out project exploits our previous experience in automatic translation of sign languages to develop a unique innovative tool that will boost an inclusive cultural environment addressing the deaf through the Inclusive Cultural Heritage Tourism (ICHT), project number POCI-01-0247-FEDER-69949. Developing an inclusive cultural environment will open doors to a significant share of global worldwide strategy for the cultural sector (Scheyvens & Biddulph, 2017).

# 3. METHODOLOGY

Figure Out aims to promote accessibility for all into our cultural heritage. Figure out is focused on creating digital tools and digital content in different languages, including sign language, to be available online, and on a mobile device.

A methodology was implemented to guide the implementation of the augmented reality application to promote cultural heritage sites in sign language. Figure Out provides an online collaborative platform to support the touristic process from end to end (promote/raise awareness, visit, follow-up/feedback).

## 3.1 Concept

The mobile application was developed to translate small pieces of text captured as an image to any given language in an augmented reality scenario. The output is also reproduced as speech. The language of the signs can be from any language. The translation is to be made to some predefined language selected by the user. The translation should be reproduced on the augmented reality application to text, sound, and sign language for deaf people. The reproduction of sign language must be implemented for any Sign Language. With the mobile diary, tool participants are enabled to quickly make diary entries whenever and wherever they use their mobile devices. This way, participants can easily document their current thoughts, actions, and surroundings. This tool should support mobile context-based co-creation in different development phases, including their prototypical technical realization and experiences of their practical application. The aim is to use this tool in a Living Lab. A Living Lab is an open innovation environment where users are integrated into the innovation process as much as possible. The best would be to get all relevant user information (ideas, feedback, concepts) from a real-world environment (not in a lab).

Thus, this mobile application is an innovative feature that allows deaf users to access information in sign language by capturing an image that contains written text of any kind. This technology is different from other options on the market that only allow the translation of written text or speech, and not from a real-time captured image.

The target audience is the daily users that want to read signs in a language different from their own. This way they can understand the signs and get continuous assistance from this mobile application. There are many situations where the user will require this kind of assistance, like translating small text snippets, reading text information from public transportation signs, timetables, tickets, receipts, or even restaurant menus (Escudeiro, et al., 2017).

Figure Out was created on top of the Virtual Sign technology, a full-developed translator that allows translation of the text to sign language (Escudeiro, et al., 2011).

## 3.2 Objectives

The scope of the Figure Out Project is to plan, design, build, and implement a system composed of a mobile application and website that enables the translation of written words to a given language.

The translated results may be presented to the mobile application users in written, audio, or sign language.

The mobile application records the word translated and the GPS position where the application was used and then these data are stored in a central database for statistical purposes.

Users can then access a website and check the stats about the application usage, such as most translated words and countries where the application is most used. Translation can be achieved with third party APIs.as for the application development, as the team has no mobile programming skills, this will be achieved with a cross-platform code generating framework using web APIs.

The scope of this project includes all requirements gathering, planning, design, development, and implementation of the Figure Out tool. In concrete, Figure Out pursued the following specific objectives:

- Development of a website to promote the product (the Website should allow the users to analyze usage statistics, analyzing the frequency and the place where the Figure Out application was used).
- Allow participants to create diary entries (Mobile Diary) at any time, from any place where they have their mobile phones, either by leaving a spoken message, picture, video, or sending a text message (a call results in multiple pieces of related data: e.g., a transcription of the voice message, an audio file, a timestamp, geo-tag, the participant ID, and the duration of the message, etc…).
- Collection of results in real-time, allowing for quick iterations on the tool and research method. This is great for customizing to individual studies (automated messages, e.g., push notifications, are sent to participants as gentle reminders to prompt an entry as well as to encourage ongoing participation).
- The possibility to analyze and easily report the data, after collecting the data.
- Support four different user types: administrator (technical and management), content specialist, mobile diary related users, casual browsers (unregistered general audience).
- Different application interfaces (layout) according to the user type. Interface language according to the user lingo. Message strings are stored in a way that allows easy translation.
- User registration is required for commenting and for submitting additional information (on submission the content specialist confirms the additional information and accepts or refuses the submission).
- Figure Out provides information on how to use the tools and the functionalities available to the user.
- The submission of additional information (photo, videos, …) will be stored in a directory on the server. All characteristics of these submissions will be stored in the database.
- Exploratory interface (search and retrieval of information given specific needs).
- Restrictions on data size, for videos and high-definition sound and images are adjusted to the user profile.

# 4. TECHNICAL RESOURCES

Given the technical knowledge required for mobile development, we saw fit to choose a framework that could serve both platforms simultaneously and with the most code re-usage possible. From the analysis of the available platforms, we ended up choosing PhoneGap.

## 4.1 Frontend Technology

The Front-end requirements can be divided into two main parts. The application and the website. Starting with the application development, we choose Ionic. Ionic is an open-source SDK for hybrid mobile application development. In simple terms, it can be used to create mobile applications, for both Android and iOS, with minimal changes, and create desktop websites, again with minimal changes to what has been done before. Regarding the website we choose Angular, as it is similar to Ionic because it is based on the same framework, making it easier, faster for the developers and most of our developer team already knew the technology.

## 4.2 Backend Server and Technology

Regarding the backend requirements, the team has a NodeJS server providing all the REST API routes to both our Application and Website. This way they have a centralized system, in which they have more control and easier maintenance. The reason for choosing NodeJS is that is widely used and quite easy to work with and find documentation. To store our data they choose firebase, given that some of our development team already had contact with the technology they found it appropriate to include.

## 4.3 APIs, Libraries, and Framework

This project requires a lot of APIs, frameworks, and libraries. For example, they will be using Adobe for the making of the promotional video, has it been a widely used software for this purpose. For capturing text with a camera, text to audio, text translation, they will use Google´s APIs. To translate from text to sign language it will be used the Virtual Sign translator (Escudeiro, et al., 2013).

## 4.4 OCR Integration

Added to the fact that the application should be able to run in both operating systems, Android and iOS should also be able to implement an OCR tool for the image to text recognition. Given the framework limitations compared to native development, the choice for an OCR was scarce and proved to be more difficult than anticipated.

After several types of testing with different OCR tools, we concluded that such tool integration with the chosen framework was not feasible. There were several types of incompatibilities and problems when trying to find a suitable OCR that worked suitably on its own, let alone being capable of working together with PhoneGap.

Given the situation, some new tests were made with a new multi-platform framework, Xamarin. This framework is based on C#, so the difference and availability of a new kind of OCR tools pointed that a new path could be opened. Sadly, although there are at least two fully functional and free OCR tools that work very well when running natively in operating systems like Windows or Windows Phone, they were not compatible with Xamarin.

## 4.5 Native Development

Even though the team lacked technical knowledge for complete native development, there was knowledge to build an application for Windows Phone, which regardless of not being in the requisites, was an opportunity to make a quick test with native development.

That test proved that native integration and availability of an OCR tool is by far the most recommended path to follow. It also added more proof to the information retrieved from the OCR search, which constantly pointed to native OCR for both Android and iOS platforms.

## 4.6 System Architecture

Figure Out was initially conceived to be centralized in a web service made available constantly and responsible for providing access to both data and resources of other components. We devised a 3-layer logical architecture, divided into UI, Server, and Data. The user interface is the layer that interacts with the user, through the mobile application or website. The web service layer is where the UI requests are attended, and the translation process takes place. The data is a persistence mechanism built for statistical purposes.

The technologies that were chosen for the development of the project were carefully selected to address the development team skills (figure 1).

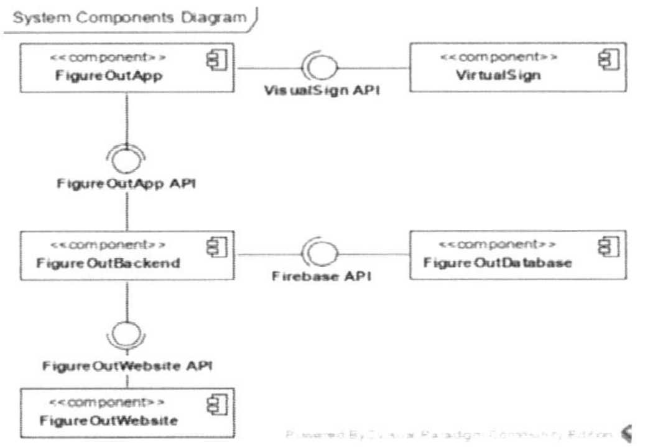


Figure 1. Logical Architecture

The technology selected for the development of the mobile application was Ionic, because of its cross-platform and the support of Android and iOS platforms. The development of the functionalities of the capture of images, text conversion to audio, and text translation to another language, can be developed with the use of Ionic plugins. For the sign language view, the VirtualSign API (Oliveira & Escudeiro, 2018) is going to be integrated with the mobile application, to allow the conversion of text to sign language.

The backend server was developed in Node.js and Express, allowing for the fast creation of a web server to communicate with the database and the Figure Out mobile application. For the database, it was used Firebase, allowing to push notifications to the mobile application and manage users.

## 4.7 The FigureOut app

The figure out mobile application aims to be intuitive so it can be used without training or any significant cognitive effort. The prototype mock-ups demonstrate the usage workflow: capture a photo using the mobile camera, configure the translation process if distinct from the default configuration previously set by the user, and proceed to translation.

The app homepage gives direct access to the translation feature in a straightforward way. From the homepage, the user may also access the About page providing access to the FigureOut webpage and additional information.

By starting a translation procedure, the user is directed to take a picture of the text to be translated with the mobile camera. The application will then identify and isolate the text area detected in the photo and present it together with the configuration panel. The user has a chance to use the default configuration or reconfigure each translation according to specific needs. The configuration of a translation involves choosing the languages pair and the output format. The output format is chosen from the three available alternatives.

An input field is also available so the user can type in the sentence to translate instead of capturing it using the camera.

# 5. PROJECT EVALUATION AND QUALITY SCENARIO CONTROL

The project evaluation followed a methodology that consists of functionality and user experience evaluation to assess a quality scenario. This is achieved with the quality efficiency framework.

The framework is called QEF (Quantitative Evaluation Framework). QEF will measure quantitatively the quality of the system being developed.

The quality scenario created was supported by the QEF framework and consisted of three major levels: dimensions, factors, and requirements. Each dimension aggregates a set of factors, and each factor includes a set of requirements.

The questionnaires which have supported the evaluation process at the Usability Dimension were based on System Usability Scale (SUS). It consists of a 10-item questionnaire with five response options for respondents; from Strongly agree to Strongly disagree (Brooke, 1995).

## 5.1 QEF Dimensions, Factors, and Requirements

The quality scenario for the Figure Out System measured with the QEF framework includes three main dimensions: Functionality (F), Adaptability (A), and Efficiency (E) (ISO 9126). The Functionality dimension is composed of four factors: functional, user interaction, content quality, and connectivity. The Adaptability dimension is composed of versatility and maintenance. Efficiency aggregates three factors: strength, consistency, and integrity (Escudeiro & Escudeiro, 2012).

The requirements identified for the quality scenario factors were:

- Functional: select the primary language; select the secondary language; navigation/position coordinates capture; avatar reproduction of sign language; audio reproduction of audio translation; translate capture to selected secondary language; download APP Android from the website; download APP iOS from the website; download User Manual from the website; language translation working on the website;
- User Interaction: android application is intuitive; iOS application is intuitive; applications have the same design in both versions; applications have the same navigation experience in both versions; scoreboard/statistics view - top five most searched words. scoreboard / Statistics view - top five highest usage countries; scoreboard/statistics view – topmost searched words in a certain period; scoreboard/statistics view – topmost searched countries in a certain period; scoreboard/statistics view - most searched word (the user can access the scoreboard/statistics view most searched word).
- Content Quality: all product information is well organized (all product information must be divided into functional areas); texts are well written and all the sentences make perfect sense (annexed standards) (the sentences are short and fulfill elementary grammar principles); all messages are easy to understand and human personified (no message presents illegible codes or similar codification form); all the contents are related to the product (all application contents must be strictly related to the product and present no dummy or irrelevant data);
- Connectivity: peripherals use permission (camera); peripherals use permission (GPS); peripherals use permission (internet); access audio repository (communication between applications and Google API); access storage repository (communication between applications and server while sending post request); Image capture (applications can capture the text on the image)
- Versatility: different desktop browsers compatibility (the application works correctly with different desktop browsers); different mobile browsers compatibility (the application works correctly with different mobile browsers)
- Maintenance: Adding the possibility of new features (Applications can add new features (for example the language))
- Strength: product has a good structure and allows users to access contents in an intuitive way to the main functions (each application has menus that allow the user to have an intuitive experience of usage); the application user interface is quick and fast responsive (the application does not freeze or lock when the user is working with it).
- Consistency: continuous operation (the application works continuously with other tasks, e.g., a call); outputs according to user inputs (the application responds according to what the user expects); all applications have a consistent audio and video experience (audio and video reproduction are timed with the operation); contents related with the product (the contents of the application meet the user expectations, meaning that they are what they should be from the user perspective).

The fulfillment level for each one of these requirements was discretized to pre-defined values that depend on the requirement. Some are simply assessed with either 0% or 100%, others rely on a 1-5 Likert scale, others are assigned to 3 (0%, 50%, 100%) to 5 percentage thresholds, such as 0, 25%, 50%, 75%, 100%. To reduce ambiguity when filling in the evaluation questionnaires all these levels are characterized for each requirement.

## 5.2 Evaluation Methodology

The project team assessed the product under development at several moments during the development lifecycle, including those reported here: alpha testing, beta testing, and final assessment. QEF provides a clear, quantitative view of the quality of a product at any stage during its development. The evaluation was based on a set of questionnaires that were designed to assess the requirements foreseen in our quality scenario (Escudeiro & Bidarra, 2008).

These questionnaires were answered by a group of twenty-two students from the Multimedia and Graphical Systems Master program from the School of Engineering of the Polytechnic of Porto. This controlled validation group used both Android and iOS mobile devices. The majority (73%) used Android. The concrete equipment used by each tester was not recorded. The following test protocol was settled and followed by all participants in the assessment:

1. On the website, create an account.
2. Watch the promotional video.
3. Scan/read the user manuals.
4. Download and install the mobile application.
5. On the mobile application, login with the previously created account.
6. Perform a text-to-text translation.
7. Use the video/image capture feature.
8. Perform a translation of the video/image captured before.
9. Provide feedback for the actions performed above.
10. Send a diary entry of any format.
11. Check the diary entries available.
12. Go further on using the application and exploring its features to provide answers to the assessment questionnaires

QEF uses the level of fulfillment of its underlying requirements to compute a quality value that lies between 0% and 100%. This quality corresponds to the percentage of achievement of the current version of the product in comparison to an ideal/perfect solution. The ideal solution is a system that fulfills at 100% all its requirements.

## 5.3 Evaluation Results

The overall FigureOut average quality, measured at each one of the formal evaluation moments, improved, as is expected, as the project evolves:

- Alpha testing: 76%
- Beta testing: 77%
- Final assessment: 96%

The overall quality is an aggregation of the quality measured at each dimension (Table *1*).

Table 1. Quality measurements

| Evaluation moment | F | A | E | Overall |
|---|---|---|---|---|
| Alpha | 51% | 85% | 74% | 76% |
| Beta | 53% | 86% | 74% | 77% |
| Final | 87% | 100% | 97% | 94% |

The evolution of the quality of the product between Alpha testing and Beta testing is marginal, from 76% to 77%. The improvements implemented from the Beta version to the last version are already significant. The boost was assured mostly by the Functionality dimension that improved 67% from the Beta version to the production version; Efficiency improved 31% while Adaptability improved 16%. This might indicate that the development team started pushing for the non-functional requirements – aiming to have a sound platform able to support the required functional features – before investing efforts in the functional requirements.

The features that are not fully met at the current version are:

- FF10 – Website – Applications can be downloaded from the website
- FF23 - Application - Replace text to the selected translation language in real-time (AR)
- FUI01 - Website – The website is intuitive
- FUI02 - Application - Android application is intuitive
- FUI03 - Application - iOS application is intuitive
- FUI06 – Application – Reduced sensory overload in AR view
- FCQ04 - Promotional Video - The storyline must be composed of two friends that go on a trip

- FCQ05 - Promotional video - Includes taxi receipt, airport sign, train station timetable, metro station placard, restaurant menu
- FCQ06 - Promotional video - Includes Portugal, UK, Slovenia, Cyprus, Greece, Germany, and Brazil
- EC05 - All applications have a consistent audio and video experience

## 6. CONCLUSIONS

Figure Out aims to cope with communication barriers of everyday users, by enabling access to information in their first language. This simplified access will improve the daily life of any tourist or individual such as a deaf student who finds it challenging to communicate in a language other than their own.

The development of this assistive technology serves not only as means to facilitate communication for everyone but also to promote the inclusion of those who use sign language to communicate and constantly strive to understand and to be understood.

We are evolving the current version of FigureOut in two fields: designing a more appealing visual identity and adding more national sign languages and International Sign into it.

## ACKNOWLEDGMENT

This work is being developed at the research group GILT – Games, Interaction and Learning Technologies from the Polytechnic Institute of Porto, with the support of FEDER – Fundo Europeu de Desenvolvimento Regional through the Sistema de Incentivos à Investigação e Desenvolvimento Tecnológico – I&D Empresas, under the frame of Portugal 2020, project number POCI-01-0247-FEDER-069949 and the Erasmus+ Programme, European Education and Culture Executive Agency, through project InSign - Advancing inclusive education through International Sign, project number 2019-1-DE01-KA203-004964.

## REFERENCES

Brooke, J., 1995. SUS: A quick and dirty usability scale. pp. 1-7.

Escudeiro, P. & Bidarra, J., 2008. Quantitative Evaluation Framework (QEF). *Revista Ibérica de Sistemas e Tecnologias de Informação,* pp. 16-27.

Escudeiro, P. & Escudeiro, N., 2012. Evaluation of Serious Games in Mobile Platforms with QEF: QEF (Quantitative Evaluation Framework). *2012 IEEE Seventh International Conference on Wireless, Mobile and Ubiquitous Technology in Education,* pp. 268-271.

Escudeiro, P. et al., 2017. *Digital Assisted Communication.* Porto, s.n.

Escudeiro, P. et al., 2013. *Virtual Sign Translator.* Beijing, Atlantis Press, pp. 290-292.

Escudeiro, P. et al., 2011. Automatic Sign Language Translator Model. *Advanced Science Letters,* Volume 4, pp. 400-407.

Escudeiro, P. et al., 2015. Virtual Sign – A Real-Time Bidirectional Translator of Portuguese Sign Language. *Procedia Computer Science,* pp. 252-262.

Gillovic, B. & McIntosh, A., 2020. Accessibility and Inclusive Tourism Development: Current State and Future Agenda. *Sustainability,* pp. 1-15.

House, J., 2016. *Translation as Communication across Languages and Cultures.* London: Routledge.

Oliveira, T. et al., 2018. *ACE Assisted Communication for Education: Architecture to support Blind & Deaf Communication.* Santa Cruz de Tenerife, IEEE.

Santa, J. G.-S. M. d. l., 2020. Tourism as a lever for a more inclusive society. *Worldwide Hospitality and Tourism Themes,* pp. 731-738.

Scheyvens, R. & Biddulph, R., 2017. Inclusive tourism development. *Tourism Geographies,* pp. 589-609.

# CRITICAL DETERMINANTS FOR LEARNING ANALYTICS ADOPTION IN HIGHER EDUCATION

Aaron Bere[1], Patrick Chirilele[2] and Rugare Chitiga[3]
[1]*Sydney International School of Technology and Commerce, 233 Castlereagh Street, Sydney 2000 NSW, Australia*
[2]*The University of Johannesburg, Cnr Kingsway & University Roads, Auckland Park, Johannesburg, 2092, South Africa*
[3]*Zimbabwe Open University, 836R+GH5, Alpes Rd, Harare, Zimbabwe*

**ABSTRACT**

The purpose of this paper is to present an empirical investigation of the critical determinants for the adoption of learning analytics in higher education. A conceptual model was proposed to understand better the adoption of learning analytics in higher education by teaching staff. Structural equation modelling is used for testing and validating the proposed conceptual model based on the survey data collected from Australia, South Africa, and Zimbabwe. Five study hypotheses were statistically significant, while two were statically insignificant. A positive relationship was revealed between user preparedness, technology preparedness, perceived usefulness, and social influence with behavioural intentions to adopt learning analytics in higher education. Hypotheses between user preparedness and perceived usefulness as well as user preparedness and learning analytics adoption were rejected. This study contributes to the learning analytics adoption research by proposing and validating a research model for the adoption of learning analytics in higher education.

**KEYWORDS**

Learning Analytics, Data Analytics, Organisational Preparedness, Behavioural Intentions, LMS.

## 1. INTRODUCTION

Learning analytics refers to using formal analysis techniques, such as machine learning and statistical techniques, to create information that improves decision-making in higher education (El Alfy, Gómez, & Dani, 2019). The adoption of learning analytics in higher education is becoming increasingly popular across the world, demonstrated not only in their rapid growth but also in the wealth of literature resulting from the active research in this area (Başaran & Daganni, 2020; El Alfy et al., 2019; Ngqulu, 2018). The popularity of learning analytics is owing to their potential benefits to active learning, improved teaching and learning approaches, implementation of early interventions for supporting student learning, better student retention, and improved student throughput (El Alfy et al., 2019; Fan et al., 2021).

The remarkable potential of learning analytics mainly is supporting student learning but has not been fully utilised. Most higher education institutions, particularly in developing countries, have not used learning analytics (Ngqulu, 2018). Those who have adopted learning analytics in higher education are still the entry-level adoptees (Başaran & Daganni, 2020; Clark, Liu, & Isaias, 2020). To effectively assist higher education institutions worldwide in their quest for learning analytics, understanding the critical determinants for university lecturers' adoption of learning analytics is significant (De Laet et al., 2020).

Few studies investigate the adoption of learning analytics (Ngqulu, 2018; Tsai, Kovanović, & Gašević, 2021). For example, Clark et al. (2020) explored the critical success factors for implementing learning analytics. Ngqulu (2018) investigated the critical determinants for adopting learning analytics in South Africa. The few studies that explored the critical determinants for learning analytics focus on limited samples, particularly from one institution with campuses in one country. This study explores the critical determinants for the adoption of learning analytics in higher education. A comprehensive review of the related studies is conducted. This leads to developing a conceptual model for exploring the criteria determinants for the adoption of learning analytics. The model is tested and validated using structural equation modelling on the survey data collected, leading to identifying the critical determinants for learning analytics. This study contributes to existing electronic learning research by enriching the understanding of the critical determinants for the adoption of learning analytics.

## 2. LITERATURE REVIEW

The rapid advancement of Learning analytics is continuously defining the significant areas of higher education (El Alfy et al., 2019). The increased acceptance and use of online learning for various reasons, including COVID-19 contact restrictions and firmer beliefs in the promises of online learning, has led to the generation of substantial amounts of data (Gibson & de Freitas, 2016). Learning analytics, and the application of data analytics in higher education institutions, have led to various benefits, including detecting at-risk students, tracking students' progress, predicting specific learning needs for an individual student, and revealing possible causes of students' academic achievement (Clark et al., 2020; El Alfy et al., 2019). Learning analytics obtains their data from Learning management systems (LMS) such as Moodle, Canvas, and Blackboard (Xin & Singh, 2021).

The LMS is developed to administer, track, report, and deliver educational courses and content. The software applications are accessible on a range of internet-enabled devices, including personal computers, laptops, iPads, Tablets, and smartphones (Xin & Singh, 2021). The high proliferation of LMS in higher education has led to the creation of massive datasets; however, obtaining relevant and accurate data from these data sets using applicable data analytics techniques has become more critical for lecturers to monitor and support students' learning (De Laet et al., 2020; Xin & Singh, 2021).

Data analytics analyses raw data to provide valuable insights to assist users in planning and implementing suitable interventions (Gutiérrez et al., 2020; Xin & Singh, 2021). There are four classifications of data analytics that can be implemented into LMS: descriptive analytics, diagnostic analytics, predictive analytics, and prescriptive analytics (Xin & Singh, 2021).

Descriptive analytics provides measured metrics and the activities in a certain period (Xin & Singh, 2021). In learning analytics, descriptive analytics enable lecturers to understand student performance patterns better and identify potential risk issues (Xin & Singh, 2021). Diagnostic analytics provide deeper insights that explain the causes of a problem under scrutiny. Diagnostic analytics are narrow and more specific than descriptive analytics (Xin & Singh, 2021).

Predictive analytics is more complex than descriptive and diagnostic analytics. They are driven by machine and deep learning algorithms for delivering a forecast of what is likely to happen. They employ descriptive and diagnostic analytics results to detect clusters and exceptions and predict future trends (Gutiérrez et al., 2020; Xin & Singh, 2021). Prescriptive analytics utilises machine learning and algorithms to prescribe a possible action that can be taken to eliminate a future problem (Xin & Singh, 2021).

The major LMS provides built-in data analytics features, which are primarily descriptive. Higher education systems that lack preparedness to adopt learning analytics often rely on built-in reporting tools based on log data. Low costs characterise these learning analytics systems, and their features and services are limited compared to data analytics plug-ins (De Laet et al., 2020; Xin & Singh, 2021). Third-party developers develop LMS plug-in learning analytics dashboards that emphasise diagnostic and prescriptive analytics to understand the cause of events and figure out solutions to improve learning outcomes. These applications are more costly than built-in. However, they are more effective and useful (De Laet et al., 2020; Xin & Singh, 2021).

Başaran and Daganni (2020) reported that learning analytics is a new technology. As a result, higher education institutions lack the capacity for staff with relevant skills. Additionally, they lack capacity in terms of technology infrastructure. This study provides insights into some of the causes of the low adoption rate s of learning analytics in higher education. Clark et al. (2020) conducted a study exploring the critical success factors for adopting learning analytics in higher education. The study results reveal five aspects of successful implementation and adoption of learning analytics, including strategy and policy at the organisational level, information technological readiness, performance and impact evaluation, people's skills and expertise and data quality. This study is valuable for highlighting critical factors for the implementation, acceptance, and use of learning analytics.

## 3. THEORETICAL FOUNDATION AND HYPOTHESES DEVELOPMENT

Learning analytics are developed through the implementation of data analytics for facilitating effective learning and teaching (Nguyen, Gardner, & Sheridan, 2020). With the rapid development of information and communications technology (ICT) and the growing adoption of online learning, learning analytics is becoming increasingly popular in higher education due to the potential benefits of learning analytics to higher education institutions (Fan et al., 2021; Tsai et al., 2021).

Many factors influence the acceptance and use of learning analytics in higher education (Tsai et al., 2021). Several studies reveal numerous theories for better understanding technology adoption, including learning analytics in higher education (Clark et al., 2020; De Laet et al., 2020; Fan et al., 2021; Jivet et al., 2020; Tsai et al., 2021). The most common theories include the technology acceptance model, task technology fit theory, theory of reasoned action, diffusion of innovation, organisation preparedness model, technology–organisation–environment framework, and Unified Theory of Acceptance and Use of Technology (Bere, 2018; Bere & Rambe, 2016; Clark et al., 2020; De Laet et al., 2020; Misra, Satpathy, & Mohanty, 2007; Tsai et al., 2021).

Due to the dynamic nature of online learning and the changing environment of higher education, the use of a single theory to investigate the critical determinants for the adoption of learning analytics in higher education is often subject to criticism due to the limitations of individual theories (Deng, Duan, & Luo, 2019). This study integrates the technology acceptance model and the organisation preparedness model. The organisation preparedness model argues that adopting a particular digital technology is much influenced by the constructs of user and technology preparedness. The technology acceptance model has been integrated to strengthen the model to understand better the user's opinions on the impact of learning analytics in higher education.

The technology acceptance model is the most widely used theory for investigating the acceptance and use of technology (Bere & Rambe, 2016). It states that technology adoption is influenced by the behavioural intention of users, which is determined by the attitude of users towards the use of technology. Additionally, the perceptions of users with regards to technology usefulness and ease of use are crucial factors in exploring the determinants for adopting a specific technology. Figure 1 presents the conceptual model for the study.

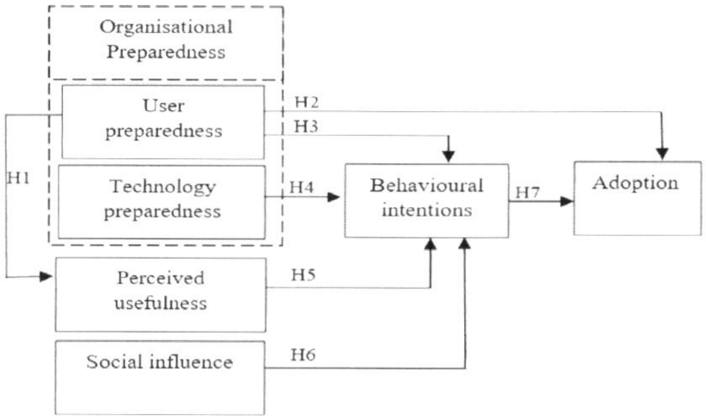


Figure 1. A conceptual model for the adoption of learning analytics

**Organisational preparedness**

Organisational preparedness refers to the ability of higher education institutions to successfully adopt, use and benefit from learning analytics (Ogunyemi & Johnston, 2012). The preparedness of users and technology are crucial contributors to organisational preparedness.

**User preparedness**

User preparedness describes how higher education staff and students are ready to productively adopt, use and benefit from specific learning analytics. User preparedness in learning analytics can be demonstrated through a display of various aspects, including tactical users showing abilities to undertake risks involving learning analytics and operational users exhibiting skills to understand the use of learning analytics for learning and teaching in higher education (Misra, Satpathy, & Mohanty, 2004; Misra et al., 2007). The following hypotheses have been developed about user preparedness:

*H1:* User preparedness positively is positively related to an individual's perceived usefulness of learning analytics.

*H2:* User preparedness positively influences the adoption of learning analytics

*H3:* User preparedness positively influences an individual's behavioural intentions to adopt learning analytics

**Technology preparedness**

Technology preparedness refers to a higher education institution's approach to managing learning analytics (Misra et al., 2007). Learning analytics involves various components, including big data, data storage, computer networks, learning analytics applications, and expertise. Higher education institutions should develop a plan for better aligning their learning analytics technology with existing information systems. The following aspects demonstrated a technology preparedness for a higher education institution (i) a standard technology and component plan to acquire learning analytics hardware and software technologies, (ii) capabilities to utilise learning analytics fully, and (iii) competence to successfully manage and assess the impact of learning analytics projects (Misra et al., 2004, 2007). The following hypothesis has been developed in relation to Technology preparedness:

*H4:* Technology preparedness positively influences an individual's behavioural intentions to adopt learning analytics

**Perceived usefulness**

Perceived usefulness refers to the degree to which individuals believe that using learning analytics would enhance their job learning and teaching performance (Bere & Rambe, 2016; Davis, Bagozzi, & Warshaw, 1989; Mafunda, Bere, & Swart, 2016). According to Davis (1989), perceived usefulness is a crucial determinant for influencing user attitude toward adopting a particular technology. The benefits of adopting learning analytics in higher education affect perceived usefulness among students and higher education staff. The following hypothesis has been developed in relation to perceived usefulness:

*H5:* Perceived usefulness positively influences an individual's behavioural intentions to adopt learning analytics

**Social influence**

Social influence states that an individual's emotions, opinions, or behaviours to accept and use learning analytics are influenced by others (Bere, 2018). The decision of higher education staff members, such as lecturers, could be influenced by their colleagues and managers. Prior researchers suggest that social influence as a variable has a significant effect on a person's intention to adopt a specific digital technology owing to attained satisfaction through conformity and identification (Amofa, 2014). The following hypothesis has been developed in relation to social influence:

*H6:* Social influence positively influences an individual's behavioural intentions to adopt learning analytics

**Behavioural intentions**

Behavioural intentions refer to motivational factors that determine the need for individuals to adopt learning analytics (Amofa, 2014). Behavioural intention is the most important predictor of an individual's behaviour in adopting learning analytics (Ajzen, 2020; Amofa, 2014). The following hypothesis has been developed in relation to behavioural intentions:

*H7:* An individual's behavioural intentions are positively related to the adoption of learning analytics

# 4. RESEARCH DESIGN

This study explores the critical determinants for the adoption of learning analytics in higher education. The study adopted a survey-based approach to achieve its objective of the study. The use of a survey is appropriate in this study because it enables the testing and validation of the proposed model while verifying the critical determinants for adopting learning analytics. Data was collected from higher education lecturers from Australia, South Africa, and Zimbabwe to better understand the critical factors influencing their acceptance and use of learning analytics for supporting student learning.

## 4.1 Demographic Characteristics

The demographic characteristics of the participants are summarised in section. The result reveals that most respondents are male (56.02%). The participant's age groups range from 30 to over 50 years. Additionally, the sample drawn comprises lecturers from Australia (43.46%), South Africa (31.94%), and Zimbabwe (24.60).

Previous studies that investigated the adoption of digital technologies employed a self-completion questionnaire (Bere, 2019; Bere & Rambe, 2016; Deng et al., 2019; Mafunda et al., 2016). This approach has been reported to be easy to manage and quickly score. This leads to faster data collection. Due to these reasons, this study employed a self-report questionnaire for data collection.

The questionnaire for the study has been developed using existing literature based on the study's objectives. It used a 7-point Likert scale format. The responses options ranged from 1 to 7, representing ''strongly disagree'', ''disagree'', ''partially disagree'', ''Neutral'', ''partially agree'', ''agree'', and ''strongly agree'' respectively. Fifteen participants comprising 8, 4, and 3 from Australia, South Africa, and Zimbabwe were randomly chosen for pilot-testing the questionnaire. Pilot testing enabled the researchers to identify and correct ambiguous statements in the questionnaire. Table 2 below presents the 21-item questionnaire measurement items used as the basis for the questionnaire developed for this study.

# 5. MAIN SURVEY DESIGN

Previous studies show that a sample of at least 175 participants would be ideal for achieving 95 % confidence (El-Gayar, Moran, & Hawkes, 2011). The questionnaire for the study was administered by a data collection online tool called survey monkey to 263 participants in 2021. A total of 197 questionnaires were returned, but six were discarded due to incomplete competition. As a result, 191 were deemed usable, comprising a response rate of 73 %, surpassing a minimum recommended sample size.

In this study, partial least squares (PLS) were used for the statistical analysis of data. PLS is suitable for this study due to its limited demand for data distribution compared to other statistical software packages used for structural equation modelling (El-Gayar et al., 2011).

The objective of using PLS is to measure the direction and strength of the relationships among model constructs. The PLS statistical analysis method has also been used to compute each item's weights and loading factors about the construct it was proposed to measure (El-Gayar et al., 2011).

Evaluating the measurement model requires assessing the internal consistency for every batch of constructs and their construct validity (Bere & Rambe, 2013). Factor loadings measure the composite reliability (CR) and average variance extracted (AVE) to evaluate internal consistency. The CR and Cronbach's alpha measure the reliability of the constructs, but CR provides a closer approximation (Bere & Rambe, 2013; El-Gayar et al., 2011).

## 5.1 Results

The mean values for this study ranged from 5.66 to 6.23, as shown in Table 3. Such mean values reveal they show that participants have a positive evaluation of the adoption of learning analytics (Fornell & Larcker, 1981). A factor loading of at least 0.7 is recommended for measured variables (El-Gayar et al., 2011). The factor loadings for this study ranged from 0.763 to 0.958, indicating that the measured variables have good reliability (Bere & Rambe, 2013; Fornell & Larcker, 1981).

The primary indicators for measuring convergent validity are CR and AVE. The recommended CR is 0.7, which covers internal constancy. The CR for this study ranges from 0.854 to 0.943, signifying a good internal consistency for each construct (Bere & Rambe, 2013; El-Gayar et al., 2011; Fornell & Larcker, 1981). AVE indicates the measure of the error-free variance of a set of convergent validity (Fornell & Larcker, 1981). A recommended AVE should be greater than 0.5 (Fornell & Larcker, 1981). In this study, the AVE for individual construct ranges from 0.793 to 0.916.

Table 1. Constructs descriptive statistics and instrument reliability and validity

| Construct | Item | Mean | Factor loading | Cronbach's α | Composite reliability | AVE |
|---|---|---|---|---|---|---|
| User preparedness | UP1 | 6.23 | .793 | .836 | .816 | .850 |
| | UP2 | | .817 | | | |
| | UP3 | | .849 | | | |
| | UP4 | | .763 | | | |
| | UP5 | | .811 | | | |
| Technology preparedness | TP1 | 5.87 | .924 | .911 | .791 | .916 |
| | TP2 | | .887 | | | |
| | TP3 | | .909 | | | |
| Perceived usefulness | PU1 | 5.66 | .841 | .915 | .875 | .793 |
| | PU2 | | .786 | | | |
| | PU3 | | .827 | | | |
| | PU4 | | .771 | | | |
| Social influence | SI1 | 6.12 | .958 | .860 | .901 | .824 |
| | SI2 | | .936 | | | |
| | SI3 | | .891 | | | |
| | SI4 | | .918 | | | |
| Behavioural intentions | BI1 | 6.61 | .862 | .936 | .779 | .831 |
| | BI2 | | .869 | | | |
| | BI3 | | .805 | | | |
| | BI4 | | .858 | | | |
| | BI5 | | .929 | | | |

Discriminant validity evaluates the extent to which assessed constructs that should be unrelated are, in reality, unrelated. The notion of discriminant validity is endorsed when the square root of AVE for each construct is greater than the correlation coefficients between the construct and the other constructs (Fornell & Larcker, 1981). The results of this study reveal, as shown in Table 2, existence due to the square roots of AVE being more significant than the correlation coefficients between the construct and the other constructs (El Alfy et al., 2019; Fornell & Larcker, 1981).

Table 2. Discriminant validity calculation

| | UP | TP | PU | SI | BI |
|---|---|---|---|---|---|
| User preparedness (UP) | **.713** | | | | |
| Technology preparedness (TP) | .324 | **.862** | | | |
| Perceived usefulness (PU) | .582 | .625 | **.796** | | |
| Social influence (SI) | .269 | .532 | .521 | **.865** | |
| Behavioural intention (BI) | .426 | .712 | .428 | .481 | **.924** |

Bold values show all the square roots of AVE, which are greater than the correlation coefficients between the construct and the other constructs.

## 5.2 Modelling Testing

The structural model analysis assesses the path coefficients (β) and $R^2$ for constructs of the research model. The β values evaluate the relative strength and sign of causal relationships amongst the constructs (Bere & Rambe, 2013; Deng et al., 2019). The $R^2$ estimates denote predictability for the research model. The combination of β and $R^2$ values provides the relationship between the structural model and experimental data (Bere & Rambe, 2016). For a path to be statically significant, a minimum β value of 0.05 is recommended (Bere & Rambe, 2016). Figure 3 indicates β and $R^2$ for this study.

The recommended acceptable β value for a path to be statically significant is at least 0.005. Figure 3 shows that H3, H4, H5, H6, and H7 are statistically significant with β values of 0.651, 0.314, 0.689,0.254, and 0.423 respectively while H1($\beta = 0.039$) and H2($\beta = 0.043$) are statistically insignificant hypotheses.

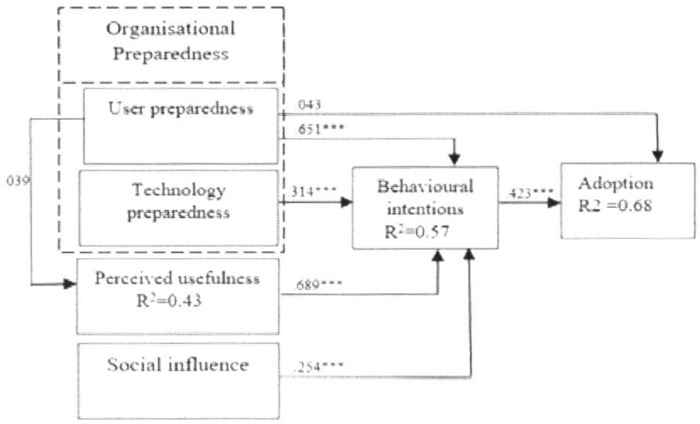


Note ***p ≤ 0.001

Figure 3. Structural model analysis

In this study, $R^2$ greater than zero ranges from 0.43 to 0.68. The $R^2$ correlations show that perceived usefulness explained 43% variance, behavioural intentions explained 57% variance, and adoption explained 68% variance. The $R^2$ attained in this study reveals that the constructs are significant.

The path coefficient β of 0.651 for H3 shows that user preparedness positively influences lecturers' behavioural intentions to adopt learning analytics. This finding is consistent with Dondorf, Pyka, Gramlich, Sewilam, and Nacken (2019)'s findings which reveal that for lecturers to develop positive intentions to adopt learning analytics, they should perceive that learning analytics application software is to be easy to use, including visualisations that are easy to access. Ifenthaler (2017) argues that the adoption of learning analytics in higher education is lacking due to the lack of lecturers with appropriate skills for using learning analytics. This finding suggests better learning analytics training programmes for lectures since trained users are highly likely to adopt learning analytics to improve their teaching and learning. Ngqulu (2018) emphasises vital staff development programmes enable high utilisation of learning analytics in higher education.

The path coefficient β of 0.314 for H4 shows that organisational technology preparedness positively influences lecturers' behavioural intentions to adopt learning analytics. This finding is consistent with Misra et al. (2007)'s claim that digital technologies available, including hardware, software, and network infrastructure, influence the lecturer's intentions to use technology. Ifenthaler (2017) argues that the adoption of learning analytics in higher education is deficient due to the lack of suitable learning analytics technology. This finding suggests that higher learning analytics adoption could be achieved with improvements in learning analytics infrastructure in higher education institutions. Dondorf et al. (2019) stated that various higher education institutions rely on built-in learning analytics of learning management systems such as Moodle. This demonstrates the higher education organisational preparedness to provide adequate technologies for learning analytics. The finding of this study suggests that higher investments in learning analytics technologies may improve learning analytics adoption by the lecturers.

The path coefficient β of 0.689 for H5 shows that perceived usefulness positively influences lecturers' behavioural intentions to adopt learning analytics. This finding is consistent with Gibson and de Freitas (2016) finding that lecturers' intentions to adopt learning analytics are driven by these technologies' ability to present insights that help understand what learners know and can do based on their interactions in digital learning spaces. Such understanding enables lecturers to implement suitable interventions for reducing supporting student learning. El Alfy et al. (2019) stated that lecturers' perceived usefulness of learning analytics is based on their ability to analyse various data, including students' test scores, demographics, and students' psychographics and gain insights into students' learning. This leads to a reduced workload for lecturers, resulting in positive intentions to adopt learning analytics.

The path coefficient β of 0.254 for H6 shows that social influence positively influences lecturers' behavioural intentions to adopt learning analytics. Ngqulu (2018) argues that management encourages lecturers to exploit their full potential by using learning analytics. This suggests that lecturers' behavioural intentions to adopt learning analytics are influenced by other people they think are essential in their careers. This finding is inconsistent with Başaran and Daganni (2020) result that reported a weak relationship between social influence and behavioural intentions.

The path coefficient β of 0.423 for H7 shows that behavioural intentions positively influence lecturers to adopt learning analytics. This finding is consistent with Başaran and Daganni (2020)'s finding that reported a strong relationship between behavioural intentions and adoption of learning analytics in higher education. This suggests that the lecturer's decision to adopt learning analytics starts with their positive intentions.

The path coefficient β of 0.039 for H1 shows that user preparedness does not affect the perceived usefulness of lecturers. This suggests that a lecturer's proficiency in learning analytics has no impact on their belief regarding learning analytics usefulness.

The path coefficient β of 0.043 for H2 shows that user preparedness does not affect lecturers' perceived usefulness. This indicates that a lecturer's proficiency in learning analytics has no direct significance in learning analytics adoption.

## 6. CONCLUSION

This study investigates the critical determinants for the adoption of learning analytics in higher education. A comprehensive review of the related studies is conducted, leading to developing a conceptual model with the integration of the organisational preparedness and technology acceptance model constructs. The model for the study is tested and validated using structural equation modelling on the survey data collected, leading to the identification of the critical determinants for learning analytics adoption in higher education. The study shows that the critical determinants of adopting learning analytics in higher education are user preparedness, technology preparedness, perceived usefulness, social influence, and behavioural intentions. Two hypotheses for the study were statistically insignificant, while five hypotheses were statistically significant.

## REFERENCES


Ajzen, I. (2020). The theory of planned behaviour: Frequently asked questions. *Human Behavior and Emerging Technologies, 2*(4), 314-324.

Amofa, K. K. (2014). *Management consultants' accceptance of internet technology: An empirical study of the determinants of web analytics technology acceptance.* Capella University,

Başaran, S., & Daganni, A. M. (2020). Learning Analytics Tool Adoption by University Students. *Learning, 11*(7).

Bere, A. (2018). Applying an extended task-technology fit for establishing determinants of mobile learning: an instant messaging initiative. *Journal of Information Systems Education, 29*(4), 239-252.

Bere, A. (2019). *Investigating the impact of digital technologies on the performance of learning in higher education.* RMIT University,

Bere, A., & Rambe, P. (2013). *Extending technology acceptance model in mobile learning adoption: South African University of Technology students' perspectives'.* Paper presented at the International Conference on e-Learning.

Bere, A., & Rambe, P. (2016). An empirical analysis of the determinants of mobile instant messaging appropriation in university learning. *Journal of Computing in Higher Education, 28*(2), 172-198.

Clark, J.-A., Liu, Y., & Isaias, P. (2020). Critical success factors for implementing learning analytics in higher education: A mixed-method inquiry. *Australasian Journal of Educational Technology, 36*(6), 89-106.

Davis, F. D. (1989). Perceived usefulness, perceived ease of use, and user acceptance of information technology. *MIS quarterly*, 319-340.

Davis, F. D., Bagozzi, R. P., & Warshaw, P. R. (1989). User acceptance of computer technology: A comparison of two theoretical models. *Management science, 35*(8), 982-1003.

De Laet, T., Millecamp, M., Ortiz-Rojas, M., Jimenez, A., Maya, R., & Verbert, K. (2020). Adoption and impact of a learning analytics dashboard supporting the advisor—Student dialogue in a higher education institute in Latin America. *British Journal of Educational Technology, 51*(4), 1002-1018.

Deng, H., Duan, S. X., & Luo, F. (2019). Critical determinants for electronic market adoption: Evidence from Australian small-and medium-sized enterprises. *Journal of Enterprise Information Management.*

Dondorf, T., Pyka, C., Gramlich, R., Sewilam, H., & Nacken, H. (2019). Learning Analytics Software Implementation for the Moodle Learning Management System. *Proceedings of the ICERI2019, Sevilla, Spain*, 11-13.

El-Gayar, O., Moran, M., & Hawkes, M. (2011). Students' acceptance of tablet PCs and implications for educational institutions. *Journal of Educational Technology & Society, 14*(2), 58-70.

El Alfy, S., Gómez, J. M., & Dani, A. (2019). Exploring the benefits and challenges of learning analytics in higher education institutions: A systematic literature review. *Information Discovery and Delivery.*

Fan, S., Chen, L., Nair, M., Garg, S., Yeom, S., Kregor, G., . . . Wang, Y. (2021). Revealing Impact Factors on Student Engagement: Learning Analytics Adoption in Online and Blended Courses in Higher Education. *Education Sciences, 11*(10), 608.

Fornell, C., & Larcker, D. F. (1981). Evaluating structural equation models with unobservable variables and measurement error. *Journal of marketing research, 18*(1), 39-50.

Gibson, D., & de Freitas, S. (2016). Exploratory analysis in learning analytics. *Technology, Knowledge and Learning, 21*(1), 5-19.

Glass, R., & Li, S. (2010). Social influence and instant messaging adoption. *Journal of Computer Information Systems, 51*(2), 24-30.

Gutiérrez, F., Seipp, K., Ochoa, X., Chiluiza, K., De Laet, T., & Verbert, K. (2020). LADA: A learning analytics dashboard for academic advising. *Computers in Human Behavior, 107*(2020), 105826-105839.

Ifenthaler, D. (2017). Are higher education institutions prepared for learning analytics? *TechTrends, 61*(4), 366-371.

Jivet, I., Scheffel, M., Schmitz, M., Robbers, S., Specht, M., & Drachsler, H. (2020). From students with love: An empirical study on learner goals, self-regulated learning and sense-making of learning analytics in higher education. *The Internet and Higher Education, 47*(2020), 100758 - 110772.

Mafunda, B., Bere, A., & Swart, J. (2016). *Establishing determinants of electronic books utilisation: An integration of two human computer interaction adoption frameworks.* Paper presented at the International Conference on Human Computer Interaction.

Misra, H., Satpathy, M., & Mohanty, B. (2004). Organisation preparedness and information technology acquisition success: An assessment model. *AMCIS 2004 Proceedings*, 466-475.

Misra, H., Satpathy, M., & Mohanty, B. (2007). Measuring user's role to assess organisation preparedness in a systems acquisition life cycle: a cognitive framework. *International Journal of Information and Communication Technology, 1*(1), 50-61.

Ngqulu, N. (2018). *Investigating the Adoption and the Application of Learning Analytics in South African Higher Education Institutions (Heis).* Paper presented at the International Conference on e-Learning.

Nguyen, A., Gardner, L., & Sheridan, D. (2020). Data analytics in higher education: An integrated view. *Journal of Information Systems Education, 31*(1), 61.

Ogunyemi, A. A., & Johnston, K. A. (2012). Towards an organisational readiness framework for emerging technologies: An investigation of antecedents for south african organisations' readiness for server virtualisation. *The Electronic Journal of Information Systems in Developing Countries, 53*(1), 1-30.

Tsai, Y.-S., Kovanović, V., & Gašević, D. (2021). Connecting the dots: An exploratory study on learning analytics adoption factors, experience, and priorities. *The Internet and Higher Education, 50*, 100794.

Venkatesh, V., Morris, M. G., Davis, G. B., & Davis, F. D. (2003). User acceptance of information technology: Toward a unified view. *MIS quarterly*, 425-478.

Xin, O. K., & Singh, D. (2021). Development of Learning Analytics Dashboard based on Moodle Learning Management System. *International Journal of Advanced Computer Science and Applications, 12*(7).

# TEACHERS' DIGITAL COMPETENCES BEFORE AND DURING THE COVID-19 PANDEMIC FOR THE IMPROVEMENT OF SECURITY AND DEFENCE HIGHER EDUCATION

Marina Marchisio[1], Fabio Roman[1], Matteo Sacchet[1], Enrico Spinello[2], Linko Nikolov[3], Malgorzata Grzelak[4], Magdalena Rykala[4] and Cristian-Emil Moldoveanu[5]

[1]*Department of Molecular Biotechnology and Health Sciences, University of Turin, Via Nizza 52, 10126 Torino, Italy*
[2]*Education and Training Command and School of Applied Military Studies, Via Arsenale 22, 10121 Torino, Italy*
[3]*Department of Communication Networks, National Military University, Karel Shkorpil 1 str., 9700 Shumen, Bulgaria*
[4]*Faculty of Safety, Logistics and Management, Military University of Technology, Poland*
[5]*Military Technical Academy "Ferdinand I", 39-49 George Cosbuc, Sector 5, Bucharest, Romania*

**ABSTRACT**

COVID-19 hastened a trend that was already ongoing before the pandemic outbreak: the progressively increasing use of distance and online teaching and learning, alongside with lectures and classes. The potentialities of online teaching allowed a didactic continuity that would have been impossible otherwise, and this approach is likely to be maintained even after COVID-19 related restrictions end. From these remarks, it immediately follows that it is of great importance that teachers, students and other personnel, such as technicians and program managers, possess digital skills devoted to education. In the context of security and defence, areas with a strong international vocation, these skills are even more valuable. This research investigates the impact of COVID-19 on education in these contexts: the changes caused by the pandemic, the teachers' perception about some aspects of their job, such as the way they relate with students, and their ability to perform the same commitments in a different scenario. The research has been conducted based on the analysis of an online anonymous questionnaire with more than 500 responses. Results suggested the importance of the development of a training devoted to improving teachers' digital skills, since they live frontline in education, and they have been directly impacted by disruptive changes. This study is part of the European project Digital Competences for Improving Security and Defence Education - DIGICODE. Pursuing to the Digital Education Action Plan, the project aims at improving education quality in security and defence, by means of digital tools in didactics, and the development of teachers' professional competences.

**KEYWORDS**

Digital Education, Distance Learning, Future Skills, Online Education, Online Teaching, Security and Defence, Teacher Training.

## 1. INTRODUCTION

Security and defence play a prominent role in the 21$^{st}$ century: new challenges such as cybersecurity and drone defence have come out, requiring nations to cooperate to cope with them. In the past most military affairs pursued the scope of national interest and prosperity. Nowadays a global perspective is necessary: the operations against terrorism constitute a well-known example characterizing international military action from the beginning of the century. As for several forms of collaboration, it is important to start in advance, to guarantee plausible proficiency and long-term duration. Internationalization in Higher Education can be strengthened using traditional and virtual modalities, experiences and training programs dedicated to young officers (Marchisio and Spinello, 2021). Such international initiatives can be enhanced with digital education. In fact, the importance of e-learning has emerged with the COVID-19 pandemic requiring an extensive rethinking of teaching and learning. Shortly after its outbreak, actions were devised in emergence (Hodges et al., 2020), but then more structured modifications were planned (Galluzzi et al., 2021). Many authors considered the potential of e-learning, becoming a support regardless of the modalities of the courses, and being a strategic tool for internationalization (Mihalova, 2006). It is possible to take full advantage of this potential only if all the stakeholders (teachers, students, technicians...) are properly competent under the digital point of view, especially in relation to education. A potentially critical issue is the overestimation of one's own and others' digital skills: the belief to be sufficiently skilled for most jobs that uses digital technologies. The belief in colleagues' digital skills can erroneously suggest that it is not particularly important to develop digital competences, since there is always someone that can compensate for others' gaps. Since both students (Buffardi and Taddeo, 2017) and educators (Tomczyk, 2021) show such tendencies, some effort could be devoted to train them about this misbelief that conditioned their perception of digital skills' importance. This applies to teachers, who in our case are university professors, module leaders in several study programs regarding the context of security and defence, for example Strategic Sciences. In 2020, the European Union published the DEAP, Digital Education Action Plan (European Education Area, 2020), which outlined the strategic value of educators' digital competences. This fostered, in 2021, the inception of Digital Competences for Improving Security and Defence Education - DIGICODE, a project within Erasmus+ Key Action 2 Strategic Partnership, aiming at the improvement of education in the security and defence context, thanks to the use of digital tools. It aims also at favoring teachers who develop the needed digital competences. The project involves several members of the European Union: Bulgaria, Italy, Poland, and Romania. Since the disciplines required to train people in security and defence cover several areas (STEM, languages, law studies...), the relative education is necessarily multidisciplinary, with teachers from divergent backgrounds taking part in courses and programs. Furthermore, in some Member States, like Italy, the agreements between armies and universities imply that some teachers are civilians while others are military, with part-time commission to academic work and teaching or research is only a part of their duty. Thus, they could take advantage from a specific kind of training.

In this paper the authors debate over these diverse topics, starting from the analysis of a questionnaire presented to university teachers involved in security and defence education, in which several aspects were rated. Many aspects, investigated before and during the pandemic, concern their approach with students, the time they took to carry out various tasks related to preparation and check, the use of PCs and electronic devices, and some open-ended questions. More than 500 instructors belonging to 15 countries responded. Data collection was part of the DIGICODE activities, thus involving specific countries, but also other teachers from countries not directly involved in the project who responded to the questionnaire. Most teachers work in security and defence, but some of them also teach elsewhere. The analysis resulted in students being exposed to more difficulties during the pandemic than before, and in more time needed to perform tasks. Both differences are significant from the statistical point of view. Therefore, a proper training could be proposed to avoid these differences and impact on teaching and learning. The paper is structured as follows: Section 2 presents the theoretical framework, while Section 3 is devoted to the research question and the methodology. Section 4 focuses on a short description of the DIGICODE project, and Section 5 reports all the results related to the discussion. Finally, some concluding remarks constitute Section 6.

## 2. THEORETICAL FRAMEWORK

The need for digital skills in the current world encourages their development. In (Van Laar et al., 2017), the authors examined the relation between 21st century skills and digital skills and they found that the list of skills is far more extensive than the list of digital skills. Moreover, they identified seven core skills: technical, information management, communication, collaboration, creativity, critical thinking, and problem solving. The development of problem solving is particularly important for officers, and there are many experiences on how to make military students develop this approach (Fissore et al., 2021). Digital skills fit into the broader concept of *future skills*, which are needed for societies to be sustainable and organizations to fit in changing environments (Ehlers, 2020, and references therein). Moreover, it is important to provide a proper balance between technical and practical aspects, since in this setting technology is a tool to pursue educational scopes (Goldin and Katz, 2009). According to 2017 data collected by the working group for the DEAP (European Education Area, 2020), while on one hand 90% of future jobs will require digital skills, on the other hand 44% of Europeans lack even the basic digital skills. Furthermore, there is still a strong gender gap, where only less than 20% of ICT professionals are women, and a digital divide, with more than 48000 schools lacking broadband connection. This brought the European Commission to the DEAP, to provide guidelines for Europeans, educational institutions, and education systems to live and work better in the digitalized world of today. The DEAP proposes three main priorities: to make greater use of digital technology for teaching and learning, to develop relevant digital skills and competences for digital transformation, to improve education systems through preferable data analysis and forecast. In fact, the gap between the use of digital technology in everyday life and in education needs to be filled, with a wide mix of digital competences being the relevant factor. Moreover, a better cooperation in data collection, data analysis and exchange of best practices could help in the formation of a collective awareness relative to the importance of such approaches.

## 3. RESEARCH QUESTION AND THE METHODOLOGY

The authors' research aims at giving an answer to the question: *How did the teachers of different countries modify their perception of higher education under the disruptive changes caused by COVID-19 pandemic?* The authors tackled the investigation mainly quantitatively, with qualitative data supporting the analysis (mixed method approach). A more qualitative study, concerning strengths, weaknesses, opportunities and threats in the evolution of digital education, as well as the most effective teachers' practices and actions to enhance education, again in relation with the area of security and defence, has been performed in (Marchisio et al., 2022). In the present work, having targeted the population of instructors in security and defence, with a prevalence of scientific professors, the authors collected data from 513 teachers. Table 1 shows the sample population divided by age and gender.

Table 1. Distribution of the teachers by age and gender

| Age range | Females | Males | Did not specify |
|---|---|---|---|
| Less than 35 years old | 23 | 37 | 2 |
| 35-45 years old | 63 | 90 | 1 |
| 46-55 years old | 60 | 94 | 1 |
| 56-65 years old | 31 | 79 | 2 |
| More than 65 years old | 6 | 23 | 1 |

Most respondents teach in the scientific area (50%), distributed among Pure Sciences, Information Technology, Engineering and Health, but several representatives of other disciplines, military and not, are present (e.g. Economics, Humanities, Languages, Law, Military Subjects, Social Sciences). Teachers' positions are almost equally distributed between full or associate professors (40%) and assistants that can be either actual professors, post-doctoral researchers, or PhD holders (40%). Instructors having only a master's or a bachelor's degree, along with some personnel with a non-academic role such as military or technical, constitute the remaining 20%. The median of experience in teaching is 15 years, with a substantial uniformity throughout time. In the questionnaire, teachers were invited to discuss how they relate with digital tools: if they are self-confident, which tools they use and own, how they rate their relationship with students, and how much time it takes them to perform specific tasks. The authors considered the reasonably expectable fact that the pandemic brought changes especially in rating and time spent, because digital tools before COVID-19 were used when teachers actually wanted to utilize them (only less than 10% of our sample did not use them at all), while during the pandemic their use often became an obligation. Comparisons were made by means of Likert scales, in which 1 stands for the lowest score and 5 for the highest one, and categorizations, where the reasonable range of time committed for a task was grouped in some intervals (e.g. "from 4 to 10 hours"), from which the respondent had to choose one. Open questions allowed the authors to deal with the qualitative part of the investigation. The use of hypothesis testing such as paired t-test and Wilcoxon signed-rank test (both normally approximate, given the large sample size), and the sign test, allowed the authors to inferentially confirm how differences brought out by descriptive means were statistically significant.

## 4. THE DIGICODE PROJECT

The project falls within the European strategic actions aimed at improving quality of education in security and defence through digital means, and it pursues the following objectives:

- the conduction of a survey, in order to collect detailed information in a group of students and lecturers from international universities, and to conduct a comparative analysis aimed at comparing processes, strategies, and methods used by the respondents, allowing to identify the best practices and competences ensuring safe and effective online teaching in security and defence;
- a handbook of best practices and solutions adopted by universities during COVID-19;
- the development of a teacher toolkit, including one for digital competences in security and defence, and open online training courses to support teachers and trainers in using specific digital learning environments for education, diverse kinds of digital tools, and in adopting innovative and adaptive methodologies like problem solving, problem-based teaching, learning by doing, formative and data-driven automatic assessment with interactive and immediate feedback, collaborative learning;
- the design and development of a curriculum for a summer school, which will help teachers have an integrated vision of the security and defence education system;
- the application of the teacher toolkit prepared especially for the digital education in order to explain the systems functionality, going beyond the classic laboratory activities;
- the improvement of digital competences and communication skills in online environment of a certain number of teachers and students from security and defence education institutions;
- the promotion of digital education among military academics, by building knowledge and resources in partner institutions.

The main activities of the project are: 4 transnational meetings, 5 intellectual outputs, 2 multiplier events, 2 staff training editions for improving the technical competences and communication skills for digital education, and 2 summer schools in digital education for learners. As a result of the activities implemented, it is expected to obtain solid results for all the participants and the organizations as part of the project, which are meant to be transferred into a better capacity for teachers to face the challenges of digitalization and of digital learning in the context of security and defence. The handbook of best practices, the methodology for the cybersecurity requirements, the teacher toolkit, the teacher digital workbook, and all the other outputs created within the project will support the context for the future organization of the staff training activities and summer schools for students. This would allow the improvement of digital competences and communication skills of teachers and students in online environments, applied to the security and defence.

## 5. RESULTS AND DISCUSSION

The authors compared pairs of questions consisting of a first question relative to the situation *before* the pandemic, and a second one where the situation *during* the pandemic is considered. As said in the Methodology, Likert scales were used for Pairs 1-4, categorical levels for Pairs 5-7.

Pair 1: how do you rate the engagement of students (in classroom before, in remote classes during)?

Table 2. Rating of students' engagement

| Engagement | Before | During | Difference |
|---|---|---|---|
| Very low (1) | 2 | 19 | +17 |
| Low (2) | 17 | 99 | +82 |
| Average (3) | 121 | 186 | +65 |
| Good (4) | 281 | 176 | -105 |
| Very good (5) | 92 | 33 | -59 |

Table 2 shows that teachers seem to perceive engagement as reduced with respect to the pre-pandemic setting: indeed, they responded by giving lower scores, averaging a score of 3.20 (standard deviation: 0.95) to the question relative to remote classes, while concerning classrooms the average was 3.87 (standard deviation: 0.75). This is confirmed by the pairing of data and analysing differences: they are significantly below zero, averaging -0.66 (standard deviation: 1.04), and having 262 of them negative, while only 49 of them are positive (202 are null). Classical tests from the inferential statistics give further confirmatory insights on the significance of declines: the z-scores of a paired Wilcoxon signed-rank test and a paired t-test are respectively 11.65 and 14.38. Note that values higher than 3 are usually sufficient to refuse the null hypothesis of insignificance. As evidence, the teachers find it difficult to adopt proper didactic strategies with technologies, being one of the aims to keep the same engagement both in classroom and remotely.

Pair 2: how do you rate communication between teacher and students?

Table 3. Rating of communication with students

| Communication | Before | During | Difference |
|---|---|---|---|
| Very low (1) | 0 | 15 | +15 |
| Low (2) | 3 | 52 | +49 |
| Average (3) | 57 | 153 | +96 |
| Good (4) | 282 | 235 | -47 |
| Very good (5) | 171 | 58 | -113 |

Table 3 shows the results. Responses resulted again in lower scores, averaging a score of 3.52 (standard deviation: 0.92) for the question relative to the communication during the pandemic, while concerning the communication before the pandemic the average was 4.21 (standard deviation: 0.65). Paired differences have average -0.69 and standard deviation 1.08, being 256 negative, 210 null, and 47 positive. Z-scores are 11.85 for Wilcoxon, and 14.37 for the t-test, thus the decline is significant. This highlights a (perceived) limitation of the communication channels when education is involved: if on the one hand our society allows us to communicate in real-time regardless of physical distances, on the other hand it seems that teachers have difficulties in feeling equally at ease if they are forced to confer with students at a distance.

Pair 3: how do you rate the degree of efficiency for the development of students' competences?

Table 4. Rating of development of students' competences

| Competences | Before | During | Difference |
|---|---|---|---|
| Very low (1) | 1 | 17 | +16 |
| Low (2) | 2 | 51 | +49 |
| Average (3) | 90 | 190 | +100 |
| Good (4) | 303 | 208 | -95 |
| Very good (5) | 117 | 47 | -70 |

Table 4 shows the results. Responses resulted one more time in lower scores, averaging a score of 3.42 (standard deviation: 0.91) for the question relative to the development during the pandemic, while concerning the development before the pandemic the average was 4.04 (standard deviation: 0.66). Paired differences have average -0.62 and standard deviation 0.93, being 249 negative, 231 null, and 33 positive. Z-scores are 12.02 for Wilcoxon, and 14.96 for the t-test, thus the decline is significant. As a matter of fact, teachers recognized that the difficulties caused by the forced changes, which forced them to look for new methodologies, made it more difficult to have the students develop their competences.

Pair 4: how do you rate the degree of implementation of the learning outcomes?

Table 5. Rating of implementation of learning outcomes

| Outcomes | Before | During | Difference |
|---|---|---|---|
| Very low (1) | 2 | 12 | +10 |
| Low (2) | 3 | 57 | +54 |
| Average (3) | 103 | 192 | +89 |
| Good (4) | 308 | 215 | -93 |
| Very good (5) | 97 | 37 | -60 |

Table 5 shows lower scores, averaging a score of 3.41 (standard deviation: 0.87) for the question relative to the outcomes during the pandemic, while concerning the outcomes before the pandemic the average was 3.96 (standard deviation: 0.67). Paired differences have average -0.56 and standard deviation 0.89, being 251 negative, 221 null, and 41 positive. Z-scores are 11.45 for Wilcoxon, and 14.29 for the t-test, thus the decline is significant. This means a greater difficulty in achieving the learning outcomes, which are usually determined before the beginning of the course, after didactics underwent the well-known changes.

Pair 5: how many hours per day do you spend at the PC for teaching/preparing teaching purposes?

Table 6. Daily time spent in front of a PC

| Daily time | Before | During | Difference |
|---|---|---|---|
| Less than 1 hour (1) | 93 | 17 | -76 |
| About 2 hours (2) | 130 | 83 | -47 |
| About 3 hours (3) | 108 | 75 | -33 |
| About 4 hours (4) | 63 | 87 | +24 |
| About 5 hours (5) | 37 | 71 | +34 |
| 6 hours or more (6) | 38 | 136 | +98 |

Table 6 shows the results. Responses, with a slightly reduced sample (469 teachers instead of 513, since a few of them said that "it was hard to say"), resulted here in higher scores, averaging a final score of 4.11 (standard deviation: 1.58), compared to an initial score of 2.86 (standard deviation: 1.49). Paired differences have average 1.25 and standard deviation 1.54, being 289 positive, 140 null, and 40 negative. Z-scores are 13.54 for Wilcoxon, and 17.58 for the t-test, thus the increase is significant. From a numerical perspective, the situation is reversed here, with increases instead of decreases. Most teachers needed more time in front of the computer during the pandemic than before, while some of them required the same amount as before, and only a few managed to perform their tasks with less time spent at the PC. The statistical significance of such increases is even stronger than for the previous pairs, and the considerably high standard deviation strengthens the opportunity to balance individual differences.

Pair 6: how much time do you spend per week preparing for classes?

Table 7. Weekly time spent preparing for classes

| Weekly time - prepare | Before | During | Difference |
|---|---|---|---|
| Less than 1 hour (1) | 12 | 7 | -5 |
| From 1 to 4 hours (2) | 237 | 161 | -76 |
| From 4 to 10 hours (3) | 181 | 194 | +13 |
| From 10 to 20 hours (4) | 68 | 103 | +35 |
| More than 20 hours (5) | 15 | 48 | +33 |

Table 7 shows higher scores, averaging a final score of 3.05 (standard deviation: 0.97), compared to an initial score of 2.68 (standard deviation: 0.84). Paired differences have average 0.36 and standard deviation 0.83, being 186 positive, 280 null, and 47 negative. Z-scores are 8.64 for Wilcoxon, and 9.89 for the t-test, thus the increase is significant.

Pair 7: how much time per week do you spend checking students' work (reports, drafts, tests, etc.)?

Table 8. Weekly time spent checking students' work

| Weekly time - prepare | Before | During | Difference |
|---|---|---|---|
| Less than 1 hour (1) | 102 | 67 | -35 |
| From 1 to 4 hours (2) | 278 | 240 | -38 |
| From 4 to 10 hours (3) | 112 | 140 | +28 |
| From 10 to 20 hours (4) | 16 | 55 | +39 |
| More than 20 hours (5) | 5 | 11 | +6 |

Responses resulted again in higher scores, averaging a final score of 2.42 (standard deviation: 0.92), compared to an initial score of 2.11 (standard deviation: 0.79). Paired differences have average 0.31 and standard deviation 0.76, being 172 positive, 293 null, and 48 negative. Z-scores are 7.93 for Wilcoxon, and 9.27 for the t-test, thus the increase is significant. Only a few teachers were able to complete their commitments more rapidly during the pandemic than before, while a relevant higher number needed more time. Most of them required substantially the same amount of time, although the subdivision of the scale (for which for example 2 hours and 3 hours, or 6 hours and 9 hours, or also 12 hours and 18 hours, referred to the same answer) could have had some impact on this. Figure 1 shows seven trends graphically: every pair of bars correspond to the averages of the scores relative to *Before* (lighter) and *During* (darker), with the standard deviations represented with the lines over them (centered on the average and 1.4 times the mean quadratic deviation wide). Figure 2 depicts the paired trends, that are the same indices, but relative to differences: their standard deviations represent how the teachers perceived the extent of the changes differently from each other.

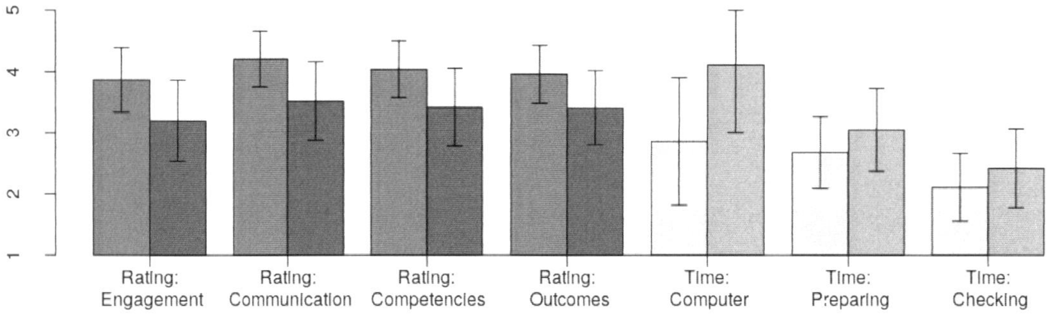

Figure 1. Comparison of ratings (Tables 1-4) and time spent (Tables 5-7) before and during the pandemic

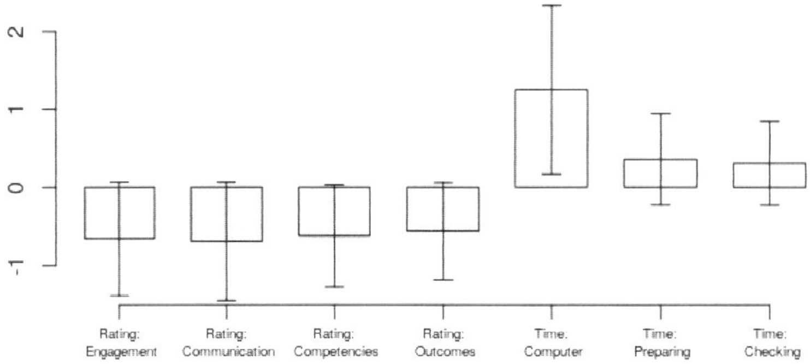

Figure 2. Comparison of ratings and time spent, in terms of differences

By relating these results with the theoretical framework and the research question, the significant decrease in the averages seen in Pairs 1-4, concerning how teachers and students do relate, can depend on various factors. A specific training in digital education can be an appropriate measure to reduce these drops. In fact, training would reasonably bring to a reduced number of teachers having difficulties in perceive comfort, which is one of the causes worsening relations with students. To strengthen this suggestion, we detected a positive difference between the standard deviation within the four pairs of questions, meaning that teachers have different reactions when asked to deal with the changes COVID-19 required. The importance of a training stands also in allowing teachers to put aside a consistent part of their personal differences, and to constitute a common basis of educational practices. Analogously, the significant increase in the averages seen in Pairs 5-7, relative to the time needed to commit various tasks, came with generally positive difference of standard deviations, addressing again differences in the teachers' reactions. Besides, most teachers would take advantage from technical support, and more in general support in things beyond didactics: less time consumption for non-didactic tasks would result in not having to reduce significantly the time dedicated to performing teaching tasks, or teachers' spare time, not affecting the quality of both teaching and life.

Qualitatively, teachers were asked some questions, such as any issues they experienced (and, if any, which ones) while integrating the practical and theoretical aspects of teaching, their sharable good practices implemented during the pandemic, and the direction in which they thought remote education should be developed. Generally, the responses infer that it is not the technology in itself to be critical, but the approach adopted by teachers and institutions. Indeed, the determinant factor is recognized to be the way technology is used by people. It is necessary to reconsider the relationship between technology and education in a wide sense. In fact, teachers perceived technology, in the simple sense of toolsets, as suitable. They were able to distinguish between the organizational difficulties and the technical issues, with a strong prominence of the former ones. This fits with one of the theoretical features depicted in Section 2, namely the balance between technical and practical aspects: it would be not so useful to concentrate only on technology itself, if our purposes are educational and the limitations detected stand for their majority outside the technical facets. Furthermore, respondents acknowledge that a proper training, considering both techniques and applications, could help in dealing with methodological and temporal issues. Specifically, on the one side limits in methodology were recognized as being an effect of lacking proper skills rather than intrinsic, thus being possible to deal with them, while on the other side time can be seen as an investment, since the training would allow to reduce (or even nullify) the impact of problems requiring a time-consuming handling. With an appropriate consideration of the relational and the methodological components, the training can be developed for aiming at the didactical scope of our study: to provide education effectively as possible.

## 6. CONCLUSION

This research allowed the authors to obtain an answer to the question regarding how, in different countries, COVID-19 pandemic forced to implement changes in higher education, and the teachers' perception of the new scenario. Various facets of teaching and learning have been affected by these pandemic-related modifications, with a particular focus on how teachers had to relate with students and work harder to complete specific tasks. It emerged that it has been almost impossible to keep the same rate of interaction with students, and to conduct the tasks without needing additional time. It is likely that the disparities in digital skills teachers possessed played a significant role in these results: those lacking experience in handling tools devoted to teaching and learning were reasonably the ones to face the most prominent effects. A proposal to tackle this issue consists in training teachers on digital competences, to make post-pandemic experiences comparable to the pre-pandemic ones. While this action can be broadly proposed, it is even more noteworthy if it concerns sectors in which the cooperation at an international level is pivotal, and this is the case of security and defence education, where the importance of digital skills is particularly marked. Once this training is proposed, it will be possible to enhance this research to detect teachers' improvements.

## REFERENCES


Buffardi, A. and Taddeo, G., 2017. The Web 2.0 Skills of Italian Students: An Empirical Study in Southern Italy. *Italian Journal of Sociology of Education*, Vol. 9, No. 1, pp. 45-76.

Ehlers, U.D., 2020. *Future Skills – Future Learning, Future Higher Education.* Springer, Karlsruhe, Germany,

European Education Area, 2020. Digital Education Action Plan. https://education.ec.europa.eu/document/digital-education-action-plan

Fissore C., et al., 2021. Development of Problem Solving Skills with Maple in Higher Education. In: Corless R.M., Gerhard J., Kotsireas I.S. (eds) Maple in Mathematics Education and Research. MC 2020. Communications in Computer and Information Science, vol 1414. Springer, Cham.

Galluzzi, F. et al., 2021. Mathematics in higher education: a transition from blended to online learning in pandemic times. *Proceedings of IEEE 45th COMPSAC Conference*, pp. 84-92.

Goldin, C.D. and Katz, L.F., 2009. *The Race between Education and Technology.* Harvard University Press, Cambridge, UK.

Hodges, C. et al., 2020. The Difference Between Emergency Remote Teaching and Online Learning. https://er.educause.edu/articles/2020/3/the-difference-between-emergency-remote-teaching-and-online-learning

Marchisio, M. and Spinello, E., 2021. Internationalization for enhancing the European Security and Defence Higher Education. *15th International Conference on e-Learning (EL2021) – Held at the 15th Multi-Conference on Computer Science and Information Systems (MCCSIS2021)*, pp. 99-106.

Marchisio, M. et al, 2022. Advantages and disadvantages of digital remote education in the security and defence contexts. *18th International Scientific Conference eLearning and Software for Education (eLSE2022)*, in press.

Mihalova, G., 2006. E-learning as internationalization strategy in higher education. *Baltic Journal of Management*, Vol.1, No. 3, pp. 270-284.

Tomczyk, L, 2021. Declared and Real Level of Digital Skills of Future Teaching Staff. *Education Sciences*, Vol. 11, paper 619.

Van Laar, E., et al, 2017. The relation between 21st-century skills and digital skills: A systematic literature review, Computers in Human Behavior, Vol. 72, pp. 577-588.

# FORCED INNOVATION IN A LEARNING ENVIRONMENT: STUDENTS' EXPERIENCE OF DISTANCE LEARNING DURING THE PANDEMIC

Edita Butrime[1], Dalija Gudaityte[1], Sigita Morkeviciene[1], Virginija Tuomaite[2]
and Antanas Vitkauskas[1]
*[1]Lithuanian University of Health Sciences, A. Mickevičiaus g. 9, LT 44307 Kaunas, Lithuania*
*[2]Kaunas University of Technology, K. Donelaičio St. 73, 44249 Kaunas, Lithuania*

**ABSTRACT**

Yesterday's situation in the universities of the world is distance teaching and learning during the COVID-19 coronavirus pandemic. Mass distance teaching and learning practices were uncommon before the pandemic. Therefore, it can be argued that the scientific sources that analyze distance teaching and learning were intended to discuss the experiences and attitudes of technology enthusiasts and visionaries. The article aims at discussing the students' distance learning experience during the pandemic, treating this experience as a kind of forced innovation. The participants of the research are the first-year English-speaking students at the X University of Lithuania (N = 110). The study revealed the diversity of the pandemic distance learning experience, the positive and negative aspects of this extreme situation, from which lessons can be learned, and the perspective of further distance teaching and learning for university teachers, IT professionals, and students.

**KEYWORDS**

Distance Teaching and Learning, Pandemic, Students' Learning Experience.

## 1. INTRODUCTION

In the spring of 2020, universities paid special attention to the transfer of teaching and learning activities to the distance teaching and learning (further, the terms *remote, virtual, online, e-teaching and learning, etc*., are used synonymously in this article), i.e., "emergency remote teaching and learning" (Hodges et al, 2020). Under such conditions, it was impossible to perform a complex analysis of what tools to choose and how to organize the study process in the most rational way. Therefore, the experience gained needs to be analyzed in order to identify the most rational solutions during the emergency distance teaching and learning and employ them in the future. With the start of the new 2020/2021 academic year, universities have already been able to organize their activities in the light of the 2019/2020 academic year spring semester experience. Therefore, some of the results may generate interesting and productive insights for higher education didactics for online studies, because, we believe, even after the quarantine is over nationally and globally, universities will transfer a larger proportion of activities online as continuing practice. The 2020 may have prompted a major transformation in higher education (Butrime and Zuzeviciute, 2021).

The pandemic has radically changed peoples' lives and activities. It is a temporary emergency, but experts in various fields of science are already predicting significant changes in various areas. Mass distance teaching and learning practices were uncommon before the pandemic. Three years ago, most teachers knew how to teach and understood how their students think and learn. Now teachers have to change the nature of their work and learn new skills themselves. And most importantly, you have to answer the questions yourself when faced with the challenge of teaching without eye contact and body language.

The aim of this article is to discuss the students' distance learning experience during the pandemic, treating this experience as a kind of forced innovation.

The research question addressed in the study is as follows: What is the attitude of university health sciences students, who have studied in a virtual learning environment (VLE) in extreme conditions, to distance learning?

The study involved 110 students who shared study experience in the fall semester of 2019 and the spring semester of 2020 (i.e., when they had to study in the conditions of forced innovation).

In this article e-learning is analyzed as a socio-cultural system (Mamardasvili, 1958; Kvedaravicius, 2006; Butrime, Zuzeviciute, 2014). Such an approach towards e-learning enabled the presentation of 'a multi-dimensionality' in the concept. The analysis of e-learning as a socio-cultural system enabled the formulation of an interdisciplinary problem, for the solutions of which it is necessary to invoke theories and outcomes of computer science, culture, and education. The analysis allowed the enumeration of the forms and contents related to educational support for the participants (lecturers) of the system.

## 2. THEORETICAL BACKGROUND OF THE RESEARCH

University studies, under the influence of contemporary information and communication technologies (ICT), are changing from the educational paradigm to the learning paradigm. What are the characteristics of e-learning (and teaching) in university academic community, and what comprises the phenomenon of e-learning as socio-cultural system?

Socio-cultural system of e-learning is a system where for the increase of efficiency in teaching and learning ICT are applied; ICT have been artificially designed by a human being; however, ICT, consequently, now influence the development and structure of this system (Butrime, Zuzeviciute, 2014). Key elements of each e-learning episode are the following: participants (teachers, students, IT profesionals); technologies (ICT); processes; relationship/connections/interaction; material/contents (information).

Modern ICT are identified as one of the factors in this system. An individual is identified as a key element of socio-cultural system, i.e., he or she is the creator of knowledge seeking to respond to the needs of knowledge society. The socio-cultural system of e-learning is disclosed as a contemporary phenomenon, as earlier classic pedagogical systems (Jovaisa, 1993; Lipinskienė, 2002; Butrime, Zuzeviciute, 2014) did not identify ICT as the element of the system.

Basilaia, Kvavadze (2020) argues that the research on the work of educational institutions during the COVID-19 pandemic is an important moment in the post-pandemic period. During a pandemic, case studies are being conducted that are "urgent". Subsequently, an in-depth research will be needed to assess the experiences of different countries, and to improve distance education. It is necessary to analyze the applied methods and improve them in further daily study practice.

The history of distance learning has been going on for two centuries (Spector et al., 2008). In the last two decades, distance learning applied in higher education has significantly improved under the influence of modern information and communication technologies (Moore et al., 2011; Butrime, Zuzeviciute, 2014). This can make higher education more attractive, personalized, practical, and flexible so that it can respond to the challenges faced by universities and colleges. Distance learning includes a variety of learning formats, such as blended learning, flipped classroom, social and collaborative learning, simulations, and game-based learning, synchronous and asynchronous video lectures, polling software or collaboration authoring tools (Casanova, Paguia, 2022; Kusel, Martin, Markic, 2020; Butrime, 2020; Petrauskienė, 2018). The development of different types of learning environments may depend on the learning objective, the target audience, the learning environment (physical, virtual and/or both), and the type of content. It is important to know how learning environments are used, and the impact of tools and methods that differentiate differences in learning outcomes/ products as technology evolves (Moore et al., 2011).

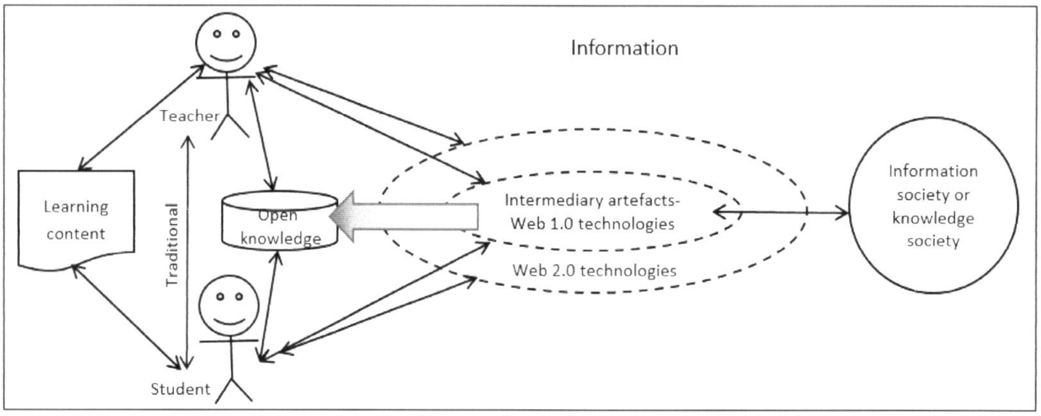


Figure 1. Teacher and student interaction. E-learning as a socio-cultural system. Blended learning as a form of e-learning (Butrime and Zuzeviciute, 2014)

According to L. Vygotsky (1978) a human and the environment cannot interact directly. People interact with the environment by the means of intermediary artifacts, i.e., the meanings, tools, or symbols formed by culture. Analyzing the interaction of teachers and students with the information and knowledge societies the intermediary artifacts are ICTs (Fig. 1.). The analysis suggests that continuous improvement of ICT determines the change in the ICT knowledge of a teacher who is an element of the e-learning (teaching) socio-cultural system. (Moore, 1998; Baltrusaitis, 2007; Hernández-Serrano, Jones, 2010; Butrime, Zuzeviciute, 2014). First, any medium is simply a way to deliver information, and one medium is not inherently better or worse than any other medium. Second, we need to better understand different media and the way people learn with different media to design effective studies. And, third, there are too many confounding variables in even the best media comparison study for the results to be valid and meaningful.

During the pandemic, all the institutions organizing studies had to change the usual way of working with students. According to G. A. Moore's (2014) law of innovation diffusion, mass application of innovation can be identified. In Moore's diffusion model, distance learners can be divided into five categories: 1) technology enthusiasts; 2) early adopters; 3) early majority; 4) late majority; 5) laggards. However, the process was forced. Hodges et al. (2020) state that in 2020 distance learning deserves the status of a special event, and proposes to call it emergency remote teaching. The authors state that the teachers had to cope with the greatest workload, as it was very important to ensure the process and access to both synchronous and asynchronous studies in a very short time. E. M. Rogers (2003) emphasizes that when designing a change, it is necessary to know how many members of the population are already using the innovation. In the case of a pandemic, there was no time to draft a change and explain how many teachers are already using distance learning. During the pandemic, the so-called "tornado" effect (according to G. A. Moore (2014)) was created by extreme conditions, i.e., forced retirement. Higher education institutions have met the challenge of 2020 in the spring, but this was done urgently and without a choice of measures. Some of the teachers worked remotely for the first time. And what about students? Some students have also tried distance learning for the first time. It is, therefore, necessary to analyze the experience of this population in distance learning.

There are many new challenges to distance learning during the Covid-19 pandemic, thus, new factors influencing student satisfaction need to be considered in the study (Chen, 2020; Kusel, et al, 2020; Butrime, 2020). Despite the proliferation of e-learning initiatives, knowledge of this experience from the point of view of students is still insufficient, although these are the main elements of the educational process (Lemos and Pedro, 2012). It should be emphasized that during the pandemic, distance learning was tried by those students and teachers who had not tried it before (according to G. A. Moore (2014) pragmatists and conservatives) or did so with great caution. Therefore, it is relevant to study the impact of distance learning planning, teacher quality, feedback, and student expectations on student satisfaction with distance learning during the Covid-19 pandemic (Butrime, 2020; Gopal, et al, 2021; Casanova and Paguia, 2022).

In higher education, the needs and expectations of the society and the individual student as a service user in terms of improving the quality of studies acquire special significance in the treatment of studies as a service and its improvement (Vilkonis et al., 2012; Bailie, 2015; Garrison, et al, 2000). According to Casanova, Paguia

(2022) higher education institutions that offer distance learning must take into account students' expectations and experiences so that all distance learning activities and resources are directed to the highest levels of student satisfaction. Distance learning is based on the theory of G. M. Moore (Moore, 1998), which explains the interaction between students and teachers, and the structure of the course, and how it affects the learning environment. Distance learning is characterized by a transaction that occurs when a student and a teacher communicate in a virtual learning environment, and that communication may not occur at the same time. This results in unique patterns of student and teacher behaviour (Nwanko, 2015). G. M. Moore's theory (Moore, 1998) distinguishes 3 types of interaction: student - teacher, student - learning content, and student - student. Casanova and Paguia (2022) distinguish the following levels of expectations of students' participating in distance learning: infrastructure (technology), teacher, learning methods, course design, and evaluation system. Many studies conducted before the pandemic sought to find out how to better adapt e-learning environment, pedagogy, objectives, content, and assessment according to the individual needs of the learners so that their learning experience is pleasant for the desired learning outcome. It should be emphasized that in the event of the pandemic distance learning involved all the students (not just those who chose this type of study themselves); those technologies were used that ensured the smooth operation of a large number of students and the institution was able to use them; there was no time and opportunity to prepare teachers for distance learning in advance; there was no time to properly prepare the content for the study subjects that were traditionally taught before the pandemic.

The paper presents a pilot study that will help describe the various aspects of distance learning that need to be considered. It is important to know which factors influence students' expectations and satisfaction with distance learning, as they can be used as normative indicators of the suitability of a course design and the suitability of a virtual learning environment. They can also help identify effective strategies and services needed for students learning in a virtual learning environment (Casanova and Paguia, 2022).

The distance learning during a pandemic can be described as a case that is different from the distance learning that has been investigated for the past 20 years. Therefore, when researching students' attitudes to distance learning during a pandemic, it is appropriate to start with a qualitative case study. The aim of this study is to describe the phenomenon under the study, i.e., distance learning during a pandemic.

# 3. THE ORGANISATION OF THE RESEARCH

The study was conducted in April 2021. The research sample is targeted. A convenient sample was used to invite volunteer students who had studied the basics of medical Latin to participate in the investigation. English-speaking students (N = 110, women - 50, men - 60) studying in Medical (MSP), Dental (DSP) and Veterinary (VSP) study programs were invited to participate in the study. It was assumed that English-speaking / international students have a better distance learning experience than Lithuanians, as distance learning was not popular in Lithuania before the pandemic. It was thought that these students could express more diverse opinions.

During the study, students were asked to rate their performance during the first (Spring 2020) and second (Autumn 2020) pandemic waves. Students were asked the following 3 closed questions:

1. Evaluate previous experience (before the COVID-19 pandemic) of learning in a VLE according to the Likert scale: 1- I have no experience at all, 2- I have almost no experience, 3- I can't answer, 4- I have enough experience, 5- I am a virtual learning expert.
2. Evaluate the experience of learning in the VLE in the autumn semester of 2020 (during COVID-19 quarantine) according to the Likert scale.
3. Evaluate the experience of learning in the VLE in the spring semester of 2021 (during COVID-19 quarantine) according to the Likert scale.

Students were also asked an open-ended question to write 3 statements as to why they rated it that way.

## 3.1 The Results of the Study: Students' Attitudes Towards Distance Learning in the Conditions of a Pandemic

The students rated their distance learning experience: the average in 2019 was 2.38; the average in 2020 was 3.6; the average in 2021 was 3.66. 39.1 percent of the students said they had no distance learning experience before the pandemic. During the pandemic, a quarter of the students said, "I am a virtual learning expert". 40 percent the students rated their ability to learn remotely sufficiently (Figure 2)

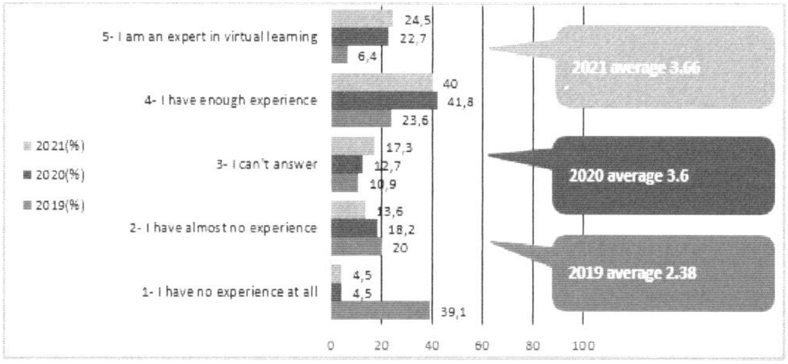


Figure 2. Students' distance learning experience before the pandemic (2019) and during the pandemic (autumn semester 2020, and spring semester 2021)

It can be said that students gained experience in distance learning during the pandemic and rated their abilities positively. About 40 percent of the study participants stated that they did not have such learning experience before the pandemic. This shows that this part of the students were not distance learning enthusiasts and chose learning methods and techniques that required contact communication. In the event of the pandemic, these students had to change their normal learning environment and learn to learn differently. This shows that the introduction of a forced innovation has led to the improvement of students' learning skills.

A total of 108 students answered the open-ended question (44 MSP; 52 DSP; 12 VSP). Some students assessed distance learning ambivalently, some - only positively, and some - only negatively.

Assessing the totality of the answers, it can be stated that most students rated their distance learning experience as causing "mixed feelings about the whole process of online learning", because "online learning has its advantages and disadvantages". Among them, only a few students stated that they "could not properly assess" their distance learning experience because they "did not experience real traditional studies" and "cannot compare ... with the normal learning process". Only a few students stated that they had a distance learning experience before Covid-19, and most respondents noticed that this way of studying was new to them.

All students' responses were examined in two sections: in terms of understanding the situation and accepting it personally. Illustrative examples of informants' responses are not edited and are provided in the original language.

Table 1. The analysis of students' distance learning experiences

| Statements | Subcategory 2 | Subcategory 1 | Category |
|---|---|---|---|
| 'enough resources and help are provided from the university's side' | | The learning resources were sufficient | **Type of Interaction: Student-Learning Content** |
| 'studies are nice but not excellent but nice', | | Students saw a possibility to improve learning content | |
| '(online) might make the studying cheaper in the future as less resources used for everyone :)' | | Studies could be cheaper | |
| 'a great advantage', 'the best thing happened to me', 'I can see more than one time or stop to make note', 'it was great to go and look back to them again', 'you have the possibility to watch lectures as often as you want to understand the content' | | Good recorded lectures | |
| 'assignments ... were very structured' | | Good learning content | |

| Statements | Subcategory 2 | Subcategory 1 | Category |
|---|---|---|---|
| 'decide at what time I want to learn', 'create my own tempo of learning', 'it saves time I spend studying', 'giving me more time practicing what is more important to me' | | Better time management | |
| 'stress levels have been a lot lower with online studies', 'convenient to stay at home', 'I am at home in my environment, and it lets me feel more comfortable', 'I am more involved in the lesson and I feel less scared to make a mistake' | Distance learning is less stressful, is closer | Their own sense of security and concentration increased because of | |
| 'I can actually see the material when in class it is hard for me to see the board' | Distance learning is more convenient physically | | |
| 'I learnt to study better on my own', 'I have more responsibility for my own schedule', 'learned study discipline in a new, more demanding way', 'optimized my study technic', 'check for myself what needs most attention' | Distance learning improves learning skills and increases personal responsibility | | |
| 'define abbreviations and acronyms the first time they are used in the text, even after they have been defined in the abstract'; 'do not use abbreviations in the title or heads unless they are unavoidable' | More difficult to understand some parts of the learning material | Negative aspects | |
| 'easier to concentrate when only the lecturer speaks and others are muted', 'no students interfere during class', 'the lectures in remote are more clear', 'easy to follow with the teacher', | Distance synchronic lectures are less stressful, is closer | Their own sense of security and concentration increased because of | **Type of Interaction: Learner-Instructor Interaction** |
| 'there is no problem of see or hear and it is easy to ask question because you can also wire them on chat and the professor answer when he can', 'it is easy to join the lectures', even straitly: 'more sleep' | Distance synchronic lectures are more convenient physically | | |
| 'good organization, clear instructions', 'great flexibility with classes', 'it was good, convenient, comfortable, flexible', 'in total a pleasant experience', 'an interesting experience', 'I feel it is more effective', 'easier transformation into university', 'great flexibility with classes' | | Good organisation | |
| 'the teachers were great and very patient', they 'looked right at home with the entire process', 'good that the professors are almost always available if you have questions' | | Teachers worked perfectly | |
| '...most teachers were able to use Moodle and Teams in a way that made learning online manageable'; 'the teachers did the best they could with the tools they had'; 'I hope we will have some digital tests in the future' | | Respondents emphasized the positive attitude towards teachers' efforts to use technical tools and the diversity of the latter | |
| 'I felt the amount of work was not well planned, practical learning was really uninspiring online'; 'feeling kind of fake, which makes it so much harder to keep up the motivation'; 'still hard to study in this way' | Assessing distance learning in the spring semester of 2021, students' feedback reflects a more | Critical approach to distance synchronic lectures | |

| Statements | Subcategory 2 | Subcategory 1 | Category |
|---|---|---|---|
| | critical approach to learning process planning | | |
| 'learning physically face to face with professor is much different than learning online; you can ask more questions, and get more visuals than online', 'it's harder than to go to the lessons in person', 'weak knowledge gaining', 'the things stay unclear', 'makes it harder to focus on the lectures', 'hard to keep focus during a long period of time', 'harder to focus on what to do school wise', 'difficult to study' | Do not like distance synchronic lectures | | |
| 'depends on the lecturer, some of them had connection problems or miss understanding with technology', 'the classes were … not adapted correctly to an online mode, 'NOT enough understanding of the situation from some teachers', '… (subject name) teachers were the worst. They just left us hard to understand pre-recorded videos, gave touch tasks and gave bad grades', 'sitting in front of a computer for an interval for 90 minutes is also not the best experience' | The lack of teachers' distance teaching experience | | |
| 'I focused more on the given material than the lectures because I often found it difficult to listen due to personal reasons as I get distracted easily', 'no real evaluation for hard worker due to some cheating', 'the teacher is good, but it is hard to have a good class when nobody is talking', 'shy to ask questions' | The students blame the situation even when in reality only they can change it themselves | | |
| 'had to attend classes well into midnight, and also attend examination well into midnight', '8 of 10 professors have good understanding of the situation, the different time zones, but some of them didn't' | The problem because of the time zones | | |
| 'you cannot really connect to others', 'you don't get to know new people', 'lack of socialising', 'no interaction, no friends', and even: 'no contact = no studies' | | The students felt discomfort because of the isolation | **Type of Interaction: Learner-Learner Interaction** |
| 'not live', 'the atmosphere in the classroom is radically different from the atmosphere in a remote audience', 'cameras opening should be mandatory', 'hiding behind the screens, cause you do other things instead of learning' | | Difficulty in performing group tasks | |
| '…Overall it was decent, but labworks, Latin and Lithuanian lessons are better in face-to-face mode' | Studying Lithuanian and Latin as negative aspects | The students pointed to the lack of practical knowledge during the laboratory work | |

The student responses indicate that distance learning is still a more positive than negative experience that has demonstrated the ability of both teachers and students to work in an emergency. Given the responses from the students and the observations made in some individual reviews, it is worth thinking about blended learning to meet the needs of many students.

This study reflects a small fraction of the world's concerns about the transformation of traditional studies into distance learning during the COVID-19 pandemic. Problems with students' preparation for distance learning are a concern in many countries. Such research is important and necessary as it will contribute to the improvement of teaching practices in the future. It is already clear today that the studies will have to transform after evaluating the experience of this global experiment.

We believe that in our case it would be appropriate to conduct further research based on the types of interaction identified by Moore (1989) (student-student; student-learning content; student-teacher) and the levels of student expectations set by Casanova and Paguia (2022) (infrastructure; teacher; learning methods, course design, assessment system). In this pilot study, we can see some aspects of these types and levels that are worth exploring further.

# 4. CONCLUSION

The findings of the study reveal a wide range of the following pandemic distance learning experiences:

• The anxiety that accompanied all of us at the beginning of the process, followed by a quick breakthrough and reorientation, allowed students to understand that they will not only need to study, but also to improve, i.e., distance learning requires different learning skills. After the first stress and confusion due to the inability to act, technical disruptions or other organizational problems, it was clear that the communication between teachers and students did not break down, gained new positive nuances, became more flexible, inclusive, and motivating, providing more opportunities to learn and innovate, i.e., create new or adapt usual methods to new conditions, plan and save time more successfully, avoid traffic congestion and rest by connecting at a convenient time.

• As for the negative, we can divide the negative aspects into two groups, i.e., technical and non-technical. As non-technical negative aspects we can name the need for live communication, faster forgetting of acquired knowledge, the desire to be in the "live" atmosphere of the university; health problems due to constant sitting and looking at the computer screen. The participants of the research also noticed the aspects of distance learning that need to be corrected at the technical level: disproportionate workload, incomplete use of software functions offered by university platforms, and lack of interactive tasks.

• And what is next? Once a certain level of unavoidable use of technologies is reached, their further mastery and use in the study process will no longer be so rapid. There will be reassurance, a certain plateau phase, i.e., the changed teacher-student relationship in the context of the pandemic will stabilize and a new impetus will be needed to re-launch the process. Could it be computer technology courses being implemented at universities, their availability, a network of consultants always available, new requirements for the qualification of university teachers?

# REFERENCES


Bailie, J. L. 2015. Perceptions and expectations of online graduate students regarding synchronous events. *Journal of Instructional Pedagogies* 17. https://files.eric.ed.gov/fulltext/EJ1102866.pdf.

Baltrusaitis, P. 2007. Theoretical assumptions of e-learning activity model. *Profesinis rengimas: tyrimai ir realijos*. 2007/13. Pages 12-19.

Basilaia, G. and Kvavadze, D. 2020. Transition to Online Education in Schools during a SARS-CoV-2 Coronavirus (COVID-19) Pandemic in Georgia. *Pedagogical Research*, 5(4), em0060. https://doi.org/10.29333/pr/7937.

Butrime E. 2020. Virtual Learning Environments and Learning Change in Modern Higher Education During the Covid-19 Coronavirus Pandemic: Attitudes of University Teachers and Students. *13th annual International Conference of Education, Research and Innovation. 9-10 November, 2020. ICERI2020 Proceedings*, pp. 8582-8589.

Butrime, E., and Zuzeviciute, V. 2021. Online Studies in Higher Education During the Covid-19 Pandemic: Students'perspective. *In International Conferences on Mobile Learning 2021 and Educational Technologies 2021*.

Butrime, E. and Zuzeviciute, V. 2014. *E- Learning as a socio-cultural system: towards a balanced development*. Saarbrücken: LAP LAMBERT Academic Publishing.

Casanova, V. S. and Paguia, W. M. 2022. Expectations, Experiences, and Satisfaction of the Graduate Students with Distance Online Learning Environment in OMSC Graduate School during the Covid-19 Pandemic. *Journal of Practical Studies in Education*, 3(1), 14-22.

Chen, T., et al, 2020. Analysis of User Satisfaction with Online Education Platforms in China during the COVID-19 Pandemic. *Healthcare 8 (3)*. https://doi.org/10.3390/healthcare8030200.

Garrison, D. R., et al, 2000. Critical inquiry in a text-based environment: Computer conferencing in higher education model. *The Internet and Higher Education*, 2(2-3), 87-105.http://dx.doi.org/10.1016/S1096-7516(00)00016-6.

Gopal, R., et al, 2021. Impact of online classes on the satisfaction and performance of students during the pandemic period of COVID 19. *Educational and Information Technologies*. https://doi.org/10.1007/s10639-021-10523-1.

Hernández-Serrano, M., J., Jones B. 2010. Innovation, Informational Literacy and Lifelong Learning: Creating a New Culture. *eLearning Studys*. N° 21 September 2010. ISSN 1887-1542.

Hodges, C. et al, 2020. The Difference Between Emergency Remote Teaching and Online Learning. *EDUCAUSE Review*. Retrieved from: https://er.educause.edu/articles/2020/3/the-difference-between-emergency-remote-teaching-and-online-learning.

Jovaisa L. 1993. *Edukologijos ivadas*. Kaunas, 192 p.

Kusel, J., et al, 2020. Students' Readiness for Using Digital Media and Online Learning—Comparison between Germany and the USA. *Educ. Sci. 2020, 10(11)*. https://www.mdpi.com/2227-7102/10/11/313.

Kvedaravicius. J. 2006. *Organizaciju vystymosi vadyba: vadovėlis* / Kaunas, 2006. 395 p. ISBN 9955-12-129-7.

Lemos, S., and Pedro, N. 2012. Students' Expectation and Satisfaction in Postgraduate Online Courses. *ICICTE 2012 Proceedings*. http://www.icicte.org/Proceedings2012/Papers/14-3-Lemos.pdf

Lipinskienė, D. 2002. *Educational Environment that Empowers the Student to Study*. Kaunas University of Technology.

Mamardasvili M., K. 1958. Procesy analiza i sinteza. *Voprosy filosofii*, No 2. Moskva.

Moore, G. A. 2014. *Crossing the Chasm: Marketing and Selling Disruptive Products to Mainstream Customers*. rev. 3rd ed., NY. HarperBusiness Publishers Inc.

Moore, G. M. 1989. The three Types of Interaction. *American Journal of Distance Education*, 3(2), 1-6.

Moore, J. L., et al, 2011. Designing for E-learn, Online, and Distance Learning Environments: Are They the Same? *The Internet and Higher Education*. Elsevier. Volume 14, Issue 2, March 2011, Pages 129-135.

Nwankwo, A. A. 2015. *Students' Learning Experiences and Perceptions of Online Course Content and Interactions*. Walden Dissertations and Doctoral Studies. 188. https://scholarworks.waldenu.edu/dissertations/188.

Rogers, E. M. 2003. *Diffusion of Innovations*. Fifth Edition, Free Press, New York.

Spector, J. M., et al, 2008. *Handbook of Research for Educational Communications and Technology* (3rd ed.). New York: Lawrence Erlbaum Associates.

Vilkonis, R., et al, 2012. E-Learning at The Higher Education Institution: Research on Students' Experience and Expectations. *Mokytojų ugdymas*. 2012. Nr. 19 (2), 114–132.

Vygotsky, L., S. 1978. *Mind in Society: The Development of Higher Psychological Processes*. Edited by Cole, M., John-Steiner, V., Scribner, S., Sourberman, E. Harvard University Press, Cambridge, MS.

# DIGITIZATION INNOVATION IN UNIVERSITY EDUCATION

Marja-Liisa Tenhunen
*Dimitrie Cantemir Christian University, Bucharest, Romania*

**ABSTRACT**

Covid-19 pandemic and post-pandemic had led to the confrontation of higher education system with enormous challenges. That necessitated the urgent transition from face-to-face –teaching to online -teaching. The change was an innovation in higher education. A comparative study of digital education based on the survey in 2020-2021 in seven different countries was conducted at Shanghai University. The study was based on grey comprehensive evaluation model. In general, developed countries had high comprehensive evaluation value, while Finland, United States of America, South-Korea and Latvia had relatively low grey correlation coefficient in several certain indicators, leading to a sharp drop in the overall score. Romania ranked last while China ranked second as a developing country as well. The study launched a conclusion that research and development personnel, infrastructure funds and university financial investment in digital education had relatively more obvious effects on improving the innovations and quality of higher education system including the leadership system of universities.

**KEYWORDS**

Learning, Innovation, Higher education, Grey Comprehensive Evaluation Model.

## 1. INTRODUCTION

Online-teaching opened up as a smart solution for future education. In the field of education, a digital leap had been made in a short notice which has encouraged universities in the development of creative and innovative solutions. Concerns about educational inequality had risen in the process especially in the countries with short prior experience in online education. Same countries had also shorter history of innovation-orientation. Despites the limitations in technological conditions, all possible efforts should have been made when pursuing equality in online-education. The global emergency of the Covid-19 pandemic confronted all people with unpredictable, disruptive situations which had changed the daily lives, economies, political decisions and universities.

Generally, online-teaching has been used to supplement the classroom teaching, which is called "blended learning". "When there is a risk, there should be an opportunity", as the saying goes. The late Austrian-American economist Joseph Schumpeter introduced the "creative destruction theory". (Schumpeter 1991, Kopp 2019) The Covid-19 pandemic was destructive, but it also, in a sense, created some creative destruction. It opened new opportunities and facilities for innovations based on the creative destruction theory. In the best scenario, teachers and students had got some benefits from online-teaching, which equipped them for the future learning and communication. For instance, teachers should have considered the issues such as how to motivate students and encourage them to be proactively participate in real-time video class discussions, how to implement innovative teaching concepts more effectively, how to maintain care and guidance for individual students, and how to share and integrate online-teaching experiences with other colleagues.

Teachers' creativity and innovation skill with online-teaching can be a vital factor for stimulating students' autonomous learning, turning the epidemic "crisis" into an "opportunity" whilst reforming teaching and learning innovative concepts. The university management should have provided support in this process and change its operating logic. During this period university leadership system changed at short notice in to the direction of Dynamic operation logic. (Aberg & Stahle, 2012). Throughout history, education has rarely been reformed or benefited from technological advances. Nowadays, with digital teaching allowing real-time interaction, many innovative teaching- and learning-methods can be attempted and implemented. The most powerful part of this new generation of real-time interactive teaching and learning is that it can simultaneously accommodate in scaling and personalized learning, which traditional classroom teaching cannot do. In traditional large classes, it is difficult for teachers to know how many of the students understand or master the contents of a class. However, if the teaching and learning activities are carried out online in real time, teachers' understanding of students' progress can change. For example, teachers can review the distribution of answers to certain multiple-choice questions. They can recognize the number of students who answered in correctly and where they went wrong through the interactive polling function. During online teaching and learning, it is possible to reduce some of the limitations of traditional classrooms, which gives room to rethink how teachers can turn "classes" into better learning experiences and enhance teachers' mentoring and coaching roles. (Hakkarainen 2004; Karna 2011; Kilpinen 2004)

## 2. AIM OF THE STUDY

Covid-19 created a digital leap in all around the world, including higher education. The starting point of online education and in innovations varied from country to country and therefore, the changes that took place in the spring of 2020 vary. In some countries, a system for providing e-learning had been acquired on a fast schedule. Teachers had been introduced to new types of teaching, and only then had provision been introduced. The leadership of university had changed. Other countries had expanded only their previous offerings of courses. It was interesting to compare the seven selected countries, China, Finland, Latvia, Mexico, Romania, South Korea and the United States at different levels of online education and to gather experiences of change for operational development and innovation.

There was no return to yesterday, so institutions needed to start from first principles, creating a vision for life after the pandemic, making hard choices based on data, creating new models, realigning priorities and entering a post-covid-19 world not in isolation but collaboration. The aim of this study is to compare the implementation, quality and quantity of online-education by a questionnaire method in seven different countries and see the innovation orientation. The survey was made in 2020-2021 at Shanghai University. (The author worked in that time as visiting professor at Shanghai University.) The countries had been selected on the basis of countries were chosen to represent different continents, different education systems and different level of innovation orientation. The first electronic survey was conducted for the management of every university and the second electronic survey was conducted for the academics including program directors. The third electronic survey in the study was conducted simultaneously for groups of students in business administration.

## 3. THEORETICAL FRAMEWORK AND RESEARCH PROBLEM

There is no single or core theory which support online education. Research is linked to educational theories, mainly constructivism or exploratory learning. Constructivism is an international concept, so it is used is this research. Exploratory learning is actually a manifestation of constructivism. E-learning is implemented in as an opportunity to individualize teaching and it provides the preconditions for the realization of a constructivist view of learning better than mass-based teaching. The main research problem was as follows: The realization of a constructivist view of learning in e-learning and in innovation at universities in seven different countries. Insightful learning combines intelligence, emotion, creativity and skill of innovation. Learning takes place not only within the human mind, but in interaction with other people. Although more and more different tools are used in learning today, the key is not technology but participatory and inspiring pedagogy. (Hakkarainen 2004).

In the light of the study, the function of human memory was the continuous drawing of conclusions and the development of contexts. When learning new things, the student develops new connections between things. This is also manifested at the brain level, with new synaptic connections between nerve cells being created and extinguished continuously. The details the student learns can be remembered as its own when they relate to some sensible whole. Memory is a very central thing in human thinking and learning. If memory doesn't work, it's impossible to anticipate or plan for the future. In the constructivism, knowledge and learning are related to action. Knowledge does not pass from the outside into the human mind, but each student constructs his or her own knowledge. Understanding cannot be transferred it is always the output of the student's own thinking.

It is the student's own active knowledge construction process, in which the student selects and interprets information based on what he or she has previously learned and expectations. Learning includes, for example, self-perceived questions, self-experimentation, problem-solving, understanding and critical thinking. According to the constructivism, the key to learning is the understanding and thinking. Learning is thus the active interpretation of an individual's observations and experiences and the construction of new meanings associated with them. Learning is situational and based on interaction. Learning requires self-direction, which must be learned and be able to learn. In order to understand the basics of own thinking, the student must grow to see himself/ herself and his/her own actions from the outside and become aware of own assumptions. The student must be able to direct his or her own selective attention to what is relevant to what he or she is learning, and the student must also feel that the questions that arise are important and meaningful to him or her. Only then does learning happen. The results of the work of the different students form the basis for the teacher's own analysis of the matter. Everyone gets to know each other's work, which varies greatly, allowing the course a learning environment where not only student´s own experiences but also other students´ issues came to the fore.

The most important skill of a teacher is to create functional, appropriate learning environments that raise questions in the student´s mind and help him or her construct answers by understanding what is being sought. In the learning environment created by the teacher, appropriate questions arise, the answers to which are sought under the guidance of the teacher on the basis of the student´s own experimentation, understanding and thinking. The teacher trains students' thinking and comprehension skills by giving them the widest possible opportunities to receive feedback on their own operational processes. The learning environment includes situations of uncertainty (confrontations) initiated by the teacher. Through these, the student gets the opportunity to develop their own abilities to learn to learn. The appropriateness of the learning environment should be a conscious goal for all involved in the process. In order for meaningful and in-depth learning to take place, one must take knowledge of one's own and shape one's own internal model of it. (Hakkarainen 2004, Karna 2011)

When we talk about constructive learning, reference is made to this constructive principle of memory. Skills are developed through long-term and goal-oriented training at a variable, gradually decelerating pace. There are occasionally different levels of skill learning, during which a certain aspect of a skill is automating, but overall performance suffers. The development of skills at the highest level means the persistent continuation of practice even after the pace of skill development has slowed down. Peak performance can be achieved by avoiding the formation of rigid routines. The student has to face challenges that break with familiar patterns and force the student to stretch his/her own skills. Simply maintaining the level of performance achieved is not enough. The most difficult of these skills are often thinking skills. In order to develop, the student must constantly and consciously refine both his/her own actions and his/her own thinking. Action and thinking develop intertwined. A well-developed and unified way of acting and thinking is typical of an expert. Self-assessment skills (metacognitive skills) are needed to develop expert thinking. The student cannot get them naturally, because the assessment and development of student´s own internal models and skills requires acceptance that the student does not yet know everything. (Hakkarainen 2004; Karna 2011)

During the pandemic university leadership changed radically. The leadership logic is basically the exercise of power, that is, power is in a way a tool of leadership. Leadership without power already seems contradictory to the idea, and in practice it is impossible. When a university leader invests in the resilience of his or her organization, he or she has to lead according to a Mechanical, Organic, and Dynamic logic - according to the current goal. This division is based on Pirjo Stale's research. (Aberg & Stahle 2012). Power and the use of power are involved all the time, albeit in very different forms. The more knowledge-intensive the organization, the more important it is for the leader and manager to understand how power is combined with results in different ways and how the university is most effectively developed in the long run.

The university's ability to innovate is based on the management of various operating logics. Operational logic refers to the principles, systems and management structures under which the activities of university staff are integrated into cooperation and further into the results of the university. In Mechanical operating logic the most important results are in teaching, degrees, secondly in research results and thirdly in impact with surroundings and society. Second logic is Organic operating logic, which produces flexible development and self-directed learning. It is based on agreed processes, human interaction, motivation and responsibility. The third one is Dynamic operating logic which produces social courage, innovation and attractiveness. It is based on networking, self-organization and strong autonomy of actors. Dynamic operating logic strengthens the university´s innovativeness and proactiveness. In dynamic action, power is paramount, as dynamics do not emerge without influencers and new perspectives that have the potential to connect creative people to work inspired by bold visions. The task of an innovative leader is to identify these people and create the conditions for them to operate. Strong dynamic operating logic is the university's attraction to innovative staff. (Cheng 2020) New creative and evolving expertise is needed when the operating environment changes and old and proven models do not work. A priori reflection on the preconditions of constructivism in e-learning provided subjects to the theoretical part and the surveys. (Hasan 2020).

# 4. METHODS

## 4.1 Data Collection

Data collection of this study was conducted as digital surveys. Target survey-takers were divided into 3 groups: (1) University management: What role did e-learning play in the current strategy of the university? How did they see the change in the future? Management was asked about their views on learning and whether they relate to some general theories or whether they exist at all. (2) Academics including program leaders: Program leaders and academics were asked about their views on learning. It was also asked whether they related to some general theories or whether they existed at all. Academics and program leaders were asked: What kind of experience had they had with e-learning technical solutions, software, content, and guidance? What was the key feedback from academics and program teachers? What were the key successes, what about failures? How did program managers and academics see the connection of e-learning to students working life after graduating? How had been the reactions of the partner companies to e-learning? (3) Students: What kind of experience had they had with e-learning technical solutions, software, content and guidance? How had their studies progressed? What were the key successes, what about failures? How did students see the connection of e-learning to working life after graduation? The collection of questionnaire data played a significant role on the application of the model. The extensiveness and reliability of the data could have ensured the model feasible with practical significance. This study selected managers, students and academics engaged in higher education as investigation object. The survey was conducted from August 2020 to March 2021, collecting data from seven selected countries. A total of 160 questionnaires were issued and collected in this survey. After eliminating 4 invalid questionnaires, 156 valid ones were obtained with an effective recovery rate of 97.50%.

## 4.2 Variable Description

Based on the existing researches, this study selected 17 indicators from *Scale of e-learning in higher education*, *Input of digital education during the Covid-19 crisis* and *Impacts of e-learning on higher education during the Covid-19 crisis* to accurately evaluate the implementation, quality and quantity of digital education in each country. First, *Scale of e-learning in higher education* reflected the basic development of digital education. Enrollment number of graduate students and number of doctor students could have represented this index. Second, *Input of digital education during the Covid-19 crisis* was the core reflecting the driving force of digital education development under the influence of the pandemic. It was not only evaluated from the indicators of physical capital such as financial investment provided by universities and online education expenditure per capita, but also taken serious considerations of human resources, including number of teachers implementing online-teaching. Among them, number of R&D personnel including innovations in digital education had attracted the special attention in terms of manpower investment in scientific research. Last, *impacts of e-learning on higher education during the Covid-19 crisis* could have reflected the ability of digital education to serve the current community. Wen's article (2013), one of the most cited articles in this field, mentioned that intensity of students' performance evaluation, grade for academics' online teaching skills and grade for managers' digital working efficiency were important indices to measure the significance of digital technologies in higher education. Furthermore, with accordance to Pan et al. (2020), number of temporary forms of academic employment and opportunities for equity, diversity and inclusion could have been selected as impact measurement indicators as well.

Table 1. Parameter List

| Primary variable | Secondary variable | Symbol |
|---|---|---|
| Scale of e-learning in higher education | Enrollment | $X_1$ |
| | Number of graduate students | $X_2$ |
| | Number of doctoral students | $X_3$ |
| Input of digital education during the Covid-19 crisis | Proportion of e-leaning in higher education | $X_4$ |
| | Number of teachers implementing online-teaching | $X_5$ |
| | Number of R &D personnel in digital education | $X_6$ |
| | Infrastructure funds | $X_7$ |
| | Financial investment provided by universities | $X_8$ |
| | Online education expenditure per capita | $X_9$ |
| | Research funds on digital technologies | $X_{10}$ |
| | Inherent assets | $X_{11}$ |
| Impacts of e-learning on higher education during the Covid-19 crisis | Total use frequency of digital technology | $X_{12}$ |
| | Intensity of students' performance evaluation | $X_{13}$ |
| | Grade for academics' online teaching skills | $X_{14}$ |
| | Grade for managers' digital working efficiency | $X_{15}$ |
| | Number of temporary forms of academic employment | $X_{16}$ |
| | Opportunities for equity, diversity and inclusion | $X_{17}$ |

## 4.3 Factor Analysis

Due to the considerable number of indicator selection, there might have been high internal correlation between different indicators and unstandardized structure of observation data resulting in inconsistent analysis results. In order to facilitate the subsequent data analysis, it was hoped to reduce the number of variables and improve the model accuracy through factor analysis first. The basic principle was to find out the representative factors that could reflect the overall characteristics in the multi-dimensional variables, and classify the same essential variables into one factor. These unobservable synthetic indicators were public factors. Grey comprehensive evaluation model was based on the entropy weight.

After the dimensionality reduction by factor analysis, grey comprehensive evaluation method was conducted to test. This method assessed the pros and cons of each comparison sequence by calculating the similarity between the comparison sequence and the reference sequence. However, the traditional grey comprehensive evaluation method simply samples the average value of the correlation coefficient of each index when solving the sample correlation degree, which obliterates the heterogeneity between the indexes. While in accordance to the background of this topic, different elements of the data had different significance to the system of digital education. Therefore, it was of great priority to distinctly set the reasonable and scientific weights for these indicators of digital education quality so as to represent different elements' value. To improve the traditional one, this study integrated the entropy weight method and the grey comprehensive evaluation method to analysis the quality of digital education in various countries.

## 4.4 Grey Comprehensive Evaluation Method

Firstly, it was needed to select the optimal sequence. All the indexes described above were positive indicators which meant that the larger the value, the better the evaluation result was. Therefore, the maximum value of the same index for each evaluation object was taken as the optimal value of the index. While the maximum value of the "Total use frequency of digital technology" was taken as the optimal value of this indicator. The sequence composed of the optimal values of each indicator was called the optimal sequence, and was denoted as $X_0 = (x_{01}, x_{02}, \ldots x_{0n})$.

Secondly, to solve the grey correlation coefficient, it was needed to set the comparison sequence and the reference sequence respectively. Continue to the previous step, the optimal sequence was taken as the reference sequence. And the sequence composed of the index values of each evaluation object as the comparison sequence, denoted as $X_i = (x_{i1}, x_{i2}, \ldots x_{in})$, i=1, 2, ...m. The grey correlation coefficient between the $i^{th}$ evaluation object and the $j^{th}$ index in the reference sequence is denoted as $\gamma_{ij}$. Here, it was taken ρ as 0.5.

Last step was to calculate the grey correlation degree which reflected the closeness of the comparison sequence to the reference sequence. The greater the degree of association, the closer the comparison sequence was to the optimal value. Therefore, the pros and cons of each evaluation object could have been evaluated according to the degree of grey correlation of each comparison sequence. Taking in to account the heterogeneity between different indicators, different weights are assigned to the indicators according to the relative importance of each indicator. Among them, $\omega_j$ was the weight of the jth index. The index weight was determined by the above-mentioned entropy weighting method. Then it was calculated the grey correlation degree of each country based on this.

# 5. RESULT ANALYSIS

## 5.1 Evaluation Results

Before factor analysis, it was necessary to judge whether the variables selected are suitable for factor analysis. According to the data, a group of observations with 5 related variables and 12 sample size were obtained for analysis. In order to prevent the occurrence of multi collinearity, it was needed to estimate the correlation between the selected variables before factor analysis. In this study, it was used SPSS 25.0 statistical software to test the collected data. Although the significance level of Bartlett sphericity test was less than 0.01, the value was 0.495, less than 0.6, which did not pass the KMO test indicating that the selected variables were not suitable for factor analysis. (In statistics, Bartlett's test, named after Maurice Stevenson Bartlett, is used to test homoscedasticity, that is, if multiple samples are from populations with equal variances. Some statistical tests, such as the analysis of variance, assume that variances are equal across groups or samples, which can be verified with Bartlett's test. The Kaiser-Meyer-Olkin KMO test is a measure of how suited your data is for Factor Analysis.)

Table 2. Comprehensive evaluation value

| Country | Comprehensive evaluation value | Rank |
|---|---|---|
| U.S. | 0.7709 | 1 |
| China | 0.5387 | 2 |
| Finland | 0.4988 | 3 |
| Latvia | 0.4751 | 4 |
| South-Korea | 0.4192 | 5 |
| Mexico | 0.3786 | 6 |
| Romania | 0.3495 | 7 |

## 5.2 Analysis of Results

It is widely accepted that developed countries tend to have high comprehensive evaluation value, including the United States of America, Finland, South-Korea and Latvia. However, Finland, South-Korea and Latvia have relatively low grey correlation coefficient in several certain indicators such as "Research funds on digital technologies" with heavy entropy weight, leading to a sharp drop in the overall score. These countries are also known as innovation-oriented countries. Notably, Romania ranked last. This is because Romania's digital education penetration is still relatively low. It can be found that the number of enrolled students (number of undergraduates, graduate students and doctoral students) is particularly low. (Liu & Yan 2018)

In general, as a developing country, all digital education evaluation index values in Mexico seemed to be tremendously low. The number of academics implementing online-teaching continued to decrease and their quality could not be guaranteed significantly. On the other hand, what was puzzling is that China ranked second as a developing country as well while the various evaluation index values had a relatively large gap, showing that China had an unbalanced level of resource development when the digital education system had obvious room for improvement. In terms of that, Liu and Ru (2018) demonstrated that for the large number of students in China, the phenomena of uneven distribution in higher education resources were increasingly obvious. For example, the resources of scientific research personnel attracted by various schools and the financial resources invested by the state were uneven. Jiang (2020) discovered that only a few universities were considered to be highly efficient and innovative in digital R&D. Since schools without national key construction projects lack national financial support, the research efficiency was relatively low. In universities the leadership was not moving toward Dynamic operating logic. According to the analysis of China's grey correlation coefficient, it could have been found that the statuses of scientific research (number of R&D personnel in digital education and research funds on digital technologies), university construction investment (infrastructure funds and inherent asset investment) as well as financial investment provided by universities are far below the optimal sequence. Furthermore, the entropy weights of R&D personnel, university financial investment and digital research funding were relatively large.

# 6. VALIDITY

When evaluating the validity of this study the differences between the target countries and the time of the survey must be taken in to account. The study was conducted at Shanghai University at a time when universities were closed everywhere. The target groups were university management, academics and students. The share of China was higher than in other countries, especially in the target group of students. Management groups, and academic groups were more balanced. However, the study was valuable because the results are indicative and showed a digital leap in developing countries as a result of the pandemic. University management' interest in responding showed that leadership was moving toward Dynamic operating logic.

# 7. CONCLUSION

Economic and cultural globalization has ushered in a new era in higher education. Because of its immersion in knowledge, higher education plays a particularly important role in global knowledge economies. However, the current Covid-19 pandemic was making it trapped in a development burden. To cope with the challenges posed by this crisis, transformation from traditional face-to-face teaching to online-teaching should have been timely implemented in higher education system. This research offered insightful analysis and established grey comprehensive evaluation model. Although Covid-19 had restricted mobility, the research result promoted the development work and internationalization of higher education institutions, which could serve as a credible reference for the higher education reform. In the future, more cross-border e-earning will be offered and implemented. The expansion of e-learning across national borders implements internationalization in an economic and efficient way. In particular, the study is likely to stimulate discussion with business representatives on issues related to employ-ability as well as on the achievement of lifelong learning objectives.

The case of the digital leap showed how universities in a short time had to change all their operating logics after the Covid-19 pandemic expanded the world. The situations at the universities were very different. Some countries had already come a long way in developing and implementing online-teaching. The necessary infrastructure was in place in the universities and the staff was able to switch to large-scale online teaching. Some countries were about to start, and the Covid-19 pandemic caused the phenomenon described by Schumpeter. Changes were needed in the leadership of universities, from more Mechanical and Organic logic of actions towards more Dynamic logic of actions. It means changes from basic decision-making to innovative solutions for teaching and research. The change was made in a very short time. In 2022, it is generally stated that there is no going back. However, the teaching of expropriation is returning, at least in part, to those countries where it is possible. Similarly, the face-to-face innovation of research teams is gradually returning to universities.

## REFERENCES


Aberg, L. & Stahle, P. (2012): How to lead the regeneration of univeristies?Voiko yliopiston uudistumiskykya johtaa? In P. Stahle & A. Ainakmo (Edit.) Innostava yliopisto: Kohti uudistavaa yliopistojohtamista. University of Helsinki, Gaudeamus. ISBN 978-952-495-222-4.

Cheng Long, Cao Xianyu & Zhang Zhigang. (2020): An Empirical Study on the impact of labor relations on the innovation and entrepreneurship willingness of University researchers -- the interactive effects of welfare, fairness and promotion. Fairness and promotion. *Journal of University of Electronic Science and Technology* (Social Science Edition) (04), 105-112.

Hakkarainen, K. & Lonka, K. & Lipponen, L. (2004): Exploratory learning, reason, emotions and culture as igniters of learning. WSOY. Finland.

Hasan, N., & Bao, Y. (2020): Impact of "e-Learning crack-up" perception on psychological distress among college students during COVID-19 pandemic: A mediating role of "fear of academic year loss". Children and Youth Services Review, 118, 105355

Jiang M.J. (2020): Assessing the research efficiency of Chinese higher education institutions by data envelopment analysis. Asia Pacific Education Review, 21.

Karna, Maija (2011): Virtual data building mode to support problem-based learning. University of Lapland. Acta electronica Universitatis Lapponiensis. http://urn.fi/URN:NBN:fi:ula-201108221152

Kilpinen Kari (2004): Reflective teacher using the computer-network in teaching; how the psycho-epistemological learning styles help to better design learning environments.

Kopp, Carol M. (2019): Creative Destruction. What Is Creative Destruction? Creative destruction can be described as the dismantling of long-standing practices in order to make way for innovation. Creative destruction was first coined by Austrian economist Joseph Schumpeter in 1942.

Liu J. & Yan X. M. (2018): One belt one road: the higher education status and development trend of the countries along the line (tenth) -- taking Latvia as an example. World education information (15), 30-33. doi: CNKI: SUN: JYXI.0.2018-15-009.

Liu, W. H.& Ru, M. A. (2018): Regional inequality of higher education resources in China. Frontiers of Education in China, 13(001), 119-151.

Pan, Xingxia & Liu, Jianfeng & Chen, Xinyun (2020): Evaluation of provincial higher education development level based on entropy weight and grey comprehensive evaluation method. Journal of Nanchang Aviation University (Social Science Edition). 022 (001). 103-110.

Schumpeter, Joseph A. (1991): The Economics and Sociology of Capitalism. Edited by Richard Swedberg. ISBN: 9780691003832. Published: Jan. 21. 1991. Princeton University Press.

Wen, F. (2013): Retracted: a mathematical model for higher education input–output efficiency analysis.

# DIGITAL TRANSFORMATION IN FINNISH HIGHER EDUCATION: A PERSPECTIVE FROM A UNIVERSITY OF APPLIED SCIENCES

Jari Multisilta and Timo Mattila
*Satakunta University of Applied Sciences*
*Satakunnankatu 23, 28130 Pori, Finland*

**ABSTRACT**

This paper describes digital transformation in Finland from the perspective of a mid-sized university of applied sciences in western Finland, outside the capital city area. Higher education institutions (HEIs) compete amongst themselves, both locally and globally, in terms of student and staff recruitment, government funding, and research funding. In addition, networking with companies and other organizations is a key part of HEIs' strategies and actions. We consider the steps that HEIs have taken toward digital transformation, the drivers behind digital transformation, and the factors that affect HEIs' management strategies. Although the digital transformation process started over 30 years ago, the COVID-19 pandemic has become a major driver of digital transformation in Finnish HEIs. The results of our case study show that an HEI's funding is of critical importance and provides the ground for setting the performance indicators in HEI management. Finally, climate change and sustainability are factors that will further affect the higher education system.

**KEYWORDS**

Digital Transformation, Digivision 2030, Management, Funding, Change.

## 1. INTRODUCTION

The Finnish higher education (HE) system employs a dual model with two types of higher education institutions (HEIs), namely universities and universities of applied sciences. Universities provide bachelor's, master's and doctoral degrees and conduct both basic and applied research. Universities of applied sciences provide bachelor's and master's degrees and conduct applied research and development in close collaboration with companies and organizations in their geographical regions. The Finnish Ministry of Education and Culture steers HEIs' activities. The HE system is primarily funded by the government and involves no tuition fees (except for non EU students). For research grants, HEIs apply for funding from multiple sources, including the private sector.

In many industry and service sectors in Finland, the need for a skilled workforce is growing, especially in technology-related fields as well as the social and health sectors. In terms of long-term projections, the decreasing birth rate suggests that Finland's population will begin to decline in 2034 (YLE News, 2021). HEIs are expected to respond to the need for more workforce by providing degree studies and continuing education.

Moreover, due to technological development and the rapid changes in our societies, jobs are constantly changing. For many jobs, workers' skills and knowledge need to be updated systematically. It is not enough to simply have a degree; rather, one must possess the latest knowledge and skills. In addition to job-specific skills, students are expected to learn the so-called future skills (see, e.g., Bakhshi et al., 2017; Ehlers & Kellermann, 2019), such as problem-solving skills, creativity, the ability to act in a self-organized manner, cooperation skills, and social and communication skills, all of which are important in today's changing work life.

The contemporary adoption of technologies in HEIs reflects a paradigm shift, whereby technology is seen as facilitating the management of complex learning environments and digital learning (Benavides et al., 2020). This paradigm shift is known as digital transformation (DT). According to Benavides et al. (2020, p. 1), "digital transformation (DT) has become a priority for higher education institutions (HEIs) in this second decade of the

21st century, and this is a natural and necessary process for organizations that claim to be leaders of change and be highly competitive in their domain."

According to Abad-Segura et al. (2020, p. 2), "digital transformation (DT) must be established according to the axioms of connectivism, to unify its commitment to meeting the expectations of the different interest groups in the economic, social, and environmental dimensions." Scholars have argued that digital learning promotes student-centered learning (Abad-Segura et al., 2020), partly because technology enables rich learning experiences. Brooks and McCormic (2020, p. 5) defined DT as "a series of deep and coordinated culture, workforce, and technology shifts that enable new educational and operating models and transform an institution's business model, strategic directions, and value proposition." The core element of DT is change (Rodrigues, 2017). An important part of DT is the "modification of business processes, procedures, capabilities and policies to take advantage of the changes and opportunities presented by new digital technologies, as well as the impact they have on society" (Sandhu, 2018).

Based on these definitions, it is clear that DT has a significant impact on HEIs' strategies, teaching, infrastructure, curricula, administration, research, business processes, human resources, and marketing.

Connectivism is a learning theory that emphasizes social learning in a networked environment. Downes (2007) described connectivism as follows: "Knowledge is distributed across a network of connections, and therefore that learning consists of the ability to construct and traverse those networks" (para. 1). In connectivism, "learning is a process of connecting specialized nodes or information sources (Siemens, 2005). Moreover, in connectivism, knowledge is constructed via social contexts and networks. Connectivism was developed because previous learning theories emerged before the growth of educational technology (Siemens, 2005). According to Siemens (2005), "the capacity to form connections between sources of information, and thereby create useful information patterns, is required to learn in our knowledge economy."

In this paper, we discuss DT in Finnish HEIs. As a case study, we discuss the experiences of a mid-sized Finnish university of applied sciences in relation to its strategy and management decisions.

# 2. DIGIVISION 2030

## 2.1 Digital Transformation in Finnish HEIs

Digivision 2030 is a joint development program for all Finnish HEIs aimed at establishing Finland as a model country for flexible learning and a global pioneer in HE. Finnish HEIs have formed a consortium that receives external funding to implement a common model for DT in Finnish HE. According to Digivision 2030 (2021), the aims are as follows:

- Learners are provided with data on their own learning in a secure manner, enabling and supporting their learning throughout their lives.
- In 2030, Finland has an open and recognized learning ecosystem that offers quality, diversity, flexibility, efficiency, and suitability for the life situation and needs, thus generating better learning results.
- The learning ecosystem also provides a platform for research and innovation activities, benefiting society and working life extensively.
- In 2030, the scientific and educational activities of HEIs are key factors in securing the high level of competence of the adult population, national competitiveness, and international impact.

Currently, all HEI's in Finland have their own information technology (IT) infrastructures and systems, and students need separate credentials to access the services provided by different HEIs. Digivision 2030 aims to establish one identity for all users for accessing all services. For the Digivision 2030 national platform, a common interface needs to be implemented to guarantee the compatibility of the existing digital services provided by HEIs.

DT will have consequences for student guidance and counseling. HEIs should support students regardless of time and place—for example, by using artificial intelligence (AI) solutions (Higher Education Institutes' Digivision 2030, 2021). However, it is not clear how best to support students studying in a complex, networked HEI. According to Edyburn (2021, p. 115), "there is an urgent need to determine how to support students that have underdeveloped self-regulation skills." More research is needed to identify students' needs and design student-centered guiding and counseling practices. Digivision 2030 represents a major DT that cannot happen without proper change management.

Digivision 2030 is a continuation of HEIs' collective and individual transformations. Digivision 2030 entails a comprehensive change in HEIs' organizational culture and thus requires knowledge of managing systemic transformations. Although an organization's subsystems strive to fulfill their own functions, only the unity of the subsystems enables the organization to achieve its goals. Therefore, management should consider the requirements and effects of change on all parts of the system as well as the relationships and dependencies between the parts (Mattila et al., 2021, pp. 171–172). In sum, Digivision 2030 is a new stage in the transformation that universities of applied sciences have been undergoing for many years (Auvinen, 2004; Nenonen, 2020).

## 2.2 Digital Transformation in Satakunta University of Applied Sciences

Satakunta University of Applied Sciences (SAMK) is a mid-sized university of applied sciences in western Finland. SAMK has over 410 staff members and over 6,000 students across 40 bachelor's and master's programs. The students represent over 60 nationalities, and 14 of the degree programs are in English. SAMK has more than 500 partner companies that participate in various research and development projects with SAMK's research centers. SAMK's vision is that all its students should find employment. The economic and industrial structure of the region where SAMK is located requires SAMK to be capable of offering extensive education and research opportunities in the fields of industry, health care and social services, business administration, and technology.

For as long as universities of applied sciences have existed (i.e., 30 years), they have been implementing changes related to the objectives of Digivision 2030. In SAMK, the transformation process has consisted of the following partly overlapping steps:

1) **Fostering enthusiasm for digitality.** Building an online learning environment to improve learning, teaching, and guidance and implementing the first steps of a digital library. In SAMK, a learning environment called Virtualia was implemented in the late 1990s.
2) **Preparing for digital learning.** Treating digital learning as part of SAMK's functions by recruiting an individual responsible for online pedagogy and the technical support assistant for teachers. At the same time, each new teacher was obliged to complete a course in online pedagogy. Since 2000, this step continued for just over 10 years and moved to step five in the early part of the 2010s.
3) **Transforming a degree program into online learning.** The next step began in the early 2000s and involved transforming one-degree program and one of the campuses into a digital campus to serve the needs of students who worked and studied at the same time. Together with multinational actors, SAMK developed an e-learning environment that enabled participation in related education and tutoring activities. Systemic change began when the administration (communication, ICT, student services, library), pedagogical solutions (teacher competence), and management realized that when constructing a digital campus, a change in one area requires modifications in all other areas to meet the learning needs of digital campus customers.
4) **Expanding digital services**. The digitality of services needs to be comprehensive. There, SAMK decided to convert all services to digital ones and to introduce the Bring Your Own Device (BYOD) concept. The systematic implementation of this change started in mid-2010 and is still ongoing.
5) **Initiating pedagogical changes**. In the fifth step of the change process, the pedagogical change became the central component of the business. The pedagogical change was fundamental and involved defining, for example, the common pedagogical starting points of the HEI and establishing the frameworks for the identification and evaluation of competences. Skill pools were established for ongoing dialogue between teachers and the administration. In response to the changes demanded by Digivision 2030, a digital leaders' group was established to develop the pedagogical framework of the future.

DT and educational organization performance require continuous development and responsivity in a changing operating environment. Digivision 2030 challenges HEIs in a new way. SAMK has responded to this challenge in an organized and proactive manner.

## 2.3 The Drivers of Digital Transformation

What are the major drivers of Digivision? We have already discussed DT and will also present climate change and sustainability as factors influencing Digivision 2030. Bakhshi et al. (2017, 12) proposed that the following trends "determine the big picture of work": environmental sustainability, urbanization, increasing inequality, political uncertainty, technological change, globalization, and demographic changes. Most of these key trends also affect Digivision 2030. However, in this paper, we study the following trends in more detail: competition for the best students, faculty, and researchers, changing work life and skills, DT caused by COVID-19, and new technological developments.

In some countries, universities are competing intensely for the best students, faculty, and researchers (Benavides et al., 2020). This is also the case in Finland. The industry and the health and service sectors need more workforce, but finding new skilled workers is not easy. The demand for professionals is greater than the number of professionals that HEIs can train; at the same time, the number of young people is decreasing. The solution to this challenge is to bring students from abroad to study in Finland and, after their graduation, to convince them to stay. Helping immigrants feel at home and develop their lives in a new culture is a well-known social challenge. It is not only HEIs' responsibility to help students settle down in Finland; rather, the community should also be strongly involved in this process by providing work, housing, health care, and safe environments for immigrants to build their careers and lives.

In addition, jobs are changing rapidly, and people need new skills to succeed. Therefore, there is a need for just-in-time courses using which people can update their skills. Online learning is one possible answer to this challenge.

In Finland, the working population is educated extensively during work life. A significant proportion of the Finnish working-age population already re-educate themselves while working. This is necessary from an individual's perspective to maintain the competence required in the work life. Changes in work and technology mean that some jobs will be lost, and new ones will emerge. Therefore, new forms of HE are required for those already employed.

The *Education Policy Report*, issued by the government and approved by parliament, states that in the future, opportunities for studying will be improved by opening up existing education institutions and creating new, flexibly targeted education programs (Finnish Government, 2021, p. 45). The solution provided by Digivision 2030 is a common learning platform for HE, using which educational opportunities can be created by third parties as well. The technical solution is the single study identity for all students, which will allow them to access this platform and will facilitate continuous learning.

The debate regarding real breakthroughs in competence building in relation to degrees is just beginning. In new areas of digital business, the importance of competence has already increased beyond formal education. However, this has not yet been the case in more traditional industries, such as health care and shipping.

Online teaching has been criticized for being a degree mill (Simonson et al., 2015, p. 18). However, quality learning means learning what is needed for a successful work life. The most important future skills in the work life include interaction skills, emotional intelligence and empathy, the ability to recognize and develop one's own competences, and networking ability. The challenge is the quality of learning and the understanding that learning takes place within a community. It remains to be seen how these requirements can be fulfilled in Digivision 2030 digital learning environments.

In Finland, universities of applied sciences have responded to these challenges by determining the shared competencies in relation to the European Qualifications Framework (EQF) competency basis, by developing competence-based evaluations, and by defining quality criteria for digital courses. Shared competences are common competence areas for different programs and degrees, and they create the foundation for operating in a workplace, cooperation and the development of expertise (Auvinen et al., 2022, p. 4). It is possible to implement all the needed work-life skills in online learning environments. In SAMK, students are encouraged to work together in a variety of ways, such as online consultations, joint tasks, discussions, presentations, peer evaluation, and the like (Kallama et al., 2019).

The DT caused by the COVID-19 pandemic can also be seen as a driver of Digivision 2030. We also know that COVID-19 has caused mental health problems for students due to long periods of university closures.

Of course, massive online open courses (MOOCs) have been around since at least 2008 (McAuley et al., 2010) and have already transformed online learning. At the same time, social media has expanded rapidly, and young people are heavy users of social media. Their use of technology reflects what they expect from their learning environments.

Finally, the development of AI can make it possible to create AI-based learning services. In many cases, AI-based tutors could guide students through the learning process and support students with underdeveloped self-regulation skills.

## 2.4 Sustainability

The Finnish Ministry of Education has introduced a sustainable development policy (Finnish Ministry of Education, 2020), and all universities of applied sciences have adopted the goal of becoming carbon neutral by 2030 (The Rectors' Conference of Finnish Universities of Applied Sciences Arene, 2020). The largest sources of CO2 emissions in HEIs are buildings and transport. In Finland, we need to heat our buildings for most of the year. In addition, buildings use energy for cooling, lights, and so on. Faculty and research staff often travel to scientific conferences or project meetings, and although video conferencing is growing, there is still a need to meet face to face. In addition, staff and students commute to campuses, and restaurants and cafeterias on campuses produce waste.

Most HEIs in Finland have taken the strategic decision to not compensate for the CO2 emissions that they produce. Instead, they aim to decrease the emissions—for example, by limiting work-related travel and using green energy. However, the biggest contribution that an HEI can make is to fight climate change in every curriculum so that when students graduate, they can use their sustainability and climate-change skills wherever they work. This is known as the carbon handprint, or positive climate impact.

# 3. STRATEGY AND MANAGEMENT ISSUES

All HEIs in Finland are currently involved in Digivision 2030. At the same time, HEIs are both jointly making decisions on how to proceed with Digivision 2030 and implementing their own strategies and competing against other HEIs.

It is quite easy to build a management system that is based on HEI's strategy and related key success factors and measure key success factors using items derived from the funding model (see Fig. 1). But managing change itself is very challenging, while changing the operating culture takes a long time. Previous funding models for Finnish HEIs have focused on the number of incoming students. Previously, an HEIs funding was based mainly on the number of students enrolled in an HEI. In negotiations with the Ministry of Education, the HEIs' goal was to secure as many student enrollment positions as possible. The enrollment brought funding, which enabled HEIs to organize their activities. In the current model, the funding is based on the output—that is, on the number of graduating students—which has been a major paradigm shift.

The current funding model puts lifelong learning at the center, together with degrees and R&D funding. The effects of this paradigm shift on teachers' work have been significant. More specifically, student groups have become larger and more heterogeneous, students' learning goals have become more diverse, and students' approach to learning and credits has changed.

When it comes to HEIs' management, perspectives are divided according to the priorities of the different groups, with performance indicators being of primary interest to management, the clarity and functionality of processes being the most important elements from an administrative perspective, and the autonomous role of teachers being seen as the most important aspects by the teachers (Auvinen, 2004, 360). These three perspectives co-exist in HEIs. Handling all three requires a strong effort on behalf of the management. When it comes to goals, it is simple to manage set metric goals and monitor their implementation. But how does one build processes, competencies, and evaluations to support the implementation of a university's strategy, and how can leadership enable teachers' pedagogical competencies to support these goals? This involves the whole organizational culture and its change. Management and supervisors must build a new culture by setting a consistent example in terms of what the management pays attention to, what they emphasize, evaluate, and control, how they react to critical events, how resources are allocated, who is rewarded, and what behavior is punished. At SAMK, the strategy, the goals, and the desired quality targets are regularly communicated via discussions with the personnel, and operations are defined and measured according to the established goals. Teachers' pedagogical freedom is guided by emphasizing competencies, such as e-learning skills, learning guidance skills, and assessment skills, and by providing training and support that lead to the successful implementation of the strategy.

| | | |
|---|---|---|
| 76% Education | 56% Batchelor's degree<br>9% Continuous learning<br>6% Number of employed graduates and quality of employment<br>3% Student feedback<br>2% Degree in vocational teaching training | |
| 19% RDI | 11% External RDI funding<br>6% Master's Degrees | 2% Publications etc. |
| 5% Other | 5% Strategic Funding | |

Figure 1. The Finnish universities of applied sciences funding model. The government funding is allocated to the universities of applied sciences based on the performance of previous three years (Ministry of Education and Culture, 2021)

According to previous research, the steering effect of a funding model on HE is considerable. Universities of applied science focus specifically on the functions highlighted by the funding model, in particular the issues related to key financial indicators (Nenonen, 2020, 29). This is what has happened at SAMK: the major indicators have all been adopted directly from the funding model. To give an example, SAMK has succeeded in implementing continuous learning, a major measure in the funding model. The number of ECTS completed in continuous learning and cooperation between universities has increased more than 100 times since 2012 and tripled between 2019 and 2021.

For HEIs not located in the biggest cities, major decisions are related to student recruitment. The constant flow of students entering an HEI and graduating on time are the most important elements in the Finnish HEI funding model. In the Finnish system, students can apply to HEIs after completing upper secondary school or vocational school. Although there are entrance exams in HEIs, entrance exams are not the only way to enter HE.

A faster transition toward HE is one of the goals of Finland's education policy. Students with high school diplomas or vocational school certificates may not yet know where they would like to work, which means that HEI enrollment should be flexible. However, after enrolling in a degree program, one should graduate from it. It is not easy to switch to another program. The idea is that one can update one's skills and learn new areas after graduation via continuous-learning opportunities. Student selection in Finnish universities is based on high school or vocational school success or entrance examinations. The universities of applied sciences have a joint entrance examination. In fact, joint entrance examinations measure the general university readiness for a specific field—that is, the same competencies as those studied during secondary education. Previous academic success thus has a major impact on whether one can enter the desired institution. Therefore, HEIs have built products that are designed to provide opportunities for demonstrating one's competency in a desired degree field by completing degree-related studies and thus earning a place to study. This option is known as pathway studies. The idea is that by completing a sufficient number of degree courses, one automatically gets degree-student status and the right to complete degree studies in the same field. According to SAMK's experience, the students chosen for degree programs after completing pathway studies often graduate on time and are satisfied with their studies. To give an example, in 2014, pathways were introduced as an experiment in one degree program. At the time, dropout rates were over 40% per class, and graduation was very rare (< 20%). Today, few students drop out, and almost 80% of them graduate on time. At SAMK, about 20% of all students start their studies through various pathways.

The goal of the government's education policy is to triple the number of international students by 2030. and to have 75% of graduates be employed in Finland. Common platforms for international HEIs, improvements in student entry and integration, co-operation in streamlining application processes, and the strengthening of foreign students' Finnish and Swedish language skills are seen as tools for achieving the employment goal. There is also a strong will to do this work together (Ministry of Education and Culture, 2022, pp. 16–17). The Ministry of Education has directed strategic funding to HEIs for joint pathway studies for foreign students. The joint pathway is an opportunity for students to see the various opportunities that Finnish HEIs have to offer. In addition to the joint pathways, Finnish HEIs have co-operated with commercial actors to recruit international students.

These tools aim to ensure that when international students arrive in Finland, they are ready for university studies, know Finnish culture, and can succeed in studies in English. There is still a lot of work to be done to make the integration of an international student a success. To give an example, SAMK presented the youragent.fi service to enable students and companies to find each other and to foster internship opportunities.

What would be the pros and cons of a national platform for common courses for all HEIs? Should HEIs open the platform to commercial players as well? It is unlikely that HEI funding will grow in the coming years. Therefore, cooperation is needed not only between educational organizations but also with commercial pedagogical operators. HEIs should accept the responsibility for the content and quality of HE.

We have already stated that the funding model is a strong tool for guiding HEIs' operations. The additional funding (research grants) comes from multiple sources and guides what kind of research is supported. For example, European Union funding emphasizes the digital and green transitions and aims to make Europe a leader in digital and climate actions. Such policies (either national or international) strongly impact HEIs' research and development.

## 4. CONCLUSION

DT is changing how HEIs operate. In this paper, we have discussed the DT of Finnish HEIs and presented a case study of the decisions and experiences of a mid-sized university of applied sciences in Finland.

Based on our case study, the DT process can be conceptualized as a five-tier process consisting of the following steps: (1) fostering enthusiasm for digitality, (2) preparing for digital learning, (3) transforming a degree program to online learning, (4) expanding digital services, and (5) initiating pedagogical changes. The process has been going on for over 30 years already.

We have identified and presented six drivers behind the DT of Finnish HEIs: (1) climate change and sustainability; (2) competition for the best students, faculty, and researchers; (3) competences and the need to organize just-in-time courses for updating skills; (4) the COVID-19 pandemic; (5) younger generations' expectations (social media and MOOCs); and (6) technological development, especially that of AI.

The factors affecting HEIs' management strategies are as follows: (1) the guidance from the ministry, especially through the funding model and the setting of performance indicators for HEIs; (2) the definition of quality in HEIs processes; (3) the interaction and balance between performance indicators, processes, and teacher autonomy; (4) student recruitment, both nationally and internationally; (5) faster transition from secondary to HE via pathway studies; and (6) the increasing number of enrolled students. Based on our case study, the funding of an HEI is a core means for guiding an HEI and provides the ground for setting performance indicators for HEI management.

There are open questions related to DT and its management in the future. First, climate change and sustainability will affect all functions in HEIs. Second, what would be the best way for HEIs to collaborate with private education service providers? Third, how can education quality be ensured in digital environments?

## REFERENCES

Abad-Segura, E., González-Zamar, M.-D., Infante-Moro, J. C., & Ruipérez García, G. (2020). Sustainable management of digital transformation in higher education: Global research trends. *Sustainability, 12*(5), 2107.

Auvinen, P., Asikainen, E., Hakonen, A. Marjanen, P., Risku, P. & Silvennoinen, S. (2022). *Recommendation on the Shared Competences of Universities of Applied Sciences and their Application.* The Rectors' Conference of Finnish Universities of Applied Sciences Arene ry. January.

Auvinen, P. (2004). *Ammatillisen käytännön toistajasta monipuoliseksi aluekehittäjäksi? Ammattikorkeakoulun-uudistus ja opettajan työn muutos vuosina 1992-2010* (From a repeater of professional practice to a versatile regional developer? Universities of applied sciences reform and change in teacher work over the years. University of Joensuu. Joensuu.

Bakhshi, H., Downing, J. M., Osborne, M. A., & Schneider, P. (2017). *The future of skills: Employment in 2030.* Pearson.

Benavides, L. M. C., Tamayo Arias, J. A., Arango Serna, M. D., Branch Bedoya, J. W., & Burgos, D. (2020). Digital transformation in higher education institutions: A systematic literature review. *Sensors, 20*(11), 3291.

Brooks, D. C., & McCormack, M. (2020). *Driving digital transformation in higher education.* ECAR research report. Louisville, CO: ECAR, June.

Duke, B., Harper, G., & Johnston, M. (2013). Connectivism as a digital age learning theory. *The International HETL Review, 2013*(Special Issue), 4–13.

Downes, S. (2007). *What connectivism is.* http://halfanhour.blogspot.com/2007/02/what-connectivism-is.html

Edyburn, D. (2021) Transforming student engagement in COVID-19 remote instruction: A research perspective. *Education Technology Research and Development*, *69*, 113–116.

Ehlers, U. D., & Kellermann, S. A. (2019). *Future skills: The future of learning and higher education*. Karlsruhe.

Finnish Government (2021). Valtioneuvoston koulutuspoliittinen selonteko. (Education Policy Report of the Finnish Government). Publications of the Finnish Government 64. https://julkaisut.valtioneuvosto.fi/handle/10024/162995

Higher Education Institutes' Digivision 2030. (2021). *Digivisio 2030. Building the future of learning.* 2030 https://digivisio2030.fi/tiedostot/higher-education-institutes-digivision-2030/

Kallama, K., & Koivisto, J. (2019). Digital Campus – ratkaisuja joustavaan oppimiseen (Digital Campus – solutions to flexible learning). Satakunnan ammattikorkeakoulu. Ulvila.

McAuley, A., Stewart, B., Siemens, G., & Cormier, D. (2010). *The MOOC model for digital practice.* https://www.academia.edu/download/43171365/MOOC_Final.pdf

Mattila, E., Kallio, T. J., & Saru, E. (2021) Sivistyksen ja soten yhteistyö kunnissa – askeleita kohti syvempää palveluintegraatiota (The collaboration of education and healt sector in muncipalities – steps towards deeper service integration). *Hallinnon Tutkimus*, 3, 170–186.

Ministry of Education and Culture. (2020). *Sustainable development policy of the Ministry of Education and Culture and its administrative branch.* http://urn.fi/URN:ISBN:978-952-263-706-2

Ministry of Education and Culture (2021). *Steering, financing and agreements of higher education institutions, science agencies and research institutes.* https://okm.fi/en/steering-financing-and-agreements

Ministry of Education and Culture (2022*). Kohti korkeakoulutuksen ja tutkimuksen kansainvälisyyden edistämisen linjausten päivitystä. KV-foorumin väliraportti.* (Updating the International Policies for Higher Education and Research. Interim report by the Forum for International Policies)

Nenonen, M. (2020). *Tulokset paranevat, miten käy laadun? Tulosperustainen rahoitusmalli koulutuksen tuloksellisuuden ja laadun kehittäjänä ammattikorkeakouluissa* (The results improve, how about the quality? A results-based funding model as a developer of the effectiveness and quality of education in universities of applied sciences). University of Eastern Finland. Joensuu (in Finnish).

Rodrigues, L. S. (2017). Challenges of digital transformation in higher education institutions: A brief discussion. In *Proceedings of the 30th International Business Information Management Association Conference, IBIMA 2017—Vision 2020: Sustainable Economic Development, Innovation Management, and Global Growth*.

Sandhu, G. (2018) The role of academic libraries in the digital transformation of the universities. *Proceedings of the 2018 5th International Symposium on Emerging Trends and Technologies in Libraries and Information Services*, 292–296.

Simonson, M. R., Smaldino, S., & Zvacek, S. (2015). *Teaching and learning at a distance: Foundations of distance education* (6th ed). Information Age Publishing Inc., Charlotte, North Carolina.

Siemens, G. (2005). Connectivism: A learning theory for the digital age. *International Journal of Instructional Technology and Distance Learning*, *2*(1).

The Rectors' Conference of Finnish Universities of Applied Sciences Arene (2020*). Sustainable, responsible and carbon-neutral universities of applied sciences. Programme for the sustainable development and responsibility of universities of applied sciences*. Arene. https://tinyurl.com/3fmd8ph7

YLE News (2021). Statistics Finland: Falling birth rates cannot maintain population. https://yle.fi/news/3-12122258

# DIGITAL TRANSFORMATION OF COMPLEX EDUCATIONAL SCENARIOS (COMPARATIVE STUDY OF FINAL QUALIFICATION ASSESSMENT FOR FOREIGN LANGUAGES PROGRAMS)

Rusudan Makhachashvili and Ivan Semenist
*Borys Grinchenko Kyiv University, Bulvarno-Kudryavska-st., 18/2, Kyiv, Ukraine*

**ABSTRACT**

The global quarantine measures and restrictions have posed a challenge to the structure and procedure of university summative assessment process. Foreign Languages Acquisition and Linguistic Education assessment are interdisciplinary processes, informed by the nature of linguistic content and types of communicative and professional activities within a framework of set and variable scenarios. The study is based on identification of various interdisciplinary competency principles, derivative of 21st century skills. This inquiry objective is to investigate the dynamic progress and results of digital transformation of final qualification assessment for students of European and Oriental Languages programs, employed in the years 2020 and 2021 through the pandemic emergency digitization measures. The study focus is on the comparison of the cases and best practices of Borys Grinchenko Kyiv University (Ukraine) Digital Final Qualification Assessment to derive contrastive results for different stages of digitization (2020 and 2021) in Foreign Languages major programs. Comparative results of the efficiency of ICT tools and practices applications across different educational activities of Final Qualification Assessment and interoperable digital literacy levels requirement are evaluated.

**KEYWORDS**

Digital Transformation, Educational Scenario, Digital Skills, ICT Tools, Final Qualification Assessment, European Languages, Oriental Languages.

## 1. INTRODUCTION

The global pandemic of COVID-19 emerged as a kind of a black swan scenario for interdisciplinary domains of social and economic life, including education. The black swan theory is a concept that describes an event that comes as a surprise, has a major effect on society, and is often inappropriately rationalized after the fact with the benefit of hindsight (Taleb, 2010). The COVID-19 pandemic amplified digitalization measures in higher education sphere, informed by the need to take quick comprehensive action in order to achieve the overarching result to transform educational scenarios into holistic digital, remote and hybrid frameworks.

The consequent functional tasks to meet this challenge are estimated as: to activate comprehensive complex skillsets, otherwise latent or underutilized in the educational process; to enhance ICT competence and digital literacy of all participants of the educational process, relocated to computer realm; to derive recommendations for increasing productivity of ICT tools implementation by all stakeholders in normative digital framework educational scenarios.

The global quarantine and subsequent emergency digital education measures have posed an array of challenges to the structure and workflow of university summative assessment process. Final Qualification assessment for Foreign Languages university-level programs in particular is chosen for analysis as an integrated cognitive and applied educational scenario, that involves interoperability of different communicative stages and activities (oral and written tests and exams, final project public presentation, internal and external review, discussion, appeal).

This study mission is to investigate the principles and results of comprehensive digital transformation of final qualification assessment for different groups of stakeholders of European (French, Italian, Spanish, English, German) and Oriental (Mandarin Chinese, Japanese) Languages programs, employed in the years

2020-2021 through several phases of lockdown measures. The study focus is on the critical review of the applied case and best practices of Borys Grinchenko Kyiv University (BGKU), Ukraine Digital Final Qualification Assessment to derive comparative results for different stages of emergency digitization measures (initial – 2020, hybrid – 2020-2021, sustainable – 2021) for Foreign Languages major programs.

The study scope permits to disclose the following tracks of findings: Introduction of a comprehensive model of digital transformation of complex educational scenarios; Comparative analysis of Final Qualification Assessment efficiency in digital format for different groups of participants (students, faculty, assessment board members, referees) according to such dimensions: Dimension A: frequency, synergy and interoperability of educational communicative activities for Final Qualification Assessment in Foreign languages; Dimension B: Soft skills and corresponding foreign language acquisition skills, activated in the Final Qualification Assessment scenario, enhanced by the use of ICT; Dimension C: digital literacy status quo and estimated requirements for different groups of Final Qualification Assessment participants in Foreign Languages programs (students, faculty, assessment board members, referees); Dimension D: efficiency evaluation of ICT tools, used for all procedures Final Qualification Assessment in Foreign Languages programs, by different groups of participants (students, faculty, assessment board members, referees);

Practical recommendations to overcome generic and specific, challenges for actual and underdeveloped skills (hard, technical and soft), that different groups of participants of the educational process encountered through Final Qualification Assessment in programs of European and Oriental Languages.

The relevant studies on various aspects of digital education, conducted across the pre-COVID-19 framework have spanned such key avenues of inquiry as 1) assessment of satisfaction with distance learning experience (Bolliger, 2009; Bekele, 2010); 2) evaluation of learning outcomes (Ni, 2013; Costareie, 2011); 3) overall attitudes to distance learning (Salyers, 2014); 4) challenges of online education (Markova et al, 2017). University-level assessment studies paradigm, for its part, adheres to such major tracks of inquiry: 1) summative assessment formats and efficiency (Kimbell, 2007); 2) measurable outcomes of summative assessment (Kuh, 2014); 3) computer-assisted assessment and the e-Scape initiative (Einig, 2013; Atkinson, 2000).

These issues require a comprehensive revisit in terms of the toll the global pandemic took on individual learning experiences, activated skillsets and subsequent shift in efficiency estimations of linguistic education in universities of the world due to the abrupt transition to exclusively digital distant or hybrid learning formats.

This inquiry estimates the knowledge gap in the cross-section of disclosing digital learning in the timespan of the COVID-19 as a comprehensive social and cognitive activity model, a holistic transformation of traditional practices and scenarios to achieve learning outcomes. As such, digital learning is determined to be a complex object system, dominated by concepts of electronic interaction and communication, acquiring the following features: ubiquity (inclusiveness); integrativity; isomorphism; normativity; communicative substantiality; information capacity; interactivity. Final Qualification assessment for Foreign Languages major programs in particular is chosen for analysis as a comprehensive practical and cognitive educational scenario, that, when digitized, involves the synergy of different of communicative types and activities (oral and written exams, final project viva, internal and external review). Qualification assessment for Foreign Languages major programs thus is a strict regimen that involves different stages, requiring interoperability of interdisciplinary soft and applied digital skills.

Foreign Languages Acquisition on university level major programs in general is a rigorous process (Miller et al, 2020) that involves different stages and a regimen of activities and competences across interconnected interdisciplinary domains. The presented study is a parcel of comprehensive institutional inquiry into aspects of innovative educational communication in the digital realm (Makhachashvili, Semenist 2021a; Makhachashvili, Semenist 2021b; Makhachashvili et al 2021) into the toll digitalization and amplified use of ICT tools put on different aspects of Oriental as well as European languages acquisition efficiency, assessment management, programmed results, communicative and digital competency formation in COVID-19 lockdown paradigm.

The outlined pre-existing studies paradigm informed the following research questions, this paper sets out to disclose: 1) What are the multi-faced aspects of Final Qualification Assessment educational scenario transformation into digital format, assisted by Information and Communication Technologies and tools? 2) What are the measurable soft skills that inform the efficiency of Final Qualification Assessment for Foreign languages programs transformation into digital format? 3) What are the measurable digital skills that inform the efficiency of Final Qualification Assessment for Foreign languages programs transformation into digital format? 4) What are the efficiency parameters of ICT tools, consistently used for Final Qualification Assessment for Foreign languages programs in the digital format?

Informed by the scope of research questions, this study objective is to review the dynamics of the complex educational scenario of Final Qualification Assessment framework transformation via digital technologies and tools through the initial (2020) and sustainable (2021) digitization measures of the Covid-19 pandemic for students of European and Oriental Languages major programs.

The survey and analysis of different ICT tools is used to estimate the efficiency and functionality of the translation of real-life qualification assessment practices into digital format. The choice of the target objective is informed by the need to elaborate comprehensive models of digital transformation of the foreign languages acquisition.

The investigation also seeks to identify the dynamics in various formats of soft skills and digital skills application, utilized through qualification assessment process by primary stakeholders (students) in Ukraine. The choice of the considered case of university Final Qualification Assessment for Foreign Languages major programs is informed by the need to estimate the dynamic parameters of digital literacy development and application in multi-cultural context.

# 2. FINAL QUALIFICATION ASSESSMENT: COMPARATIVE STUDY OF DIGITAL TRANSFORMATION AT BGKU, UKRAINE

## 2.1 Methodology and Design

The study employs the combination of mixed methods (Almaki 2016) – a proportional arrangement of quantitative and qualitative inquiry to assess in-depth aspects efficiency estimation of digital Final Qualification for Foreign Languages programs. The comprehensive study design methodology included the following consecutive steps: 1) Qualitative soft and digital skills framework profiling to identify indicators of that inform the efficiency of Final Qualification assessment activities, performed via ICT tools; 2) Qualitative Finale Qualification Assessment framework profiling (Makhachashvili et al 2021; Nelson et al 2014) and structuring of framework transformation of this educational scenario into digital format; 3) Quantitative assessment of the efficiency and expediency of The Final Qualification Assessment for European and Oriental languages programs, conducted in digital and hybrid format, performed based on the online survey method.

Final Qualification assessment for Foreign Languages major programs in particular is chosen for analysis as a comprehensive practical and cognitive educational scenario, that involves interoperability of different of communicative stages and activities (oral and written exams, final project viva, internal and external review). The survey method and analysis of different ICT tools is used to assess the parameters of efficiency of transforming real life qualification assessment practices into digital and hybrid format.

The benchmarking survey was conducted through the academic semesters of 2020 and 2022, spanning the Covid-19 quarantine measures applied to HEI in Ukraine.

This inquiry *methodological groundwork* is founded on identification of ICT competency principles, derivative of various paradigms of soft skills (Dos Reis, 2015; Morze et al, 2016): 21st century skills framework (Davies 2011; Abbot 2013), Competences 2020 (European Commission 2020a) framework and the newly devised Global Skills framework (World Econimic Forum 2020 has been devised.

The projected digital literacy requirements for educational purposes in Liberal arts are consequently elaborated across UNESCO ICT Competency Framework (UNESCO 2018), European e-competence framework guideline (European Commission 202b), and Digital Competence 2020 framework (European Commission 2020a).

A complex skill is generally understood as a skill requiring to process lots of information and make lots of decisions simultaneously (Wulf et al, 2002). That way, a comprehensive correspondence between 21st century skills framework, Skills of the Future framework, and Global Skills 2025 framework has been devised and upgraded. In this study it is suggested to revise and augment the model of integration between the corresponding skillsets across various frameworks could be referred to the following key interdisciplinary domains of human activity: COMMUNICATION; COGNITIVE ACTIVITY; PERSONAL INTERACTION; SOCIAL ACTIVITY; HEURISTICS; DIGITAL INTERACTION:

The core cross-sectorial domain (Slater 2013; Callaos 2020) that is referential for primary skills (social skills, emotional intellect, collaboration, communication, ICT-literacy), necessary for educational goals achievement, is COMMUNICATION.

The fundamental interdisciplinarity that COVID-19 digital procedural transformations imposed on the educational process in the area of Foreign languages acquisition, is verified by a unified interoperable framework of correspondence between the components of communication (Shannon 1948) and communicative competence (Dell 1972), comprising of a diverse skillset, and various aspects of digital (ICT) competence in Arts and Humanities (specifically, in foreign languages education) (European Commission 2020a, European Commission 2020b, UNESCO 2018), utilized in the educational process, elaborated for the purposes of this study.

Subsequently, the study estimates, that the educational activities, correlated with these types of soft skills, serve as **indicators for activation of such groups of digital competency elements** as: 1) ICT practitioner skills, e-business skills, ICT user skills (European e-competence framework guideline); 2) Understanding ICT in education, ICT for Curriculum development and assessment, ICT for Organization and administration, ICT for Teacher professional learning (UNESCO ICT Competence Framework); 3) information and data literacy; communication and collaboration through digital technologies; digital content creation; safety; problem solving through digital technologies (Digital Competence 2020).

## 2.2 Final Qualification Assessment for Foreign Languages Programs as a Complex Scenario of Interdisciplinary Activities

Qualification assessment for Foreign Languages major programs is a mandatory procedure, involves different stages of foreign language acquisition skills assessment (oral and written exams, final project viva, internal and external review).

The generic form of summative state qualification of students is defined by the state standards of education and is reflected in the curricula in the countries across the world. Usually state qualification has two forms, combined or separate: 1) Qualification/final exam; 2) Defense (viva) of qualification (bachelor's or master's) paper. State standards of education in countries of Europe typically provide for the existence and observance of rules and requirements for the procedure of Final Qualification Assessment. Moreover, the defense of the qualification work contains propaedeutic procedures designed to obtain the basis for admission of students to the defense.

The qualification assessment regimen was adapted to digital format as a framework (a rigorous legal procedure that results in the degree confirmation of a student), the string of consecutive cross-sectorial activities according to the legal procedure described in the profile above, the "ritual" scenario (and experience for the student that is emotionally uplifting and somber in nature, connects with the traditions of the university culture of Europe).

As such, the framework transformation of Final Qualification Assessment enticed the elaboration of adequate and equivalent digital formats and digital communicative settings, substituting each type of activity in the procedure regiment on each level of the Final Qualification Assessment framework: PRE-ASSESSMENT REGIMEN; ASSESSMENT PROPER REGIMEN; POST-ASSESSMENT REGIMEN (Makhachahsvili et al, 2021).

According to the study observations, based on the case study of BGKU through the timespan of 2020-2021, the conversion of Final Qualification Assessment for Foreign Languages programs as a complex framework educational scenario into the digital format is subject to the educational goals taxonomy 2.0 (Churches, 2008) structuring in terms of activities, employed on each stage of the procedure and ICT tool utilized.

Assembled schemes of the Final Qualification Assessment procedure transformation into digital technology assisted format comprise a comprehensive framework, informed by the application of ICT tools and digital communication practices, corresponding to different tiers of educational goals and different interdisciplinary domains.

## 2.3 Evaluation of Final Qualification Assessment Digital Transformation: Comparative Survey Results

Informed by the Final Qualification Assessment activity profile, an iterative survey was conducted among the stakeholders of the Final Qualification Assessment at Borys Grinchenko Kyiv University, (Kyiv, Ukraine) Foreign languages programs, in order to assess the efficiency of dynamics and sustainability of results of qualification assessment transfer into digital format via various ICT tools. The survey was conducted several times in 2020 and 2021 respectively, over the span of Covid-19 digitization measures, after the wrap up of all academic year Qualification Assessment procedures.

The survey comprised of 12 questions total (variable and invariable multiple choice and Likert scale score), divided into such evaluation dimensions: 1) Questions on overall experiences of Final Qualification Assessment participants in all procedures, conducted via ICT tools; 2) Questions on digital literacy skills, required of Final Qualification Assessment stakeholders; 3) Questions on soft skills, required of Final Qualification Assessment stakeholders; 4) Questions, aimed to conduct Efficiency Ranking (Dos Reis 2015; Morze, Makhachashvili et al 2016) of crucial ICT tools for Final Qualification Assessment.

The following participants of the digital Final Qualification Assessment were respondents of the survey overall: Students of senior year of bachelor's program; Assessment board members; Faculty members (who took part in digital qualification assessment preparation and conduct); Bachelor project referees and supervisors.

For the purposes of this paper we singled out student respondents, as primary subject of Final Qualification Assessment. Sizable samples of 45 students (senior year Bachelor's and Master's programs graduates) of Foreign European and Oriental languages programs at Borys Grinchenko Kyiv University, Ukraine took part in the survey in 2020 and 34 students participated in 2021. Respondents of all groups spanned the foreign language Bachelor's programs in proportional distribution measures: Spanish major program- 33%; Japanese major program- 15%; Mandarin Chinese major program - 21%; French major program - 16%; Italian major program- 15%. In the year 2020 (initial digitization measures) the overall digital qualification assessment experience on the Likert scale of 1 to 5 was defined by respondents from BGKU as predominantly mostly agreeable (4) by 50% of respondents, most agreeable (5) by 29% of respondents. In the year 2021 (ongoing digitization measures) were assessed as equally mostly agreeable (4) by 38,2% and most agreeable (5) by 38,2% of respondents. The standard deviation in FQA digital transformation through the sustainable digitization measures has diminished to 0.

The Likert scale ranking 1-5 of the ICT tools employed through digital qualification assessment process yields following tools getting the highest scoring (5) among all ICT tools identified and used by respondents in 2020: email services; google suite tools; video conferencing services; Microsoft Office tool-kit and various social media platforms. In the year 2021 respondents gave the following set ICT tools the highest scoring (5): e-mail services; Videoconferencing services; google suite tools; LMS Moodle; Microsoft Office tool-kit; screen sharing services (whiteboards); social media platforms (Table 1).

Table 1. Comparative scoring of highest ranking ICT tools for Final Qualification Assessment in 2020-2021

| ICT tools ranking 5 | 2020 BGKU (Ukraine) | Score | 2021 BGKU (Ukraine) | Score |
|---|---|---|---|---|
| **E-mail services** | + | 40% | + | 65% |
| **Google Suite** | + | 38% | + | 53% |
| **Videoconferencing services** | + | 43% | + | 62% |
| **Screen sharing services** | + | 21% | + | 44,1% |
| **Microsoft Office tool-kit** | + | 47% | + | 50% |
| **Social media platforms** | + | 46% | + | 44,2% |
| **LMS Moodle** | - | - | + | 50% |

Through the progress of digitization measures it is an observable increase in the progressively positive assessment of more complex, communication/collaboration-based digital tools in the Final Qualification Assessment Scenario (LMS Moodle – a 50% increase in positive evaluation; e-mail services – 25% increase; Whateboard tools – a 23% increase; Google Suite – a 15% increase).

The data on implementation of ICT tools for Final Qualification assessment in Foreign languages testifies to the **activation of such predominant groups of digital competency elements**: 1) ICT practitioner skills; 2) communication and collaboration through digital technologies; 3) digital content creation; 4) problem solving through digital tools.

Activation of digital competency elements allowed to identify the following most prominent activities across all ICT tools used throughout the digital qualification assessment process by respondents in the 2020-2021 timespan: Communication (synchronous); Communication (asynchronous); Collaboration; Information/file sharing; Summative assessment; Formative assessment; Peer review; Presentation; Speech quality assessment; Brainstorming. The activities are related to the key interdisciplinary domains of human activity (Communication, Cognitive Activity, Personal Interaction, Social Activity, Heuristics) and required the activation of interoperable interdisciplinary skills across all ICT tools used throughout the digital qualification assessment process.

Across all ICT tools, used consistently throughout the digital qualification assessment process in 2020 and 2021, the respondents of all groups identified the following most prominent education activities: Communication – 99%; Collaboration; Information/file sharing – 97%; Presentation – 94%; Summative assessment – 89%; Speech quality assessment – 46%; Peer review – 34%; Brainstorming – 24%; Formative assessment – 20%.

Information sharing and presentation are scored sustainably as dominant for such types of tools as Google services (mean score of 46% of respondents across 2020 and 2021 benchmarking), email (31% of respondents), Microsoft Office Toolkit (24,3% of respondents). These parameters correspond to such elements of digital competence as **ICT practitioner skills and digital content creation**.

Synchronous and asynchronous communication and collaboration is distributed as prominent among video conference services (mean score of 53,2% of respondents), email services (35% of respondents), and learning management systems (20% of respondents). These parameters indicate *activation of such elements of digital competence* as ***communication and collaboration through digital technologies*** **and** ***information and data literacy.***

The tools that feature summative and formative assessment as a prominent activity are Videoconferencing services (mean score of 27% of respondents), LMS Moodle (22,3% of respondents), Google suite (19% of respondents). These parameters indicate *activation of elements of digital competence, customized for in-training teachers of Foreign languages,* such as ***understanding ICT in education*** **and ICT for** ***curriculum development and assessment.***

The following technical and user requirements, most prominent for ICT/digital tools employed throughout the digital qualification assessment process were identified through the educational scenario profiling: Bandwidth; Specialized software; Specialized hardware (webcam, mic, PC type etc.); Intuitive interface; Advanced digital literacy; Intermediate digital literacy; Elementary digital literacy; Customized training before use. Through the year 2020 the students of Foreign languages programs prioritized the following technical and user requirements: intuitive interface (30,3%), elementary digital literacy (29,3%), specialized software (17,3%).

Through the sustainable digitization measure the following technical requirements for Final Qualification Assessment tools were prioritized: intermediate digital literacy (79,4%), intuitive interface (53%), advanced digital literacy (44,1%), specialized hardware (35,3%). These parameters testify to the consistent activation of such elements of digital competence as information and data literacy on the sustainable level of education scenarios digitization (2021) – Figure 1.

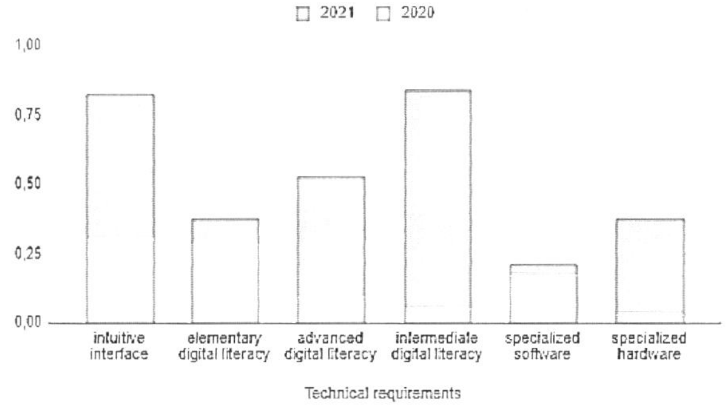


Figure 1. Compared technical and user requirements for ICT tools in digital qualification assessment process

Intuitive interface is a technical requirement to that features consistently through all digitization stages in education across the board of ICT digital tools that have been analyzed (mean score 42% of respondents). It is considered a leading technical requirement for such ICT tools as email (21%), LMS (20%), Google services (19%), video conferencing services (20%) and social media platforms (21%). There is a dramatic observable shift from the initial perceived requirements of elementary digital literacy to intermediate digital literacy (by 50,1%) and advanced digital literacy (by 35%) In and of itself this parameter is indicative of an apparent digital literacy gap and an ongoing need for specialized digital training in educational sphere, that the sustainable COVID-19 digitization measures verify as the ICT tools for educational scenarios transformation get consistently more complex.

According to skills of the 21st century frameworks, various levels of digital literacy have been identified in the survey. Digital literacy is understood primarily as the ability to use information and communication technologies to find, evaluate, create, and communicate information, requiring both cognitive and technical skills [3; 9]. Advanced digital literacy as the requirement for qualification assessment ICT tools efficiency is in average attributed to such instruments as learning management systems (18%), Microsoft Office toolkit (11%) and Automated testing systems (10,5%). Intermediate digital literacy is required for such instruments that are used for final qualification assessment as google suite, screen sharing interface, online randomizer, automated testing system, learning management system are evaluated (15-20% of respondents), which is indicative of an inherent challenge in this range of ICT tools application. Elementary digital literacy level is assessed as dominant for such tools as email (21%), Microsoft Office Toolkit (20%), social media platforms (19%), video conferencing (7%).

The comparative distribution of various levels of digital literacy requirements for ICT tools used for Final Qualification Assessment procedures by respondents through the years 2020 and 2021 is presented as follows (Table 2):

Table 2. Distribution of various levels of digital literacy requirements for ICT tools used for Final Qualification Assessment procedures (2020-2021)

| Digital literacy level | ICT tools for Final Qualification Assessment | 2020 | 2021 |
|---|---|---|---|
| Advanced digital literacy | Learning management systems, Microsoft Office toolkit, automated testing systems, google suite | 13,1% of respondents | 50% of respondents |
| Intermediate digital literacy | Microsoft Office Toolkit, screen sharing interface, online randomizer, social media platforms stem, learning management system | 13% of respondents | 83% of respondents |
| Elementary digital literacy | email, video conferencing, speech to text interfaces, social media platforms | 22% of respondents | 22% of respondents |

Across various ICT tools for the digital qualification assessment process the *following complex skills and competences most widely implemented and practiced, drawn from various relevant 21st century skills frameworks* have been identified: Communication; Collaboration; Team work; Digital literacy; Emotional intellect; Interdisciplinary skills; Critical thinking; Leadership; Flexibility and Adaptability; Decision making; Learning and Innovation skills.

Different priorities in complex soft skills are identified to fulfill the digital qualification assessment of the Foreign Languages program of through the years 2020 to 2021 (Figure 2). *Through the year 2020* the following soft skills are identified as overwhelmingly important for fulfilling Final Qualification Assessment in the digital format: Communication (65% of respondents), Collaboration (19% of respondents), Team Work (78%), Flexibility/Adaptability (10,5%), Digital literacy (5,2%). *Through the year 2021* the following soft skills are prioritized for Final qualification scenario adaptation into digital format: Digital literacy (85,3% of respondents), Communication (79,4% of respondents), Collaboration (44,11%), Interdisciplinary skills (41,2%).

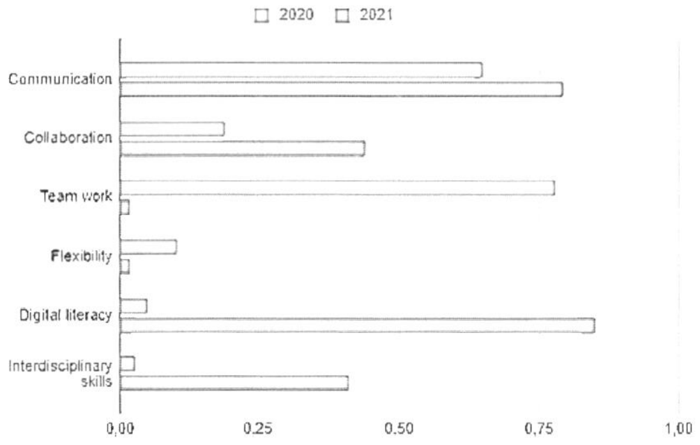


Figure 2. Comparison of skills in digital qualification assessment process for Foreign languages programs (2020-2021)

The dynamic distribution of core soft skills, necessary to apply ICT tools for Qualification assessment is as follows. Communication, collaboration rank by respondents as a type of skills most widely applied for the use of such instruments as email, Google services, video conferencing services and social Media platforms. Subsequently, the application of soft skills across these ICT tools for Qualification assessment entices activation of *such elements of digital competence* **as communication and collaboration through digital technologies**; **digital content creation**. Interdisciplinary skills rank most prominent for the use of Google Suite, Learning management systems and Videoconferencing services. Application of the soft skill across ICT tools for Qualification assessment entices activation of *such elements of digital competence* **as ICT practitioner skills, ICT user skills, problem solving through digital technologies.** Digital literacy features as a priority relevant in the use of such ICT tools as a learning management systems, automated Testing System (offline, online and cloud based), Android apps and Microsoft Office tools. Application of these soft skills across relevant ICT tools for Qualification assessment entices activation of *such elements of digital competence* **as ICT practitioner skills, ICT user skills, information and data literacy.**

# 3. CONCLUSION

The study results attest to the argument that all procedures and scenarios of the Final Qualification Assessment activities for foreign languages have been successfully transferred to digital remote format with the use of various sets of ICT tools in the framework of the COVID-19 pandemic adjustments.

The inquiry findings indicate the highest interoperability between such elements of digital competence as communication and collaboration through digital technologies; digital content creation; ICT practitioner skills and information and data literacy across all educational activities that comprise digital Final Qualification Assessment for Foreign languages programs. Subsequently, highest scoring educational activities, implemented by the ICT tools used for Final Qualification Assessment of Foreign Languages, necessitate the activations of such soft skills as: communication, collaboration, interdisciplinary skills, digital literacy.

The survey results conducted among students as participants of Final Qualification Assessment for European and Oriental foreign languages in BGKU across various stages of emergency digitization have yielded contribution as to representative data on the customized efficiency of various ICT tools implementation for rigorous assessment procedure scenario.

The comprehensive transference process of the Final Qualification Assessment procedure for European and Oriental languages programs in Ukraine from face-to-face into all-digital and hybrid format can be accompanied by the following recommendations across various socio-cultural contexts: the need for customized digital literacy training for participants of the Final Qualification Assessment process for all stages of the procedure; overcoming digital divide in accessibility of computer and Web technologies, necessary for all stages of Final Qualification Assessment; customized training to diversify the activation of soft skills through application of digital competence in comprehensive educational contexts.

Various levels of digital literacy demands have been identified corresponding to different digitization stages of 2020 and 2021. Across the board, implementation of Final Qualification Assessment via various

ICT tools requires of participants of educational process upper intermediate digital literacy. There's a significant observed discrepancy in digital literacy and ICT competence requirements between Final Qualification Assessment stakeholders of European and Oriental languages programs in 2020 and 2021 (elementary to intermediate digital literacy in 2020, advanced to intermediate digital literacy in 2021 required for efficient use of crucial ICT tools). This progression is informed by the implementation of increasingly more complex digital tools for educational scenarios adaptation.

The survey results will be furthered and elaborated in assessment of ICT tools efficiency and digital skills adaptability for separate groups of Final Qualification Assessment (students of foreign languages programs in countries of Europe and Asia, Assessment board members, staff members, reviewers) according to roles and tasks performed, as well as according to age and entry digital literacy level.

## ACKNOWLEDGEMENT

Empirical findings and survey procedures have been conducted under the auspices of the Integrated Research framework of Romance Languages and Typology Chair of Borys Grinchenko Kyiv University European Languages And Literatures Development In Cross-Communication Context (0116U006607) and Integrated Research framework of Oriental Languages and Translation Chair of Borys Grinchenko Kyiv University Oriental Studies Development in the framework of Higher Education Internationalization (0116U007073). Special gratitude is extended to the Armed Forces of Ukraine for providing security to complete this study.

## REFERENCES

Abbott, S. 2013. *The Glossary of Education Reform.* Retrieved from Edglossary: http://edglossary.org/hidden-curriculum

Al-Jardani, Khalid Salim. 2020. E-Learning in Higher Education: Challenges and Opportunities. *International Journal of Innovation, Creativity and Change*, 14 (11), pp. 58-64.

Almalki, S. 2016. Integrating Quantitative and Qualitative Data in Mixed Methods Research - Challenges and Benefits. *Journal of Education and Learning*, 5(3), pp. 288-296.

American Library Association. 2020. *Digital Literacy*. Retrieved from: https://literacy.ala.org/digital-literacy (accessed July 2020).

Bekele T. A. 2010. Motivation and satisfaction in internet-supported learning environments: A review. *Educational Technology & Society*, 13(2), pp. 116–127.

Bolliger D. U., & O. Wasilik. 2009. Factors influencing faculty satisfaction with online teaching and learning in higher education. *Distance Education*, 30(1), pp. 103–116.

Callaos, N., & Marlowe, T. 2020. Inter-Disciplinary Communication Rigor. *Rigor and Inter-Disciplinary Communication: Intellectual Perspectives from Different Disciplinary and Inter-Disciplinary Fields*. TIDC, LLC. pp. 4-29.

Costareie S. 2011. Assuaring quality based on the assessment of learning outcomes. *5th International Technology, Education and Development. Conference (INTED)*, Mar. 07-09, Valencia, Spain, pp. 3235–3236.

Davies, A., & Fidler, D. 2011. *Future Work Skills 2020.* Retrieved from Institute for the Future for University of Phoenix Research Institute: https://www.iftf.org/uploads/media/SR-1382A_UPRI_future_work_skills_sm.pdf

Dell H. Hymes. 1972. Communicative competence. In *Sociolinguistics: selected readings*. Harmondsworth: Penguin, 269-293.

Dillman, D. A., Smyth, J. D., Christian, Leah Melani, 2014. Internet, Phone, Mail and Mixed-Mode Surveys: The Tailored Design Method, 4th edition. John Wiley: Hoboken, NJ.

DosReis, A. 2015. To Be a (Blended) Teacher in the 21st Century - Some Reflections. *International Journal of Research in E-learning, 1*(1), pp. 11-24.

DQ Global Standards. 2019. *World's first global standard for digital literacy, skills and readiness launched by the Coalition for Digital Intelligence.* Retrieved from DQ Global Standards Report: https://www.dqinstitute.org

European Commission. (2020). *European E-Competence Framework Guideline.* Retrieved from European Commission: https://www.ecompetences.eu/

European Commission. 2020. *Digital Competence 2020.* Retrieved from European Commission: https://ec.europa.eu/jrc/en/digcomp/digital-competence-framework

Kuh G.D., N. Jankowski, S.O. Ikenberry. 2014. *Knowing What Students Know and Can Do: The Current State of Learning Outcomes Assessment in U.S. Colleges and Universities*. Urbana: University of Illinois and Indiana University.

Miller A. H., B. W. Imrie & K. Cox. 1998. Assessment in Higher Education: *A Handbook for Assessing Performance*. Abingdon, Routledge.

Nassim Taleb. 2010. *The Black Swan: The Impact Of The Highly Improbable* (2nd ed.). London: Penguin. ISBN 978-0-14103459-1.

Nataliia Morze, Rusudan Makhachashvili, Eugenia Smyrnova-Trybulska. 2016. Communication in education: ICT tools assessment. *Proceedings from DIVAI*, Sturovo: University of Nitra, pp. 351-354.

Nataliia Morze, Rusudan Makhachashvili, Eugenia Smyrnova-Trybulska. 2016. Research in Education: Survey Study. *Information and Communication Technologies in Education*, 3, pp. 114-123.

Ni A. Y. 2013. Comparing The Effectiveness Of Classroom And Online Learning: Teaching Research Method. *Journal of Public Affairs Education*, 19(2), pp. 199–215.

Richard Kimbell. 2007. E-assessment in project e-scape. Design and Technology Education: an International Journal, 12(2).

Robert Nelson, Phillip Dawson. 2014. A contribution to the history of assessment: how a conversation simulator redeems Socratic method. Assessment & Evaluation in Higher Education, 39 (2), pp. 195–204.

Rusudan Makhachashvili, Ivan Semenist, Anna Bakhtina. 2021. ICT tools for final qualification assessment survey study for european and oriental languages programs 8th International Conference on Educational Technologies 2021, ICEduTech 2021 and 17th International Conference on Mobile Learning 2021, ML 2021, 107-115.

Rusudan Makhachashvili, Ivan Semenist. 2021. Digital Competencies and Soft Skills for Final Qualification Assessment: Case Study of Students of Foreign Languages Programs in India. *7th International Conference on Frontiers of Educational Technologies*, ICFET 2021, pp. 21-30.

Rusudan Makhachashvili, Ivan Semenist. 2021. Interdisciplinary Skills Development Through Final Qualification Assessment: Survey Study for European and Oriental Languages Programs. *Proceedings of the 12th International Multi-Conference on Complexity, Informatics and Cybernetics*, 1, pp. 144-152.

Rusudan Makhachashvili, Ivan Semenist, Yuliya Shtaltovna, Anna Bakhtina. 2021. Soft Skills and ICT Tools for Final Qualification Assessment in Universities of Ukraine and India in COVID-19 Framework. *Psychology and Education*, 58 (2). pp. 849-861.

Salyers V., L. Carter, A. Carter, S. Myers, & P. Barrett. 2014. The Search for Meaningful E-Learning at Canadian Universities: A Multi-Institutional Research Study. *The International Review of Research in Open and Distributed Learning*, 15(6), pp. 313–347.

Sandra Einig. 2013. Supporting Students' Learning: The Use of Formative Online Assessments. *Accounting Education*, 22 (5), pp. 425–444.

Shannon, C. E. 1948. A Mathematical Theory of Communication. *Bell System Technical Journal, 27* (3), pp. 379–423.

Supriyatno T., Kurniawan F. 2020. A New Pedagogy and Online Learning System on Pandemic COVID 19 Era at Islamic Higher Education. *6th International Conference on Education and Technology (ICET)*, pp. 7-10.

Tatiana Markova, Irina Glazkova and Elena Zaborova Quality. 2017. Issues of Online Distance Learning. *Social and Behavioral Sciences*, 237, pp. 685–691.

Terry Atkinson, Graham Davies, 2000. *Computer Aided Assessment (CAA) and language learning*. March 2021 from: https://web.archive.org/web/20111026051400/http://www.ict4lt.org/en/en_mod4-1.htm(accessed)

Troussas C., Krouska A. and Sgouropoulou C. 2021. A Novel Teaching Strategy Through Adaptive Learning Activities for Computer Programming. *Transactions on Education*, 64 (2), pp. 103-109.

UNESCO. 2018. *ICT Competency Framework for Teachers.* Retrieved from UNESCO: https://unesdoc.unesco.org/ark:/48223/pf0000265721

World Economic Forum. 2020. *The Future of Jobs Report.* Retrieved from World Economic Forum: http://www3.weforum.org/docs/WEF_Future_of_Jobs_2020.pdf

World's first global standard for digital literacy, skills and readiness launched by the Coalition for Digital Intelligence. 2019. The DQ Global Standards Report. Retrieved from: https://www.dqinstitute.org/

Wulf, G., & Shea, G. 2002. Principles derived from the study of simple skills do not generalize to complex skill learning". *Psychonomic Bulletin & Review, 9*, pp. 185–211.

# MARKETING IMPULSE TO PROMOTE E-LEARNING IN BASIC AND SECONDARY EDUCATION

Nuno Sotero Silva and Luís Valadares Tavares
*Universidade Lusiada, COMEGI, Portugal*

**ABSTRACT**

This research focuses on e-learning and its specific evolution applied to Basic and Secondary Education, taking into account new technological approaches, as evidenced by the marketing of school publishers in Portugal. Marketing strategies depend on educational complexity, and this research explores the possible impulse to promote e-learning in such environment. The research methodology focuses on the needs and motivations for a conceptual framework, including the development of e-learning supply processes, demand formation, and the interaction between supply and demand, which can be enhanced with appropriate public policies. The results of qualitative interpretations confirmed that beliefs about e-learning are generally influenced by most previous implementation processes and are still generally considered an unsurpassed failure. However, the evidence is modified by the new data on the impact that COVID-19 has on the entire educational organization process, specifically on technological dissemination and innovation. Price or free access and training offers forms the basis for the "mise en valeur" while marketing emphases the values of generosity, empathy and sharing of emotions.

**KEYWORDS**

Marketing, e-Learning, Education, COVID-19, Portugal.

## 1. INTRODUCTION

The COVID-19 pandemic could create enormous potential and opportunity for the e-learning market by changing the culture of using computers in families for education, improving technical conditions and boosting digital literacy (Saraiva & Silva, 2021). In this sense, an interruption of face-to-face education demonstrated the importance of "openness" in education. Open Educational Practices (OEP), Massive Open Online Courses (MOOC), and many others in Educational Youtube Channels are valuable examples in a time of crisis and routine life. A better way to promote open education is to foster and support a culture of openness, in face of ambiguity and uncertainty of educational settings. However, the current literature seems to neglect a vital discussion: considering the impacts of COVID-19 and marketing on the "mise en valeur" of e-learning.

It is crucial to define realistic goals, present proposals that consider the current moment and implement e-learning with simplicity, commitment and empathy. Prioritizing issues of care, empathy and emotional support should not be limited to the e-learning environment directed at students but also embodied in educational policy and decision-making with an impact on teachers and parents.

Alves and Cabral (2021) suggest that it be reflected more in the learning of those far away than the simple and generous information about the "mise en valeur" of distance learning consummated in training offers, tips, and warnings shared in the community. Students can learn actively through their computers, tablet, or mobile phone. More evidence is the potential of using games and simulators, augmented reality, the Internet of things, didactic robotics, remote laboratories and artificial intelligence capable of helping the teacher chat, job correction, etc.

This study focuses on the development of e-learning in Basic and Secondary Education. The case of Portuguese education system is divided into pre-school education (from the age of 3), basic education (6 to 15 years old) and upper secondary education (15 to 18 years old) (Eurydice, 2022). Empirical evidence was analysed and evaluated in six aspects: the school and the impact that business marketing has on its options, the e-learning tools and their potentiation, and the ability to monitor results in the face of teachers' digital training and skills.

Based on school management and educational policies, the school enables the use of e-learning tools in the form of platforms and Internet access, with results that require monitoring by teachers and parents. Business marketing actions are based on the studies that suppliers make on the needs and motivations of both schools and teachers. While training forms the basis for the "mise en valeur", dissemination and use of e-learning instruments, the COVID-19 pandemic has contributed to a context of resilience, generosity, empathy and sharing of emotions. So, the following question is required:

What business marketing actions did e-learning providers adopt in the context of COVID-19?

A qualitative case study methodology explored the needs and motivations based on a conceptual framework, including the development of e-learning supply processes, demand formation, and the interaction between supply and demand, which can be enhanced with appropriate public policies. To this end, suppliers, and teachers with different levels of responsibility in schools and groups of schools were interviewed. In addition, news and statistical documents from the public domain has been analysed. Thus, qualitative interpretations and classifications were, whenever possible, combined with quantitative confirmations.

To recognize "mise en valeur" of e-learning and disseminate from a right-based approach, marketing actions will go together as part of one big action plan.

## 2. E-LEARNING APPROACH

Implementing distance learning by e-learning in the context of Basic and Secondary Education is a complex task that begins with a strategy for developing basic technical infrastructure, as in any other implementation.

Clark and Mayer (2016) define e-learning as education delivered on a digital device (computer, laptop, tablet, or phone) intended to support learning. Ways of e-learning can include electronic storage of content on external drives, in the cloud, or in local memory.

E-learning certainly has a place in the curriculum for the future of Basic and Secondary Schools. However, it is necessary to know that younger and full-time compulsory school-age students need planned parental involvement to work from home (Hasebrink et al., 2009), along with tutorial support and collaborative work opportunities. For this research, the above definitions imply a formal scope of educational design. New learning environments challenge continuous thinking, from "technology" on one side to "social" on the other.

The impacts of COVID-19 on e-learning emerged in contextual situations characterized by ambiguity and uncertainties. Previous technologies and humans faced challenges never expected. Fast developments and adaptations (like in Zoom, or Teams tools) to educational environment, in parallel with massive fast training (like in Youtube) to resolve many problems of digital illiteracies, changed the values in context.

## 3. MARKETING ISSUES

The commercialization of education is a controversial issue. If there is no sales team, school publishers rely heavily on marketing! Ultimately, marketing makes selling unnecessary (Kotler & Keller, 2006). It is essential to distinguish which marketing responsibilities can be divided and which strategies have been considered successful (Eastman & Saulnier, 2019). This can be done while in frame definitions of marketing because they have been revised according to the evolution of technologies and the market. The American Marketing Association is an example, and in 2017 approved the latest definition as follows: "Marketing is the activity, set of institutions and processes of creation, communication, delivery and exchange of offers that have value to customers, partners and society in general." (AMA, 2017).

Business marketing is based on much more personal and direct relationships between organizations. Jobber and Fahy (2019) identify organizational or business-to-business (B2B) purchasing three main types of buyers: the industrial market, the dealer market, and the government market. In business marketing, schools should interactively develop educational services in cooperation with key stakeholders (e-learning system providers, teachers, pupils, parents, local authorities, etc.). Indeed, in Basic and Secondary Education, the market is influenced by government agencies that buy products and services, covering the needs of teaching instruments and thus helping schools carry out curricular activities.

Nie et al. (2020) suggest e-learning sustainability models based on a 4Es table, which correspond to the dimensions of effectiveness, efficiency, economy, and equity. Pine and Gilmore (1999) also discussed 4Es that are intended to add value and unique competitive advantages for the following domains of experience, which are educational, aesthetic, escapist, and entertainment experiences. Nevertheless, Graham (2018) proposed the 4Es model of mentoring (experience, exposure, enthusiasm and empathy) to ensure value-added teaching.

Any of these models have their validity for the "mise en valeur" of e-learning, pertinent to relating some tools and techniques to digital marketing actions. Given that e-learning is a service, teachers and students are the main focus of suppliers. Marketing models in this context use a set of "marketing mix" variables, such as Li and Hung's 5P's (2009): Product - distance education service; People - ability, skill, knowledge, experience, and teachers' care for students; Pricing - complex decision given independent price negotiation for each school, or grouping of schools, or households; Promotion - school media, or others (radio, television, newspapers, social networks, websites), or relational sale (teachers); and Place - the Internet.

Although, according to Mahajan and Golahit (2017), this set of variables can still be broader if we apply the 11P's: Program (Product); Price (I am going to price it); Place; Promotion; People; Process; Physical evidence (Physical Evidence / Infrastructure s and Technology); Performance; Positioning; Pleasure; and Meeting point.

All these variables may be relevant. Nevertheless, in the case of e-learning, while infrastructure and technology are essential, the price is the most important, given the sensitivity of online consumers (Pricebench, 2020). In general, e-learning providers offer free or minimum-priced courses associated with brand messages, such as "Online courses at the best price" (Traininghouse, 2021) or "Online courses for less" (Udemy, 2021). Jobber and Fahy (2019) state that addressing the needs of clarity, coherence, credibility and competitiveness in a positioning strategy is vital. More than products or services, positioning is the key to conveying the benefits of a supplier.

Competition between Basic and Secondary Schools occurs mainly in the private sector, while the public sector remains a prisoner of government decisions and national educational strategies. Thus, producers of e-learning platforms and content face several challenges. First, who should be the client: student, teacher, school, or parents and educators. In addition, the COVID-19 pandemic creates a new environment and has opened new horizons. Marketing actions depend on this complexity, and this research explores the possible drive to promote e-learning in these environments.

For instance, Paiva, Morais and Moreira (2015) suggest marketing by course unit. In this specific case, they refer to partnerships with organizations that produce knowledge in teaching and sciences (ClicMat and Physical and Natural Sciences) and chemistry (Portuguese Society of Chemistry).

According to Bonilla Segura (2014), to make a promotional analysis, the following aspects should be considered:

- promotion is a tool or set of techniques that constitute one of the controllable variables of marketing;
- promotion is to disclose a product or service;
- communication in the promotion is made in the spirit of informing, influencing, persuading or convincing an audience or consumer;
- the promotion always applies to a specific location or time.

Moreover, in order to promote e-learning in Basic and Secondary Education, it is suggested to consider the following factors:

- market-driven (Social marketing);
- teacher training (People);
- price policies (Promotion);
- image issues (Pointing-Out as a Reference);
- infrastructure (Physical Evidence);
- availability class (Performance);
- resilience (Digital identity).

Finally, Wang et al. (2021) found that electronic-word-of-mouth significantly influences consumer decision-making for products of high personal involvement. Learning by observation or social will reinforce the extrinsic motivations of consumers associated with the surrounding context, situations and external factors. In the period of closure of schools in the face of COVID-19, communication through social networks may have generated the benefits of word-of-mouth or viral. However, on a larger scale, online free videos in the form of training for teachers may have reached a high number of potential customers or influenced school management.

Meanwhile, generosity, empathy, and sharing of emotions are essential factors for any marketing activity to be effective (Godin, 2019).

According to Maughan (2019), school publishers need to appeal to the gatekeepers (teachers, librarians, parents, and booksellers), and marketing teams have kept pace with technological advances to connect with educators through such digital tools as social media platforms, videos, and podcasts. From one side, the design elements of marketing campaigns must grab kids' attention even if they do not purchase their course materials. On the other side, the free competition and the free choice of schoolbooks should not be eliminated (Barna & Zentai, n.d.).

Following Eurydice (2022), the digital transition of schools is a holistic integration of three contexts:

- Organisational - leadership, teamwork, professional development of school human resources;
- Pedagogical - curriculum development and assessment, pedagogical practices, use of digital educational resources;
- Technological and digital - infrastructure, equipment and Internet access; digital platforms.

Any marketing model should follow digital ambassadors with technical-pedagogical advisory roles and responsibilities for organizing training allocated to training centres. In addition, the nature of the educational environment requires specific marketing and strategic communications, advertising, and public relations. That influences the variables for each contractual context (specific supplier to a specific type or form of Government), and different alternatives can emerge to attribute weights for the multicriteria decision-making model influenced by marketing actions.

# 4. METHODOLOGY

This research highlights the qualitative case study of e-learning, in which participants enriched the description and increased the perspective of a similar context (transferability), which implies a complete explanation of all the actual circumstances.

Berg and Lune (2012) claim that the case study can reflect nuances, patterns and other underlying parts that previous research may neglect. Yin (2017, p. 18) defines it as "an empirical survey that investigates a contemporary phenomenon within its real context, especially when the boundaries between phenomena and context are not evident". There are numerous previous investigations on e-learning, but few specifically address Basic and Secondary Education and the context of the state of emergency caused by COVID-19 pandemic. Thus, the case study is the most appropriate option for this investigation.

The choice of participants, or people to be interviewed, followed Amado's recommendation (2014) so that "because of their experience of daily life, their responsibilities, status, etc., they are involved or in very close contact with the problem one wants to study". For the recruitment of participants in this investigation, a purposive sampling technique was adopted, and proportionality was not the primary concern, but rather the understanding of the categories of participants of a small representative group. Contacts were developed with Basic and Secondary Education teachers and with School Publishers marketers.

Silva (2022) performed semi-structured interviews enabling a long period of recording and transcription time. The case study selection also echoes the work of Creswell and Poth (2018), namely the "purposeful maximum sampling" approach. Twelve participants were interviewed "online" and contributed their observations and testimony, providing a rich volume of data and a pluralistic view. Collaboration and participation were the assumptions of the networks of contacts that allowed the selection of participants in this research. By deliberate choice, participants sought to bring more meaningful information in a diversified way. All participants were previously informed about possible data collection procedures. In this sense, informed consent was discussed individually, ensuring anonymous and voluntary participation.

The authors believe it is vital to differentiate the perceptions of the problem by the participants, process or event of the case study. The use of qualitative tools promotes teachers to sharing of sensitivity and ability to distinguish the details of phenomena in particular circumstances. The selection of participants in Portugal also denotes ordinariness, unusual circumstances, or accessibility. However, it is vital to understand a case study as a method of investigation through a comparative analysis of each participant, not of particular organizations (or even the Portuguese Government). In addition, for quantitative confirmatory data, several public information and documents were collected longitudinally from the media or government entities. So, this research represents a different contribution because other studies are usually only quantitative, with data collection based on online questionnaires and samples of low representativeness (CNE, 2021). Quantitative analysis shows an increase that already reflects the use of e-learning.

The free access to platforms that school publishers gave as a result of COVID-19 pandemic significantly impacted the use of e-learning. Even more than the previous offer of the Government for all students from 1st to 12th grade who attend public schools (according to the certified statistics database of Portugal, Pordata website https://www.pordata.pt), and access to digital resources developed in conjunction with manuals, designated as a Digital License. Moreover, public procurement of e-learning is observed in contracts made by regional and local Governments (register of Portugal, BASE website https://www.base.gov.pt/).

The school publishers' market is not exactly the sale of e-learning courses, but it works as a complement to school books in digital form to support and impulse the e-learning in Basic and Secondary Schools. Conclusions from the excerpt:

... when you talk about e-learning, it's distance learning services... for a value of 100€, a course on X... we don't have this market, we have a tool that supports our school projects, from the first cycle to the secondary... that in a free version allows them to use many services, in the paid version can access more services.

On the one hand, the main clients are the Government and private colleges (B2B):

... actually it is a platform of things and takes on a characteristic a little modelling in the sales process, come on, first of all, there is the model with the Government... there is an institutional client here; on the other hand, another is the ok college, the private college.

However, on the other hand, the first customers are parents, which always have in the business model teachers as mediators:

... I present this solution to teachers, and they choose our books. In addition to using my books, they have access to a digital platform... business model always has teachers to mediate... parents so that students can use them autonomously. (E1_M_I)

Finally, in market analysis, the quantified analysis of potential customers should also be considered. For this investigation, the public data from the Pordata website (see above) was relevant concerning the number of students and teachers in Basic and Secondary Education. This universe is essential to make a relationship or ratio with the public information about the use of the e-learning platforms of each school publisher and their potential. In addition, this could be released with a training offer. For instance, the CFAE (School Association Training Centre) websites are also not uniform, and there is no general list of all courses available at the national level. Following what is quantifiable, it is concluded that only a tiny percentage of the available courses are focused on content relevant to e-learning. Still, there is no uniformity in the designations nor the reference number of courses.

## 5. INTERPRETATION AND DISCUSSION

Business marketing actions come from a direct relationship between school publishers and the Government. A teacher has not been considered as "the school" but rather an intermediary for school publishers to reach the market of "students". The buyer teacher represents a market that is insignificant or null. Nevertheless, business marketing related to generosity paved the way for the communication process, empathy, and the sharing of emotions, as verified by the involvement of providers of e-learning systems and communication systems, and educational technologies. A supplier/school relationship was found, safeguarding cases in which teachers worked outside the professional sphere, for example, as parents. In this relationship, ethical aspects such as security, reliability, equity and transparency of platforms were evidenced.

In response to the above research question, school publishers' first clients are teachers and parents, but always having different marketing models to mediate. However, the main clients are the Government and private colleges. The public procurement and different type of contracts made by regional and local Governments are generally observed, but e-procurement or digital marketing actions could not be quantified (at least in above mentioned BASE website). Anyway, the medium price by digital license is different between public contracts. This way, an ethical analysis may be necessary if equity of access is put in evidence.

For parents, the marketing actions of publishers appear in the form of online gradual discounts throughout the school year and focus mainly on the Internet, email, and social networks, which are considered the influence of teachers and the concern of parents. The teacher, not usually a potential client, emerges in the market as an intermediary potential or influencer.

Price differentiation by e-learning tools and tools that maximize usage success is also relevant. On the one hand, specific and differentiated negotiation between e-learning providers, schools, school groups, or municipalities is relevant. The incidence of business marketing for these prices, so to speak, is often the discount. On the other hand, and as an example, Zoom was only free until 40 minutes... the schools had to buy! Everything indicates that it is promotional marketing or the attempt to generate the need in the consumer that leads to the subsequent purchase.

With COVID-19, opportunities arose for differentiated, directed marketing or level of segmentation by course unit. The new marketing actions should consider what teachers already intend to use and have already mobilized students and families. Any reason for disappointment can lead to a setback, for example, if the pricing policy is abusive, as it will be more natural for more users to lower prices. One supplier stated that he did not want to make a profit at this time (COVID-19 pandemic), just wanted them to be widely used. He said, therefore, "it was the moment to add the usefulness and pleasant... you need, and we have here for you to use, for us it was significant from a communication point".

How did teachers feel about this business marketing, or how did the product of these publishers come to them? One participant replied, "It is like this; they showed it by opening for free to everyone, made many people know some materials they did not even know these publishers had, didn't they!"

With the teacher specifically as a focus, the offer of formal and informal training was widely used mainly through digital communication. On Youtube, it is also possible to see and review testimonies and recorded sessions, webinars, seminars, digital dating cycles, tutorials, etc. It is usually possible to see the impact of these short videos, given the number of views being recorded and added over time. For example, the analysis of the ratio between the total potential users (Basic and secondary school students, Pordata data) and the number of views can reveal the levels of general interest and adherence to these technologies.

The improvement of marketing strategies should focus on the person in charge of education as a client and not only use the teacher as a direct or indirectly influencer. Thus, marketing aimed at each family will be more efficient because it enables empathy and paves the way for generosity and sharing of emotions. The big question is if the investment of human resources would be necessary or whether this will be possible with virtual agents and artificial intelligence. At the moment, much more fruitful collaboration between the Government's social action mechanisms, e-learning providers, and families will be one of the most viable hypotheses.

As for teachers, business marketing related to training offers should focus more on rewards, for example, with the allocation of micro-credentials that are certified by educational institutions (Kato, Galán-Muros & Weko, 2020; French & Berry, 2017). In this case, and in an indirect way, not counting for career progression if there is no government reconsideration may elevate the feeling of self-esteem and strengthen leadership capacity.

Since business marketing is focused only on suppliers with profit as its goal, product improvement requires constant analysis. For this, it is necessary to contact by sampling key users. For example, in the evaluation of teachers who already used the platforms of school publishers before COVID-19, it was mentioned that they often did work with links that later students did not have access to open. That was one of the reasons they quit. On the other hand, bonus or premium systems that are awarded to students are referred to as sources of motivation in the early stages but lose influence over time of use.

Finally, the power of innovation is one of the characteristics of the human being, which in nature, in general, is manifested by the changes, changes, etc., which we call evolution. Business marketing does not escape this rule, and all the experiences originated by COVID-19 should be leveraged. Teaching has undergone changes that may not return, especially through the forms of synchronous digital communication. The use of mobile phones is one of the most promising areas. The strict collaboration between telecommunications providers and publishers gives rise to joint enterprise marketing products and actions of great added value.

The e-learning market has expanded with COVID-19. The widespread supply of e-learning services was the main change in existing marketing actions and focused primarily on promotional discounts sent by email to subscribers of limited free access who were registered. With this offer, there was a significant increase in registered users and consequent access to personal data. This consent allows stratification and segmentation of the target audience, especially if used techniques such as data mining. Thus, digital marketing done within the platform itself, both internal and external, was also benefited.

Finally, open or free access to platforms due to COVID-19 has allowed fundamental competitive analyses for e-learning suppliers. The work of cooperation between suppliers to offer unique solutions designed together that solve equity problems can bear fruit based on business marketing, but for now, it is non-existent. That fails to enhance e-learning by communicating and giving knowledge about new tools, creating increasingly accessible resources, and being attentive to the needs of teachers and pupils (i.e. schools), taking into account all socio-economic contexts.

## 6. CONCLUSION

Research work should never be considered a finished product but rather an opening of new possibilities. In the emerging context of COVID-19, even more relevant is to consider that much is to be done. Moreover, this remarks the originality of this paper on a school publishers' terrain, where marketing issues are not usually under contest of school leadership or families as customers.

From a methodological point of view, the theoretical contribution responds to the gap in qualitative studies in this research that has based data collection on semi-structured interviews.

From these results, it was possible to infer recommendations about the initiatives that are considered most relevant to enhance better e-learning in favour of Basic and Secondary Education in Portugal. It should also be said that this theme is essential in all countries. However, in Portugal, it gains additional priority since the weaknesses of the educational system are well known, greatly aggravated by the pandemic context and the growing asymmetry of the socio-economic conditions of many students. It is therefore understood that this problem deserves special attention in the Digital Education Action Plan (2021-2027).

COVID-19 forced the use of e-learning as a response to the personal and collective protection that humanity needs. All the actors in Basic and Secondary Education were confronted with new instruments, uncertainty, and fear. As a rule, human being tends to be more generous in sharing means, resources, and knowledge— especially given whether or not basic needs are met. A spirit of survival has led to teachers, students, families and suppliers being more empathetic to each other. Educational culture, ethics and equity will have to be reconsidered in the context of the digital transformation of schools.

Business marketing actions are mainly focused on the teacher as an influencer and increasing discounts on prices throughout the school year for families. There is no clear boundary between the school environment as a final or intermediate consumer.

On the one hand, the training was offered, particularly for the platforms of the publishers, and took place mainly online and with recording for later review. On the other hand, suppliers opened their platforms for free access, which was just a marketing opportunity for many of the participants. Promotional marketing in the form of training offered by publishers, plus the usual product discounts, was the biggest revelation. The registration process enabled the possibility to contact further around 100% of the universe of potential users.

In any case, competition in the publishers/producers of content and e-learning platforms market is limited to a small number of brands. Moreover, competition between private Basic and Secondary Education institutions is almost non-existent, and the public sector remains a prisoner of government decisions. Conversely, public procurement of e-learning is observed in contracts made by regional and local Governments, and even marketing actions are missing or not quantifiable.

Finally, because of the diversity of tools and instruments in use revealed, it is suggested that the focus of future work is the specific contribution each of these tools has in the face of the potentiation of e-learning. Thus, the marketing impulse of a specific product from a specific supplier to a specific type or form of Government can be considered a potential contribution to the "mise en valeur" of e-learning.

## ACKNOWLEDGEMENT

This work is supported by national funding's of FCT - Fundação para a Ciência e a Tecnologia, I.P., in the project «UIDB/04005/2020».

# REFERENCES


Alves, J. M., & Cabral, I. (2021). *Ensino Remoto de Emergência. Perspetivas Pedagógicas para a Ação. Serviços de Apoio à Melhoria da Educação*. Faculdade de Educação e Psicologia, Porto. https://www.fep.porto.ucp.pt/sites/default/files/files/FEP/SAME/Livro_Ensino_Remoto_de_Emerge%CC%82ncia_VF_mar21(1).pdf

AMA. (2017). Definitions of marketing. American Marketing Association. https://www.ama.org/the-definition-of-marketing-what-is-marketing/

Amado, J. (2017). Manual de Investigação Qualitativa em Educação. Imprensa da Universidade de Coimbra.

Barna, I., & Zentai, P. L. (n.d.). The end of educational book market in Hungary. Federation of European Publishers. https://fep-fee.eu/The-end-of-educational-book-market

Berg, B. L. & Lune, H. (2012). *Qualitative research methods for the social sciences* (8th ed.). Pearson. ISBN-13: 9780205809387

Bonilla, L. (2013). *E-Learning marketing*. E-marketing.

Clark, R. C., & Mayer, R.E. (2016), *E-learning and the Science of Instruction: Proven Guidelines for Consumers and Designers of Multimedia Learning*, John Wiley & Sons, Hoboken, NJ.

CNE (2021). *Educação em Tempo de Pandemia: problemas, respostas e desafios das escolas*. Conselho Nacional de Educação. https://www.cnedu.pt/content/iniciativas/estudos/Educacao_em_tempo_de_Pandemia.pdf. ISBN: 978-989-8841-37-7.

Creswell, J. W., & Poth, C. N. (2018). Qualitative inquiry and research design: Choosing among five approaches (4th ed.). Sage Publications.

Eastman, T., & Saulnier, J. (2019). State of *e-learning* Marketing: Results and Recommendations from a Nationwide Survey. *Journal of Library Administration*, *60*(3), 235-249.

Eurydice (2022). European education systems: Portugal Overview. https://eacea.ec.europa.eu/national-policies/eurydice/content/portugal_en

French, D., & Berry, B. (2017). Teachers, Micro-Credentials, and the Performance Assessment Movement. *VUE- Voices in Urban Education, 46*, 37-43.

Godin, S. (2019). Isto é marketing. Ideias de Ler. ISBN: 978-989-740-067-4

Graham, D. (2018). PESTEL factors for *e-learning* revisited: The 4Es of tutoring for value-added learning. *E-learning and Digital Media*, *15*(1), 17-35.

Jobber, D. & Fahy, J. (2019). *Foundations of marketing* (6th ed.). McGraw-Hill Higher Education. ISBN-13: 978-1526847348.

Kato, S., Galán-Muros, V., & Weko, T. (2020). The Emergence of Alternative Credentials. OECD Education Working Paper No. 216.

Kotler, P. & Keller, K. L. (2016). *Marketing management* (15th ed.). Pearson Education.

Li, C. & Hung, C. (2009). Marketing tactics and parents' loyalty: the mediating role of school image. *Journal of Educational Administration*, *47*(4), pp. 477-489. https://doi.org/10.1108/09578230910967455

Mahajan, P., & Golahit, S.B. (2017). Incorporating 11 P's of Service Marketing Mix and Its Impact on the Development of Technical Education. *Journal of Entrepreneurship Education*, *20*, 1.

Maughan, S. (2019). Taking Middle Grade to Market. Publishers share their strategies for capturing the interest of preteens. PW publishersweekly.com

Nie, D., Panfilova, E., Samusenkov, V., & Mikhaylov, A. (2020). *E-learning* Financing Models in Russia for Sustainable Development. *Sustainability*, *12*(11), 4412. https://doi.org/10.3390/su12114412

Paiva, J., Morais, C., & Moreira, L. (2015). *O multimédia no Ensino das Ciências: Cinco anos de investigação e ensino em Portugal*. Fundação Francisco Manuel dos Santos.

Pine, B. J., II, & Gilmore, J. H. (1999). *Experience economy: Work is theatre and every business a stage*. Harvard Business School Press.

Pricebench (2020). *Marketing Mix: tudo sobre o Preço e outros Ps, Set 1*. https://www.pricebench.pt/blog/marketing-mix/

Saraiva, A. C., & Silva, N. S. (2021). The COVID-19 Impact on Online Education – Opportunities and Challenges in a SWOT Analysis. International Journal of Research in E-learning. 7(2), 01–18. https://doi.org/10.31261/IJREL.2021.7.2.03.

Silva, N. S. (2022). "Mise en Valeur" of E-learning in Basic and Secondary Education: the impact of COVID-19 (Unpublished Ph.D. thesis).

Traininghouse (2021). *Cursos online ao melhor preço*. https://traininghouse.pt

Udemy. (2021). *Cursos online por menos*. https://www.udemy.com

Wang, Y., Zhang, M., Li, S., McLeay, F., & Gupta, S. (2021). Corporate Responses to the Coronavirus Crisis and their Impact on Electronic-Word-of-Mouth and Trust Recovery: Evidence from Social Media. *British Journal of Management*, 10.1111/1467-8551.12497. https://doi.org/10.1111/1467-8551.12497

Yin, R. K. (2017). *Case Study Research: Design and Methods* (6th ed.). Sage.

# UNIVERSITY TRAINING FOR FUTURE PRIMARY SCHOOL TEACHERS ON AUTOMATIC FORMATIVE ASSESSMENT

Vittoria Bonanzinga[1], Francesca Casasso[2], Cecilia Fissore[3], Valeria Fradiante[2] and Marina Marchisio[2]
*[1]Dipartimento di Ingegneria dell'Informazione, delle Infrastrutture e dell'Energia Sostenibile, Università Mediterranea di Reggio Calabria, Italy*
*[2]Dipartimento di Biotecnologie Molecolari e Scienze per la Salute, Università di Torino, Via Nizza, 52, 10126 Torino TO, Italy*
*[3]Dipartimento di Lingue e Letterature Straniere e Culture Moderne, Università di Torino, Via Giuseppe Verdi Fronte 41, 10124 Torino TO, Italy*

**ABSTRACT**

From 2020/2021 the evaluation of students' learning in primary school is no longer expressed through a decimal-based score, but through a descriptive assessment, in a more formative perspective of evaluation. In addition, the widespread use of technological tools in school has changed the teaching/learning process and it has highlighted the need to adopt new teaching methodologies. In this context, it becomes fundamental to train teachers and future teachers on the use of digital resources and innovative teaching methodologies, such as automatic formative assessment. This article presents a training module on automatic formative assessment which involved 153 university students of the Master's Degree course in Primary Education and aims to answer the following research questions: Were students able to design questions with formative assessment and interactive feedback? What were the most adopted strategies? All the forms and the questionnaire completed by students during the training course were analyzed. Even if most of the students had some difficulties in designing the interactive feedback, they really appreciated the development of the training module and the proposed methodologies. They find formative assessment very effective in several aspects.

**KEYWORDS**

Automatic Formative Assessment, Future Teacher Training, Interactive Feedback, Primary School.

## 1. INTRODUCTION

In Italy, starting from the 2020/2021 school year, the periodic and final evaluation of students' learning in primary school is expressed, for each discipline, through a descriptive assessment and no longer through a decimal-based score. This change is characterized by a formative perspective of evaluation and by an enhancement of the improvement of learning paths and teaching methodologies. The perspective is that of assessment for learning, which has a formative nature since the information collected is also used to adapt teaching to the concrete educational needs of students and their learning styles, modifying the activities according to what has been observed and starting from what can be valued. This evaluation method allows to represent, in transparency, the articulated cognitive and meta-cognitive, emotional and social processes through which the learning results are manifested. Descriptive assessments refer to the learning objectives that are the subject of evaluation and that are defined in the school curriculum. Each assessment is related to a specific learning level. Formative assessment is a process in which students are active protagonists and have the opportunity to understand what has been or has not been learned and how to learn it. Students can also understand the progress made and the difficulties they have in learning (Beatty & Gerace, 2009). Formative assessment differs from summative or standardized assessment, where the goal is to measure students' learning outcomes generally at the end of a learning path. The best-known example of national standardized assessment in Italy are the INVALSI tests (https://invalsi-areaprove.cineca.it/) in the Mathematics, English, and Italian disciplines (Bolondi et al. 2018, Cascella et al. 2020). The new digital culture and the widespread use of technological tools have changed the teaching/learning process, forcing the school to adopt an innovative teaching model. Technologies also play a fundamental role in the evaluation process and in the implementation of adaptive teaching strategies, supporting both teachers and students. For several years, the Italian Ministry of Education has supported projects for the introduction of innovative methodologies through the use of technologies in the classroom and their integration with traditional resources, such as the PP&S project (www.progettopps.it) for training and continuous support to teachers of all types and disciplines from all over Italy (Fissore et al., 2020a-2020b). In fact, in this new scenario, teachers have a key role, as they can effectively use technologies for educational purposes to make the entire training process more efficient. It therefore becomes essential to train teachers and future teachers on the use of digital resources and innovative and interactive teaching methodologies, in order to integrate them into ordinary teaching. The Delta Research Group of the University of Turin has successfully developed and tested a model for designing automatic formative assessment activities through the use of an Automatic Assessment System –AAS - for STEM (Barana et al., 2020a; Barana, 2021) and other disciplines (Corino et al., 2022; Marello et al., 2019). This article presents a research connected to a training module on automatic formative assessment which involved 153 university students of the Master's Degree course in Primary Education for a total of 8 hours held during the Academic Year 2021-22 at University Mediterranea of Reggio Calabria, in collaboration with University of Turin. The course was delivered in hybrid mode, i.e. a part of the students attended the lessons in presence and a part of the students attended remotely due to the Covid pandemic. The teachers carried out the lessons in presence while the tutors managed the Digital Learning Environment remotely from the University of Turin. In this course, the concepts of formative assessment and automatic formative assessment with immediate and interactive feedback were presented to university students, who will become primary school teachers. After a theoretical introduction and the presentation of several examples of activities with automatic formative assessment, the students were guided in the design of two activities with automatic formative assessment. The first request was the transformation of an INVALSI question (the same one for all) for standardized assessment into a question for formative assessment. The second request was the design of a new question with formative assessment. The design was guided through a form with reflection questions. At the end of the design, the students carried out a peer evaluation activity. The course was held in presence using a Digital Learning Environment integrated with an automatic assessment system. At the beginning and at the end of the course, all students submitted a satisfaction questionnaire. The research question is: Were students able to design questions with formative assessment and interactive feedback? What were the most adopted strategies?

# 2. STATE OF THE ART

## 2.1 Formative Assessment and Feedback

The definition of formative assessment that we adopt is that of Black and Wiliam (2009), well known in the literature: "Practice in a classroom is formative to the extent that evidence about student achievement is elicited, interpreted, and used by teachers, learners, or their peers, to make decisions about the next steps in instruction that are likely to be better, or better founded than the decisions they would have taken in the absence of the evidence that was elicited". Assessments become formative when the information is used to adapt teaching and learning to meet students' needs. When teachers know how students are progressing and where they are having trouble, they can use such information to make necessary teaching adjustments, such as reteaching, trying alternative didactic approaches, or offering more opportunities for practice (Sadler, 1989). These activities can lead to improved student success (Boston, 2002). Black and Wiliam (2009) conceptualize formative assessment through the following five key strategies: clarifying and sharing learning intentions and criteria for success; engineering effective classroom discussions and other learning tasks that elicit evidence of student understanding; providing feedback that moves learners forward; activating students as learning resources; activating students as the owners of their own learning. The first strategy concerns the sharing of learning objectives. To do so, it is first of all necessary to have a clear understanding of how to formulate the learning objectives. According to the Italian legislation, but which refers to theoretical assumptions well studied in the literature, the learning objectives must contain: a reference to the cognitive process (written through a verb to explain what the student must do) and a reference to the disciplinary content. It is possible to add something about the conditions under which this cognitive process must be implemented. There are six cognitive processes, written using Bloom's taxonomy revised in 2001 by Anderson and Krathwohl (Anderson & Krathwohl, 2001): remember, understand, apply, analyze, evaluate, create (from the simplest to the most complex). An example of a learning objective of the "understand" cognitive process is: compare two decimal numbers and find the greater number. It is important that evaluation and feedback are coherent with the learning objectives established and shared with the students from the beginning of the teaching activity. Feedback plays an essential role in reducing the discrepancy between current and desired understanding (Hattie & Timperley, 2007; Kluger & DeNisi, 1996). It should indicate what the learning goals are, what progress is being made toward the goal, and what activities need to be undertaken to make better progress. In fact, effective feedback must answer three main questions: "Where am I going?", "How am I going?", "Where to next?". Formative assessment is one of the most important methods for developing students' self-determination, self-efficacy, autonomy, and self-esteem. It can help students increase their motivation to study, acknowledge their strengths and weaknesses, be aware of the level reached, proceed step by step, following the feedback received, which must always be numerous and immediate (Nicol & Macfarlene-Dick, 2006). The development of new technologies, and in particular the use of an AAS, can support the possibility of giving feedback (Bennet, 2002; Nicol & Milligan, 2006). An AAS is often used for summative assessment, because it offers the opportunity to automatically evaluate, collect and analyze students' responses. However, it can also offer support for a formative assessment, giving immediate and personalized feedback, guiding students in an exercise, and proposing adaptive exercises (Giraudo et al., 2014). Moreover, teachers in the classroom deal with a large number and variety of students. They can have concrete support in offering all students personalized feedback and teaching from educational technology.

## 2.2 Automatic Formative Assessment and Interactive Feedback

The practice of formative assessment in a Digital Learning Environment integrated with an automatic assessment system allows the automatic processing of students' answers and the provision of feedback. We conceptualize interactive feedback as a step-by-step interactive process guiding the learner in the resolution of a task after one or more autonomous attempts (Barana et al., 2021). Our model requires the use of an automatic assessment system and it is supported by theories on formative assessment and feedback (Barana et al., 2020b). Interactive feedback is a step-by-step interactive solving process which shows a path to the solution after one or more autonomous attempts by the learner. It begins immediately after answering one question, when students are working on an online test. After showing the correctness of the answer, the system proposes a step-by-step resolution that interactively shows a possible process for solving the task. This interactive feedback can be displayed only to the students who failed to answer autonomously to the main question, or even to those who made it correct (Barana et al., 2021). This type of questions also allows the student to try a simpler version of the question, guiding them through the exercise one step at a time, and presenting whatever other approach the instructor thinks is appropriate. Fig. 1 shows an example of an activity with automatic formative assessment and interactive feedback. The first part of the question is taken from an INVALSI question for the second grade of primary school. After reading the text of the problem, students must select their answer from the three proposed options. In the case of the INVALSI question created for standardized assessment, if the students choose the wrong answer, the teacher has no information on the difficulties encountered by the students and the mistakes they made. Consequently, effective and educational feedback cannot be provided. It is different when using interactive feedback, in this case divided into two sub-questions. This step-by-step guided path is proposed in case of wrong answer (as in the example shown). In the first sub-question, the operation to be performed in order to answer the first question is requested. In the second part, students are guided to solve the problem by filling in the blanks by entering the problem data and the result of the operations. In both cases, students have three attempts to answer the question. After choosing their answer they can click on the "verify" button to get immediate feedback on its correctness. In case of correct answer, students go to the next part; in case of wrong answer, they can try to change their answer and repeat the check. The possibility of having more attempts available through a guided and interactive path is very important for students' self-confidence, and it can help to overcome the errors due to the incorrect insertion of the written answer. The teacher can view the students' answers and all attempts to answer, thus becoming aware of the most frequent errors and any difficulties encountered. Finally, this is an Algorithm-based question. The random values and parameters in the question text, answers, and feedback randomly change at every attempt and for each student. At every attempt, an algorithm generates new data for the number of bags and candies, and updates correct solutions accordingly. In this way, students can try to answer the question several times to consolidate the solution process learned and the knowledge acquired. The importance of immediate and interactive feedback is essential for both students and teachers. Through continuous and formative feedback, the student can focus not on the result, but on the progress made, on the mistakes made, and on the actions to be taken in order to improve (Barana et al., 2019). At the same time, teachers can progressively monitor students' learning levels and obtain valuable feedback.

Figure 1. Example of activity with automatic formative assessment

To ensure that teachers implement this type of questions with automatic formative assessment, it is important to train teachers in designing this type of activity and in acquiring formative assessment methodologies.

## 3. METHODOLOGIES

The purpose of the training module is to introduce future primary school teachers to the concepts of formative assessment and automatic formative assessment and to adopt these methodologies in the teaching of Mathematics. Through the acquisition of educational-didactic tools and strategies before taking up service, they will be able to disseminate good practices of educational action in schools. The training module involved a total of 153 university students (future primary school teachers). The duration was 8 hours for each group of students. In the 4-hour meetings a Digital Learning Environment was used. The didactic methodologies adopted were frontal explanations with discussions, learning by doing, and peer evaluation. The training module was organized as follows: a first part of theoretical explanation with discussions; a second part of planning activities with automatic formative evaluation by filling in a form; a third part of peer evaluation in which students evaluated the activity planned by one of their classmates by answering questions. In the design module, the first request was the transformation of an INVALSI question (the same one for all) for standardized assessment into a question for formative assessment. The question asked to observe a line in which two numbers were marked and to find the number placed halfway between the two (choosing between three options). Students had to design a possible interactive feedback to guide students in answering the question in case of an error. They were then asked how the question was adapted for the formative assessment and what they thought was the goal of the question. The second request was the design of a new question with formative assessment. The question had to be a contextualized problem to be solved through a guided procedure. The students had to pay particular attention to the choice of context, which must be close to the experience of the primary school students. Then they had to design the various parts of the question indicating the sub-questions texts, the correct answers, and the number of attempts to answer. Again, they had to indicate the objective of the question. The peer evaluation activity was guided through the following questions: "Did you find it difficult to understand the question requests? If so, which ones?"; "Was the contextualization you chose effective?"; "What difficulties do you think students may encounter in interpreting the requests of the question and in answering the question?"; "Is the question pertinent to the stated objective?". Students completed an initial questionnaire at the beginning of the workshop and a final questionnaire at the end. In the initial questionnaire, students were asked if they were using automatic assessment as students and what benefits they think it provides. Then they were asked, on a scale from 1 (not at all) to 5 (very much), to what extent they considered the use of automatic formative assessment to be effective for various aspects, such as: understanding and reviewing knowledge; developing problem solving skills; raising awareness of one's knowledge and skills; increasing interest in the subject; understanding one's mistakes; and adapting teaching activities. In the final questionnaire, the latter question was asked again and the satisfaction about the proposed activities and methodologies was discussed. To answer the research question, the activities planned by the students and the students' responses to the initial and final questionnaires were analyzed. The questions designed by the students in both parts of the form were analyzed and classified into three different categories: effective interactive feedback, not fully effective interactive feedback, ineffective interactive feedback. The analysis also reported the reasons for the classification made. The strategies adopted for formative assessment, the learning objectives indicated by the students and the context chosen for the activity they invented were also analyzed.

# 4. RESULTS

## 4.1 Design of the Activity with Automatic Formative Assessment

Following the analysis of the 153 design forms, three types of interactive feedback emerged:

- not very effective feedback: the sub-questions do not guide the students in the solution process;
- quite effective feedback: the sub-questions guide students in finding the solution, but they do not allow students to think about the solution procedure;
- very effective feedback: the sub-questions guide students gradually, stimulating them to think about their mistakes, about the possible solutions and about the meaning of the final result.

Regarding the first request of the form: 54% of the students designed a not very effective feedback, 41% a quite effective feedback, and 5% a very effective feedback. We want now analyze the cases in which students have project a not very affective feedback. 77% of the not very effective feedback has sub-questions in which the student is asked what operations are needed to reach the solution (For example: "What operation is needed to arrive at the solution?"). In this case, there are two main issues. The first one is that it leaves no room for different solution strategies (not all students solve the problem in the same way or in the teacher's way). The second problem is that this type of feedback does not guide the student in the solution process and whoever made the first question wrong does not have the information to reflect on the mistakes made. The remaining 33% of the not very effective feedback consisted of sub-questions not related to each other, which did not allow to build a logical reasoning. The interactive feedback that has been classified as "quite effective" allows the student to get to the solution, but it does not make them reflect adequately on the solution process. An example of this category is given by the two sub-questions "If we add the value 2 to the value 10, what number do we get?" and then "If we divide the number 12 by 2, what number do we get?". Following the interactive feedback, the students do a calculation exercise but do not think about the operations to be carried out and with which data of the problem to carry them out. In questions with very effective interactive feedback, the sub-questions gradually guide students towards the solution by making them reflect on the solution strategies. An example of this category are the following sub-questions: "What are the numbers between 2 and 10?" and "Represent numbers on a straight line and indicate the number that is in the middle". When students reflected on how they adapted the question for formative assessment, most (73%) declared a strategy that was inconsistent with the one implemented. This result may reflect the students' difficulty in understanding the request and the difficulty in transforming a standardized evaluation question into a formative evaluation question. Regarding the second designed activity, invented by the students, 49% of the interactive feedback was not very effective, 36% of the interactive feedback was quite effective and 15% of the interactive feedback was very effective. By analyzing all the different types of feedback designed by students, even in the second form, 53% of the not very effective feedback focuses exclusively on the operations necessary to reach the solution. The remaining students have designed some interesting sub-questions which, however, do not make the question formative. 61% of the students who designed a quite effective interactive feedback created sub-questions with the aim of solving the problem mechanically, asking them to complete the operation and the solution formula, rather than dwell on the meaning of the problem, on the most important data, on the construction of the solution process and on the meaning of the result obtained. In these cases, the students manage to reach the solution, but they are not aware of the procedure used. 18% of future teachers have devised sub-questions that ask to argue the chosen strategy to solve the problem, but in this way students who cannot answer the question correctly are not guided in the resolution. 21% of not very effective feedback has sub-questions that are too articulated and complex and which could therefore be unclear and confusing. The future teachers who designed a very effective feedback did not just lead the students towards the correct result, but asked the students to think about their mistakes, the solution procedure followed and the meaning of the result obtained. The goal of interactive feedback is to show the student a possible solution process and induce him to think about his mistakes, rather than simply obtaining a correct result. A very positive aspect was the choice of context. 89% of future teachers were able to find a real context and very close to the students in such a way as to stimulate their interest and involvement. Among the most used contexts are: candy distribution, games, stickers, birthday parties, Christmas decorations and dessert recipes. Here is an example of a captivating context: "Alessandro wants to go to a toy store to buy Christmas presents. Alessandro finds a train for € 16, a helicopter for € 18, a doll for € 12 and a Lego for € 6. Alessandro's mother gave him a maximum of € 39. What can Alessandro buy without exceeding the money limit imposed by his mother?". The students also reflected on the objective of the problem, and in most cases the objectives indicated do not correspond to the real purpose of the problem. This highlights the need to deepen the definition of learning objectives, also referring to what is contained in the National Guidelines. This is both in terms of the disciplinary contents to be addressed and in terms of the goals that the students must reach, in order to design adequate activities and make the correct learning objectives explicit. From the analysis of the deliveries of the two papers, it clearly emerges that, in designing the questions for the formative assessment, only few have managed to create very effective interactive feedback. The reasons for this difficulty may derive from the fact that, being the first time they have found themselves designing interactive feedback, most of the students took inspiration from the examples shown to apply formative assessment strategies without taking into account that the feedback of such examples cannot always be generalized to other problems, with the result that the feedback they design is not entirely effective. For example, many students have focused on the operations to be done (adding and dividing by the formula of the midpoint, or difference) by binding the student to a solution strategy imposed by them. The results revealed the need to increase the references to National Guidelines, in particular regarding the declaration of the learning objectives to be achieved with a specific activity and the target they address, in particular paying attention to the words used, to clarity of the text and the reference context of the problem.

## 4.2 Students' Observations on the Training Module

Only 35% of the students knew and used automatic assessment tools (google forms and web applications like Kahoot) before the training module. This shows that formative assessment, and even more the automatic formative assessment, is unfortunately an educational practice still little used by teachers in service. According to the students, some of the aspects that are favoured by automatic assessment are: interest, involvement, attention, verification of the level of learning, self-assessment, correction of homework (speed and comfort), analysis of results and monitoring of learning, immediate feedback, objectivity and impartiality of evaluation, enhancement of teachers 'and pupils' digital skills. Table 1 shows the students' considerations on the effectiveness of automatic formative assessment in teaching in various aspects indicated. For each aspect, students had to choose a score from 1 (not at all) to 5 (very much). The table shows the mean scores and standard deviation before and after the training module. According to the students, automatic formative assessment was very effective in various aspects even before the training module. After the training module all scores increased and the standard deviation decreased. In particular, according to the students, automatic formative assessment is especially effective for remedial actions, to make students autonomous in solving problems, to increase students' autonomy and increase their awareness, and to facilitate study autonomy. The course, in addition to inviting students to design and implement a question for the formative evaluation with interactive feedback, was an important moment of reflection and meta-reflection on this teaching methodology.

Table 1. Students' considerations on the effectiveness of automatic formative assessment in teaching

| | Mean before | Dev.St. before | Mean after | Dev.St. after |
|---|---|---|---|---|
| Review your knowledge | 3,99 | 0,93 | 4,28 | 0,75 |
| Improve understanding of content | 4,13 | 0,87 | 4,42 | 0,72 |
| Develop problem solving strategies | 4,16 | 0,90 | 4,43 | 0,71 |
| Develop autonomy in solving problems | 4,25 | 0,86 | 4,46 | 0,62 |
| Develop argumentative skills | 3,83 | 1,00 | 4,15 | 0,82 |
| Facilitate recovery actions | 4,19 | 0,91 | 4,33 | 0,74 |
| Valuing excellent students | 3,79 | 1,10 | 4,00 | 0,99 |
| Raise awareness of one's knowledge and skills | 4,35 | 0,78 | 4,47 | 0,72 |
| Facilitate autonomy in the study | 4,27 | 0,86 | 4,38 | 0,78 |
| Promote metacognitive reflection | 4,11 | 0,93 | 4,28 | 0,78 |
| Increase motivation for the matter | 4,16 | 0,89 | 4,29 | 0,80 |
| Allow the inclusion of students with SEN-SLD | 4,08 | 0,99 | 4,15 | 0,96 |
| Understanding your mistakes | 4,44 | 0,88 | 4,54 | 0,62 |
| Personalize educational activities | 4,16 | 0,95 | 4,42 | 0,70 |

Students positively assessed the congruence of the training contents and the clarity of the proposed material (both with an average score of 3.6 out of 4). Table 2 shows the students' scores on different aspects of the training module and the proposed methodologies. The results are very positive. Students find the proposed methodologies clear and interesting, and they think they can support innovative and interdisciplinary teaching. The proposed methodologies help "collaborative learning", student learning and their development of skills. They intend to use the methodologies proposed in the classroom in the near future and to deepen the proposed methodologies.

Table 2. Students' considerations on different aspects of the training module and the proposed methodologies

| | Mean | Dev.St. |
|---|---|---|
| The proposed methodologies are interesting | 4,53 | 0,67 |
| The proposed methodologies are clear | 4,31 | 0,78 |
| The proposed methodologies support innovative teaching | 4,55 | 0,62 |
| The proposed methodologies support interdisciplinary teaching | 4,27 | 0,80 |
| The proposed methodologies support "collaborative learning" | 4,47 | 0,70 |
| The proposed methodologies help students' learning | 4,49 | 0,71 |
| The proposed methodologies help students develop skills | 4,50 | 0,70 |
| I intend to use the methodologies proposed in the classroom | 4,50 | 0,64 |
| I intend to deepen the proposed methodologies | 4,49 | 0,65 |

## 5. CONCLUSIONS

In this paper we have presented a training module on automatic formative assessment which involved 153 university students of the Master's Degree course in Primary Education (future primary school teachers). In this course, the concepts of formative assessment and automatic formative assessment with immediate and interactive feedback were presented. Students designed effective, not fully effective and ineffective interactive feedback. Most of the students had some difficulties in designing the interactive feedback, but those struggles are understandable, since it was their first time dealing with the topic. Most of the students had never used an automatic assessment system before, and this did not facilitate them in the design of the questions and related answers. The results revealed the need to increase the references to the National Guidelines (MIUR, 2012), in particular regarding the declaration of the learning objectives to be achieved with a specific activity, also paying attention to the words used, the clarity of the text and the context of the problem. Students really appreciated the development of the training module and the proposed methodologies. They find formative assessment very effective in several aspects. This type of training can also be very useful for teachers already in service. We believe it is important to train teachers of all levels on an important topic such as automatic formative assessment and on the strategies to be implemented to carry it out. For primary school teachers (in service or pre-service), this training is particularly effective according to recent regulations. This type of training can be deepened by training students on the use of the automatic evaluation system and having them implement the planned questions. A further possible fallout can be the creation of a database of activities with automatic formative evaluation that can be shared among future teachers and with primary school teachers.

# REFERENCES


Barana, A., 2021. From Formulas to Functions through Geometry: A Path to Understanding Algebraic Computations. *In European Journal of Investigation in Health, Psychology and Education,* Vol. 11, No. 4, pp. 1485-1502.

Barana, A. et al, 2020a. Automatic Formative Assessment Strategies for the Adaptive Teaching of Mathematics. *International Conference on Computer Supported Education.* Online, pp. 341-365.

Barana, A. et al, 2020b. From Standardized Assessment to Automatic Formative Assessment for Adaptive Teaching. *Proceedings of the 12th International Conference on Computer Supported Education*. Online, pp. 285–296.

Barana, A. et al, 2019. Empowering engagement through automatic formative assessment. *2019 IEEE 43rd Annual Computer Software and Applications Conference*. Milwaukee, Wisconsin, USA, Vol. 1, pp. 216-225.

Barana, A. et al, 2021. Interactive feedback for learning mathematics in a digital learning environment. *In Education Sciences*, Vol. 11, No. 6, p. 279.

Beatty, I.D. and Gerace, W.J., 2009. Technology-Enhanced Formative Assessment: A Research-Based Pedagogy for Teaching Science with Classroom Response Technology. *In J. Sci. Educ. Technol.*, Vol. 18, pp. 146–162.

Black, P. and Wiliam, D., 2009. Developing the theory of formative assessment, *In Educational Assessment, Evaluation and Accountability*, Vol. 21, No. 1, pp. 5-31.

Bennett, R.E., 2002. Inexorable and inevitable: the continuing story of technology and assessment. *In The Journal of Technology, Learning, and Assessment*, Vol. 1, No. 1.

Bolondi, G. et al, 2018. A quantitative methodology for analyzing the impact of the formulation of a mathematical item on students learning assessment. *In Studies in Educational Evaluation*, Vol. 58, pp. 37–50.

Boston, C., 2002. The concept of formative assessment. *In Practical Assessment, Research, and Evaluation*, Vol. 8, No. 1, p. 9.

Cascella, C. et al, 2020. An analysis of Differential Item Functioning on INVALSI tests, designed to explore gender gap in mathematical tasks. *In Studies in Educational Evaluation*, Vol. 64.

Corino, E. et al, 2022. Adaptive Exercises and Formative Assessment for English Remedial Action. *Orchestration of Learning Environments in the Digital World.* pp. 3-19.

Fissore, C. et al, 2020a. Secondary school teacher support and training for online teaching during the covid-19 pandemic. *Proceedings of EDEN Conference*, No. 1, pp. 311-320.

Fissore, C. et al, 2020b. Digital competences for educators in the Italian secondary school: a comparison between DigCompEdu reference framework and the PP&S project experience. *Proceedings of the International Conference E-Learning*, pp. 47-54.

Giraudo, M. et al, 2014. Tutoring con le nuove tecnologie per ridurre l'insuccesso scolastico e favorire l'apprendimento della matematica nella scuola secondaria. *In Mondo Digitale*, Vol. 13, No. 51, pp. 834-843.

Hattie, J. and Timperley, H., 2007. The Power of Feedback. *In Review of Educational Research*, Vol.77, No.1, pp. 81–112.

Kluger, A. N. and DeNisi, A., 1996. The effects of feedback interventions on performance: A historical review, a meta-analysis, and a preliminary feedback intervention theory. *In Psychological Bulletin*, Vol. 119, No. 2, pp. 254–284.

Marello, C. et al, 2019. Automatic assessment to enhance online dictionaries consultation skills. *16th International Conference on Cognition and Exploratory Learning in the Digital Age.* Cagliari, Italy, pp. 331-338.

MIUR, 2012. *National Guidelines for the nursery school curriculum and the first cycle of education.*

Nicol, D. and Milligan, C., 2006. Rethinking technology-supported assessment practices in relation to the seven principles of good feedback practice. *Innovative Assessment in Higher Education*, pp. 1-14.

Nicol D. and Macfarlane-Dick D., 2006. Formative assessment and self regulated learning: A model and seven principles of good feedback practice. *In Studies in Higher Education*, Vol. 31, No. 2, pp. 199-218.

Sadler, D. R., 1989. Formative assessment and the design of instructional systems. *In Instructional Science*, Vol. 18, pp. 119-144.

# CONVERGENT VALIDITY OF INVIGILATED, SUMMATIVE ONLINE ASSESSMENTS IN BUSINESS MATHEMATICS COURSES AND STUDENTS' COMPARATIVE PERFORMANCE IN ONLINE AND OFFLINE ASSESSMENTS

Victor K. Y. Chan and Hio Man Lei
*Macao Polytechnic University*
*Rua de Luís Gonzaga Gomes, Macao SAR, China*

**ABSTRACT**

The validity and specifically the convergent validity of a course's online assessments (i.e. the extent to which the online assessments really measure what is measured by other assessments meant to measure the constructs of the course's learning outcomes) so far receive little attention, especially for business mathematics courses. Based on a business mathematics course at the authors' university, this article aims to verify the convergent validity of an invigilated, summative online assessment by evaluating the extent to which the online assessment measures what is measured by an invigilated, summative offline assessment meant to measure the construct of the course's learning outcomes. In addition, this article attempts to deduce whether the students performed better in the online assessment than in the offline assessment or vice versa. Findings was that such convergent validity was just scarcely acceptable and that students in the online assessment drastically outperformed themselves in the offline assessment. Reasons are proposed for the findings, for example, students' computer anxiety, perceptions of and attitudes towards online assessments as well as some distinctive features of online assessments in mathematical courses.

**KEYWORDS**

Summative Online Assessment, Invigilated, Comparative Performance, Mathematics Courses, Offline Assessment.

## 1. INTRODUCTION

Alongside the phenomenal proliferation of e-learning applications in universities and other tertiary education institutions across the globe over the past two decades, summative online/electronic assessment of students (e.g. through tests and examinations on electronic e-learning platforms) has been piloted, launched and even institutionalized in the realm of tertiary education. Vis-à-vis offline/traditional (pen-and-paper) counterparts, online assessments are inherently superior in the sense of:

- cost and time savings in view of the automated administration, grading/marking/scoring and storage of students' works,
- possibly customised and/or immediate feedback to students, which is of pedagogical benefit,
- enhanced student engagement due to the novelty and appeal of this assessment modality,
- geographical flexibility of students in submitting their works on campus or off campus and
- minimised human errors in grading/marking/scoring.

(Hewson, Charlton and Brosnan, 2007; Hewson, 2012).

Nevertheless, ever since their advent, the validity of online assessments has loomed large and been controversial among tertiary educationists (Hewson, 2012). Validity refers to the extent to which the online assessments in a particular course (or module dependent on the specific terminology adopted in a particular tertiary institution) turn out to measure what they are meant to measure, i.e. specifically the learning outcomes of the course (Dennick, Wilkinson and Purcell, 2009; Whitelock, 2009; Hewson, 2012). Traditionally and generally, validity of any instrument to measure any construct (i.e. abstract variable), be the construct a course's learning outcomes or otherwise, covers hierarchical perspectives as follows:

- content validity
    - face validity
- criterion-related validity
    - concurrent validity
    - predictive validity
- construct validity
    - convergent validity
    - discriminant/divergent validity

(Heale and Twycross, 2015).

In particular, convergent validity concerns the extent to which the instrument really measures what is measured by other instruments meant to measure the construct (Heale and Twycross, 2015). Therefore, for an online assessment (as an instrument to measure the construct of a course's learning outcomes) to achieve high convergent validity, it should at least measure what is measured by an offline assessment broadly recognised as an instrument to measure the construct of the course's learning outcomes. In other words, such high convergent validity can be manifested by consistency between the online assessment scores and the offline assessment scores when both assessments are administrated to the same student sample.

To the knowledge of the authors, consistency between online and offline assessment scores in the form of a high correlation coefficient or otherwise for the purpose of substantiating convergent validity of an online assessment has still not been conclusively established generally across multiple disciplines. This is especially true of the business mathematics discipline. As a matter of fact, there are appreciable empirical studies hitherto on validity of online assessments and effectiveness of e-learning specific to courses in such disciplines as psychology (Hewson, Charlton and Brosnan, 2007; Hewson, 2012) and medicine (Pei and Wu, 2019; Hope *et al.*, 2021). In contrast, comparable studies in business mathematics disciplines are relatively the minority. As Pei and Wu (2019) contend, curriculum types (and thus disciplines) may dictate the outcomes of e-learning (and thus online assessments), so it is pointless to miss out business mathematics disciplines as such. In fact, online assessments in mathematical disciplines may deserve particular heed in the sense that not only are online assessments most prevalently adopted in mathematical (or numerate) disciplines (Hewson, 2012) but also they are characterised by the following distinctive features setting them apart from other disciplines in the context of online assessments:

(a) On top of serving solely as content repositories, content retrieval systems and operational media for the assessment and learning of any disciplines, computer platforms for online assessment and e-learning at large are direct assistive tools for the computation-intensive content of mathematical disciplines (Hussain *et al.*, 2014).

(b) Students may take advantage of such computer platforms to countercheck their answers during online assessments of mathematical courses by means of commonplace spreadsheet software or other computational software presumably bundled with these platforms (Hussain *et al.*, 2014).

(c) Students may even utilise such commonplace software to work out their answers, for example, in plotting graphs during online assessments of mathematical courses (Hussain *et al.*, 2014).

(d) Cumbersome input of mathematical notations and expressions into the computer platforms may impede students during online assessments (Anthony, Yang and Koedinger, 2005).

(e) The computer platforms' communication facilities may facilitate student cheating (Fask, Englander and Wang, 2014; Arnold, 2016; Dendir and Maxwell, 2020; Bilen and Matros, 2021), and mathematical courses typified by their absolute answers preclude most cheating accusation (Trenholm, 2007).

Moreover, even in the prior empirical researches that claimed to be on validity of online assessments in disciplines like psychology (Hewson, Charlton and Brosnan, 2007; Hewson, 2012) and medicine (Hope *et al.*, 2021), most of them simply compared students' online assessment mean scores to their offline assessment mean scores based on statistical tests of independent samples with scant regard for the consistency between online and offline scores in the same student sample. In other words, most such researches did not directly intend to verify convergent validity of online assessments.

The current study is to fill these gaps by evaluating the consistency between the online assessment scores (specifically, the invigilated, summative online assessment scores) and the offline assessment scores in the same student sample having taken a business mathematics course at the authors' university. State differently, the current study aims to verify the convergent validity of the invigilated, summative online assessment, i.e. the extent to which the invigilated, summative online assessment (as an instrument to measure the construct of the business mathematics course's learning outcomes) measures what is measured by an offline assessment broadly recognised as an instrument to measure the construct of the business mathematics course's learning outcomes. Further to convergent validity's verification, the current study additionally compares these two series of scores in order to deduce whether the students performed better in the invigilated, summative online assessment than in the offline assessment or vice versa. The comparison is based on statistical tests of paired samples as opposed to those of independent samples so as to compare the two assessment modalities with respect to the same student sample instead of, say, two randomly allocated samples.

## 2. THE STUDY

This study focused on evaluating the convergent validity of the invigilated, summative online assessment of a business mathematics course at the authors' university and the comparison between the online assessment scores and those of a corresponding offline assessment.

### 2.1 Materials and Methods

The course for this study concerned introductory business mathematics for year 1 students at the then School of Business and was delivered in the first semester of the academic year 2020/2021from September to January 2021. The total enrolments were 109. Instruction was offered offline and traditionally through classroom lectures but was complemented by the learning management system Canvas, which "tripled" as a course content repository (electronically storing all course materials), a course content retrieval system (for the students to retrieve all course materials) and an operational medium (for professor-student electronic communication, online assignment/test submission, mark announcement, etc.).

There was a mid-semester test conducted online through Canvas temporally around the middle of the semester and accounting for 40% of the course's overall assessment marks. This online test was the online assessment of which the convergent validity was to be verified in this study. It was in the form of a "quiz", which was a standard Canvas facility through which the professor could post the test questions and the students could answer by typing or uploading files. The files uploaded could be in the PDF, JPEG, PNG or Microsoft Word format and contain typed answers or scans/photographs of hand-written answers. Composed of "essay-type" mathematical questions asking for mathematical steps to arrive at mathematical solutions, the online test was invigilated (or proctored) and lasted one and a half hours in designated computer laboratories. It was graded/marked also online on Canvas afterwards partly automatically and partly manually by the professor in charge of the course, the marks of and the professor's comments for individual students also being announced to and accessible by the corresponding students on Canvas.

Towards the end of the semester, there was also an offline final examination, making up half the course's overall marks. Also comprising "essay-type" mathematical questions, the offline final examination was literally an offline assessment in that it was a traditional pen-and-paper examination with both questions from the professor printed and answers from the students hand-written on paper and was invigilated inside a physical hall/pavilion over a duration of three hours. Likewise, grading and commenting were performed on paper alongside students' answers manually by the professor in charge of the course. The topic coverage of the online test roughly constituted two-thirds of that of the offline final examination. In other words, only a third of the latter's topic coverage was on top of the former's. That is to say, the online test's contents resembled two-thirds of the offline final examination's, so the latter could act as a reference for the verification of the former's convergent validity.

## 2.2 Methods

By the close of the semester, the students' online test scores and their offline final examination scores became available, enabling the computation of the correlation coefficient between these two series of scores. A high coefficient would verify consistency between the online test scores and the offline final examination scores and to a large extent imply strong convergent validity of the online test in that the online test (as an instrument to measure the construct of the course's learning outcomes) measured what was measured by the offline final examination broadly recognised as an instrument to measure the construct of the course's learning outcome.

Then, a paired-sample $t$-test was performed to verify the hypothesis that students in the online test outperformed themselves in the offline final examination or vice versa. In the case of the hypothesis turning out to be statistically acceptable, one might be able to conclude that either of these two assessment modalities was to the students' benefit in terms of their scores.

# 3. RESULTS

Disregarding students absent from either the online test or the offline final examination, 99 out of the 109 students were qualified for the correlation analysis and the paired-sample $t$-test.

The correlation analysis gave rise to a correlation coefficient of 0.367 with a $p$-value of 0.000187, which was statistically significant even at the 1% significance level. With such a coefficient slightly below +0.5 and thus mildly on the low side, the implication was that the online test scores and the offline final examination scores were merely moderately consistent despite the substantial overlap between the coverage of the two assessments which were barely around two months apart. Stated differently, students scoring highly in the online test were only moderately likely to score highly in the offline final examination and vice versa. As such, the convergent validity of the online test, at least when gauged by the traditional, offline final examination, was just scarcely acceptable. Having said that, the $p$-value indicated that the correlation coefficient differed from zero even at the 1% statistical significance, attesting to the ability of the online test score being a proxy for the offline final examination score even if not a very faithful one.

As regards the paired sample *t*-test for the differences between the online test scores and the offline final examination scores for all the 99 students, the mean difference was 33.51 marks, its 95% confidence interval was from 28.189 to 38.832 marks, and the *p*-value of the *t*-test was 0.0000 and thus statistically significant even at the 1% significance level. The implication is that notwithstanding the appreciable overlap between coverage of the online test and the offline final examination which were marginally two months apart, students in the former outperforming themselves in the latter is almost undeniable, at least at the 1% significance level if put technically. On average, they scored 33.51 marks more highly in the former than in the latter. In other words, the online test favoured students in comparison with the offline final examination in that students scored drastically more highly in the former.

## 4. DISCUSSION

Prior literature does not accentuate the convergent validity of online assessments, or equivalently, the consistency between online assessments and traditional, offline assessments (or any alternative well-established and broadly recognised assessments). Instead most previous literature simply determines whether the mean scores of online assessments statistically differ from those of comparable offline assessments, presuming that online assessments are "fair and equitable" and worthy of pedagogical application as long as their mean scores do not deviate excessively from their offline counterparts (Hewson, Charlton and Brosnan, 2007; Hewson, 2012; Hope *et al.*, 2021). In fact, even if such differences between mean scores are negligible, there is no guarantee that online assessments truthfully reflect what offline assessments should reflect in respect of students' performance. For instance, even if there are zero mean score differences between online and offline assessments, it may be that eminent students ironically score lowly in online assessments but highly in offline assessments while less competent students happen to score conversely in the two assessment modalities, zeroing out the differences between the mean scores of the two. In contrast, even if the mean scores differ by a large margin, as long as online assessments render high scores for eminent students and low scores for less competent students as offline assessments supposedly do, the mean score disparity by no means prejudices online assessment's "fairness and equity" or debases online assessments one way or another at least when benchmarking against traditional, offline assessments. If optionally desired, the minor issue of mean score disparity can be muffled by simply scaling all students' scores across the board. In summary, it is the convergent validity of online assessments (or any assessment modalities else in question), or equivalently, the consistency between online assessments (or any assessment modalities else in question) and traditional, offline assessments (or any alternative well-established and broadly recognised assessments) instead of any mean score disparity between them that substantively determines the former's pedagogical worthiness.

This study exactly delved into the convergent validity of online assessments as exemplified by the scenario of a business mathematics course at the authors' university. It was found that such convergent validity was just scarcely acceptable. Additional findings were that students in the online assessment drastically outperformed themselves in the offline assessment, the two assessments being around two months apart.

Existing literature purports a students' computer anxiety and perception of and attitude towards online assessments to be exogenous/confounding variables/factors causing his/her online assessment score to deviate from his/her offline assessment score (Hewson, Charlton and Brosnan, 2007; Hewson, 2012). These variables/factors are considered exogenous/confounding in view of their not being any of the learning outcomes of the courses in question (unless in the currently irrelevant case of computer submersion courses whose learning outcomes may be computer proficiency, etc.) and thus are not supposed to be reflected in any assessment scores. Different students are prone to different levels of computer anxiety and possess different perceptions of and attitudes towards online assessments and thus are advantaged or disadvantaged differently in online assessments but not at all in offline assessments not involving computer platforms and/or online operations. Such anxiety, perceptions and attitudes might be some of the reasons for the different discrepancies between online assessment scores and offline assessment scores across different students and thus degraded convergent validity found in this study. Different students being advantaged or disadvantaged to different degrees in online assessments and thus degradation of online assessments' convergent validity in this study might have been strengthened by different students leveraging or being hindered by the five distinctive features (a) to (e) of online assessments in mathematical courses (as enumerated in Section 1) to different extents. All such preliminary reasoning is to be investigated in further research.

By the same token, one may reason that the students in this study's online assessment drastically outperformed themselves in the offline assessment because students on average leveraged the five distinctive features (a) to (e) of online assessments in mathematical courses more than they were hindered. This reasoning is again subject to further research.

Besides, extension of this research to disciplines other than business mathematics for broader generalisation may be worthwhile just as what Pei and Wu (2019) hint.

# 5. CONCLUSION

Invigilated, summative online assessments for business mathematical disciplines are merely consistent with and can thus serve as proxies for invigilated, summative offline assessments to a limited extent. In addition, such online assessment scores substantially exceed their offline counterparts.

It is worth investigating whether computer anxiety and perception of and attitude towards online assessments, alongside distinctive features of mathematical courses' online assessment, are exogenous/confounding variables/factors underlying the disparity between online and offline assessment scores in this study and the convergent validity of online assessments falling short of impeccability. (Hewson, Charlton and Brosnan, 2007; Hewson, 2012).

# REFERENCES


Anthony, L., Yang, J. and Koedinger, K. R. (2005) 'Evaluation of multimodal input for entering mathematical equations on the computer', in *Conference on Human Factors in Computing Systems - Proceedings*. Portland, OR: Association for Computing Machinery, pp. 1184–1187. doi: 10.1145/1056808.1056872.

Arnold, I. J. M. (2016) 'Cheating at online formative tests: Does it pay off?', *The Internet and Higher Education*, 29, pp. 98–106. doi: 10.1016/J.IHEDUC.2016.02.001.

Bilen, E. and Matros, A. (2021) 'Online cheating amid COVID-19', *Journal of Economic Behavior and Organization*. Elsevier B.V., 182, pp. 196–211. doi: 10.1016/j.jebo.2020.12.004.

Dendir, S. and Maxwell, R. S. (2020) 'Cheating in online courses: Evidence from online proctoring', *Computers in Human Behavior Reports*. Elsevier Ltd, 2. doi: 10.1016/j.chbr.2020.100033.

Dennick, R., Wilkinson, S. and Purcell, N. (2009) 'Online eAssessment: AMEE guide no. 39.', *Medical teacher*. England, 31(3), pp. 192–206. doi: 10.1080/01421590902792406.

Fask, A., Englander, F. and Wang, Z. (2014) 'Do Online Exams Facilitate Cheating? An Experiment Designed to Separate Possible Cheating from the Effect of the Online Test Taking Environment', *Journal of Academic Ethics*, 12(2), pp. 101–112. doi: 10.1007/s10805-014-9207-1.

Heale, R. and Twycross, A. (2015) 'Validity and reliability in quantitative studies', *Evidence-Based Nursing*, 18(3), pp. 66–67. doi: 10.1136/eb-2015-102129.

Hewson, C. (2012) 'Can online course-based assessment methods be fair and equitable? Relationships between students' preferences and performance within online and offline assessments', *Journal of Computer Assisted Learning*, 28(5), pp. 488–498. doi: 10.1111/j.1365-2729.2011.00473.x.

Hewson, C., Charlton, J. and Brosnan, M. (2007) 'Comparing Online and Offline Administration of Multiple Choice Question Assessments to Psychology Undergraduates: Do Assessment Modality or Computer Attitudes Influence Performance?', *Psychology Learning & Teaching*, 6(1), pp. 37–46. doi: 10.2304/plat.2007.6.1.37.

Hope, D. *et al.* (2021) 'Candidates undertaking (invigilated) assessment online show no differences in performance compared to those undertaking assessment offline', *Medical Teacher*. Taylor & Francis, 43(6), pp. 646–650. doi: 10.1080/0142159X.2021.1887467.

Hussain, M. A. *et al.* (2014) 'The Impact of Technology in Mathematics Education: A Case Study of Pakistan', *Journal of Basic & Applied Sciences*, 10, pp. 67–72. doi: 10.6000/1927-5129.2014.10.10.

Pei, L. and Wu, H. (2019) 'Does online learning work better than offline learning in undergraduate medical education? A systematic review and meta-analysis', *Medical Education Online*. Taylor & Francis, 24(1). doi: 10.1080/10872981.2019.1666538.

Trenholm, S. (2007) 'A Review of Cheating in Fully Asynchronous Online Courses: A Math or Fact-Based Course Perspective', *Journal of Educational Technology Systems*, 35(3), pp. 281–300. doi: 10.2190/y78l-h21x-241n-7q02.

Whitelock, D. (2009) 'Editorial: e-assessment: developing new dialogues for the digital age', *British Journal of Educational Technology*, 40(2), pp. 199–202. doi: 10.1111/J.1467-8535.2008.00932.X.

# AN IMPACT STUDY ON THE ARDUINO PROGRAMMING TRAINING FOR BEGINNERS

Charito G. Ong, Josan C. Fermano and Albert Christopher P. Daniot II
*University of Science and Technology of Southern Philippines, Lapasan, Cagayan de Oro City, Philippines*

**ABSTRACT**

This study reports an impact assessment of the basic Arduino programming training conducted among select Junior High School Students in a National High School in Cagayan De Oro City. The Focus Group Discussion sessions and survey questionnaires via goggle form complemented the content of the impact study table. The researchers aimed to determine the impact of the training towards the perception of the trainees in programming, skills development and learning gain. Furthermore, the training program used was evaluated by both trainers and trainees in terms of content, strategies and activities used. Research results showed the respondents' negative perception on Arduino programming yet manifested positive views on the training for programming skills development and enhancement of learning. The training material was rated high ranging from format to organization and content.

**KEYWORDS**

Assessment, Arduino Programming, Training.

## 1. INTRODUCTION

Song Seng (2019) posits that student competence is a vital factor for achieving educational excellence. Emphasis has been placed on academic training. This is to ensure that students become more accountable and extra knowledgeable about the courses they take. As the core component in any educational system, these students need training to assure learning efficiency. Thus, educational institutions should be driven by the need to achieve efficiency, effectiveness and equity. This highlights the importance of training students, supplementary to the lessons they receive in classes.

Recently, Alam (2020) found a considerable surge among industries to attract skillful people. The significant development in technologies, working skills, and learning method increased the competition level. Hence, the academe needs to enhance student competence by providing trainings; thus addressing the students' needs to keep abreast with technological changes.

However, involving students in various trainings is not an end in itself. To further assess whether they really had enhanced their competences, the primacy of conducting an assessment is indeed high. In her study, Organtini (2018) concludes that an after training evaluation provides information whether a program has achieved or failed its objectives. Moreover, she adds that analyzing the training event by using appropriate evaluation tools can improve the outcome of future trainings to a considerable extent.

In 2019, this University conducted an extension program among select Junior High School students of Lapasan National High School. The training offered an introduction to Arduino programming, working with analog and digital sensors and building Arduino project leading to Robotics. To measure the impact of the implemented training, the researchers proposed for the conduct of this study. Specifically, the study scrutinized and described the skills developed among the respondents, including the motivation and focus which aided their programming performance. These are founded from Basarmak's (2021) study which recommends that training should help in updating skills and increase confidence level which strengthens the students' competitiveness.

Furthermore, the researchers administered this impact study to determine one important factor, change. For formative purposes, this impact evaluation was undertaken to analyze the given training intervention and gauged whether to continue, replicate or scale it up by examining the piloted training content.

# 2. BODY OF PAPER

## 2.1 Research Design and Instruments

This paper employed both descriptive and diagnostic research designs. In the research process, the researchers gathered data from both trainers and trainees. The training material/program were evaluated by both trainers and trainees; with emphasis on content, strategies and activities. Furthermore, this impact assessment took a process that included four basic components: 1) described training improvement over time, 2) motivated students to evaluate the training process, 3) evaluated the training materials and 4) ranked the trainees and trainers' evaluation of the entire training process.

## 2.2 The Instruments

This research made use of the prepared focus group discussion prompts modified from Sparks (2016), questionnaire and Ong's (2017) evaluation tool for assessing the training material used. These validation instruments served as basis for further recommendation on the training material enhancement.

## 2.3 The Respondents

The participants of the study were the USTP trainers involved in the 2019 Arduino programming for beginners' training. This was also inclusive of the thirty-six Graders who served as respondents in the training from Lapasan National High School. As the study was conducted during the COVID-19 pandemic, they were reached out via Facebook, group chats and zoom video conferencing.

## 2.4 Data Gathering Procedure

The researchers of this study conducted separate focus group discussion sessions among the trainers and trainees of the 2019 Arduino training program conducted at Lapasan National High School. The modified FGD prompts was utilized. These respondents likewise answered via google form, an adopted questionnaire which focused on the assessment of the training areas. An impact assessment table was likewise completed in this regard.

This qualitative research, which is based on the impact method; examined the impact of the conducted training in terms of the respondents' perception on programming, development of their programming skills and learning gain. Their ideas on how to enhance the training program used were likewise sought. An evaluation tool was modified which served as baseline instrument for the assessment.

# 3. RESULTS AND DISCUSSION

Table 1 shows that out of 36 respondents, majority perceived programming negatively or difficult. This data was taken through the focus group discussion and survey questionnaire. Similarly, results from the study of Arslan & Tanel (2021) manifested the same outcome. The paper presented a new approach to teaching programming to undergraduate computer science students. A dedicated Arduino board along with custom application programming interface (API) was introduced into programming classes with a view to strengthen students' engagement and improving the attractiveness of the course. The students were presented with basic functionalities of the board, which gave them a possibility to accomplish their own projects, typically video games; without any background in electronics. The level of engagement of the participants was observed by the tutors during classes and also reviewed based on questionnaires filled by 347 first, second, and third year undergraduates. The results indicated that the proposed approach was well received by nearly 80%, while nearly 75% of the participants expressed a wish to continue their Computer Science education using Arduino. Hence, the negative perception did not affect the students' ability to learn programming in this study.

Table 1. Respondents' Perception of Programming

| Perception on Programming | Frequency | Percentage | Rank |
|---|---|---|---|
| Easy to understand | | | |
| Negative | 35 | 97.2 | 1 |
| Positive | 1 | 2.7 | 2 |
| Interesting to Learn | | | |
| Negative | 2 | 5.5 | 2 |
| Positive | 34 | 94.4 | 1 |
| Needed in higher g-level | | | |
| Negative | 5 | 13.8 | 2 |
| Positive | 31 | 86.1 | 1 |
| Needed formal training | | | |
| Negative | 0 | 0 | 2 |
| Positive | 36 | 100 | 1 |

Another study of Perenc et. al (2019) aimed to examine the effect of robotic design with Arduino on students' attitudes towards programming and on their perceptions of self-efficacy in programming. The study group consisted of 25 sophomore students attending the Department of Computer Education and Instructional Technologies in a state university located in the south of Turkey. The study lasted 12 weeks and the participants performed robotic design activities with Arduino throughout the process. Firstly, participants prepared a prototype and then programmed it for 8 weeks, and they created their own designs in the remaining 4 weeks. The Computer Programming Attitude Scale and Computer Programming Self-Efficacy Scale were utilized as the data collection tools in this pretest-posttest experimental study. The findings revealed that robotic design activities with Arduino significantly improved the participants' attitudes towards programming and programming self-efficacy. In addition, according to the participants' views, the factors that cause this improvement can be listed as activities' being enjoyable, facilitating and concretizing the process, being interesting and practical. Moreover, these robotic design activities were found to contribute to students' understanding of finding bugs and the logic of programming.

Table 2. Respondents' Perception of the Training Impact on the Development of their Skills

| Development of Skills | Frequency | Percentage | Rank |
|---|---|---|---|
| Programming for beginners | | | |
| Negative | 0 | 0 | 2 |
| Positive | 36 | 100 | 1 |
| Basic Electronics | | | |
| Negative | 1 | 2.7 | 2 |
| Positive | 35 | 97.2 | 1 |

The researchers looked into these two areas in the development of programming skills: programming for beginners and basic electronics. When the respondents were asked about their views as to whether Arduino training will develop their programming and basic electronics skills; majority of them were on the positive side. They believe that indeed, when they receive the training, they will be able to develop such skills.

The study of Darmawan (2017) proves that Arduino programming develops both basic programming and electronics skills. Accordingly, electronic devices have become a part of human life today that cannot be ignored. The Community Service Program conducted by Prodi Electrical Engineering, Maranatha Christian University aimed to increase knowledge, increase interest, form the ability of cooperation, improve creativity and improve the fighting power of high school students on the operation of electronic devices, in the form of Arduino programming training. Arduino was referred to as an open source electronic kit specifically designed as a controller that regulates the working process of electronic circuits. The method used in this PKM was Participatory Action Research (PAR) in the form of lecture method to describe the material that had been prepared by PKM team, the method of practice in the form of Arduino programming and assembling the electronic component connected with Arduino, the method of mentoring when the students do the programming and stringing electronic components, and discussion methods in the form of inter-group cooperation to solve the case given. The results of this training became a provision for high school students in the form of programming skills, the ability to assemble electronic components, the ability to work with groups to solve existing problems, and increase confidence in designing and operating electronic devices.

Table 3. Respondents' Perception of the Training Impact on Learning Gain

| | A Lot | Quite | Some | A Little | Nothing |
|---|---|---|---|---|---|
| Did you learn in the Arduino lectures and training? | 95% | 5% | 0% | 0% | 0% |
| Did you find the Arduino lectures interesting? | 95% | 5% | 0% | 0% | 0% |
| Did you learn in the activities you performed? | 100% | 0% | 0% | 0% | 0% |
| Did you find the series of Arduino activities interesting? | 100% | 0% | 0% | 0% | 0% |

Table 3 manifests that the trainees were able to learn a lot from the training conducted. They found the activities and the lectures interesting too. Enjoyment was manifested when they shared that they found the activities on lighting up bulbs and circuits among others fun. This is supported by Rubio's (2013) study which found that the training modules they developed enhanced the students learning. Seventy-four percent of the students attained a good programming level, a 32% increase compared to the traditional learning. Attitudes improved also: sixty four percent of the class felt confident programming by themselves, a 21% gain. Only 55% that received the traditional approach asserted their satisfaction with programming. The Arduino platform was received well by the students. Over 95% of student found the laboratory sessions interesting and over 85% enjoyed the lecture demonstrations.

Albatish's (2018) paper aimed at helping trainees to overcome the difficulties they face when dealing with Arduino platform by describing the design of a desktop based intelligent tutoring system. The main idea of this system is a systematic introduction into the concept of Arduino platform. The system shows the circuit boards of Arduino that can be purchased at low cost or assembled from freely-available plans; and an open-source development environment and library for writing code to control the board topic of Arduino platform. The system is adaptive with the trainee's individual progress. The system functions as a special tutor who deals with trainees according to their levels and skills. Evaluation of the system has been applied on professional and unprofessional trainees in this field and the results were good.

Table 4. The Trainers' Evaluation of the Training Activities

| Areas | Large Extent | Some Extent | Not at All |
|---|---|---|---|
| Correlated with the skills developed | 4 | 0 | 0 |
| Practical and Feasible | 4 | 0 | 0 |
| Encourage active involvement | 4 | 0 | 0 |
| Logically arranged | 4 | 0 | 0 |
| Suitable to the grade level | 4 | 0 | 0 |

All of the four trainers evaluated the training activities positively. They rated large extent the five areas identified as basis of the evaluation which are: correlation of the activities with the skills developed, practicality and feasibility, encourage active involvement, logically arranged and suitable to the grade level. Similarly, using the same evaluation tool, the trainees gave a positive rating. This is presented in the table that follows.

Table 5. The Trainees' Evaluation of the Training Activities

| Areas | Large Extent | Some Extent | Not at All |
|---|---|---|---|
| Correlated with the skills developed | 34 | 2 | 0 |
| Practical and Feasible | 35 | 1 | 0 |
| Encourage active involvement | 36 | 0 | 0 |
| Logically arranged | 36 | 0 | 0 |
| Suitable to the grade level | 36 | 0 | 0 |

Majority of the trainees believe that the training activities manifest a large extent on these five areas: correlation of the activities with the skills developed, practicality and feasibility, encourage active involvement, logically arranged and suitable to the grade level. Only two out of thirty-six ticked some extent for the area correlation of the activities with the skills developed while one chose some extent for the activities' practicality and feasibility.

In a study conducted by Garcia et al (2019), it was cited that several countries have usually adopted several priorities for developing ICT competences from kindergarten to secondary education. Most of them were focused on the development of key competences and/or coding skills. It was suggested that although coding may be very attractive for young students and a very good practice or experience, it could be more interesting to develop students' logical thinking skills and problem-solving skills throughout programming approaches or computational thinking. The paper presented a very exciting challenge with lots of possibilities regarding coding, robots, mobiles devices, Arduino-based application, game-based learning and so on. Thus it is very important discuss the experiences that are being developed worldwide in specialized for a with researchers that are working on this field, such as for example European Union TACCLE 3 - Coding project. This track is devoted to identify, share and valorize best practices and experiences (including technological and methodological issues) that focused on the development of computational thinking and related skills in any level of pre-university education.

## 4. CONCLUSION

In conclusion, the researchers found a strong positive impact between the trainee-respondents' perception on programming, the development of their programming skills, and the learning gain from the conducted training. All trainees agreed that the training had a huge effect on their perception on basic Arduino programming. The training significantly improved their competency and abilities to perform excellently in programming related activities.

The trainers developed an introductory Arduino programming teaching resource that enhances students learning. These modules composed of topics on programming codes, IDE, analog sensors, digital sensors and Arduino project application. The results obtained from the respondents show that when using these modules more students learn to program and more students enjoy programming.

Although teaching computer programming to Junior High School and Elementary students is a challenge, the respondents found the subject related to their core interests and felt comfortable during the course of the training conduct. The application of the physical computing paradigm engaged students more effectively and enhanced their learning. These are reasons why the evaluation of the training program was positively skewed.

## REFERENCES


Alam, M. (2020). Arduino for Chemical Engineering Students via Game-based Learning. *ASEAN Journal of Engineering Education*, *4*(1).

Albatish, I., Mosa, M. J., & Abu-Naser, S. S. (2018). *ARDUINO Tutor*: An Intelligent Tutoring System for Training on ARDUINO.

Arslan, K., & Tanel, Z. (2021). *Analyzing the effects of Arduino applications on students' opinions, attitude and self-efficacy in programming class*. Education and Information Technologies, 26(1), 1143-1163.

Basarmak, U. (2021). Views of Pre-service Teachers in Different Disciplines about Coding with Arduino. *Malaysian Online Journal of Educational Technology*, *9*(2), 1-14.

Darmawan, A., Ratnadewi, R., Sartika, E. M., Pasaribu, N. T. B., & Arlando, R. (2017). Basic Arduino Programming Training for High School Students. *The Spirit of Society Journal*, *1*(1).

García-Peñalvo, F. J., & Cruz-Benito, J. (2016). *Computational thinking in pre-university education*. In Proceedings of the Fourth International Conference on Technological Ecosystems for Enhancing Multiculturality (pp. 13-17).

Ong, C. G. (2017). *College Communicative Teaching and E-Learning: A Training Scheme*. International Association for Development of the Information Society.

Organtini, G. (2018). *Arduino as a tool for physics experiments*. In Journal of Physics: Conference Series (Vol. 1076, No. 1, p. 012026). IOP Publishing.

Perenc, I., Jaworski, T., & Duch, P. (2019). Teaching programming using dedicated Arduino educational board. *Computer Applications in Engineering Education*, *27*(4), 943-954.

Rubio, M. A., Hierro, C. M., & Pablo, A. P. D. M. (2013). *Using arduino to enhance computer programming courses in science and engineering*. In Proceedings of EDULEARN13 conference (pp. 1-3). IATED Barcelona, Spain.

Sparks, G. M. (2016). The effectiveness of alternative training activities in changing teaching practices. *American educational research journal*, 23(2), 217-225.

# SHORT PAPERS

# A STEM FAMILY E-LEARNING FRAMEWORK TO INCREASE FAMILY ENGAGEMENT IN DISADVANTAGED COMMUNITIES

Kate Darmody[1], Julie Booth[1], Fergal O'Toole[1], Alexandra Alcala[1], Josephine Bleach (PhD)[1], Paul Stynes (PhD)[1] and Pramod Pathak (PhD)[2]

[1]*National College of Ireland Mayor Street, IFSC, Dublin 1, Ireland*

[2]*Technological University Dublin, Grangegorman, Dublin 7, Ireland*

**ABSTRACT**

STEM family e-learning involves increasing the engagement in STEM home learning activities. STEM home learning activities range from exploring subjects such as science technology, engineering, and maths through a fun play based K-6 STEM curriculum. The family are trained to act as teachers, mentors, and coaches to the K-6 members. Families from educational disadvantaged areas are typically early school leavers and having the STEM capacity to support their children is a challenge. This research proposes a STEM Family e-Learning framework to increase family engagement in supporting the K-6 members engaged in STEM learning activities. The proposed framework combines training for volunteers and STEM learning activities provided to families. Training for volunteers focuses on how to work with families in disadvantaged communities. STEM learning activities involve providing the family with STEM programmes such as Virtual Robotic Coding Clubs, Card Challenges, e-Learning Programme, STEM Play and Learn, STEM Workshops, Showcases and Events. Parent and child evaluation data indicate that the activities stimulated interest in STEM for both children and their parents and increased confidence in STEM subjects. This research can potentially enhance the mainstreaming and extension of STEM e-learning to disadvantaged communities.

**KEYWORDS**

STEM, e-Learning, Family Engagement, Disadvantage, Action Research.

## 1. INTRODUCTION

Research consistently highlights early learning as the foundation for all subsequent learning (Heckman, 2006) and the importance of Science, Technology, Engineering and Mathematics (STEM) as an indicator of future academic success. Competence in STEM is essential for functioning in everyday life, and for success in our modern technological workplace. Children today will be applying for jobs in STEM areas such as advanced robotics, autonomous transport, artificial intelligence, and biotechnology. Student achievement in STEM education is attributed to a complex interrelationship of socioeconomic factors, home influences, and home-school relationships (Duch & Gennetian, 2018). Families in educationally disadvantaged communities do not have the knowledge or skills required to encourage or help young people with STEM subjects (ELI, 2012; Gunning, Marrero and Morell, 2016), and student engagement has been found to be lower in schools in disadvantaged communities (Bray et al., 2021; Devitt et al., 2020). In the context of e-learning, Bray and colleagues found that the primary barriers teachers noted in student engagement online were lack of student interest and a lack of support at home. These social and motivation barriers had greater significance in disadvantaged community settings (Bray et al., 2021).

Parental attitudes and involvement influence their children's interest, motivation and sense of personal efficacy (Bandura, 1997) and reinforce outcomes in a positive or negative feedback loop. For students in disadvantaged communities, it has an impact on their choice of and persistence in a STEM career. Parents involvement in their children's STEM education may accelerate achievement of learning or mitigate risk factors that threaten it (Henderson & Mapp, 2002). Families' feedback is a critical element in developing opportunities for STEM learning (Henríquez, 2018).

Recognizing agency of the participants (Bandura, 2001) and individual home learning context is important. Gunning, Marrero & Morell (2016) provided the opportunity for low-income families to do science and engineering activities together. Their findings indicate that the opportunity successfully altered the families' view and practice of science outside of school. It is claimed that learning educational robotics can be a gateway for children's engagement with scientific concepts and mathematical thinking as well as developing their understanding of technology (Elkind, 2008). Individualized, active, explorative and child-directed learning (Casad & Jawaharlal 2012) is important to giving young children positive STEM experiences in order to maintain their interest. High-quality long-term integrated science experiences build a critical foundation to support future science knowledge and interest (Gerde, Schachter, & Wasik, 2013; Patrick, Mantzicopoulos, Samarapungavan & French, 2008).

STEM programmes with disadvantaged communities have been running since 2008 in the Early Learning Initiative (ELI, 2012) in Dublin's Inner-City. An initial survey of need (Dartington Social Research Unit, 2006) found that while local parents had high educational aspirations for their children, they did not understand their pivotal role and were not confident that they had the skills to support their children's learning. With support for parents as the primary educators of their children a priority, involving local people as co-constructors of programmes and in the decision-making processes is perceived as key to educational change and student achievement (Bleach, 2013). These programmes were initially delivered in-person through schools and services or integrated within home visiting and parent engagement programmes. In 2020 the STEM K-6 programmes transitioned to e-Learning delivery in response to the COVID19 emergency restrictions. The present study investigated the impact of introducing K-6 e-learning activities on family engagement in a disadvantaged community. The major contribution of this research is a novel STEM Family e-Learning Framework that combines family engagement, training and activities in order to promote family and community engagement with e-learning. Engagement is defined as the combination of three dimensions namely, participation, confidence and interest.

## 2. STEM FAMILY E-LEARNING FRAMEWORK

ELI designed multiple holistic family interventions ranging from workshops and events on STEM subjects to Virtual Robotic Coding Clubs through K-6 e-learning programmes. Community Action Research (Bleach, 2016) is used to design, implement, and evaluate the multi-faceted e-learning programme. Time to plan, engage, implement and evaluate is a central component of the process. The STEM Family e-Learning Framework is shown in figure 1. The framework combines three components, family engagement, training, and activities each of which are detailed below.

Figure 1. STEM family e-Learning framework

Family engagement consists of family recruitment and family needs analysis and support. Family recruitment uses multiple methods to recruit participants namely, referral from ELI's home visiting, family engagement programmes, along with local schools and services. Families may also self-refer hearing of programmes through social media, and word of mouth. Family needs analysis and support involves first identifying the barriers individual families might face to engagement. A family's access to technology, digital literacy, proficiency in English and confidence to engage in STEM are all taken into consideration. The level of support is then determined based on these needs. Engaging directly one-to-one with families may be important with support to access the technology and materials provided in advance of an activity. The number of participants should be kept low to address the cognitive and affective difficulties of mastering STEM concepts and enable more intense engagement and support. Discussions around on-screen etiquette along with allaying concerns around internet safety requires continuous conversations and check-ins throughout the programme. Ongoing support should be provided to discuss any difficulties families are having with e-learning, and so parents have a voice in the development of the programme, ensuring it is family-friendly and fit for purpose.

Training involves building staff capacity to recruit and engage families which feeds back into the family recruitment, needs analysis and support processes. Induction training for volunteers, workshops for volunteers and Home Visitors (staff delivering one-to-one programmes) are provided prior to beginning activities and, finally, Home Visitor supervision is provided for STEM Play & Learn. These training components enable best practice and to ensure professionals are supported. Staff are trained in how to engage with families, this can be individualized depending on the needs of the family. Guidance on content development is provided and experienced staff model STEM activities for the one-to-one sessions, explaining the benefits of the activities and resources for a child's development. One-to-one introduction meetings are arranged for each family with their Home Visitor or volunteer. In keeping with best practice from the Home Visiting Model ongoing programme support is provided to Home Visitors and volunteers through supervision and programme reviews.

The STEM family e-Learning activities, detailed below, are designed to appeal to a range of age groups. The Virtual Robotic Coding Club (8-12 years) aims for children to learn about basic robotics, programming and electronics with mbots and micro bits which they program using Makeblock software. The activities re-enforce children's coding skills over the 6-week programme, culminating in a competition event where children can participate in a coding challenge.

Card Challenges (8-12 years) aims to raise awareness of the role that the family and community can play in improving and promoting literacy and numeracy with fun activities and building parents' confidence in participating in learning activities with their children. Families were paired with a corporate volunteer to play card games each week for 4 weeks with a virtual card challenge competition at the end.

The aim of the e-Learning Programme (5-12 years) is to raise parent's awareness of STEM educational and career expectations and to increase parental educational capital facilitating their ongoing involvement in their child's education and learning. This 4-lesson program is developed with a focus on the environment, through four subtopics: food, water, energy, and climate, and activity packs are provided for each topic. Creating a Google platform of engagement provides a space for peer learning and discussion amongst families.

The STEM Play & Learn programme (4-6 years) aims to upskill parents as home educators to have the confidence, understanding, skills and knowledge to continue to support their children's education in this new everchanging situation. This 6-week programme supports children's early literacy, numeracy, language, and social/emotional development, in fun and interactive way. The blended learning approach through phone/video contact; e-Learning programmes and resources; home learning packs including books and toys to explore STEM concepts suitable for this age.

STEM workshops (5-11 years) are one off opportunities for families to engage in fun learning educational activities to explore STEM. The workshops are delivered in collaboration with other organizations and professionals with a STEM background.

## 3. METHODOLOGY

The development of the activities, framework and their evaluation follow a community action research approach (Bleach 2016). This research was approved by the Ethics Committee. Informed consent was sought prior to participation.

Prior to beginning the programme parents are asked to complete an intake form. Information provided in the form along with conversations with the programme coordinator form the basis of the family's needs analysis. In the case of STEM Play & Learn, parents completed a short pre-programme survey identifying the frequency to which the family engage in home learning activities.

167 children and 167 parents participated in the e-learning activities from August 2020 to December 2021. All families were from an area of socio-economic disadvantage in Dublin's Inner City. All e-learning activities were delivered online in the family home. Children's and parents' attendance were collected in order to measure participation.

Parents and children were invited to complete online post-programme surveys designed by ELI to evaluate the engagement of the family based on examining children's and parents' interest and confidence in STEM. Participants were asked to rate their levels of confidence and interest on a five-point scale in a number of questions. For example, parents were asked to rate the level to which participating in the STEM activity increased their confidence in their ability to support their child's learning in STEM and their involvement in their child's STEM learning. Children were asked to rate the level to which their confidence in STEM skills increased and if participating increased their interest in STEM. 68 parents and 64 children responded. Parents participating in the STEM Play & Learn also completed the same home learning environment questions that were asked at pre-programme.

## 4. RESULTS AND DISCUSSION

This section examines the findings and discusses key components to measuring successful family engagement as well as the challenges. Data were analysed in Microsoft Excel. Average percentage of attendance in e-learning activities used to measure participation. Interest and confidence in STEM were measured by frequency of children and parents rating 4 or 5 on a 5-point scale. Qualitative data was analysed by identifying recurring themes in children and parents' responses.

Children participated online from their homes accompanied by their parents. The average percentage participation of both children and their parents in the programmes are outlined in Table 1.

Table 1. Average percentage participation of parents and children in each activity of STEM Family e-Learning Framework

| Programme | Parent avg. % attendance | Child avg. % attendance |
|---|---|---|
| Virtual Robotic Coding - 6 weeks | 26% | 68% |
| Card Challenges - 4 weeks | 92% | 92% |
| STEM Play & Learn - 6 weeks | 54% | 54% |
| STEM Workshops - 1 session | 92% | 100% |

From child and parents' attendance in Virtual Robotic Coding Clubs it is evident that engaging with children and parents directly for this virtual robotic coding club had a positive impact on parental participation with 26% of parents participating compared to previous years when 0-4.9% engaged in person (ELI, 2018, 2019). Participation, however, was a challenge with the self-directed e-Learning module due to parental capacity, time and digital literacy issues. As is indicated in the results presented above, programmes that are parent directed and involve one-to-one attention to families such as the Card Challenges and STEM Play & Learn result in high levels of participation and engagement, particularly regarding parents.

Parents and children highlighted the relationships and connection, with professionals and peers as a beneficial aspect for engaging in the programmes, and for some parents was their sole contact outside the home. For one child the favourite part was *"[been] online with familiar faces, learning new things in a fun way"*. Participation in the programmes coupled with the connection with staff also encouraged engagement in further programmes: *"Thank you for thinking of my child for coding club, he really enjoyed the STEM event back in August. He has his experiment on show in his bedroom, he even brought his experiments into school for science week to show what he has done."* Finally, parents noted that the resources provided also encouraged engagement in their children.

Survey data indicated that the e-learning activities stimulated both children's and parents' interest in STEM. On being involved in helping their child learn about STEM after the activities parents participating in Virtual Coding Club (95%, n=18), Card Challenges (100%, n=7), and the STEM workshops (96%, n=27) reported an increased interest. Furthermore, data from STEM Play & Learn indicates parents engaging in home learning activities daily increased by 16-38%. Children's interest in STEM was also stimulated through the activities with children or parents reporting a greater interest in their learning STEM after Virtual Coding Club (94%, n=17), Card Challenges (100%, n=7), and the STEM workshops (66%, n=27). As the STEM workshops are individual events and not over multiple sessions it may have resulted in the lower rate of interest. It must also be noted that this was reported by parents and not by the children directly. In relation to their child's increased interest, one parent noted *"it was a new area of learning for my child. He didn't know anything about microscopes but the event really got him thinking and sparked his interest."*

Confidence in STEM was measured in children in the Virtual Robotic Coding Club. 67% (n=12) of children reported high levels of confidence in their coding skills after participating and 61% (n=11) in their computer skills. 94% (n=17) of the children also indicated that both their coding and computer skills had improved while participating in the activities. Parents also noted children's enhanced confidence and ability in qualitative responses across activities. One parent commented that their *"5 year old has had huge enjoyment from it, and his confidence to create things on his own has soared as a result of the initiative."* Parents' own confidence in supporting their child to learn STEM was also enhanced through engagement in the e-learning activities. Parents noted high levels of confidence after Virtual Coding Club (84%, n=16), e-Learning Programme (100%, n=2) and STEM Play & Learn (93%, n=14). Increasing parents' confidence and involvement through these activities can develop opportunities for children's future STEM learning (Henríquez, 2018) and potentially accelerate children's learning (Henderson & Mapp, 2002).

This study has some limitations. Firstly, as mentioned previously, ELI has been engaging with the community since 2008. Prior relationships have been established with some of the families in the study and this prior engagement may have previously influenced children and parents' interest and confidence in STEM. Additionally, these prior relationships coupled with the self-report nature of the surveys may have led to response bias.

## 5. CONCLUSION AND FUTURE WORK

This research investigated the impact of a novel, holistic STEM Family e-Learning Framework to promote family engagement with STEM e-learning. Results demonstrate that creating fun and enjoyable e-learning activities for children to engage in STEM increases interest and confidence, with children's skills in coding (94%) and interest in STEM (66% in workshops and 94% in Virtual Coding Club) improving. It is evident that building children's self-efficacy of STEM through these e-learning activities stimulates their engagement and desire to further participate in STEM (Bandura, 1997), with parents noting their children continuing the STEM activities and increased creativity, for example one parent noted *"it is a very good programme and my child is continuing what she learnt by having a weekend card game with her cousins... It is great fun for them and a great way of learning."* Upskilling parents as coaches and co-participants built their capacity as educators and increased family interest, confidence and participation in STEM. It offered rich K-6 STEM family learning opportunities through the application of skills in context but also through an apprenticeship-like enculturation into the language and norms of a particular domain. Furthermore, it is evident that engaging in an e-learning approach increases parent participation in their child's STEM learning, as can be seen in the 21% increase in parental engagement in Coding Clubs since the programme was last delivered in person. Research has shown that the teaching approach in online learning can impact on student engagement (Keane, 2013). The delivery and relationship with staff were noted in the qualitative data as factors of engagement in the e-learning activities. One parent whose child has delayed speech stated their Home Visitor *"was brilliant with working with X. She held X's attention through the virtual calls so well... He absolutely loved her and as a result of the good connection we heard more words."* This research can potentially enhance the mainstreaming and extension of STEM e-learning to disadvantaged communities. This work can be improved by exploring how territorial development action research process (Karlson and Larrea, 2014) combined with threshold theory can change STEM cultural cognitive frameworks within educationally disadvantaged communities.

## ACKNOWLEDGEMENT

This work was supported by grant 20-DP-8252 from the Science Foundation of Ireland.

## REFERENCES


Bandura, A., (1997). *Self-Efficacy: The Exercise of Control.* W. H. Freeman and Company.

Bandura, A., (2001) Social Cognitive Theory: An Agentic Perspective. *Annual Review of Psychology, 52,* 1-26. https://doi.org/10.1146/annurev.psych.52.1.1

Bleach, J., (2013). Improving Educational Aspirations and Outcomes through Community Action Research, *Educational Action Research Journal, 21*(2), 253-266.

Bleach, J., (2016). Community Action Research in Ireland: Improving Educational Outcomes through Collaboration in the Dublin Docklands. In L. Rowell, C. Bruce, J. Shosh, & M. Riel, (Eds.), *Palgrave International Handbook of Action Research* (pp. 177-188). Palgrave Macmillan.

Bray, A., Banks, J., Devitt, A. and Ní Chorcora, E., (2021). Connection before content: using multiple perspectives to examine student engagement during Covid-19 school closures in Ireland. *Irish Educational Studies*, *40*(2), 431-441.

Casad, B. J., & Jawaharlal, M., (2012). *Learning through guided discovery: an engaging approach to K-12 STEM education.* [Conference paper]. ASEE Annual Conference, San Antonio, Texas. https://peer.asee.org/21643.

Dartington Social Research Unit, (2006). *National College of Ireland Early Learning for Children in North Docklands: Report of Findings.* [Unpublished Report]. National College of Ireland.

Devitt, A., A. Bray, J. Banks, and & E. Ní Chorcora, (2020). *Teaching and Learning During School Closures: Lessons Learned. Irish Second-Level Teacher Perspectives*. Trinity College Dublin. http://hdl.handle.net/2262/92883

Duch, H. and Gennetian, L.A. (2018). Using a behavioral economics perspective to boost family engagement in the getting ready for school preschool intervention. In Caspe, M., Woods, T. A., & Kennedy, J. (Eds.). *Promising practices for engaging families in STEM learning* (pp.65-80). Information Age.

Early Learning Initiative (ELI), (2012). *Submission to the Joint Committee on Jobs, Social Protection and Education on Educational Disadvantage.* [Unpublished Report]. National College of Ireland.

Early Learning Initiative (ELI), (2018). *End of Year Report 2017/18.* National College of Ireland. https://www.ncirl.ie/Portals/0/ELI/ELI%20End%20of%20Year%20Report%202017-2018_Final.pdf?ver=2019-06-26-091433-083

Early Learning Initiative (ELI), (2019). *End of Year Report 2018/19.* National College of Ireland. https://www.ncirl.ie/Portals/0/ELI/Final%20End%20of%20Year%20Report%202018-19%20-%20Updated.pdf

Elkind, D., (2008). Forward In Bers, M.U. *Block to Robots*, Teachers College Press.

Gerde, H.K., Schachter, R.E. and Wasik, B.A., (2013). Using the scientific method to guide learning: An integrated approach to early childhood curriculum. *Early childhood education journal*, *41*(5), 315-323. https://doi.org/10.1007/s10643-013-0579-4

Gunning, A.M., Marrero, M.E. and Morell, Z., (2016). Family learning opportunities in engineering and science. *The Electronic Journal for Research in Science & Mathematics Education*, *20*(7). https://files.eric.ed.gov/fulltext/EJ1188035.pdf

Heckman, J. J., (2006). Skill Formation and the Economics of Investing in Disadvantaged Children, *Science, 312* (5782), 1900-1902. https://doi/10.1126/science.1128898.

Henderson, A.T. and Mapp, K.L., (2002). *A New Wave of Evidence: The Impact of School, Family, and Community Connections on Student Achievement. Annual Synthesis 2002.* National Center for Family & Community Connections with Schools. https://sedl.org/connections/resources/evidence.pdf

Henríquez, A. (2018). NYSCI neighbors: creating locally-driven authentic opportunities for immigrant parents in s STEM ecosystem. In Caspe, M., Woods, T. A., & Kennedy, J. (Eds.). *Promising practices for engaging families in STEM learning* (pp. 137-146). Information Age.

Karlson, K. and Larrea M., (2014) *Territorial Development and Action Research Innovation Through Dialogue*. Routledge

Keane, E., (2013). *Widening Participation in Higher Education in the Republic of Ireland.* HEFCE (Higher Education Funding Council for England).

Patrick, H., Mantzicopoulos, P, Samarapungavan, A. and French, B.F. (2008). Patterns of young children's motivation for science and teacher-child relationships. *The Journal of Experimental Education*, *76*(2), pp. 121-144. https://doi.org/10.3200/JEXE.76.2.121-144

# VTS+: A VISUAL THINKING STRATEGIES VARIANT FOR LOW-INTERACTIVITY DISTANCE LEARNING

Raymund Sison
*De La Salle University, Philippines*

**ABSTRACT**

The COVID-19 pandemic has forced governments and educational institutions around the world to look for viable alternatives to campus-based education. However, pedagogical methods such as Visual Thinking Strategies (VTS) might need to be adapted to low-interactivity distance learning environments, such as datacasting. This paper describes VTS+, a version of VTS that, in addition to asking the three VTS foundation questions, involves getting the student to iteratively write down his or her answers to the three foundation questions of VTS until no further details could be observed, and finally writing down what the visual text is communicating to the student. These innovations were designed to increase the degree of learner-self conversation and, through prolonged engagement with the teacher-selected visual text, also the degree of learner-teacher conversation. Quasi-experimental results indicate the effectiveness of VTS+ and a surprising outcome: the conciseness of final interpretations.

**KEYWORDS**

Visual Thinking Strategies, Distance Learning, Datacasting, English Language Learning.

## 1. INTRODUCTION

The COVID-19 pandemic has forced government and educational institutions around the world to shift to distance or remote teaching and learning. In developed countries, where most students have computers and Internet access at home, remote learning has largely taken place over the Internet. However, in developing countries, such as the Philippines, much of the remote teaching and learning is implemented using a paper-based approach, in which printed modules are picked up at schools by parents at the start of each quarter, and answer sheets are brought by parents to the schools at the end. Unfortunately, paper-based distance learning has several disadvantages, including unsustainability, especially when used in mass education.

Though less than one-fifth of the households in the Philippines have Internet access, more than four-fifths (83%) of the households have television (TV) sets (DICT, 2019). Through datacasting, which is the broadcasting of data over television signals, learning materials could therefore be delivered inexpensively to students in these households. Compared to the Internet, communication via datacasting might be more limited in that it is primarily one-way, but this is still better in terms of transmission speed and economies of scale than paper-based communication in traditional distance education. The use of datacasting to transmit learning materials is being examined in several United States pilots in South Carolina, Indiana, Pennsylvania (Modan, 2020) and New Mexico (Griswold, 2021).

In the Philippines, while waiting for datacasting infrastructure to be put in place, we have begun developing a framework and set of materials for distance learning via datacasting (DOST-PCIEERD, 2022). This paper focuses on the English learning materials for Grade 6, particularly the design of learning materials for visual comprehension, which is an important English competency taught from Grade 5 onwards. Specifically, the author has developed a version of Visual Thinking Strategies (VTS), called VTS+, for low-interactivity distance learning environments, such as datacasting. The rest of the paper discusses VTS, VTS+, and the pilot test results.

## 2. VISUAL THINKING STRATEGIES (VTS)

Visual Thinking Strategies (VTS) is a facilitation method for building visual literacy (Yenawine, 2013, viii). Created by Abigail Housen, a cognitive psychologist, and Philip Yenawine, a former education director of the Museum of Modern Art, VTS has become one of the most popular educational methods for viewing art in recent years, whether in museums or in schools (Ishiguro, et al., 2020).

The protocol of a VTS session involves presenting a carefully selected image, posing three specific questions, facilitating discussion, and concluding the session (Hailey, Miller, and Yenawine, 2015). The three "foundation" (Housen, 2001) questions that the VTS facilitator asks are: 'What is going on here (in this picture)?', 'What do you see that makes you say that?', and 'What more can you find?' VTS is designed to be carried out in an environment of group discovery (Housen, 2001).

The length of VTS interventions has been shown to correlate not only with aesthetic development, for which it was designed, but also with the development of elementary students' critical thinking skills, which transferred from art images to science artifacts (Housen, 2001). It has also been shown to correlate with improvements in medical image interpretation skills of medical and nursing students (see Hailey, Miller, and Yenawine, 2015). More recently, the use of VTS is being explored in fields other than the humanities and healthcare, such as engineering (Campbell, et al., 2021) and leadership (Kakim and Priest, 2020).

## 3. VTS+

As mentioned earlier, datacasting provides a way to deliver distance education in areas with low Internet penetration but high TV penetration. However, the technology-mediated communication in datacasting is primarily *one-way*, from the teacher to the learner. Pedagogical methods such as VTS, which require a great deal of learner-teacher and learner-peer interaction, will therefore need to be adapted for use in low-interactivity distance learning environments, such as those that rely on datacasting.

In the learning materials that the author has designed, VTS is used as the framework for teaching visual comprehension in Grade 6 English, in which images are considered as texts to be "read" or interpreted. Therefore, in their English lessons, students not only "read" paintings, but also diagrams, editorial cartoons, infographics, visual narratives, traffic signs, maps, and other visual images.

In the author's adaptation of VTS, called VTS+, students are shown a picture on their TV or similar device and then asked to fill out a VTS+ Table, shown in Table 1. The first three questions in the VTS+ Table are the same three foundation questions in (Housen, 2001). To compensate for the low degree of learner-teacher conversation inherent in datacasting, the author added a fourth question, which involves the student's *iteratively* asking himself or herself the first three questions until he or she could no longer find anything new in the visual text.

Table 1. VTS+ Table

| Question | Your Answer |
|---|---|
| 1. What is going on in this picture? | |
| 2. What do you see that made you say that? | |
| 3. What more can you find? | |
| 4. Repeat steps 1-3 until you could not find anything else. How many times did you repeat steps 1-3? | |
| 5. What is the picture saying to you? | |

The addition of this fourth question has two benefits. First, it increases the degree of learner-self (L-S) conversation in distance learning (Sison, 2003). L-S conversation involves implicitly or explicitly developing, executing, and/or monitoring a learning plan, no matter how small, partial, or tentative it is, and reflecting on one's learning. L-S conversation is related to self-regulated learning (SRL) (Zimmerman, 2005), which has been associated with improvements in students' academic performance as well as strategic behavior and motivation at the primary (e.g., Dignath et al., 2008), secondary (Dignath and Buettner, 2009), and tertiary education levels (Theobald, 2021). L-S conversations are arguably as important to the learning process as learner-teacher (L-T) and learner-peer (L-P) conversations, especially in distance learning. Second, it lengthens the student's engagement with the visual text. If we view the visual text that the teacher has selected or created as a complex message (Sison, 2003) from the teacher to the learner, then increasing engagement with that text can be viewed as also strengthening the L-T conversation.

The author also added a fifth question, 'What is the picture saying to you?' which is similar to the first question, but framed in a more personal way. This not only enables the student to provide an overall interpretation of the visual text after performing an iterative analysis of it, but also enables the student to compare her final interpretation of the visual text against her initial impression of it, possibly triggering self-satisfaction reactions (Zimmerman, 2005) as she realizes how her efforts resulted in new discoveries about the text leading to a final interpretation that is better than the first. The fifth question's being framed in a personal way also paves the way for further analysis of persuasive visual texts, such as editorial cartoons.

# 4. RESEARCH METHOD, RESULTS, AND DISCUSSION

The learning materials were piloted with a group of volunteer students from the De La Salle University - Integrated School (DLSU-IS). Specifically, these were Grade 5 students who were taking Grade 6 lessons in science and mathematics (on top of their Grade 5 lessons in these subjects). Prior to their participation, we obtained the students' assent and their parents' consent using assent and consent forms. We also obtained permission from the school principal. A pretest and a posttest were then administered before and after the students took four lessons on interpreting visual texts (Lesson 1: Formal Elements of Visual Texts; Lesson 2: Symbols in Visual Texts; Lesson 3: Visual Texts as Narratives; and Lesson 4: Making Connections with Visual Texts). Each lesson is essentially a sequence of lesson presentation-worksheet activity pairs; that is, a lesson is composed of mini-lessons, at the end of each of which is a worksheet activity. Each worksheet activity includes writing down answers to questions (such as the VTS+ questions in Table 1) on an answer sheet. The VTS+ Table was explicitly taught in Lessons 3 and 4, but VTS+ questions 1 and 2 in Table 1 were introduced in Lessons 1 and 2.

Because the datacasting facilities are not yet in place, datacasting was simulated by uploading the learning materials to a shared Google Drive every Monday morning, which students would then download to their devices via the Internet. Nevertheless, the learning materials have been tested and found transmissible via the prototype datacasting setup of the project's partner agency (DOST-ASTI). No other lesson-related communications with the students were performed, in keeping with the limitations of datacasting technology. The students would then email photos of their answer sheets every Friday. The pre- and posttests were administered via Google Forms.

Though there were 13 students who took the pretest, only five were able to take the posttest and all the four lessons on visual comprehension. Part 1 of the pretest/posttest involved interpreting five images. Part 2 involved making connections between five images and one's background knowledge. Neither the pretest nor the posttest required the students to use VTS+ to interpret the images. The students' Part 1 pretest and posttest scores for completeness and accuracy are shown in Table 2. Completeness is measured as the number of salient details in a student's answer; accuracy is measured as the number of details in a student's answer that are correct.

Table 2. Pretest and posttest scores of student participants

| Student ID | Pretest Score | Posttest Score |
|---|---|---|
| S01 | 11 | 12 |
| S05 | 9 | 11 |
| S08 | 9 | 14 |
| S12 | 7 | 7 |
| S13 | 6 | 6 |
| Average | 8.4 | 10 |

As Table 2 shows, there was a 19% increase in the average student score after the participants took our lessons, where they used VTS+. This increase is significant at alpha=0.1, test statistic=0, using the Wilcoxon Rank Test.

Surprisingly, the author also noticed while doing qualitative analysis that the students' posttest answers were more concise. For example, here is S05's pretest interpretation of a diagram of the life cycle of a butterfly:

> *What I see in this picture is how a butterfly is made. Its like its life circle. Because it is indeed the life cycle of a butterfly.*

Here is the same student's posttest answer:

> *This is a life cycle of a butterfly. It represents how a caterpillar transforms to a butterfly.*

It will be noted that not only is the posttest answer less verbose; it also contains an additional detail (caterpillar). Table 3 shows the number of words used by the participants in their pretest and posttest answers.

Table 3. Number of words used in pretest and posttest answers

| Student ID | Pretest Answer Length | Posttest Answer Length |
|---|---|---|
| S01 | 85 | 74 |
| S05 | 105 | 55 |
| S08 | 54 | 45 |
| S12 | 28 | 17 |
| S13 | 13 | 9 |
| Average | 57 | 40 |

As Table 3 shows, there was 30% decrease in the average answer length after the participants took our lessons, where they used VTS+. This decrease is significant at alpha=0.1, test statistic=0, using the Wilcoxon Rank Test.

Conciseness is, of course, not just a matter of using less words. However, if a decrease in answer length is accompanied by an increase in the completeness and accuracy of these same answers, then the answers might indeed be more concise. The author was surprised by this result because nowhere in any of the four lessons were the students told to use less words or to be more concise in their interpretations. In fact, the VTS+ protocol, which asks the students to iteratively do steps 1-3, i.e., iteratively observe and interpret an image, would cause students to generate more words as they observe more details in an image. However, it could be that step 5 of VTS+, coming at the end of a potentially exhausting series of iterations of steps 1-3, taught the students to produce a final interpretation of an image that not only synthesizes all their observations and intermediate interpretations, but also one that does so efficiently.

# 5. CONCLUSION AND FURTHER WORK

The COVID-19 pandemic has forced governments and educational institutions to look for viable alternatives to campus-based or in-person education, such as distance learning via datacasting. This paper described VTS+, a version of VTS adapted to a low-interactivity distance learning environment, particularly datacasting. The adaptation involves getting the student to iteratively write down his or her answers to the three VTS foundation questions until no further details could be observed, and writing down what the visual text is communicating to the student. These were designed to increase the degree of learner-self conversation and, through prolonged engagement with the teacher-selected visual text, also the degree of learner-teacher conversation.

Pilot-test results showed that posttest interpretations of images were more complete, accurate, and concise than pretest interpretations, indicating that VTS+ might be effective. However, further studies are needed because the sample size of the pilot is small and the students in the pilot test might have above-average intelligence or SRL skills. There are plans underway to do a second pilot run of the lessons at a public elementary school in the new academic year, during which the author also plans to revise the first two lessons on visual comprehension to explicit teach VTS+, thereby increasing exposure of the students to VTS+. As noted earlier, the length of VTS interventions has been shown to correlate with image interpretation skills. It will also be interesting to unpack the VTS+ innovations to determine whether improvements in performance indicators are due to the increased degree of learner-self conversation or the student's increased engagement with the teacher's selected visual text, which in turn can be viewed as an increased degree of learner-teacher conversation.

## ACKNOWLEDGEMENT

This study is part of a project titled "Development of Framework and Materials for Distance and Remote Learning via Datacasting," funded by the Department of Science and Technology - Philippine Council for Industry, Energy, and Emerging Technology Research and Development (DOST-PCIEERD) of the Philippines, and De La Salle University. The author also wishes to acknowledge the members of the project team, especially Ryan Dimaunahan and his subteam of instructional technologists, and Honeylen Libunao, who wrote one of the four lessons on interpreting visual texts based on the author's framework, and administered the four lessons and two tests to the volunteer students.

## REFERENCES

Campbell, et al., 2021. Visual Thinking Strategies (VTS) for Promoting Reflection in Engineering Education: Graduate Student Perceptions. *Proceedings of the 2021 ASEE Annual Conference,* Virtual Meeting.

DICT, 2019. National ICT Household Survey Results. Department of Information and Communication Technology, Philippines.

Dignath, C., & Buettner, G., 2018. Components of fostering self-regulated learning among students: A meta-analysis on intervention studies at primary and secondary school level. *Metacognitive Learning*, Vol. 3, pp 231-264.

Dignath, C., Buettner, G., & Langfeldt, H., 2008. How can primary school students learn self-regulated learning strategies most effectively? A meta-analysis on self-regulation training programmes. *Educational Research Review*, Vol. 3, pp 101-129.

DOST-PCIEERD, 2022. Development of Framework and Materials for Distance and Remote Learning via Datacasting. [Online] Available from: https://www.youtube.com/watch?v=0IajMHrrDOw [Accessed 20th June 2022].

Griswold, S., 2021. New Mexico PBS to Broadcast Educational Materials to 100 Students' Computers. Source NM. [Online] Available from: https://sourcenm.com/2021/10/21/new-mexico-pbs-to-broadcast-educational-materials-to-100-students-computers/ [Accessed 20th June 2022]

Hailey, D., et al., 2015. Understanding Visual Literacy: The Visual Thinking Strategies Approach. In Baylen, D., et al. (Eds.), *Essentials of Teaching and Integrating Visual and Media Literacy.* Springer, Switzerland.

Housen, A. 2001. Aesthetic Thought, Critical Thinking, and Transfer. *Arts and Learning Journal*, Vol. 18, No. 1, pp 99-131.

Ishiguro, C., et al., 2020. Comparing Effects of Visual Thinking Strategies in a Classroom and a Museum. *Psychology of Aesthetics, Creativity, and the Arts*, Vol. 15, No. 4, pp. 735-745.

Kakim, S., et al., 2020. Developing Leadership Capacity Using Visual Thinking Strategies. *Journal of Leadership Education,* Vol. 19, No. 3.

Modan, N., 2020. States Invest in Datacasting to Bridge the K-12 Divide. *Education Dive.*

Sison, R., 2003. A Conversational Model of Online Learning. *International Journal of Continuing Engineering Education and Lifelong Learning*, Vol. 13, Nos. 3/4, pp 336-349.

Theobald, M., 2021. Self-regulated learning training programs enhance university students' academic performance, self-regulated learning strategies, and motivation: A meta-analysis. *Contemporary Educational Psychology*, 101976.

Yenawine, P., 2013. *Visual Thinking Strategies: Using Art to Deepen Learning Across School Disciplines*. Harvard Education Press, Massachusetts, USA.

Zimmerman, B., 2005. Attaining Self-Regulation: A Social Cognitive Perspective. In Boekaerts, M., et al. (Eds.), *Handbook of Self-Regulation.* Elsevier.

# DESIGNING A PEER-MEDIATION SERIOUS GAME

Nikolaos Kiriazis[1] and Thanasis Hadzilacos[1,2]
[1]*Open University of Cyprus, Cyprus*
[2]*The Cyprus Institute, Cyprus*

**ABSTRACT**

Peer-mediation in a school environment, when carried out correctly, can benefit not only the parties of the conflict, but also their environment, including the school, the team, the family and the mediator. A serious same has been designed and a prototype developed for the training of minors and young adults as mediators. The core of the game is a simulation of mediation dialogues in which the trainee mediator is presented with choices of action along a conflict story. These choices affect the development of three variables that are instrumental to the mediation outcome: they are the trust of each party to the mediator, their feeling of anger about the conflict, and the validity of the information that the mediator gathers about the conflict.

**KEYWORDS**

Peer-Mediation, Mechanism, Trust, Anger, Information, Serious Game.

## 1. INTRODUCTION

The contribution of this paper is to present a framework of standards, on the basis of which micro-scenarios will be developed in a Serious Game (SG). The SG to be developed is aiming to educate and evaluate minors as mediators in conflicts that take place in the digital world.

Many definitions have been formulated for SGs and many gather common elements, such as those described as "*interactive computer applications*" and more specifically "*virtual game simulation*", which emphasize their dual role, educational and recreational (Mestadi et al., 2018).

There are several ways to resolve disputes (ADR: Alternative Dispute Resolution), such as negotiation where the parties in conflict negotiate with each other, arbitration where a third party decides (on behalf of) the parties in conflict, mediation where a third party facilitates the solution, as well as combinations of the above, and so on (Menkel-Meadow, 2015). Mediation has a wide scope (Condette, 2020), as it resolves conflicts concerning the workplace, the business field, States (Hartmann-Piraudeau, 2022), school (Artinopoulou, 2010) etc. Peer-mediation or School-based mediation is observed practised between peers, where the parties in conflict and the mediator are minors. Peer mediation training is provided through mediation programs. However, it does not have to be part of the school curriculum (Artinopoulou, 2010).

Conflicts between peers, such as classmates, friends or strangers, are largely unavoidable in adolescence and the treatment of these challenges varies, sometimes with a restorative action neutralizer (e.g. humour, a distraction etc.) and sometimes seeking resolution through demonstrations of resentment, outbursts, arguments, and even the use of physical force. The challenges of conflict faced by young people in the real world can also be addressed in the digital world (Novin et al., 2018).

## 2. MICRO-SCENARIOS IN MEDIATION

Different mediation models (e.g. Facilitative mediation, e-Mediation, court-mandated Mediation) are identified in the literature, which differ from each other according to various criteria (e.g. the scope, the number of intermediaries, the nature of the argument, the type of relationship) and the "best" model is what adapts and / or what combines models to meet the conflict needs. According to the type of the parties' relationship, there are at least two different models of mediation: the direct one, where the parties are met together with the mediator, and the indirect model where the mediator meets each of the parties separately, in order to talk about the conflict and find potential solutions (Lohvinenko et al., 2021). Despite the existence of numerous studies related to factor for effective mediation training programs, there is no agreement on what these programs should include (Devinatz, 2018). One of the ingredients is the experiential activities with which mediators are practised, such as role play, analysis of case studies, supervised practice, etc. (Gentry, 1992). The simulation of mediation is made by case studies and role play studies, where the trainers give feedback to the mediator to be enhancing his understanding and choices (Walker, 1988).

SG, which is planned to be developed in the future, consists of 4 roles, the mediator, the two conflicting parts and the narrator. The player has the role of the mediator, who interacts with both parts of the conflict and the narrator provides information to the player.

More specifically, the narrator gives information to the player to create a "tactic" scenario scene. The information of the narrator may be the time of the conflict, the allegations of the involved parties, the previous actions of the mediator, the previous actions of the two parties, etc. That is, the narrator is responsible for presenting the situation in which mediation is located before the player takes on a role in the game. In addition, the narrator gives feedback to the player after completing their actions in mediation.

The player carries out individual-private sessions with parts of the conflict and if the result of these sessions allows, then the group session is carried out with a view to resolving the conflict by reaching an agreement between the parties.

The above brief descriptive interaction of the roles of SG mediation are similar to the education/training of the chess players with screenshots of chess games. In these snapshots the pawns in the Chess Board are depicted, while the moves the pawns have previously taken, are unknown to the player when asked to play. This type of workout is called "tactics", a subject which is broadly researched in the literature (Petrovic & Koprivica, 2014). The chess player is asked to play so as to achieve a specific goal (e.g. to attack Queen) with a specific number of movements (e.g. with 2 movements) (Lane & Chang, 2018). Mediation micro-scenarios, which are to be developed for the game are like to the Chess Tactics scenarios.

## 2.1 The Mechanism in Peer-Mediation Serious Game

Various models have been proposed, describing "mechanisms" in SGs, such as MDA (Mechanics, Dynamics, Aesthetics), where engineering refers to actions, behaviors and control mechanisms (e.g. bluff, bet) (Wigdor & Wixon, 2011), while the player understands the mechanisms in the game as "rules" (Pendleton & Okolica, 2019), the Game Experience Model, which refers to actions by objects of the game for various situations (e.g. Interactive storytelling) (Suovuo et al., 2020). This section describes the mechanism, which will be used to manage "actions" in mediation.

At the beginning of the mediator's session with one part of the conflict, the narrator informs with evidence describing the "regular" scene of the scenario. In the dendrogram of Image 1 the player is located at the Node1.

The player has two options, either to choose Acme-1.1, leading to Node-1.1 or to select Acme-1.2, leading to Node-1.2. The acmes describe to the player the acts, which can be carried out at every session with the party of the conflict. At the node that the player is driven, he/she can see the results that his/her choice of acme has caused in the party of the conflict. In the same way, from the new Node the player is located, they chooses a new acne from the two that are at his disposal, so as to be taken to the next new Node, which is the final one for the session. As the player is on one of the final Nodes, the narrator provides feedback.

Subsequently, the player proceeds to the 2nd session with the second part of the conflict, which takes place in the same way as the first. Finally, after the completion of the 2nd session, the player proceeds to the group session with both parts of the conflict.

The result of the 1st individual session with the first part of the conflict will judge whether to allow the player to proceed to the 2nd individual session with the second part. The results at 4 final nodes either approve or reject access to the next session. Rejection means that mediation stops while approval does not mean that the conflict is result. For the mechanism, "results" means an influence of variables, which is Trust, Anger and Information.

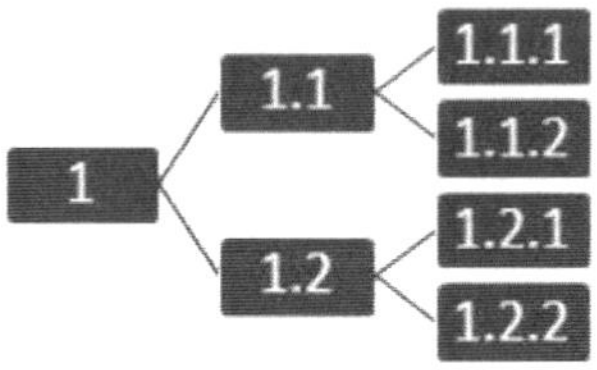


Figure 1. Evolution of the session in a "tactic" scene of mediation

It was reported that the "result" of a session will determine the access to the next session, whether it is going to be done with the 2nd part of the conflict, whether it is the group session. The result arises from the prices of variables, "Trust", "Anger" and "Information", which are in the mechanism.

Trust is a key factor in creating a conflict but equally important for its resolution. The appeal of the parts of the conflict to a mediator takes place because confidence has been disturbed (Stimec & Poitras, 2009). In mediation, the parties utilize the mediator's confidence as the means for achieving cooperative benefits between them. The mediator seeks to create a level of confidence, as it is necessary for a successful mediation (Mcgovern, 2016). Since mutual descriptions often occur in mediation, the mediator must be cautious, listen to the parties' information but also keep they reasonable doubts about their accuracy (Stulberg & Love, 2013). Understanding emotions is a regulatory factor in the process of mediation, as emotions affect but are also affected by the conflict. The feeling is not central in all contexts of mediation (e.g. interpersonal, international), but when this is central, the mediator also takes care of the emotions of the conflicting parties, comprehension and impacts (Jones & Bodtker, 2001). There are numerous and extensive studies on emotions, some more and some less complicated (Strongman, 2003), in which disagreement is found in the number of emotions, but most of them include the feeling of anger. (Gu et al., 2019) Regarding "Anger", there is no commonly accepted definition, but scholars, who examine the negotiations, the causes of anger, indicatively report the Low-Power position, promises, time pressure, feeling of mistreatment, etc. (Hunsaker, 2017).

The "Trust" variable in the mechanism is influenced by the factors that the Trustor's factors of perceived trustworthiness is discerned by the Trustee. These factors are Ability, Benevolence and Integrity. Ability is summarized as the group of skills and characteristics, which can affect specific areas, such as special knowledge / specialization (e.g. explanatory in the process, advise, focuses on finding solutions, etc.). Benevolence is a positive orientation, where for Trustee is believed to want to do good for Trustor, without any profit incentives for them (e.g. the parties to feel comfortable, courtesy, the instinct of the parties for trust by the beginning etc.). Integrity is the practice of being honest, sincere and display solid ethics, such as Trustor's belief that Trustee is fair and that his/her words coincide with his/her acts (e.g. impartiality, respect, right to choose without enforcement, etc.) (Mayer et al., 1995; Poitras, 2009).

The variables of the mechanism can take integer values 0 to 5. When Trust = 0, the part of the conflict has no confidence in the mediator. When Trust = 5, the part of the conflict has absolute confidence in the mediator. When Anger = 0, the part of the conflict is not exhausted by the feeling of anger. When Anger = 5, the part of the conflict has a strong anger. When the player selects acne seeking to collect information from the parts, the variable value is increased. As the mediator retains his doubts about the accuracy of the information, this is reflected in the difference between the information between the parties. If the difference in variable information values for the two parties is 0, then at the group session, resolving the conflict problem can be accepted by the parties. If the difference is 5, then the effort to resolve will fail, as the solution will not satisfy any place. However, the combination of variables may not allow acceptance of the collision solution, such as if Trust = 0 and Information = 5, the part of the conflict will reject the solution, as if Anger = 5 and Information = 5, the part of the conflict will leave mediation.

However, there is also the information collected by the mediator from which he could ascertain a misunderstanding either of the intention or the event, which is attributed to the erroneous communication channel and / or the incorrect encoding / decoding of the messages (e.g. by increased tone voice, misunderstanding when processing the message, unclear message of the transmitter) (Edwards et al., 2017). In addition, it can be found from the information that the dispute does not matter to the parties. In these cases, the difference in value of the variable remains great, but it is permissible to resolve misunderstanding rather than dispute.

To understand the functioning of the mechanism, the following example is listed and then commented. The node includes 3 "Trust, Anger, Information" variables. Let the player start at the 1st session with the 1st part of the conflict.

Table 1

| Session with the 1st part of the conflict conferences | | |
|---|---|---|
| Narrator: *X mentions that Y publishes snapshots of the game in social media, of his worst moments of the game.* | | |
| Node | Acmes | Nodes |
| Node Number: 1<br>1,4,1 | Acme Number: 1.1<br>You make clarifying questions like: In which social media groups does he publish? Does this also happen to other members of your social group? (Trust through Ability +) (Information +) | Node Number: 1.1<br>2,4,2 |
| | Acme Number: 1.2<br>You ask him about his feelings. When discussing with him, you explain to him that anger is possibly caused by distress, injustice, etc. Moreover, you make clear to him/her that resolving the problem and restoring the relationship will create happy feelings (Anger -). You ask if this is also happening to other teammates, that is snapshots of their bad moments in the game to be published without their permission. (Information +) | Node Number: 1.2<br>1,3,2 |

Annotations: The narrator gives information to put the player into a conflict problem. The player starts the session with X and knows that the variables for trust, anger, information is 1, 4 and 1 respectively. His/her two options, Acme-1.1 and Acme-1.2. The choice that the player will make will alter trust prices, anger, information and go to the next node. In the new node that the player will go, either at Node-1.1 or Node-1.2, will be invited to make a new choice in order to go to a following node, and so on.

## 3. DISCUSSION AND FUTURE WORKS

The aim of this paper is the presentation of a Framework of Standards. According to this, a number of micro-scenarios will be written which will meet the specifications mentioned. The purpose of the mechanism designed is to manage the micro-scenarios, which will be included in SG. Our next objective to carry out studies to determine the number of the micro-scenarios required for SG, designed / developed SG, to be given to the final users, and then to record SG results aimed at the training and evaluation of minor mediators in the conflicts of the digital world.

## REFERENCES


Artinopoulou, V. (2010). *I sholiki diamesolavisi: Ekpedevondas tous mathites sti diahirisi tis vias ke tou ekfovismou [School Mediation: Training pupils in dealing with violence and bullying]*. Nomiki Bibliothiki.

Condette, S. (2020). *The Contribution of Peer Mediation to the Implementation of Human Rights Education* (pp. 159–172). https://doi.org/10.1007/978-94-024-1913-9_8

Devinatz, V. G. (2018). What Makes a Good Mediator? Insights from a Mediation Training Program Participant. *Employee Responsibilities and Rights Journal*, *30*(3), 181–201. https://doi.org/10.1007/s10672-018-9315-y

Edwards, R., Bybee, B. T., Frost, J. K., Harvey, A. J., & Navarro, M. (2017). That's Not What I Meant: How Misunderstanding Is Related to Channel and Perspective-Taking. *Journal of Language and Social Psychology*, *36*(2), 188–210. https://doi.org/10.1177/0261927X16662968

Gentry, D. B. (1992). Using computer aided interactive video technology to provide experiential learning for mediation trainees. *Journal of Divorce and Remarriage*, *17*(3–4), 57–74. https://doi.org/10.1300/J087v17n03_04

Gu, S., Wang, F., Patel, N. P., Bourgeois, J. A., & Huang, J. H. (2019). A model for basic emotions using observations of behavior in Drosophila. *Frontiers in Psychology*, *10*(APR), 1–13. https://doi.org/10.3389/fpsyg.2019.00781

Hartmann-Piraudeau, A. (2022). Mediation. In *Mediators in the Leading Role - Understanding and Actively Managing Mediation* (pp. 1–15). Springer Fachmedien Wiesbaden. https://doi.org/10.1007/978-3-658-36253-9_1

Hunsaker, D. A. (2017). *Anger in Negotiations: A Review of Causes, Effects, and Unanswered Questions*.

Jones, T. S., & Bodtker, A. (2001). Mediating with heart in mind: Addressing emotion in mediation practice. *Negotiation Journal*, *17*(3), 207–244. https://doi.org/10.1023/A:1013283710190

Lane, D. M., & Chang, Y. H. A. (2018). Chess knowledge predicts chess memory even after controlling for chess experience: Evidence for the role of high-level processes. *Memory and Cognition*, *46*(3), 337–348. https://doi.org/10.3758/s13421-017-0768-2

Lohvinenko, M., Starynskyi, M., Rudenko, L., & Kordunian, I. (2021). Models of mediation: Theoretical and legal analysis. *Conflict Resolution Quarterly*, *39*(1), 51–65. https://doi.org/10.1002/crq.21315

Mayer, R. C., Davis, J. H., & Schoorman, F. D. (1995). An Integrative Model of Organizational Trust. *The Academy of Management Review*, *20*(3), 709–734. https://doi.org/10.2307/258792

Mcgovern, F. E. (2016). Trust and the SRBA mediation. *Idaho Law Review*, *52*, 335–340. https://scholarship.law.duke.edu/cgi/viewcontent.cgi?article=6374&context=faculty_scholarship

Menkel-Meadow, C. J. (2015). Mediation, Arbitration, and Alternative Dispute Resolution (ADR). *International Encyclopedia of the Social & Behavioral Sciences: Second Edition*, 70–74. https://doi.org/10.1016/B978-0-08-097086-8.86083-3

Mestadi, W., Nafil, K., Touahni, R., & Messoussi, R. (2018). An Assessment of Serious Games Technology: Toward an Architecture for Serious Games Design. *International Journal of Computer Games Technology*, *2018*. https://doi.org/10.1155/2018/9834565

Novin, S., Bos, M. G. N., Stevenson, C. E., & Rieffe, C. (2018). Adolescents' responses to online peer conflict: How self-evaluation and ethnicity matter. *Infant and Child Development*, *27*(2). https://doi.org/10.1002/icd.2067

Pendleton, A., & Okolica, J. (2019). Creating serious games with the game design matrix. In *Lecture Notes in Computer Science (including subseries Lecture Notes in Artificial Intelligence and Lecture Notes in Bioinformatics): Vol. 11899 LNCS*. Springer International Publishing. https://doi.org/10.1007/978-3-030-34350-7_51

Petrovic, A., & Koprivica, V. J. (2014). *Tactics Factors in Chess: Theoretical-Empirical Aspects*. https://www.researchgate.net/publication/339253534

Poitras, J. (2009). What makes parties trust mediators? *Negotiation Journal*, *25*(3), 307–325. https://doi.org/10.1111/j.1571-9979.2009.00228.x

Stimec, A., & Poitras, J. (2009). Building trust with parties: Are mediators overdoing it? *Conflict Resolution Quarterly*, *26*(3), 317–331. https://doi.org/10.1002/crq.235

Strongman, K. (2003). *The Psychology of Emotion* (Fifth). John Wiley & Sons Ltd.

Stulberg, J., & Love, L. (2013). *The Middle Voice : Mediating Conflict Successfully* (2nd ed.). Carolina Academic Press.

Suovuo, T. "bgt," Skult, N., Joelsson, T. N., Skult, P., Ravyse, W., & Smed, J. (2020). *The Game Experience Model (GEM)*. 183–205. https://doi.org/10.1007/978-3-030-37643-7_8

Walker, G. B. (1988). Training mediators: Teaching about ethical concerns and obligations. *Mediation Quarterly*, *1988*(19), 33–42. https://doi.org/https://doi.org/10.1002/crq.39019881906

Wigdor, D., & Wixon, D. (2011). Mechanics, Dynamics, and Aesthetics. *Brave NUI World*, 107–114. https://doi.org/10.1016/b978-0-12-382231-4.00016-2

# GENERATING GLOBAL MODEL TO PREDICT STUDENTS' DROPOUT IN MOROCCAN HIGHER EDUCATIONAL INSTITUTIONS USING CLUSTERING

Khalid Oqaidi[1], Sarah Aouhassi[2] and Khalifa Mansouri[1]
[1]*Laboratory SSDIA ENSET of Mohammedia University Hassan II of Casablanca, Mohammedia, Morocco*
[2]*Laboratory SSDIA ENSAD University Hassan II of Casablanca, Mohammedia, Morocco*

**ABSTRACT**

The dropout of students is one of the major obstacles that ruin the improvement of higher education quality. To facilitate the study of students' dropout in Moroccan universities, this paper aims to establish a clustering approach model based on machine learning algorithms to determine Moroccan universities categories. Our objective in this article is to present a theoretical model capable of identifying higher education institutions that are similar in the dropout phenomenon. To avoid making Educational Data Mining Analysis on each higher educational programs predict students' performance, with such a classification we can reduce the number of studies to be done on one institution in each category of universities.

**KEYWORDS**

Students' Dropout, Higher Education, Machine Learning Prediction, Clustering.

## 1. INTRODUCTION

Students' dropout of higher educational institutions is an issue that gets more attention from the decision makers in the last years. In Morocco this problem is blatant especially in open access universities. The most common way to try to solve this problem is to predict students' dropout using machine learning. The prediction of "at risk students" allows the decision makers to take early actions before the abandonment. The problem that researchers face is that every dropout prediction study is different from other similar studies even in the same country or in the same university, which make it hard to an institution to benefit from other institutions actions. In this article we develop a global model that will automatically generate the best machine learning algorithm in dropout prediction our main contribution is providing a global model that will reduce time and give best results in higher educational dropout prediction in Moroccan institutions.

In section II we present recent related works that concentrate on higher educational dropout using machine learning algorithms and specifically clustering algorithms, in section III we comment these works and show that lacking points that lead to our contribution, in section IV we present our model, and in the section V we conclude with a summary and perspectives of our work.

## 2. RELATED WORKS

### 2.1 Moroccan Context

Students' dropout is one of the biggest problems that face the higher education in the world. In Morocco this issue is present by force, especially in open access institutions. In the report of (Higher Council of Education, Training and Scientific Research, 2018) it is stated that more than one quarter of bachelor students drop out only in their first year at the university.

We noticed the lack of a global model to predict students' dropout prediction using machine learning algorithms, and the need of grouping higher education institutions into groups depending on their dropout nature.

## 2.2 Surveys and Synthetic Studies

In (Kumar, 2017) the authors analyze different contributions of students' dropout prediction in India between 2009 and 2016, and present the results in a survey. They conclude that there are four Educational Data Mining categories: Classification, Clustering, Prediction and Association Rule mining. The most used machine learning classifiers are: Support Vector Machine, Decision Tree algorithms, Artificial Neural Networks, Logistic Regression, Naïve Bayes and Random Forest.

In a systematic literature done on 67 papers selected from 1681 ones the authors in (Alban, 2019) identified the techniques used in the literature to realize data pre-processing, the factors affecting the dropout, the techniques used to select these factors, the techniques used for prediction, their levels of reliability and the tools used.

A detailed review of 12 studies in educational data mining that use clustering algorithms is presented in (Dutt, 2015). The goal is to compare these studies according to their objectives, their algorithms, and their sources of data.

To classify students into natural groups depending on their characteristics, a review of clustering in (Iam-On, 2017) helped to develop a use case as practical guideline to facilitate detecting students at risk of dropping out.

Studying dropout in 160 Tunisian higher education institutions between 2013 and 2018 (Srairi, 2022) revealed the importance of contextual factors such as university accommodation in helping students to complete university education.

## 2.3 Use Cases

The authors in (Manrique, 2019) classified the representations of students into Global Features-Based, Local Features-Based and Time Series with the appropriate learning algorithm for each of them. The best approach to predict the dropout was the Local Feature.

To evaluate the efficiency of higher education institutions dropout in Brazilian universities, the authors in (Marilia, 2020) provide a comparative analysis between the three combined models in the first side: K-Means with Linear Regression, K-Means with Robust Regression, and K-Means with Support Vector Regression and the classic algorithms in the other side: Support Vector Regression, Bagging, Linear Regression, and Robust regression in the other side. The combined models gave satisfactory results in comparison with classic algorithms.

Another case study that uses clustering and decision tree in higher educational data mining is described in (Križanić, 2020). The clusters are selected here according to their similarities in learning behaviors.

The authors in (Kabók, 2017) study competiveness in higher education institution by clustering analysis to come up with groups of countries that share some similarities in this subject.

Making the Tinto's model (1973) operational in a way that it could be implemented by universities as an academic computational support system for predicting dropouts is the subject of (Nicoletti, 2019).

To detect students at risk of dropping out in German universities an Early Detection System (EDS) was developed in (Berens, 2019) by predicting their performance in an early stage using AdaBoost.

Our Model is divided in two parts: A clustering study of the higher education institutions based on institutional data "Figure 1", and a machine learning prediction study using students' data "Figure 2".

# 3. GLOBAL MODEL TO PREDICT STUDENTS' DROPOUT

Every higher education institution has its particular characteristics different from other institutions. There are differences relative to the programs, the students' background, the enrollment conditions, the administrative data, and the academic staff etc. That's why there are almost as many dropout prediction studies as the number of institutions. In our work we propose a model that brings together all dropout prediction use cases in one study.

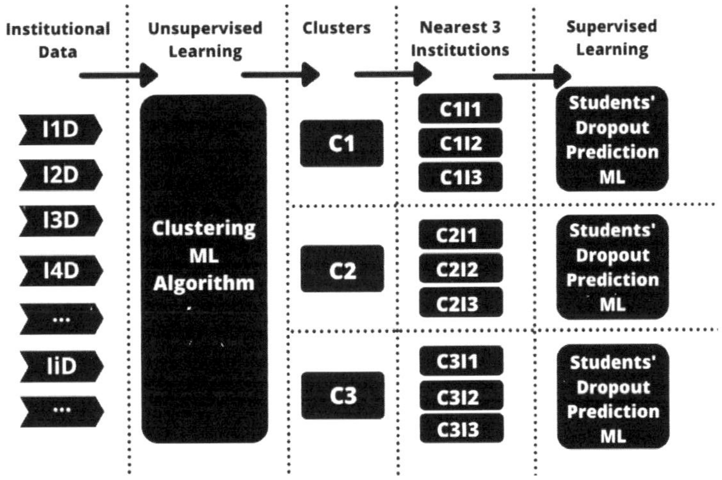


Figure 1. Identification of the nearest 3 institutions to the clusters' centers using the data of the institutions

## 3.1 Clustering the Higher Education Institutions

The goal of this step "Figure 1" is to come up with reduced number of clusters and figure out the best predicting algorithm of each cluster.

- First, we fit the machine learning algorithm with Data of the Institution j (IjD): information about the institution only. We gather all the available features such as: End degree, Start year, End year, Degree, Certified program, Start course date, End course date, Study program of enrollment, School shift, Pupil classroom ratio, Pupil teacher ratio etc. We can add all the details about the institutions that we can get access to.
- Then we use unsupervised machine learning algorithm to obtain institutions grouped by similarities.

We use the most frequent clustering machine learning algorithm in the literature: The K-Means Clustering (Mannor, 2011). We need to determine groups of institutions knowing only the dependent quantitative variables that concern the institutions. The qualitative variables must be converted to fit the model.

The first step is to choose a number of groups of institutions, and a number of arbitrary centers (institutions that represent the group) of the groups to initiate the algorithm. The algorithm decides for each center the closest institutions to build a cluster around. In each cluster the algorithm recalculates the distances to update the centers (it may be the Euclidian distance using the features' values). Now we repeat the process since we have new centers to redistribute the institutions on the clusters, so we update the institutions that belong each cluster. We obtain the same number of clusters, but this time they contain different institutions.

- Given one cluster i (Ci), we take three nearest institutions CiIj ($CiI_1$, $CiI_2$ and $CiI_3$) to the center of the cluster i. If the center itself is an institution we add two others, if it is fictive we add three.

## 3.2 The Best Machine Learning Algorithm per Cluster

- We use now supervised machine learning to predict the students' dropout in each CiIj "Figure 1".

To do so we gather all the students' data CiIjSD "Fig. 2" and we fit the most used machine learning algorithms in dropout prediction: Linear Regression, Decision Tree, Random Forest, Artificial Neural Networks, k Nearest Neighbors, Support Vector machine, and Naïve Bayes. Through the evaluation metrics in we sort the algorithms according to their performance; we retain the first one CiIjA.

- For each cluster we combine the three best algorithms CiIjA with AdaBoost as in (Berens, 2019) to come up with one machine learning prediction algorithm of the students' dropout per cluster CiA "Figure 2". Now we have for each cluster of higher education institutions in Morocco the most performing algorithm in term of students' dropout prediction.

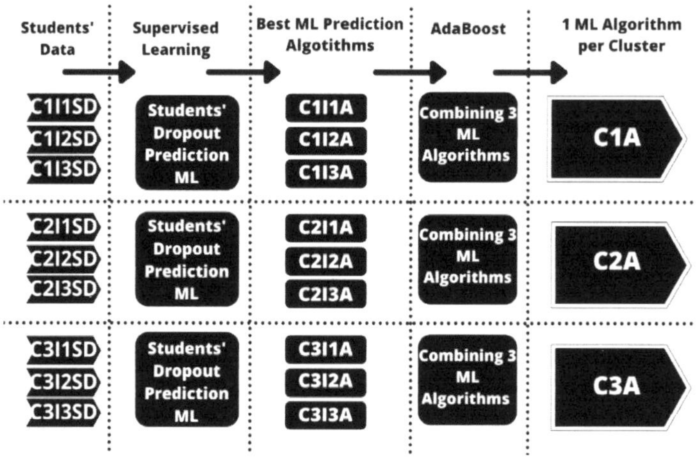


Figure 2. Generating the best dropout prediction algorithm per cluster using the students' data

## 3.3 Summary of the Model

Returning to "Figure 1" and "Figure 2" we started from the data of the institutions, which is by far smaller as students' data (it contains as many rows as the number of higher education institutions by a country). Then we apply clustering to reduce the number of institutions. We choose the three nearest institutions to the cluster's center by using Euclidian distance or equivalent. At this level we use machine learning to predict the dropout in each institution to come up with one algorithm per institution.

- To obtain the best algorithm per cluster we combine the three algorithms of the three institutions that represent the cluster (the nearest to the cluster's center). Now we have one algorithm per cluster.

## 3.4 How to Use the Resulting Model

When this model will be built in Morocco, given a new higher educational institution i (Ii) we collect just the data relative to the institution IiD "Figure 3", then we apply the first part of the model "Figure 1" to decide Cj. The model will generate automatically the best machine learning algorithm relative to this cluster CjA. We apply the second part of the model "Figure 2", we fit CjA with all the data available in this institution to predict students' dropout.

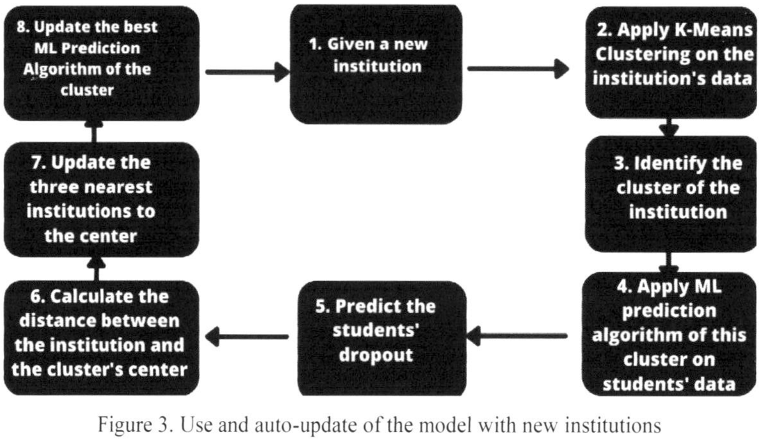


Figure 3. Use and auto-update of the model with new institutions

### 3.5 Model Application Scenario

According to (Ministry of Higher Education and Scientific Research of Morocco, 2020) there were 409 higher education institutions in Morocco in the season 2019-2020. We consider a scenario of 400 institutions.

- We consider 10 arbitrary institutions as initial centers of the clusters.
- We fit the K-Means Clustering algorithms with the institutional data of the 400 institutions.
- We have now 10 final centers, we take the three nearest institutions to each center including the centers if they are not fictive points. The result number is 30 institutions.
- We fit the supervised machine learning algorithms (Linear regression, Random Forest, Decision Tree…etc.) with all the available students' data to predict the dropout.
- After applying the evaluation metrics to these algorithms we obtain one best algorithm per institution, and in each cluster we have three best algorithms.
- To get the best algorithm per cluster we combine the three algorithms with AdaBoost to have just one performing better than each one CiA of the three. We have now 10 clusters with 10 machine learning dropout prediction algorithms: C1A, C2A… C10A.
- Given new institution in Morocco: number 401. We use just I401D, the model will determine the cluster of I401D. Let's suppose it is C7. Now we know that the best algorithm to predict the students' dropout in I401 is C7A. We fit C7A with the independent variables to predict the abandonment.

## 4. DISCUSSION

### 4.1 The Use Cases of the Model

Instead of trying to make a dropout prediction study in each higher education institution of the country, with such a model we make the machine learning prediction in less than 10%. The main contribution of this idea is to prepare a model for the researcher and the decision makers to not repeat the dropout prediction for any new institution even if it was not founded at the time of the development of the model.

This Model can be implemented in other countries to unify the dropout studies that use machine learning. The theoretical part still convenient even with a clustering algorithm different from K-Means and with different supervised machine learning algorithms.

### 4.2 The Model's Limitations

The main idea with this approach is that we do the effort once to make it easier for the studies that come after.

The first limitation is that institutional data must be available in all the institutions, and a convenient data must be available in all the institutions near to the clusters' centers.

The second limitation is the sustainability: once we decide the clusters for the country, new higher education institutions will be founded after. They may be with very different characteristics and far from any cluster. Considering the nearest cluster is not a perfect solution.

## 5. CONCLUSION AND FUTURE WORKS

Using machine learning to predict students' dropout in higher education institutions is largely used by researchers. Most of cases supervised machine learning algorithms are applied to tell in the output either a student will or not drop out. The problem of this approach is that every study stays local and the results concern only the institution in case.

To prepare a common ground on which all the dropout prediction studies in Morocco can start, we generated a global model based on clustering. The idea is to reduce the number of institutions to a smaller number of clusters, and then decide the best prediction supervised machine learning algorithm for each cluster.

Once we want to study the dropout in a given new institution we use the model to determine the cluster of this one, then we have already the best algorithm that can be used according to the model, so we fit it with the students' data to predict the abandonment.

Our next step is to implement this model in the Moroccan context to validate it. We will collect institutional data from all higher education institutions if it is available, otherwise we will collect the data of a representative sample of institutions. We have two objectives from that:

- Applying the model subject of this article to provide higher education decision makers in Morocco with groups of institutions based on some similarities.
- Deciding the best dropout prediction machine learning algorithm of each cluster. That can be obtained after collecting students' data from some institutions and applying our model.

Considering the second limitation of the model, we will work on the auto-correction of the model: once a new higher education institution is far from all the clusters we will affect it to the nearest cluster and update the cluster best algorithm. That will be subject of our future works.

# REFERENCES


Alban, M. et al. (2019) "Predicting University Dropout Trough Data Mining: A systematic Literature," Indian journal of science and technology, 12(4), pp. 1–12. doi: 10.17485/ijst/2019/v12i4/139729.

Berens, J. et al. (2019) "Early detection of students at risk - predicting student dropouts using administrative student data from German universities and machine learning methods." doi: 10.5281/ZENODO.3594771.

Dutt, A. (2015) "Clustering algorithms applied in educational data mining," International journal of information and electronics engineering. doi: 10.7763/ijiee.2015.v5.513.

Higher Council of Education, Training and Scientific Research (2018) "L'enseignement supérieur au Maroc," Csefrs.ma. Available at: https://www.csefrs.ma/wp-content/uploads/2018/10/Rapport-Enseignement-sup--rieur-Fr-03-10.pdf, (Accessed: January 20, 2022).

Iam-On, N. and Boongoen, T. (2017) "Generating descriptive model for student dropout: a review of clustering approach," Human-centric computing and information sciences, 7(1). doi: 10.1186/s13673-016-0083-0.

Kabók, J., Radišić, S. and Kuzmanović, B. (2017) "Cluster analysis of higher-education competitiveness in selected European countries," Economic Research-Ekonomska Istraživanja, 30(1), pp. 845–857. doi: 10.1080/1331677x.2017.1305783.

Križanić, S. (2020) "Educational data mining using cluster analysis and decision tree technique: A case study," International journal of engineering business management, 12, p. 184797902090867. doi: 10.1177/1847979020908675.

Kumar, M. et al. (2017) "Literature survey on educational dropout prediction," International journal of education and management engineering, 7(2), pp. 8–19. doi: 10.5815/ijeme.2017.02.02.

Mannor, S. et al. (2011) "K-Means Clustering," in Encyclopedia of Machine Learning. Boston, MA: Springer US, pp. 563–564.

Manrique, R. et al. (2019) "An analysis of student representation, representative features and classification algorithms to predict degree dropout," in Proceedings of the 9th International Conference on Learning Analytics & Knowledge. New York, NY, USA: ACM.

Marilia et al. (2020) "A combined model based on clustering and regression to predicting school dropout in higher education institution," International journal of computer applications, 176(34), pp. 1–8. doi: 10.5120/ijca2020920396.

Ministry of Education, Vocational Training, Higher Education, and Scientific Research, (2020) " L'enseignement supérieur en chiffres," Gov.ma. Available at: https://www.enssup.gov.ma/storage/statistique/1.l'enseignement%20sup%C3%A9rieur%20en%20chiffre%20%202019-2020.pdf (Accessed: January 07, 2022).

Nicoletti, M. do C. (2019) "Revisiting the Tinto's theoretical dropout model," Higher education studies, 9(3), p. 52. doi: 10.5539/hes.v9n3p52.

Srairi, S. (2022) "An analysis of factors affecting student dropout: The case of Tunisian universities," International journal of educational reform, 31(2), pp. 168–186. doi: 10.1177/10567879211023123.

# VIRTUAL AND IMMERSIVE LEARNING ENVIRONMENTS USING ARTSTEPS: EXPLORATORY STUDY WITH TEACHERS

Sara Cruz[1] and Alexandre Torres[2]
[1]*Polytechnic Institute of Cávado and Ave, Portugal*
[2]*National Teachers Association, Portugal*


### ABSTRACT

ArtSteps is an immersive virtual exhibit tool that is attractive and versatile; the user can present objects, artefacts, and art, whether it is work they have created or found in public resources. This paper presents an exploratory study on digital teacher empowerment using ArtSteps to promote innovative pedagogical methodologies involving Virtual and Immersive Learning Environments. The study involved thirty-five professors from different subject areas. The study was a qualitative and quantitative investigation aimed at understanding how virtual and immersive learning environments such as ArtSteps can promote teachers' engagement and whether teachers are receptive to using virtual environments and immersive environments in their professional practice with students. Findings suggest that teachers are receptive to introducing virtual learning and immersive environments in their teaching practice with students. Teachers' exploration of ArtSteps involved them in a virtual and immersive learning experience that motivated them to experiment with their students. A didactic proposal promotes an immersive gallery experience where different types of work can be showcased and viewed using curriculum content.



### KEYWORDS

Virtual Environments, Immersive Environments, Virtual And Immersive Learning Environments, Projects, ArtSteps.


## 1. INTRODUCTION

In an educational context, several digital tools have emerged that allow the use of Virtual Reality and Augmented Reality applied to education. The evolution of digital resources in Virtual Reality has improved the experience of simulation and interaction in real-time, which can be used in multiple sensory channels to facilitate learning by the student. Several technological tools have also emerged that allow students to experience Augmented Reality, putting them in contact with an interface that superimposes virtual objects on the student's physical environment. The student can interact with the virtual objects and use technological devices to visualize the mixed climate in real-time. It is, therefore, relevant to adopt different forms of teaching, attending to individuals with appropriate pedagogical interventions to raise the level of learning. Our article arises in this context and describes an in-service training course for teachers from different education levels. The training course was conducted in eLearning and involved thirty-five teachers. This training course aimed to promote innovative pedagogical methodologies involving Virtual and Immersive Learning Environments (VILEs).

The article introduces the concept of virtual and immersive learning environments and briefly introduces ArtSteps as a virtual gallery, an immersive and virtual learning tool. Then we present the methodology adopted in the exploratory study and its description. Finally, we present a brief discussion of the results, main conclusions and some proposals for future investigations.

## 2. VIRTUAL AND IMMERSIVE LEARNING ENVIRONMENTS

The proliferation of Virtual Worlds in different fields has also enabled their insertion into the educational field, from which new possibilities for using these computing resources emerge as an element of support and even motivation in the educational process (Voss et al., 2014). The Virtual and Immersive Learning Environments (VILEs) encapsulate all the online environments that constitute learning situations that are constructed using various techniques and software tools, including game-based learning, simulation-based learning and virtual 3D worlds. In our study, an immersive learning environment is a learning space but with forms of virtual learning. They are distinguished from other learning methods by their ability to simulate realistic scenarios and environments that allow learners to practice skills and interact in a real-life environment.

The ArtSteps virtual gallery is a web-based application for viewing and creating virtual exhibitions. It is helpful for artists and art organizations to model actual and virtual exhibits. In our study, we used ArtSteps, a freely available application that allows the development of 3D virtual learning environments (Fokides & Sfakianou, 2017). The ArtSteps is accessible through the link (http://www.artsteps.com/). Through this tool, we promote with a group of teachers the use of innovative pedagogical methodologies involving Virtual and Immersive Learning Environments. It is accessible via a web browser, and through an individual registration, the user can access their works in progress or completed without any additional software requirements. The virtual and immersive learning environments built through ArtSteps may include 2-dimensional items like photos and posters or 3-dimensional items like small installations or streaming videos. ArtSteps is an innovative, web-based application that empowers creators to build virtual exhibitions, virtual events and a virtual storytelling environment. It allows a wide range of combinations of virtual learning environments, such as (i) exploring and discovering art in 3D virtual galleries; (ii) creation and design of your 3D virtual exhibitions; (iii) embedding and distributing your digital creations on blogs or websites (Gimnazială & Turda, 2017). Using ArtSteps is relatively easy; the users can design their own spaces and rooms and add information to them through web links, text, audio and video (Fokides & Sfakianou, 2017).

## 3. METHOD

This study occurred during the COVID-19 pandemic, where in-service training course for teachers took distance classes through videoconferencing platforms. This work presented an intensive in-service training course for Portuguese teachers. The study has been developed using a quantitative methodology through quasi-experimental research designed around the idea of digital teacher empowerment in immersive and virtual environments with ArtSteps. The teachers answered a diagnostic questionnaire to understand their knowledge about virtual learning environments, immersive environments and their perceptions about integrating these pedagogical methodologies in an educational context.

In a subsequent phase of the training course, the teachers designed and created their pedagogical resources in Artsteps. At the end of the process, the teachers answered a questionnaire with which we intend to compare answers and understand the evolution of teachers in understanding the methodology of Virtual and immersive learning environments in education. In our study, we guided students through the following procedure: (i) teachers made a knowledge diagnosis; (ii) are involved in an activity that involves using ArtSteps as resource users; (iii) students investigated solutions to solve the problem; (iv) each teacher builds a resource, a 3D gallery on ArtSteps; (v) teachers tested resource in own students and (vi) teachers made a final reflection about the pedagogical methodology. In the first training moment, the teachers experienced ArtSteps as technology users (Figure 1).

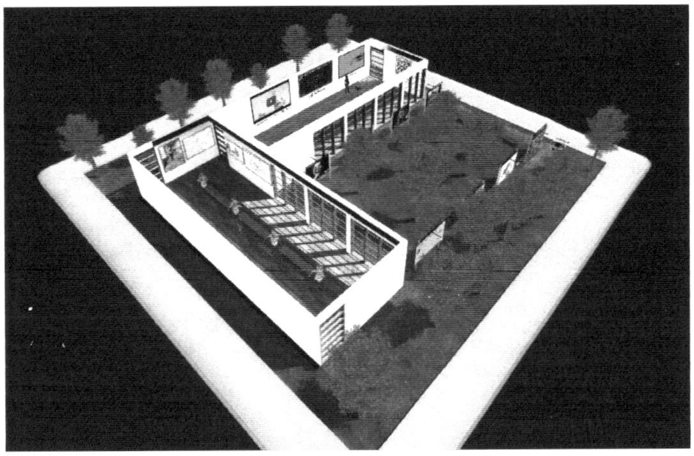

Figure 1. Pedagogical resource created in ArtSteps in exploitation by teachers

Teachers were challenged to design and develop a pedagogical resource for their subject area in ArtSteps. The process was mediated by the Zoom platform and the ArtSteps web-based app, which supported all phases of the process described above to communicate with teachers. Different methods were applied to collect the data: (i) system logs on the platform, (ii) a diary to collect direct observations, (iii) a diagnostic and final questionnaire.

## 4. RESULTS

The diagnosis showed that teachers most of the teachers involved (56%) did not know and had never heard of immersive learning environments. We noticed that some of these teachers had already heard about virtual reality (44%), but few had heard about augmented reality applied to education (18%). Most teachers who claimed to have heard about immersive environments applied to education never used them in their professional practice (82%). Only a few of these teachers claim to have used virtual reality (15%) or augmented reality (6%) in their classes with students.

All teachers (100%) were receptive to using ArtSteps, and they learned how to create a project in ArtSteps from templates available in the application and how to structure and assemble a new project from scratch. In addition, each teacher designed a Virtual and immersive learning environment to implement in their students and created a pedagogical resource in ArtSteps to work on a curricular theme in their subject area.

In the final reflection, all teachers admitted that using virtual and immersive environments in an educational context can motivate students to learn. Also, all the teachers involved stated that they consider that using virtual and immersive environments can promote active learning of the contents by the students, leading them to have a more active role in their education. The use of virtual learning environments enhances understanding and, at the same time, creates opportunities for students to interact socially and apply knowledge in situations that are close to real (Vieira & Brazão, 2022). We noticed that some of the teachers involved (13%) say that they do not find a reason to start using immersive virtual learning environments in their classes. However, it is also verified that all the teachers involved (100%) intend to use virtual and immersive learning environments in future classes as a motivating factor for their students. All teachers (100%) consider that using VILEs environments can promote active learning of the contents by the students. From the teachers' answers, we also noticed that a part of the teachers (37%) had already used and showed a desire to use VILEs again in their teaching practice. Also, all teachers (100%) consider that the use of VILEs environments can promote an active learning of the contents by the students. From the teachers' answers, we also noticed that a part of the teachers (37%) had already used and desired to use VILEs again in their teaching practice.

## 5. DISCUSSION AND CONCLUSION

In this article, we present a pedagogical experience involving thirty-five teachers in a Virtual and immersive learning environment. It should be noted that most teachers had never heard of the term immersive learning environment or virtual learning environment. At the end of this exploratory study, teachers were excited about the idea of being able to use Virtual and immersive learning environments in their context of working with students. All teachers created a teaching resource in ArtSteps to work on content from their curricular area with their students. It should be noted that some of the teachers involved applied the pedagogical resource in their classes and managed to create virtual and immersive learning environments. In this way, our objective is to promote innovative pedagogical methodologies involving Virtual and Immersive Learning Environments among teachers.

In line with Cruz et al. (2014), we realize that technology is an ally of pedagogy through the use of devices that most teachers have at their disposal. Also, according to Vieira & Brazão (2022), we realized that virtual and immersive learning environments could play an essential role in developing dynamic, interactive, engaging, customizable learning environments that enhance the learning and application of content in a real or simulated way. From the results obtained, we realized that 50% of the teachers involved recognize that they do not know how to create and implement an immersive virtual learning environment in their professional practice. However, all teachers consider that using these environments can promote active learning of the contents by the students. Furthermore, it should be noted that many teachers who have already tried using virtual and immersive learning environments in their pedagogical practice intend to use them again to enhance student-centred teaching, allowing them to play a more active role.

Our work shows teachers' lack of technical experience and, consequently, the massive gap in reaching students with innovative applications, given the problems generated by the pandemic. Although with this exploratory study, we could understand the teachers' receptivity to the use of Virtual and Immersive Learning Environments, it seems relevant to us in future studies to understand its impact on students in a practical application of curricular contents.

The digital training of teachers has aroused the interest of researchers and governments. An attempt has been made to create conditions for teachers to integrate technologies in different curricular areas with a view to continuous improvement in the quality of learning and innovation in the educational system. In this sense, it seems relevant to us to understand in future investigations whether teachers' reflection around teaching with an immersive learning environment or virtual learning environment promotes a change in teachers' practices. It also seems relevant to understand whether an immersive or virtual learning environment promotes deeper learning of the topics covered, translating into effective teaching and learning.

## ACKNOWLEDGEMENT

We would like to thank the Directorship of National Association of Teachers, in particular, Doctor Paula Carqueja the possibility of carrying out data collection on a training course. We also would like to sincerely thank all teachers from the online training course who agreed to participate in the study.

## REFERENCES

Cruz, S., Lencastre, J. A., & Coutinho, C. (2015). Edição criativa de vídeos e sua partilha em ecrãs públicos na escola: um estudo exploratório. In Tomé, Irene (coord.), Proceedings of the X International Symposium EUTIC 2014 The Role of ICT in the Design of Informational and Cognitive Processes (pp. 279-288). Lisbon: CITI – Centro de Investigação para Tecnologias Interactivas / FCSH / Universidade Nova de Lisboa.

Fokides, E., & Zampouli, C. (2017). Content and Language Integrated Learning in OpenSimulator Project. Results of a pilot implementation in Greece. *Education and Information Technologies*, 22(4), 1479-1496. https://doi.org/10.1007/s10639-016-9503-z.

Vieira, L. M. S., & Brazão, J. P. G. (2022). Learning Environments: from real to immersive. *Journal of Research and Knowledge Spreading*, 3(1), e13486. http://dx.doi.org/10.20952/jrks3113486.

Voss, G. B., Nunes, F. B., Herpich, F., & Medina, R. D. (2014). Ambientes Virtuais de Aprendizagem e Ambientes Imersivos: um estudo de caso utilizando tecnologias de computação móvel e web viewers. *Tecnologias, Sociedade e Conhecimento*, 2(1), 24-42. https://doi.org/10.20396/tsc.v2i1.14448.

# ANALYSIS OF LEARNING OBJECTS FOR OPTIMIZATION AND DIGITAL TRANSFER REPORT OF INTERMEDIATE RESULTS ON LEARNING PATH IDEAS – FIRST SURVEY

Fabian Dillenhöfer, Bernd Künne
*TU Dortmund, Department of machine elements, Leonhard-Euler-Street 5, 44227 Dortmund, Germany*

**ABSTRACT**

This paper is a progress report about a project that consists of five stages starting with an analysis of the current state of application of higher educational learning material with regards to structural format and media didactics. The aim of this analysis has been accomplished through an initial survey with the motivation to analyze didactic and digital aspects of final study competencies as well as individual learning styles. The next stages include a digitalization process and an upcoming evaluation section. The results of the initial survey show that key competence goals that are formulated by teachers are not always comprehended and accepted by students. Students sometimes do not understand the purpose of the teachers' learning path ideas and, thus, do not accept some subjects and intermediate goals. These lacks of acceptance provide a fundamental basis of refining teaching courses. This report summarizes an approach to optimize learning goals and digital transfer so that precise evaluation helps finding these misconceptions and therefore both course structure and learning materials can be improved. Furthermore, it advices teachers to focus on teaching relevant topics not only for exam purposes but also for future professional competencies. Finally, this paper serves an example for teachers, especially of higher education level, to find weaknesses in a teaching objective and how to prioritize optimization, thereby clarify the learning path to students. This increases motivation and improves digital transfer.

**KEYWORDS**

E-Learning, Distance Education, Higher Education, Scientific Survey, Didactic, Competence Learning, COVID-19.

## 1. INTRODUCTION

Covid-19 has led to a rise in digitalization of teaching objective in global education due to the closure of many schools (Statista 2020). Since then, digitalization has become essential with new challenges to tackle. Institutions and experts advise higher education materials to be open access and call for wider cooperation (DAAD/DIE, 2018). Consequently, a project between six high schools in North-Rhine-Westphalia has been started promoting digital OER[1]-learning materials for public use and discussion. In this project, six universities, namely TU Dortmund University, Dortmund University of Applied Sciences, Bochum University of Applied Sciences, South Westphalia University of Applied Sciences, Hamm-Lippstadt University of Applied Sciences and University of Wuppertal, revise the learning materials used in higher education. Through surveys, didactic and digital aspects of study competences and individual learning styles were analyzed. Altogether, this paper evaluates the initial situation including the first survey, while the digitalization process is still going on. A second survey will follow in early 2023.

Previously, the course Technical Drawing, a basic module of higher education for engineers, has been restructured in terms of didactics to aim for competency-based learning. Here, constructive alignment ensures that learning objectives, success contributions, and teaching/learning activities are aligned (Biggs, J. & Tang, C., 2011). Then, a digitalization project was launched to offer OER-material (open educational resources) for the higher education platform of North-Rhine-Westphalia (ORCA.nrw). To obtain knowledge about the needs of students and lecturers, questionnaires have been prepared. The focus of this survey is to find out which competences are important to reach certain learning goals/objectives. Both the students and the lecturers' thoughts on the acquirement of these competences are considered. A majority of students in higher semesters were surveyed. The students have predominantly participated in the exam at the end of the course, so that they are able to answer with a much broader knowledge in terms of competences needed for their future study. This article is structured as follow: at first, the project cycle is shown to understand the purpose of the report. Then, the structure of the questionnaire is depicted and the inspected parameters of the first survey are presented. Next, the results are analyzed by comparing the answers of the students with the expectations of the lecturers and are discussed. Finally, a conclusion regarding the presented optimization process is given.

# 2. PROJECT CYCLE

Before the teaching module is digitalized, an initial survey is applied to analyze both the students' and teachers' opinion on how learning materials should be provided to reach competence goals (Figure 1). The first questionnaire was handed out at the beginning of the Covid-19 pandemic in 2020 and the second one will be introduced in February 2023 in order to indicate possible changes. They should reveal the student's assessment of educational goals and whether these competences needed for further studies are attained. For this reason, mostly students of higher semesters were consulted.

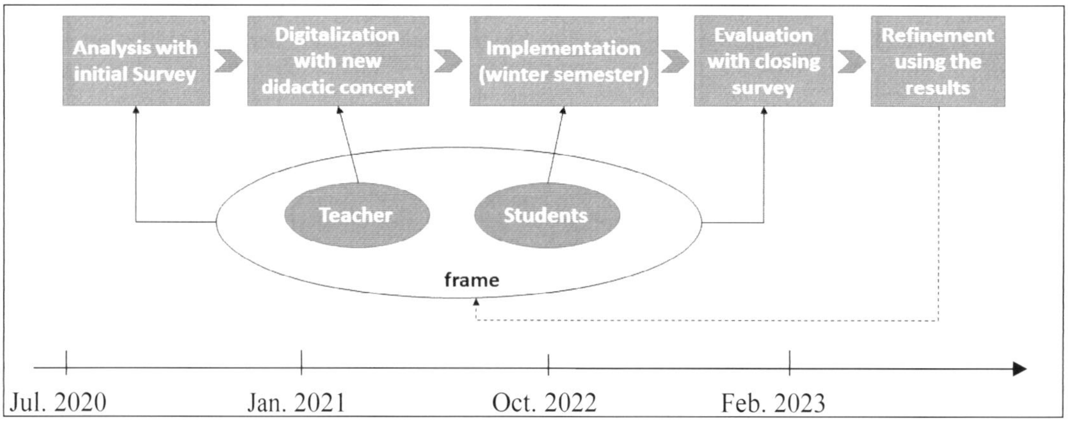


Figure 1. Project cycle with timetable

At the moment, new digital materials with innovative and interactive characters are generated. To reach learners' full motivation, as suggested by Shabbir et al., providing personalized intervention will be considered (Shabbir et al. 2020). After the completion of this stage, the new proposal will be offered locally at the universities that are participating in the project by implementing it in teaching courses. At the end of the trial, the evaluation with the second survey will be executed. The results will be analyzed afterwards and the digital course offer will be passed through a refinement process. Last but not least, the final results will be published in a full paper. The upcoming paper will analyze the sufficiency of the measures presented in this paper and will also conclude the acceptance of digital OER-material using modern didactics backtracking. Moreover, the digital learning materials will be published at the online portal of North-Rhine-Westphalia.

## 2.1 Questionnaire Structure

The questionnaire is provided digitally to the students, which makes it easier to automate the evaluation. It consists of eight questions that are to be answered within five minutes. These questions target specific facets such as the gained skill level or the importance of the gained knowledge for their further study that is displayed in further detail in table 1. In order to determine the degree of agreement regarding the questions, the Likert scale, developed by Rensis Likert (1931), from one to five (strongly agree-strongly disagree) is implemented. It is used in various sciences using questionnaires (e.g. Croasmun JT & Ostrom L. 2011; Gay, L. et. al., 2009). The questions also provide the assessment of their own skill level. It is convenient to link these self-assessments to the competence goals written down in the module manual. On the other hand, the survey delivers not only direct topics and ideas that are very suitable to refine, but also reveals lacks of skill or competence that should be addressed to fill a desideratum.

Table 1. Construction of questionnaire

| Dimension | Facet | Option |
|---|---|---|
| exam | skill level/experience | Yes/no |
| extent | perception | 1-5 |
| complexity | previous knowledge | 1-5 |
| Media usage | digital media-savvy | 1-5 |
| topics | Importance for further study | 1-5 |
| topics | Suited for digitalization | 1-5 |
| Skill level | Gained in course | 1-5 |
| digitalization | Innovative ideas | Open response |

# 3. SURVEY RESULTS AND DISCUSSION

259 people from the six universities mentioned above participated in the survey. The majority of the participants (95 %) relate to a semester greater than two. 89 % of the students have also participated in the course exam, so that they are able to assess their exam grade, which is correlated to the competence level obtained in the course. The results show that the extent of the course is estimated as reasonable.

Based on the following Figure 2, it can be seen that the students do not entirely agree to whether the media used to contribute better understanding. This circumstance could have two reasons. First, this could relate to different learning styles in general or the degree of proficiency. Hence, the skill level of first semester engineer students differs tremendously due to individual internships before studying and possible vocational training completed in advance. Secondly, the knowledge of innovative media available and technological possibilities is different among the students.

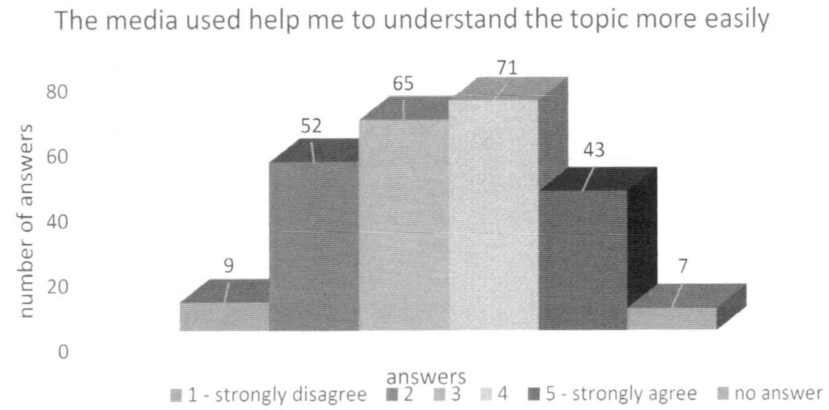


Figure 2. Opinions on media usage

Furthermore, it is asked whether the skills gained could and should be applied in their study. The answers correlate directly to the next question, which topic should be focused on in a broader way related to competences needed for studying and jobs in the future. The results relating to the question about the suitability of topics for digitization with a virtual teaching approach in particular are coherent in terms of the lecturer's expectation on the student's answers.

The last question targets ideas for both technical and didactic digitalization solutions to offer new innovative learning and teaching materials. There is one interesting point where teachers and students contradict each other. Drawings made by hand are considered unimportant by students and the focus should be more on CAD (computer aided design) drawings, because technical drawings made by hand will not be needed any more in the future. The teachers strongly disagree on this point, because it does not only help them to learn effectively with simple examples, but it is also a basic comprehensive competence needed in many engineering situations like a strategy department meeting to sketch ideas or examples by hand, so that the communication between engineers is simplified.

## 4. CONCLUSION

The survey points out which topics should be focused on when creating new digital learning objectives. It shows where learning objectives are presented poorly, for example the strong disagreement on drawings by hand. It leads teachers to where and how misconceptions are to be processed. The first idea that comes into mind is to outline important competences in a motivation section to show important skills that are urgent for future tasks to come. Moreover, it locates possible weaknesses in teaching courses that can be tackled through didactic approaches for example through gamification improving student's and teacher's satisfaction.

In general, students prefer videos as digital preparation especially to be able to learn independent of time and place, also mentioned in LinkedIn (2019). Nevertheless, there is also a fraction of students that need a schedule that is set up by the lecturer for motivation and organization purpose. These different opinions also prevail over students in terms of teaching in presence vs. teaching digitally. These results suggest that hybrid learning or blended learning is a reasonable model that is able to fulfill everyone's needs. It should be mentioned that these models should provide both options (physical and virtual presence) simultaneously.

E-learning with digital media is able to set up a learning environment that is much more effective, but also bears more risks that need to be tackled. On the one hand, some students lose their motivation quickly while studying at home (Islam, S et al., 2018). On the other hand, time saved through higher efficiency can be used elsewhere, for example to close the gaps mentioned above. These measures lead to the establishment of a better basic understanding for both teachers and students. By applying those changes mentioned in the article, it is expected that the misconceptions between teachers and students decrease and the formulated competence targets coincide. This thesis will be researched after the second survey in early 2023.

## ACKNOWLEDGEMENT

We would like to thank our partners named Dortmund University of Applied Sciences, Bochum University of Applied Sciences, South Westphalia University of Applied Sciences, Hamm-Lippstadt University of Applied Sciences and University of Wuppertal for providing the data and supporting the analysis. We gratefully acknowledge financial support through the DH.NRW with funds provided by the Ministry for Culture and Science of the state of North Rhine-Westphalia (MKW) under Grant No. 214-5.01.03.02 - 145504.

## REFERENCES

Biggs J. & Tang, C. (2011): Teaching for Quality Learning at University: What the Student Does (4th ed.): Maidenhead: Open University Press.

Croasmun JT & Ostrom L. (2011): Using Likert-type scales in the social sciences. Journal of Adult Education. Volume 40:19-22.

DAAD/DIE (2018): Digital Transformation: Higher Education and Research for Sustainable Development. Position paper. Bonn, November 2018.

Gay, L. R., Mills, G. E., & Airasian, P. (2009). Educational research: Competencies for analysis and applications. Columbus, OH: Merrill.

Islam, S., Baharun, H., Muali, C., Ghufron, M. I., Bali, M. E. I., Wijaya, M., & Marzuki, I. (2018). To boost students' motivation and achievement through blended learning. Paper presented at the Journal of Physics: Conference Series, 1114(1) doi:10.1088/1742-6596/1114/1/012046 Retrieved from www.scopus.com, May 6, 2022

LinkedIn. (February 27, 2019). Share of learners who want fully self-directed and independent learning in the United States in 2019, by generation [Graph]. In Statista. Retrieved April 29, 2022, from https://www.statista.com/statistics/988933/workplace-learning-independent-learning-united-states-generation/

Statista (2020). COVID-19's Staggering Impact On Global Education. Statista. Statista Inc. Accessed: March 18, 2022. https://www.statista.com/chart/21224/learners-impacted-by-national-school-closures/

Shabbir S., Ayub M. A., Khan F.A., Davis j. (2020). Short-term earners' motivation modeling in web based Education system; IADIS International Conference e-Learning 2020, ISBN: 978-989-8704-17-7 © 2020

# GENESIS OF AN E-PLATFORM FOR LANGUAGE ENHANCEMENT

Adam Forrester
*English Language Centre, The Hong Kong Polytechnic University*
*Hung Hom, Kowloon, Hong Kong*

**ABSTRACT**

This paper covers the work in progress of an e-platform being developed for language enhancement at a tertiary institution in Hong Kong. There is an actual or perceived concern about the English and Chinese language ability of undergraduate students at certain universities in Hong Kong. One reason for this is that a significant proportion of students with a lower language proficiency enter university in their third year of the four-year degree. Their first two years are spent at other tertiary institutions, and they are then able to articulate to finish their studies at university and gain a degree level qualification. Given their crowded timetable from the third year, there are very limited opportunities for extra credit space in order to enhance the language skills of these students. As a result, an e-platform which students would utilise through the informal curriculum to improve their English and Chinese language ability was proposed by senior management. This paper will examine the beginnings of the e-platform, including results from a large-scale survey of undergraduate students about the preferences for an e-platform, and initial discussions among language experts as to the design of the e-platform. This paper will consider the decision to use H5P to create interactive content within the platform and discuss some of the features that are expected on the e-platform. Problems that have been encountered and expected will be discussed with an outline of the next steps that will be taken. The paper concludes with the observation that an e-platform alone is unlikely to significantly enhance the language ability of learners.

**KEYWORDS**

Instructional Design, e-Platform, eLearning, Language Enhancement.

## 1. INTRODUCTION

### 1.1 Need for and Focus of e-Platform

Given the packed timetable of undergraduate students in Hong Kong, it is unlikely that extra credit space can be provided to students in order to enhance their language capabilities. It was therefore proposed that an e-platform is developed for students so as to help them to improve their language skills through informal means. As indicated by a student survey conducted within the university, 75% of students are already using an e-platform of some sort (e.g., Grammarly, Duolingo) to enhance their language learning, with nearly half accessing the platform several times per week. Research has shown a positive, moderate correlation between the amount of time spent on a language learning platform and learning gains (Loewen et al., 2019), so it is important that (1) students access any platform frequently, and (2) the platform is informative, effectively designed and built to encourage ease of use.

The focus of the proposed e-platform has been discussed in depth within the university. Considerations include a desire not to duplicate existing platforms while also providing students with an easy-to-use platform that can enhance their language skills. It is believed that the e-platform should provide students with opportunities for practice, input and feedback, and it is agreed that the e-platform should aim at improving the vocabulary of students, including vocabulary usage and pronunciation, which would facilitate them to have better standard language test scores. It was noted that in the survey that students self-rated English vocabulary among the lowest. The e-platform would not treat vocabulary in isolation, but rather consider it in context so that students can enhance their overall writing skills and integrate vocabulary into workplace English and Chinese (including Putonghua) and daily communication.

In order to develop the e-platform, a project team was formed from various members of the Faculty of Humanities in the university. Members had varying levels of experience of developing different language learning tools using different technologies. This paper first provides a short overview of other platforms and studies related to the topic. It then gives an overview of the requirements of the e-platform, both technical and pedagogical. It will give a brief overview of H5P, before considering the findings of an online survey among students as to their habits and preferences towards learning online. The final section will consider progress towards the e-platform as well as problems encountered and possible solutions.

## 2. EXISTING STUDIES

A literature review was conducted to examine similar platforms. Probably the most popular language learning platform today, with 500 million users in 2020 (Blanco, 2020), is Duolingo. This gamified mobile-assisted language learning (MALL) application has numerous features that attract users, including challenging activities, incentives, different levels, and the ranking of users. A study by Shortt et al. (2021) is useful on understanding how the design of Duolingo has an impact on how the platform is used. One key feature of Duolingo is it use of gamification, and Dehganzadeh and Dehganzadeh (2020) in a review of previous studies, point out that gamification-based learning can have benefits. Regarding the use of H5P to design language learning tasks, recent literature reviews have shown it is conducive to increasing attention and interest of learners (Addhiny, 2022).

## 3. REQUIREMENTS OF E-PLATFORM

The experience of members of the university and the results of the survey informs this section of the paper. In order that an effective e-platform is developed, it is important that it meets different requirements.

### 3.1 Requirements (Technical)

- Single Sign-on (SSO) for users
- Link to existing university systems
- Tracking of student usage and performance
- Learning Tools Interoperability (LTI)
- Push notifications
- Simple, easy and clear to use
- Leaderboard of top performing users
- Consideration of the user

Given the short time frame, a 'mobile first design' (Schmidt, 2010) might be used rather than a responsive or adaptive e-platform. SSO is a requirement so that users do not need to create an extra account. By using SSO it is also hoped that the platform can also be linked to other university systems. It is important to track student usage and performance to gather data analytics about the system and feedback to further enhancements. LTI is a method for a learning system to invoke and to communicate with external systems; this would allow us to host course content and tools provided by external, third-party systems on the platform. Push notifications would allow users to be 'pushed' or reminded to use the platform more with a simple, easy and clear to use design also meaning users are more likely to return. A leaderboard with top performing users is a possible requirement if we want the system to have a gamification element on the platform.

## 3.2 Requirements (Pedagogical)

- Adaptive materials based on users' performance
- Instant feedback
- Language can be taught in context (e.g. academic and workplace writing skills, workplace and daily communication)

The pedagogical requirements are also important. Adaptive release is a mature technology that allows content to be released after certain conditions are met, for example, a certain score achieved, or a time period has passed. Instant feedback is important to students, although to be instant, it needs to be automated. In addition, rather than having isolated exercises (e.g. fill in the blanks, matching), we would want the language to be taught in the context that it is used.

## 3.3 H5P

The project team recommended that activities on the platform are built using H5P (H5P Organisation, 2022). H5P is an open-source content collaboration framework based on JavaScript. H5P is an abbreviation for HTML5 Package, and aims to make it easy for the creation, sharing and reuse of interactive HTML5 content. Interactive videos, interactive presentations, quizzes, interactive timelines and other activities can be developed and shared using H5P. H5P content is also sustainable in the case of future changes in the LMS supported by the University. In order for the content to be shared via the LMS (e.g. Blackboard or MS Teams) a package needs to be purchased from Joubel (Joubel, 2022) so a budget must be available for this.

By using H5P, the university would have flexibility on using the materials created for language enhancement on a standalone e-platform or by integrating them into a LMS. The advantages of integrating into the existing LMS include students would already have access and that there are already data analytics built into the LMS. On the other hand, a standalone e-platform can be built and designed to meet the specific needs of PolyU students.

## 3.4 Online Survey

An online survey on Student Digital Media Use and Foreign Language Learning was conducted in November 2021. It aimed at finding out the digital media habits and preferences for learning languages by PolyU undergraduates. All undergraduate students at the PolyU were sent an email inviting them to participate in the survey. An incentive coupon of HK$20 (approximately US$ 2.5) was provided to the first 250 students to successfully complete the survey. The sample was self-selecting, but overall representative of the student body as a whole. There were 248 survey respondents who came from all the eight Faculties and Schools within the university, with around 80% being local Hong Kong students.

### 3.4.1 Key findings

- 75% of respondents have experience on using online platform for language learning, with Grammarly (55%) and Duolingo (28%) being the most popular platforms.
- The majority learned English (44%) as foreign language, followed by Cantonese (12%), Japanese (11%), Mandarin (10%) and Korean (10%).
- Mobile phone (43%) and notebook computer (31%) were the most often used electronic devices.
- Students spent 2-4 times (41%) to 5-7 times (21%) on accessing one online platform per week, whereas they only spent less than 15 minutes (24%) to 15 – 30 minutes (42%) per visit.
- Most students used the online platform for language learning when they were at home (52%), commuting (22%) or in the library (19%).
- Students liked the online platforms mostly because of practical/informative contents, user-friendly interface and useful feedback.
- For the interface design features of online platform (full scores: 5), students rated simplicity (4.24), instruction (4.22), flexibility (4.21), visibility (4.19) and adaptive learning (4.07) the most important.

- Students agreed to a large extent that online platforms could stimulate their interests in language learning (3.92) and enhance their ability in self-learning (4.06).
- Students were most eager to get help with their English and Chinese in the areas of writing essays, job interviews, writing CVs and presentations.
- The respondents self-rated their language proficiency (full scores: 10) in both English and Chinese. The scores were relatively higher in listening and reading (Chinse reading: 7.45; Chinese listening: 7.82; English reading: 6.60; English listening 6.52) but lower in writing and vocabulary (Chinese writing: 6.77; English writing: 6.16; English vocabulary: 5.93).
- Respondents preferred watching movies, using online platforms and chatting with friends when learning languages outside classroom.

## 3.5 Problems Encountered and Anticipated

### 3.5.1 Recruitment Issues

The first issue encountered was being unable to hire a suitable technical staff member to help build the e-platform. This was likely due to a number of reasons including: (i) a general shortage of qualified web developers in Hong Kong (Westbrook, 2021), (ii) the relatively short time frame of the contract, and (iii) the unclear job title and description which did not fully represent the job nature. The project team decided that while it would be possible to re-advertise with a more suitable job advert, the focus should be instead to build pilot materials using H5P and launch them through the LMS in the next academic year.

### 3.5.2 Attracting Users

While it is relatively straightforward to build content using H5P and launch on a LMS, there is no guarantee that students will come to the course site to use the content. As already noted, senior management intend that students should improve their language skills through the "informal curriculum", and this means that no time, and no credits would be given to students who complete different activities on the platform. It is perhaps expected that students will be using intrinsic (e.g. an internal desire to improve their language skills) or extrinsic (e.g. improving language skills to do better in language tests) motivation if they are to use the proposed e-platform (Lamb, 2017), as there will be no requirement to use it.

In terms of attracting the users, and mixture of traditional, proven methods, and more out of the box ideas will be used. Traditional methods include sending mass emails, distributing posters advertising the platform around campus, producing short videos promoting the e-platform, and asking teachers to promote the e-platform to their students – a personal recommendation. The last method has been found to be more effective in the past, with emails unread, posters unseen, and videos unwatched. We plan to expand the 'personal recommendation' by employing 'student ambassadors' from different departments with a strong social presence (Haenlein et al. 2020). These ambassadors would be initially paid to use the platform and then post their progress on their social media platforms. If the ambassadors are able to attract more student users from their department to use the platform, then they would receive a bonus payment as recompense.

### 3.5.3 University and Faculty Expectations

The project team has experience of developing a range of elearning applications related to language learning including web-based materials, LMS modules, instructional videos, MOOCs, chatbots and VR applications (Forrester & Chan, 2021). These have all been created with the student end user foremost in mind and while we have attempted to incorporate advanced features, we would be more cautious if they features had not been proven to be stable. There is pressure from the university and faulty for the e-platform to include more advanced features, (e.g. AI elements, natural language processing, VR/AR) and be a standalone platform not linked to a LMS. The project team has already taken the decision to launch initially on the LMS in order to gather feedback on the student experience. It is envisaged that expectations will need to be managed given the timeframe and budget, and technological capabilities of the moment.

### 3.5.4 Next Steps

During summer 2022 material writers will be recruited to start building language activities using H5P. It is envisioned that these activities will follow a learning sequence in which students will follow a number of different steps. This is in contrast to traditional computer graded quizzes such as multiple-choice questions or matching exercises. These learning sequences will be piloted with a small number of staff and students before their launch on the LMS in the next academic year (September 2022). Learning analytics data will be collected form the students using the 'e-platform' in the third quarter of 2022, as well as their being focus group interviews with users. This data will be further analysed in the fourth quarter 2022, with a plan to start developing a standalone e-platform in early 2023.

## 4. CONCLUSION

There is clearly a need for different initiatives to help students improve their language skills. An e-platform could provide one element that can help students. However, past experience tells us that an e-platform by itself is not enough to significantly improve the language skills of students. Instead, a multifaceted approach is needed including e-learning, face-to-face learning and commitment from those controlling timetable space and credits, if there is to be a significant improvement in language skills. The team members behind this e-platform are experienced and creative enough to ensure that it will be built. However, if it is to be a success, it needs university commitment in other areas.

## REFERENCES


Addhiny, T. (2022). The Use of H5P Interactive Content in English Language Learning. *PANRITA: Journal of Science, Technology, and Arts*, *1*(1, Desember). Retrieved from https://journal.dedikasi.org/pjsta/article/view/16

Blanco, C. (2020). 2020 Duolingo Language Report: Global Overview. *Duolingo Blog*. https://blog.duolingo.com/global-language-report-2020/

Dehganzadeh, H., Dehganzadeh, H. (2020). Investigating effects of digital gamification-based language learning: A systematic review. *Two Quarterly Journal of English Language Teaching and Learning University of Tabriz*, 12(25), 53-93. doi: 10.22034/elt.2020.10676

Forrester, A., & Chan, C. H. J. (2021). Virtual Reality (VR) - possibilities for use in tertiary language centres, TESOL International Journal, 16(8), 7-16. https://www.elejournals.com/tij-2021/tij-volume-16-issue-8-2021-2-2/

H5P Organisation. (2022). https://h5p.org/

Haenlein, M., Anadol, E., Farnsworth, T., Hugo, H., Hunichen, J., & Welte, D. (2020). Navigating the New Era of Influencer Marketing: How to be Successful on Instagram, TikTok, & Co. California Management Review, 63(1), 5–25. https://doi.org/10.1177/0008125620958166

Lamb, M. (2017). The motivational dimension of language teaching. *Language Teaching, 50*(3), 301-346. doi:10.1017/S0261444817000088

Loewen, S., Crowther, D., Isbell, D., Kim, K., Maloney, J., Miller, Z., & Rawal, H. (2019). Mobile-assisted language learning: A Duolingo case study. *ReCALL*, 31(3), 293-311. doi:10.1017/S0958344019000065

Joubel. (2022). https://h5p.com/

Shortt, M., Tilak, S., Kuznetcova, I., Martens, B. & Akinkuolie, B. (2021) Gamification in mobile-assisted language learning: a systematic review of Duolingo literature from public release of 2012 to early 2020, *Computer Assisted Language Learning*, doi: 10.1080/09588221.2021.1933540

Schmidt, E. (2010, Feb 16). Eric Schmidt at Mobile World Congress. [Video]. https://youtu.be/ClkQA2Lb_iE

Westbrook, L. (2021, Mar 13). *Hong Kong's IT sector facing shortage of skilled talent as Covid-19 keeps foreigners away and locals mull migration*. The South China Morning Post. https://www.scmp.com/news/hong-kong/hong-kong-economy/article/3125233/hong-kongs-it-sector-facing-shortage-skilled

# AN E-LEARNING ENVIRONMENT FOR INFLUENCING CHILDREN'S ATTITUDES TOWARD ULTRAVIOLET PROTECTION

Sotiroula Theodosi and Iolie Nicolaidou
*Department of Communication and Internet Studies, Cyprus University of Technology*
*P.O. Box 50329, Limassol 3603, Cyprus*

**ABSTRACT**

This paper describes a work in progress to design and evaluate an e-learning intervention that utilizes the Internet of Things (IoT) to increase awareness of the dangers of ultraviolet (UV) radiation exposure and promote sun protection practices early in life. The authors' previous work in a pre-test post-test control group study (Study 1) involved children in using IoT devices to collect and analyze real-time UV radiation data. Preliminary data were promising in this small-scale study, but the latter did not use a validated instrument to measure children's UV knowledge, attitudes, and behaviors. This second study has a dual aim. First, it reports on the results of a systematic literature review that aimed to identify validated questionnaires that a) measure attitudes toward UV light protection, b) are appropriate for primary school, and c) are suitable for evaluating e-learning prevention interventions if they are used as a pre-test and post-test. Second, it describes how the intervention of Study 1 will be re-enacted through an e-learning platform that allows for deepening student understanding and engagement through gamification and allows for visualizing students' understanding in real-time.

**KEYWORDS**

e-Learning Environment, Ultraviolet (UV) Protection, Children, Attitudes, Validated Instruments, Systematic Literature Review.

## 1. INTRODUCTION

Prolonged exposure to ultraviolet radiation (UV) is linked to skin cancer, and children are considered a more vulnerable group to UV harmful effects than adults. The most proactive and effective way of preventing skin cancer is through education. Increasing awareness of the dangers of UV radiation exposure and promoting sun protection practices early in life through prevention interventions is essential (Cercato et al., 2013) particularly for countries with a high UV index year-round.

This paper describes a work in progress to design and evaluate an e-learning intervention that utilizes the Internet of Things (IoT), specifically UV light sensors, to collect data that reflect real time environmental conditions. IoT technologies are not yet applied in primary education for data collection, processing and visualization and their potential benefit and impact in the learning process has not yet been realized. The authors' previous work involved designing an intervention for $6^{th}$-grade children in a STEM inquiry-based learning environment following a sequence of four eighty-minute ultraviolet radiation and protection course. During the course students studied multimodal sources, experimented with UV beads, and utilized commercially available sensors connected to tablets for precise measurements of UV radiation levels in their schoolyard (Study 1). Data sources included questionnaires on UV knowledge, attitudes, and behaviors administered pre- and post-intervention. Preliminary results of this first pre-test post-test control group study with 31 participants were promising, as statistically significant learning gains, and positive behavioral changes were found only for the experimental group (Theodosi & Nicolaidou, 2021).

However, Study 1 did not use a validated instrument to measure children's UV knowledge, attitudes, and behaviors. In fact, most of the studies that focused on measuring young children's sun-related attitudes followed a survey design (Aquilina et al., 2004; Wright et al., 2008; Saridi et al., 2012) and used questionnaires that were not tested for validity (Koster, 2017), which is a limitation in the literature. Moreover, most prevention behavioral interventions for increasing sun-protective attitudes were not technologically supported.

Prevention interventions designed and delivered through e-learning platforms are expected to have significant benefits. These include having all learning activities in one place, providing the teacher with real-time visualization of students' understanding, and the ability to enhance interventions with gamification elements. The purpose of this study is twofold: a) to identify validated questionnaires that measure UV sun exposure habits and participants' propensity to increase sun protection through a systematic literature review, and b) to describe added pedagogical affordances which will be made possible in a second enactment of the intervention using an e-learning delivery platform to increase children's awareness of UV protection.

## 2. METHODOLOGY

This study's first aim is to identify validated questionnaires, which measure UV sun exposure attitudes and participants' propensity to increase sun protection, through a systematic literature review. The framework used by Neira (2017) for conducting systematic reviews was followed. Google Scholar was used to enable a broad search for scientific studies across various disciplines.

For the studies to be selected, inclusion criteria were set as follows: (a) peer reviewed and fully accessed papers, (b) empirical studies following a survey design and addressing UV exposure attitudes and participants' propensity to increase sun protection and (c) have students as participants. Throughout the searching procedure, the following keywords were used "UV questionnaire AND attitudes AND children", "UV instruments AND attitudes AND children", "UV exposure AND students' attitudes", "Sun exposure attitudes AND primary school", "validated questionnaire AND UV attitudes", resulting in 126 relevant studies. Selection criteria were applied to each study, with the final number of studies, summing up to 70. Fifty-six studies were excluded as follows: duplicated studies (n=15), reviews (n=13), PhD theses (n=4), irrelevant studies (n=1), not fully accessed papers (n=1), theoretical articles regarding UV radiation (n=2), papers developing questionnaires (n=1), studies applied in a general population (n=19). Data was analyzed quantitatively following thematic content analysis regarding each study's research aim, number of participants, educational level, and the use (or not) of validated questionnaires for data collection. All data was coded in these categories and imported in a Microsoft Excel coding sheet.

For the study's second aim, a critical comparison was performed between activities included in Study 1 (Theodosi & Nicolaidou, 2021) and enhanced activities that will be included in its re-enactment in Study 2, in which a commercial e-learning platform (Nearpod) will be used so students can access their learning materials online and work at their own pace.

## 3. RESULTS

Literature searches resulted in 70 relevant studies that met inclusion criteria. Nine out of 70 studies used a descriptive research design aiming to investigate sun protection behaviors adopted by students of different age groups. With the focus in this paper being placed on studies conducted in primary education, the previously mentioned studies were excluded from any further analysis. An overall analysis was performed with respect to participants' educational level to the remaining 61 studies. As the literature review revealed, studies were conducted at all educational levels with 18 studies in total focusing on students' attitudes and behaviors regarding sun protection in primary education. Specifically, 7 studies were conducted in early childhood, 21 in secondary education and 15 in higher education.

Results focusing on primary education (n=18) are presented in this paper. Six surveys aiming to investigate both parents and their children's sun exposure habits and sun-protective behaviors with data deriving from questionnaires completed by parents were excluded from the present review (Balato et al., 2007; Cercato et al., 2012; Dixon et al., 1999; Nyiri, 2005; Stanganelli et al., 2019; Thoonen et al., 2019). Out of the remaining 12 studies, eight of them stated the use of validated questionnaires for measuring UV attitudes. Five studies used Cronbach's alpha to assess the reliability and internal consistency of the questionnaires used (Ergul & Ozeren, 2011; Hewitt et al., 2001; Kubar & Hoffman, 1995; Saridi et al., 2012; Saridi et al., 2014). Cronbach's alpha for the attitudes scale ranged from 0.62 (Hewitt et al., 2001) to 0.85 (Kubar & Hoffman, 1995).

Validated questionnaires were used both to record UV attitudes and sun protective behaviors of primary school students (Ergul & Ozeren, 2011; Kubar & Hoffman, 1995; Saridi et al., 2012) and to record a change in knowledge, attitudes, and sun protective behaviors before and after an educational intervention aiming at higher knowledge and healthier attitudes and behaviors (Duarte et al., 2018; Geller, 2003; Hewitt et al., 2001; Rouhanni et al., 2009; Saridi et al. 2014). The number of participants used for validation purposes was stated in four studies (Duarte et al., 2018; Ergul & Ozeren, 2011; Geller, 2003; Saridi et al., 2012; Saridi et al. 2014) ranging from 50 participants (Duarte et al., 2018) to 1472 participants (Saridi et al. 2014).

For instance, Duarte et al. (2018) conducted a survey to compare primary school students' sun-related knowledge and behavior during school and holiday periods. A questionnaire about sun exposure and behavior was given to 2114 students after educational sessions were held with educators, and an educational activity book regarding sun exposure and protection was administered to all participants. The questionnaire contained: (a) demographic questions, (b) questions on sun-exposure behavior during school and holiday periods, and (c) seven true or false questions to test their knowledge. The questionnaire was designed specifically for children following a review of the relevant literature and was validated with 1,472 students in 2003.

Similarly, Geller (2003) conducted a survey aiming to evaluate the Sun Wise School Program in 102 primary schools in 42 states with a validated questionnaire derived from other studies, revised by educational and child development experts, and pilot-tested for readability and length. The questionnaire included demographic questions and items assessing knowledge, attitudes, practices, and intended practices before and after a paper-based intervention. Rouhanni et al. (2009) followed the same method for evaluating an educational intervention, focusing on sunscreen's use. Similarly, Saridi et al. (2014) used a questionnaire to evaluate the Sun Smart program in Australia, aiming to address students' knowledge, attitudes, and behaviors. Contrary to the previously mentioned interventions, Hewitt et al. (2001) assessed effectiveness of the "Sun Safe" computer-supported intervention by measuring the change in knowledge, attitudes, and behaviors prior and after the intervention. A critical comparison of instruments selected in this review, including an evaluation of their difficulty level for completion by primary school students, will identify an instrument for validation in the children's native language as part of future work.

For the study's second aim, the e-learning platform that will be utilized in the second enactment of the learning environment to increase awareness of the dangers of ultraviolet (UV) radiation exposure (https://nearpod.com/) will allow for several added affordances, including interactivity and increased student engagement. Students will be able to easily access and study multimodal sources of information focusing on the question "Why is the sun dangerous?" which will be uploaded by the teacher in the structured environment of the platform (Lesson 1). Students' individual responses to this question, as well as students' observations regarding UV radiation (Lesson 2), will be available to the teacher in real-time, a functionality that allows for visualizing students understanding in real-time and using insights from formative assessments to guide the teaching and improve student outcomes. Students can input their measured UV radiation levels collected using sensors during the lesson and asynchronously in the e-learning platform (Lesson 3). Students can be scaffolded to interpret sensor-collected data regarding UV radiation levels at their school. They can input their suggestions of products and actions they consider sun-protective through collaborative work in small groups, and participate in gamified activities in the platform (Lesson 3). Students can present the results of their testing of sun-protective products using sensors to determine their level of protection through the e-learning platform (Lesson 4), allowing the teacher to adapt instruction or address misconceptions during lessons based on feedback from real-time data.

# 4. CONCLUSION

This study's primary contribution refers to identifying several validated instruments measuring attitudes towards UV protection that can be used to evaluate the effectiveness of e-learning prevention interventions aiming to affect young children's attitudes towards UV protection. Future short-term research steps will focus on validating a selected instrument in the children's native language and designing the intervention in a specific commercial e-learning platform (Nearpod) for increased interactivity, engagement, the addition of gamified activities, and the ability to adapt instruction based on real-time data. Long-term research goals include using the validated instrument in a pre-test, post-test control group design with a larger sample of students who will participate in an e-learning re-enactment of the prevention intervention to positively affect children's attitudes towards UV protection.

# REFERENCES


Ackermann, S., Vuadens, A., Levi, F., & Bulliard, J-L. (2016). Sun protective behaviour and sunburn prevalence in primary and secondary schoolchildren in western Switzerland. *Swiss Medical Weekly*, 1-11. http://doi.org/10.4414/smw.2016.14370

Aquilina, S., Gauci, A. A., Ellul, M., & Sceritt, L. (2004). Sun awareness in Maltese secondary school students. *European Academy of Dermatology and Venereology, 18*, 670 – 675. http://doi.org/10.1111/j.1468-3083.2004.01046

Cercato, M. C., Nagore, E., Ramazzotti, V., Sperduti, I., & Cuillen, C. (2013). Improving sun-safe knowledge, attitudes and behaviour in parents in primary school children: a pilot study. *Journal of Cancer Education,28*, 151-157. http://doi.org/10.1007/s13187-012-0413-5

Duarte, A. F., Picoto, A., Pereira, AdC., & Correia, O. (2018). Sun protection in children: a behavioural study. European *Journal of Dermatology, 28*(3), 338-342. http://doi.org/10.1684/ejd.2018.3290

Ergul, S., & Ozeren, E. (2011). Sun protection behavior and individual risk factors of Turkish primary school students associated with skin cancer: a questionnaire-based study. *Asian Pacific Journal of Cancer Prevention, 12*, 765-770.

Geller, A. C., Rutsch, L., Kenausis, K., Selzer, P., & Zhang, Z. (2003). Can an hour or two of sun protection education keep the sunburn away? Evaluation of the environmental protection agency's sunwise school program. *Environmental Health: A Global Access Science Source, 2*(13), 1-9. http://ehjournal.net/content/2/1/13

Hewitt, M., Denman, S., Hayes, L., Pearson, J., Wallbanks, C. (2001). Evaluation of "Sun-safe": a health education recourse for primary schools. *Health Education Research, 16*(5), 623-633.

Koster, B., Sondergaard, J., Nielsen, J. B., Christensen, K. B., Allen, M., Olsen, A., & Bentzen, J. (2017). Knowledge deficit, attitude and behavior scales association to objective measures of sun exposure and sunburn in Danish population based sample. *PLoS ONE 12(*5), 1-17. https://doi.org/10.1371/journal.pone.0178190

Kubar, W. L., Rodrigue, J. R., & Hoffman III, R. G. (1995). Children and exposure to the sun: relationships among attitudes, knowledge, intentions, and behavior. *Psychological reports, 77*, 1136-1138.

Neira, S.A.E., Salinas, J., & De Benito, B. (2017). Emerging technologies (ETs) in education: a systematic review of the literature published between 2006 and 2016. *International Journal of Emerging Technologies in Learning, 12*(5), 128-149.

Rouhani, P., Parmet, Y., Bessell, A. G., Peay, T., Weiss, A., Kirsner, R. S. (2009). Knowledge, attitudes, and behaviors of elementary school students regarding sun exposure and skin cancer. *Pediatric Dermatology, 26*(5), 529-535. http://doi.org/10.1111/j.1525-1470.2009.00908.x

Saridi, M. I., Rekleiti, M. D., Toska, A. G., & Souliotis, K. (2014). Assessing a sun protection program aimed at Greek elementary school students for malign melanoma prevention. *Asian Pacific Journal of Cancer Prevention, 15*, 5009-5018. http://dx.doi.org/10.7314/APJCP.2014.15.12.5009

Saridi. M., Toska, A., Rekleiti, M., Wozniak., G., Liachopoulou, A., Kalokairinou, A., Souliotis. K., & Birbas, K. (2012). Sun protection habits of primary students in a coastal area of Greece. *Journal of Skin Cancer, 2012*, 1-9. http://doi.org/ 10.1155/2012/629652

Theodosi, S. & Nicolaidou, I. (2021). Affecting young children's knowledge, attitudes, and behaviors for ultraviolet radiation protection through the internet of things: A quasi-experimental study. *Computers, 10*(137), 1-15. https://doi.org/10.3390/computers10110137

Wright, C., Reeder, A. I., Gray, A., & Cox, B. (2008). Child sun-protection: sun-related attitudes mediate the association between children's knowledge and behaviours. *Journal of Paediatrics and Child Health, 44*, 692-698. http://doi.org/ 10.1111/j.1440-1754.2008.01408.x

# ASSESSMENT OF DISTANCE LEARNING MODES FOR TERTIARY EDUCATION IN PAKISTAN

Jalil Raza[1], Tahira Anwar Lashari[1,*], Sana Anwar Lashari[2,**], Hira Raza[1] and Saima Anwar Lashari[3,***]

[1]*School of Electrical Engineering and Computer Sciences (SEECS), National University of Sciences and Technology (NUST), Pakistan Islamabad, Pakistan*

[2]*School of Applied Psychology, Social Work and Policy, University Utara Malaysia (UUM) 06010 Sintok, Malaysia*

[3]*College of Computing and Informatics Saudi Electronic University, Riyadh, Saudi Arabia*

**https://orcid.org/0000-0003-0474-1650*

***https://orcid.org/0000-0002-2707-9017*

****https://orcid.org/0000-0001-6209-491X*

**ABSTRACT**

In this study, two modes of communication for distance learning are discussed -Broadcast Media Technologies (one-to-many) and Communicative Media Technologies (many-to-many). In addition, the study sheds light on Synchronous Versus Asynchronous modes of communication. Further, the study evaluates the effectiveness of Digi skills' (an initiative by the government of Pakistan for Information Technology courses) mode of communication and its possibilities of deploying the same in tertiary education in Pakistan. For the accessibility, affordability and acquaintance with tools and software, this research has conducted a survey through Google forms in order to assess an availability of internet connectivity and availability of devices for distance learning amongst Students. Finally, the researcher proposes a Hybrid Solution for distance education for tertiary Education in Pakistan.

**KEYWORDS**

Distance Learning, Hybrid Modes of learning, HyFlex mode of learning, synchronous and asynchronous modes of learning.

## 1. INTRODUCTION

The recent trend of online learning has increased due to COVID-19 pandemic that has caused a massive disruption in the academic field. To cope with the situation universities shifted to electronic learning (e-learning) which has affected universities, instructors and understudies at all levels. The quantity of schools and colleges around the world, giving distance learning programs has risen emphatically and numerous nations have seen an increase in distance learning. The United Nations Educational, Scientific, and Cultural Organization (UNESCO) announced that more than 1.37 billion understudies (80% of the worldwide understudy populace) have been impacted by the emergency. The interruptions have constrained learners to migrate from actual school grounds and adjust to new internet based instructive settings. Hence, to provide alternative solutions several software houses and Edu-Tech companies tried to impart uninterrupted education. Consequently, digital learning tools are in high demand.

Adegbija, Fakomogbon, & Adebayo (2013) claimed that institutions where teachers are completely naive about the technological modes and lack of training towards basic understanding of frameworks like Technology Pedagogy Content and Knowledge (TPACK). Consequently, leads in poor lecture delivery and resulted in incomplete attainment of desired learning outcomes. Nevertheless, videoconferencing and online discussion forums and social media are examples of communicative technologies. This educational communicative media allows interaction between learners and teachers, and perhaps creates even more significant learning impact on a learner, without the participants needing to be present in the same place. In addition to this, there are two main types of distance learning: synchronous and asynchronous. Synchronous mode of distance learning requires all those participating in the communication to participate together, at the same time, but not importantly in the same place. Videoconferencing tools such as, Zoom Meeting, Skype, and MS Teams and webinars are examples of a synchronous mode of interaction. On the other hand, asynchronous Mode of learning enables members to access information or communicates at different time zones, usually at the time and place of choice of the participant. Broadcast mode and all recorded media are asynchronous (such as YouTube videos). Similarly, Learning Management Systems (LMS); a vital software platform enables educator and trainers to deliver, create, and manage educational content; thus, providing the alternative approach to internet connectivity issues, lack of proper online communication discussions and lack of availability of LMS. More than 70,000 universities, corporations and schools in over 200 countries and 100 different languages are utilising learning management systems for improving educational outcomes for students. Yet, a majority of institutes in Pakistan still use conventional methods without realizing the changes taking place around them. Moodle is a free online LMS that allows educators creating grading systems, securing content, tracking attendance, creating quizzes, and maintaining a platform with a wealth of instructional material that connects students to critical educational resources. It aids teachers in providing better education to students and allows students to learn more quickly while staying on top of their schoolwork and extracurricular activities. LMS has become an essential part of academic activity in Europe and the United States. Pakistan, on the other hand, is far behind in this regard.

Pakistan - a developing country - is also fostering its field of information technology. Recently, Ministry of Information Technology Government of Pakistan jointly with Virtual University started e-learning program: Digi Skills, for the youth of Pakistan. The program offered various courses of 12 weeks duration: Digital Marketing, E-commerce Management, Freelancing and so forth. Trainees were equipped with the latest skills in various fields of information technology. As a result, Pakistani youth would use their learned skills and earn by working virtually. The Digi Skills Mode of learning is an asynchronous mode in which learner's watches the video uploaded on LMS and the Communication between instructor and students takes place in same platform and each communicate as per their availability, ease and accessibility to the internet. This approach is names as Hyflex (Hybrid Flexible) which is a combination of hybrid and flexible modes of distance learning. This method integrates physical, virtual and face to face interaction in the online learning. The program has an efficient way of assessing the trainees through quiz and hands-on-exercise. This will help the under-resourced youth by exposing them to a greater world of technology. In Pakistan, most students pursuing higher education have access to the internet for social purposes. LMSs can easily be used to turn things around for both teachers and students if adequately implemented. Therefore, the current study aims at assessing the modes of learning using HyFlex model for tertiary education in Pakistan.

## 2. LITERATURE REVIEW

Smallhorn, et al., (2015) revealed that learning management systems might be critical for efficient management. Few campuses utilized open-source software which facilitates teachers and students in maintaining the various tasks. This Moodle-based system relieves students stress by producing speedy, accurate results. For instance; Erfurt University has 5,000+ students enrolled on average for an academic year, while an ordinary department employs no more than 10 people in the management and 10 in the faculty. That is how technology helps managing academic life of students and teachers. However, Bates (2019) claimed that lecture capture recordings may be less effective than an online course incorporating collaborative learning and online discussion forums. Interaction is considered crucial to learning experiences in the constructivist learning perspective. Learning in a group, is an integrated approach for students to get experience with collaboration and improve skills in knowledge co-construction.

Adegbija, et al., (2013) revealed the importance of Open Distance Learning (ODL) and its synchronization with ICT tools. Literature shed light on the significance of broadcast communication model (television and radio) particularity the use of broadcast in the historical perspective of BBC in Nigeria. In 1932, BBC started its first radio broadcast subsequent started its first education program in West Africa. Moreover, in 1957, Nigeria broadcast service started education programs. In the initial years, TV was limited only to primary, secondary and teacher training. However, with the help of the UNESCO institution of education, university of Ibadan in 1962 established the first audio-visual system. Onwards, tertiary education started to begin and implemented two modes of leaning namely open and distance learning. These terms are interrelated. Basically, this broadcast mode is self-pace learning mode where learners are responsible for their learning activities. Nonetheless, the observations of United Nations Educational, Scientific and Cultural Organization (UNESCO) the inequality between developing and developed digital divides pointed out the challenges. Few of them are campus radio or other TV stations do not have proper education broadcaster, instructional designers, scriptwriter for ODL (Open and Distance Learning) programs. Laboratories need to be redeveloped according to the guided enquiry so that learning outcomes can be analyzed.

Wahab et al (2021) stated that technology which best fits in the in the pedagogical approach in the classrooms nourished students learning. Streaming digital video on demand increased math achievement scores statistically significantly. Such educational programs facilities learners with better reading skills, higher visual processing and spatial perceptual skills, increased knowledge of critical thinking about a particular issue are all part of the cognitive domain, and there is plenty of research on how video can help with mental growth and academic achievement. Moreover, the integration of Edu domain can be deemed through the example of Substitution, Augmentation, Modification, Redefinition (SMAR) model which can be resulted as a ladder to improve students learning from basic to advance level of learning difficulties. At the substitution level, lecture may ask the outcomes of replacing a certain task with technology. For the augmentation level, the question which arises is about new features that technology can provide. Moreover, at the modification level, they may ask about the changeability of task with the integration of technology. Lastly, at redefinition, they may ask if the technology can help in achieving the inconceivable tasks. In conclusion, SMAR model does not work as magic bullet rather it does replace scaffolding approach. In a way, the access to learning anywhere and anytime, time and money-saving and offering flexibility. However, there is a limitations of distance learning include distraction, technology awareness, and the less communication between instructor and student. In-addition, Moodle platform for uploading resources highlights the right set of limitations and advantages that can be considered while conducting research on distance learning. Therefore, blend of both tools should be used in learning. Moreover, the dynamics of online discourse and pedagogical techniques in cyberspace implies all communication that shared ground of information facilitates the holistic approach of learning.

## 3. RESEARCH METHODOLOGY

A comparative assessment survey was conducted on Google forms in order to assess the availability of access to digital tools, reliable internet access, connectivity issues, intermittent power outages and acquaintance with communication software. The survey was conducted from two public universities in Pakistan namely Shaikh Ayaz University Shikarpur (SAUS), Sindh and PAF-IAST (Pak-Austria Fachhochschule- Institute of Applied Science and Technology) Haripur, KP (Khyber Pakhtunkhwa). Both of the universities are located in the rural areas of the two provinces. The aim behind selecting these universities was to examine the ground realities of the educational institutes situated in the far-flung areas of the urban centers. The total number of responses collected was 750. The questionnaire designed was closed ended. The research has also observed the model used by Digi Skill in teaching various digital skills.

## 4. DATA VISUALIZATION AND ANALYSIS

A statistical tool was used to analyze data collected in the survey. The data was presented in the form of pie and bar charts that made easier to analyze statistically. The readiness assessment survey had four questions. The finding of each posed survey questions is sequentially represented in the following section. The first question was on inquiring the reliable access to the internet. To the question on availability of internet, the responses showed that 72.1% students have Wi-Fi from PAF-IAST (Pak-Austria Fachhochschule: Institute of Applied Science and Technology) whereas 34% from SAUS claims to have Wi-Fi. The results of Figure 1 showed similarity between both universities.

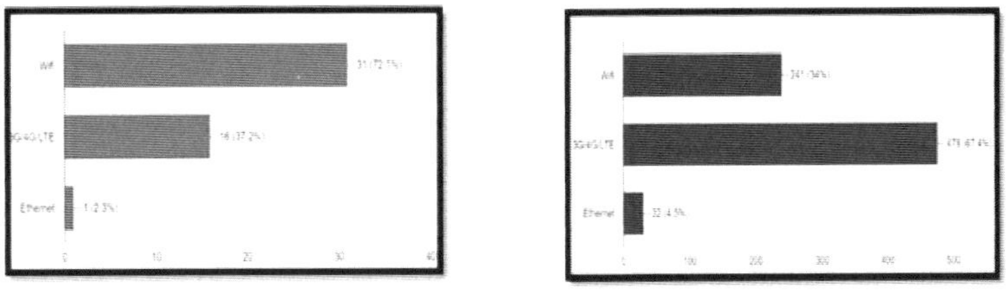


Figure 1. Access to Internet

Secondly survey question was related to difficulty faced during internet connectivity. The students were asked if they have used various communication softwares for online education. The results showed that PAF-IAST (Pak-Austria Fachhochschule: Institute of Applied Science and Technology) students were more familiar with MS Teams however; SAUS students were more familiar with Skype.

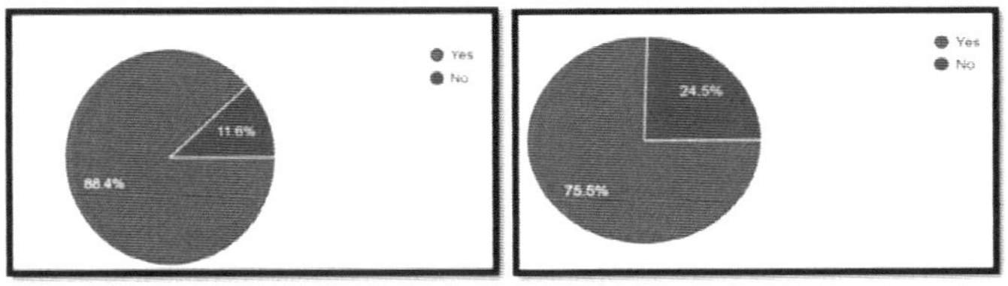


Figure 2. Internet connectivity issues

To the question on readiness for online classes, students were asked to inform regarding their opining on online classes. The results showed that students from both universities were not ready for online education.

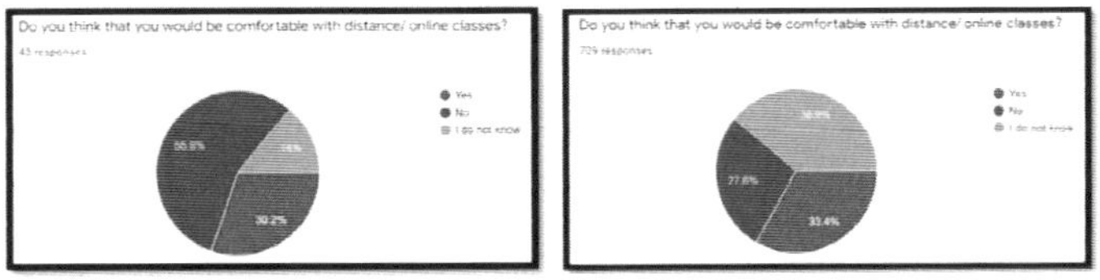


Figure 3. Usage of softwares

Lastly, their expertise in operating computer was inquired. The data from the survey shows the differences and similarities between the two universities. One is equipped with the latest instructional technologies of smart classroom (PAF-IAST) and the other one has traditional classrooms without any instructional technologies (SAUS). The result from both universities showed that the students were not ready and satisfied with the complete transition from face to face to online classes. The reasons for dissatisfaction found through the survey were electricity power outages, internet connectivity issues, access to the internet and so forth.

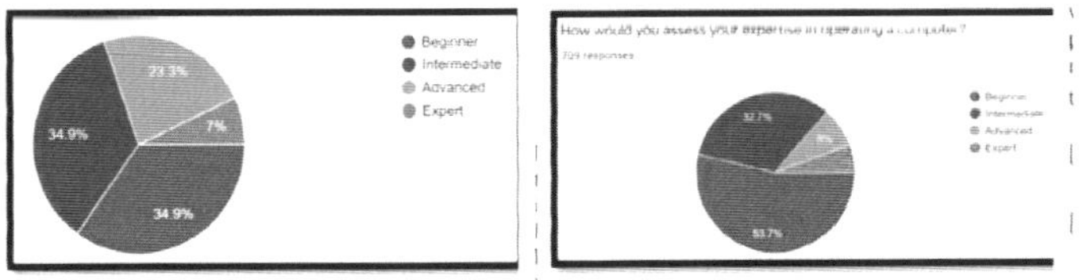


Figure 4. Expertise in operating a computer

## 5. CONCLUSION AND RECOMMENDATIONS

Considering the results gathered from the survey, this research proposes that aggregation of Broadcast and Communicative mode for online or distance learning is superlative communicative platform for online learning. This study has discussed the two modes of technologies in distance learning; broadcast media and communicative media. The effectiveness of Digi skills mode of technology is considered as the solution to tertiary education problems in Pakistan. The mere limitation of current study is data is collected for two universities in Pakistan and future studies could extend the sample. Moreover, the current trends practiced in the distance learning in Pakistani universities could also be explored. Moreover, due to the unfortunate Covid-19 pandemic, teaching and learning modes have witnessed a drastic transition from the traditional classroom to distance learning. Higher education in Pakistan is in the process of transitioning the new modes of earning and teaching. Higher Education Commission (HEC) has been deliberating on designing instructional technologies with the inclusion of smart classroom facilities. This research benefits the country's higher education sector with the proposed hybrid mode of learning. The suggested hybrid mode should address the needs of learners in terms of access o content, lectures and assessment.

## ACKNOWLEDGEMENT

The authors would like to express their gratitude to the Office of Research, Innovation and Commercialization and School of Electrical Engineering and Computer Sciences (SEECS), National University of Sciences and Technology (NUST) for technical support and funding.

## REFERENCES

Adegbija, M. V., Fakomogbon, M. A., & Adebayo, M. S. (2013). Roles of broadcast media for instructional delivery in open and distance learning: Nigeria as a case study. European Scientific Journal, 9(23).

Bates, A. T. (2019). Choosing and using media in education: the SECTIONS model. Teaching in a Digital Age-Second Edition.

Leijon, M., & Lundgren, B. (2019). Connecting physical and virtual spaces in a HyFlex pedagogic model with a focus on teacher interaction. Journal of Learning Spaces, 8(1).

Lim, F. P. (2017). An analysis of synchronous and asynchronous communication tools in e-learning. Advanced Science and Technology Letters, 143(46), 230-234.

Miller, J., Risser, M., & Griffiths, R. (2013). Student choice, instructor flexibility: Moving beyond the blended instructional model. Issues and trends in educational technology, 1(1), 8-24.

Sabharwal, R., Chugh, R., Hossain, M. R., & Wells, M. (2018, December). Learning management systems in the workplace: A literature review. In 2018 IEEE International Conference on Teaching, Assessment, and Learning for Engineering (TALE) (pp. 387-393). IEEE.

Trail, L., Fields, S., & Caukin, N. (2020). Finding flexibility with HyFlex: Teaching in the digital age. International Journal of the Whole Child, 5(2), 22-26.

Wahab, A., Lashari, T. A., Lashari, S. A., Mamoon, J., & Afzal, E. (2021). Teaching Code of Ethics through Interactive Videos to Enhance Learner's Engagement, Interest, and Performance. Turkish Journal of Computer and Mathematics Education (TURCOMAT), 12(6), 4856-4866.

# RECOGNIZING REAL EMOTIONS THROUGH INDUCTIVE WRITING TEACHING

Li Li
*School of Languages and Cultures, Shanghai University of Political Science and Law, Shanghai, China*

**ABSTRACT**

It is of great importance to identify students' negative emotions so as to avoid accidents. However, most of the students with mental problems seldom express their emotions in some ways, which makes it more difficult for the emotion recognition system to obtain the emotional data of these students. To solve the problem of the lack of data acquisition approaches in emotional monitoring of special student groups, this paper proposes a method to obtain students' real emotions based on emotion-induced writing teaching. First, the channel for acquiring emotion data of the special students is established through writing teaching. Second, students are guided to express their emotions through essays by purposeful writing exercises. At last, this paper proposes an emotion calculation method, which comprehensively analyzes a student's real emotion according to the emotions of a group of essays on positive, neutral and negative themes. The experimental results show that the proposed method can obtain students' real emotions effectively and is much better for students with optimistic and pessimistic personalities.

**KEYWORDS**

Emotion Recognition, Writing Teaching, Mental Health.

## 1. INTRODUCTION

The COVID-19 pandemic is sweeping the world. The fear of the virus, the depression of isolation and the pressure of employment have affected many people's emotions. Comparatively speaking, college students, a special group, have weak emotional control ability, and psychological breakdown will lead to more serious consequences. It is of great significance for students' healthy development and social stability to accurately perceive students' negative emotions and effectively ease them so as to avoid unexpected situations.

The emotion recognition task mainly includes two sub-tasks. First, obtaining raw data for emotion recognition. It is usually obtained through conversations, social media, audio and video surveillance. These data include conversations, texts, tones, facial expressions, body movements, web behaviors, etc., which may explicitly or implicitly contain the emotions of the subjects. Second, emotion recognition. It is mainly achieved by emotion dictionary (Kim, 2004), statistical machine learning method (Wang, 2012) or deep learning method (Liu, 2015; Ouyang, 2015). Current studies mainly focus on the second sub-task, while the first task is rarely studied.

In the context of COVID-19, the primary problem faced by college student emotion recognition task is that it is difficult to obtain emotion data. Due to the necessity of fighting against the epidemic, there are fewer group activities in school and less face-to-face communication between students. In particular, for the special emotional students, they are not good at communicating with others or active on social networks. They lack the way of emotional release, and are more prone to have some psychological problems, which makes it difficult for us to obtain emotional data of the special student group through traditional means.

In order to solve the above problems, we propose English writing teaching as a channel for perceiving students' emotions. Because of the special status of English writing teaching in Chinese universities, it is a compulsory course for freshmen and sophomores in almost all majors. Some third and fourth grade students also need to take English writing courses because of the Graduate Entrance Examination, TOEFL and so on. Therefore, student essay as emotion recognition data is a possible approach. Compared with social media and other ways of expressing emotions directly, the emotions expressed by essay are not necessarily students' current emotions, so it is more difficult to identify students' real emotions based on essays. To solve the problem, we propose an emotion-guided writing exercise, which allows students to write essays on different emotion topics in a short period, and integrates the emotions expressed by students in essays on positive, negative and neutral emotion topics, so as to better acquire students' real emotions.

The main contributions of this paper are as follows:

1) This paper proposes a method to acquire students' emotion data based on English writing teaching, and establishes a channel for acquiring emotion data of the special emotional students.
2) This paper puts forward a method of obtaining students' emotions by emotion-guided writing training, which improves the ability to obtain students' real emotions from essays.

# 2. METHOD

The proposed framework to induce and recognize students' real emotions based on writing exercises is shown in Figure 1. The framework mainly includes a writing task generation module, an essay emotion recognition module, and a student emotion recognition module. The modules and the work process of the framework are shown as follows.

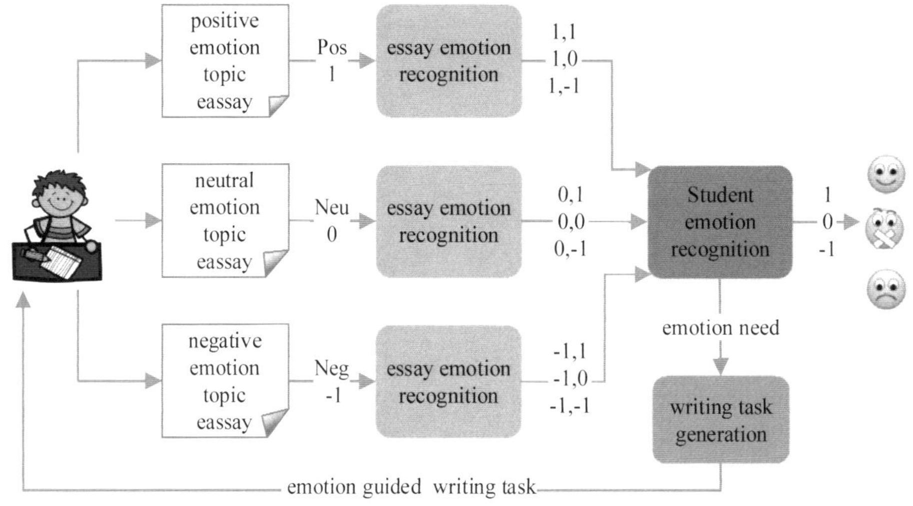


Figure 1. Real emotion recognition framework of a student

## 2.1 Writing Task Generation Module

The writing task generation module generates three different writing tasks which involve positive, negative and neutral topics for a student. An effective way is to label each writing task in the existing writing practice database with an emotion, and then randomly select writing tasks according to the task requirements and emotion labels in the database. The number of writing tasks is relatively limited, so we make the emotional labeling of writing tasks manually to obtain a more accurate result.

## 2.2 Essay Emotion Recognition Module

The essay emotion recognition module classifies the emotion of each essay. When the essays are completed by the student, emotion recognition module obtains the emotion of each essay based on emotion classification method. The text emotion classification method based on deep learning has become the mainstream, and there exist many methods with good effect, such as RNN (Recurrent Neural Network) (Topbaş, 2021; Zhang, 2016), BI-LSTM (Bi-directional Long-Short Term Memory) (Tareq, 2021). This module directly employs the BI-LSTM + CRF model as the emotion classifier.

## 2.3 Student Emotion Recognition Module

The student emotion recognition module identifies the real emotion of a student by comprehensively considering the emotions of three essays belonging to three writing tasks. This module is the key to the proposed method. We use three categories of emotions, among which positive emotion is 1, neutral emotion is 0, and negative emotion is -1. Each essay may be classified as positive, neutral, or negative emotion by the essay emotion recognition module. There are nine possible combinations shown in matrix (1), each of which is represented by a two-tuples. For example, (1, -1) indicates that a student writes an essay on a positive emotion topic into a negative emotion essay, which may indicate that the student has severe negative emotions.

$$\begin{bmatrix} (1,1) & (1,0) & (1,-1) \\ (0,1) & (0,0) & (0,-1) \\ (-1,1) & (-1,0) & (-1,-1) \end{bmatrix} \tag{1}$$

Each of these two-tuples is simplified by subtracting the first item from the second item to get the following matrix.

$$\text{mim} = \begin{bmatrix} 0 & -1 & -2 \\ 1 & 0 & -1 \\ 2 & 1 & 0 \end{bmatrix} \tag{2}$$

In (2), -2 means the most negative motion, 2 means the most positive motion, and the other values means middle motion. We call (2) as the motion inductive matrix for writing. Assume that the emotions of a student's three essays are -1, -1, 0 respectively, which are mapping to the mim matrix and get the position matrix, as shown in (3).

$$\begin{bmatrix} -1 \\ -1 \\ 0 \end{bmatrix} \Rightarrow \begin{bmatrix} 0 & 0 & 1 \\ 0 & 0 & 1 \\ 0 & 1 & 0 \end{bmatrix} \tag{3}$$

Finally, the emotion of the student $es$ can be gotten by (4). $es$ values range from -3 to +3 for a total of seven emotional states. We convert them to three emotional states -1, 0, and 1 as the final output of the method., namely the student's real emotion.

$$es = sum\left( \begin{bmatrix} 0 & 0 & 1 \\ 0 & 0 & 1 \\ 0 & 1 & 0 \end{bmatrix} \circ \begin{bmatrix} 0 & -1 & -2 \\ 1 & 0 & -1 \\ 2 & 1 & 0 \end{bmatrix} \right) = -2 \tag{4}$$

## 2.4 Work Process

The real emotion recognition framework of a student works circularly. Each round of student emotion recognition works as follows.

1) According to the emotional need and the writing teaching need, the writing task generation module selects three writing tasks of positive, negative and neutral topics from the labeled writing tasks database.

2) When the essays are completed by the student, the emotion recognition module obtains the emotion of each essay based on text emotion classification method.

3) Finally, the student emotion recognition module comprehensively considers the emotions of three writing tasks and the emotions of three essays, and finally obtains the student's emotion.

To avoid the uncertainty of the single-round emotion recognition, the above emotion recognition process can be repeated many times according to the frequency of practice in writing teaching. If the recognition results of multiple rounds in a short period of time are conflicting, the result should be ignored. On the contrary, if the recognition results of multiple rounds in the short term are consistent, the recognition results are of great reference value.

## 3. EXPERIMENT

### 3.1 Experimental Design

**Experiment Participants:** We select 30 none-English major students from different majors and grades in a university as the participants. The emotions of these students can be observed. They either have social media accounts and update frequently, or they can be observed with the help of surrounding students, or they can be observed by teachers in class. These observations are transparent, and the participants are not aware of participating in the experiment, so as not to affect the experimental results.

**Experimental Process:** The processes of the experiment are as follow,

(1) Observe and obtain the real emotion of a student manually;

(2) Generate writing tasks, choose three essays which involve positive, negative and neutral topics respectively, and release them to the student one by one;

(3) Collect the three essays one by one, and recognize the emotion of each essay;

(4) Calculate the student's emotion based on the emotions of three essays.

(5) Observe and obtain the real emotion of the student again, and compare it with the emotion obtained in step1. If there is no change in emotion, this round of experiment is over and the results are available. Otherwise, the results of this round are discarded and then a new round of experiment starts. The goal of this step is to eliminate the influence of writing on student's emotions.

(6) Repeat the above steps for all 30 students to complete a complete experiment.

(7) Take the emotion of each student obtained in step (1) as reference, and calculate the correctness of the emotion of all students obtained by the method.

### 3.2 Experimental Results and Analysis

We repeated the experiment three times, and the results are shown in the first line of Table 1, with an average accuracy of 74.5%. Although there is still a lot of room for improvement in accuracy, the proposed method has been proved to be effective. Further, we try to find out whether there exists a difference of the proposed method in the emotion acquisition of different personalities. Based on the personality analysis of the participants, we classified them into optimistic, pessimistic and neutral groups. The results of the experiment are recalculated in each group. The final results are shown in lines 2, 3, and 4 in Table 1. The experimental results show that the proposed method has the best effect on optimistic student, followed by pessimistic student and neutral student.

Table 1. Results of real emotion recognition of students through essays

| Personality type | Exp1 | Exp2 | Exp3 | Average |
|---|---|---|---|---|
| all students | 0.739 | 0.786 | 0.711 | 0.745 |
| optimistic students | 0.800 | 0.900 | 0.800 | 0.833 |
| pessimistic students | 0.750 | 0.875 | 0.750 | 0.792 |
| neutral students | 0.667 | 0.583 | 0.583 | 0.611 |

To explore the reasons for the differences among different personality, we conducted a further analysis of the experimental data to observe whether a student's emotions are consistent with the emotions expressed in his/her essays. The emotion consistency degree is equal to the ratio of the number of emotionally consistent essays to the total number of essays, which is also calculated in personality groups and the results are shown in Table 2. The results show that optimistic students have the highest emotion consistency degree, followed by neutral students, and pessimistic students have the lowest emotion consistency degree. The high emotion consistency degree means that students' emotions can be expressed more through the essay, which also makes students' emotion recognition algorithm perform better.

Table 2. Comparison of emotion consistency of different personality students

| Personality type | Emotion consistency degree |
|---|---|
| All students | 0.758 |
| optimistic student | 0.853 |
| pessimistic student | 0.689 |
| neutral student | 0.734 |

Through the above analysis, it can be seen that the proposed method of obtaining students' real emotions through guided writing is effective. Although the method has a certain tendency that the emotion recognition of optimistic students is better than that of pessimistic students, the emotion acquisition of pessimistic students has also been proved to be effective.

## 4. CONCLUSION

It is meaningful to monitor the psychological impact of COVID-19 on college students by using emotion analysis systems to avoid some unexpected accidents. However, most of the students with mental problems seldom express their emotions in some ways, which makes it more difficult for the emotion recognition system to obtain the emotional data of such students. This paper proposes the method of obtaining students' real emotions based on writing exercises, which effectively solves the problem of lacking emotion data in the emotion monitoring of special student groups. The experimental results show that the proposed method can obtain students' real emotions effectively and is much better for students with optimistic and pessimistic personalities. The proposed method can be used not only in student emotion perception and analysis system, but also in feedback and evaluation of writing teaching after making little changes.

The paper presents the preliminary result of the proposed method of obtaining students' emotion through inductive writing teaching. There are still more improvements to be made in the next step of the paper, such as trying to use more methods to improve the accuracy of emotion recognition in individual essays, design more step experiments to verify the effectiveness of the proposed method.

## ACKNOWLEDGEMENT

This research was financially supported by the fund from China National Institute for SCO International Exchange and Judicial Cooperation (No.20SHJD021)

## REFERENCES

Kim, S., and Hovy, E., 2004. Determining the sentiment of opinions. *Proceedings of the International Conference on Computational Linguistics*. Geneva, Switzerland, pp. 1367-1373.

Liu, P. et al, 2015. Fine-grained Opinion Mining with Recurrent Neural Networks and Word Embeddings. *Proceedings of the Conference on Empirical Methods in Natural Language Processing*. Lisbon, Portugal, pp.1433-1443.

Ouyang, X. et al, 2015. Sentiment Analysis Using Convolutional Neural Network. *Proceedings of the IEEE International Conference on Computer and Information Technology; Ubiquitous Computing and Communications; Dependable, Autonomic and Secure Computing; Pervasive Intelligence and Computing*. Liverpool, UK, pp. 2359-2364.

Tareq, A., and Hewahi, N., 2021. Sentiment Analysis of Tweets During COVID-19 Pandemic Using BLSTM. *Proceedings of the International Conference on Data Analytics for Business and Industry*. Sakheer, Bahrain, pp. 245-249.

Topbaş, A. et al, 2021. Sentiment Analysis for COVID-19 Tweets Using Recurrent Neural Network (RNN) and Bidirectional Encoder Representations (BERT) Models. *Proceedings of the International Conference on Computing, Electronic and Electrical Engineering*. Quetta, Pakistan, pp. 1-6.

Wang, S., and Manning, C. D., 2012. Baselines and Bigrams: Simple, Good Sentiment and Topic Classification. *Proceedings of the Annual Meeting of the Association for Computational Linguistics Volume 2*. Jeju Island, Korea, pp. 90–94.

Zhang, Y. et al, 2016. Sentiment classification using Comprehensive Attention Recurrent models. *Proceedings of the International Joint Conference on Neural Networks*. Vancouver, BC, Canada, pp. 1562-1569.

# REFLECTION PAPER

# HOW ARTIFICIAL INTELLIGENCE HAS CHANGED E-LEARNING EDUCATION IN THE META ERA

Kyriakos Kouveliotis[1] and Maryam Mansuri[2]
*[1]Prof. Dr., Provost & Chief Academic Officer*
*[2]Dr., Lecturer & Head of Postgraduate Studies*
*Berlin School of Business and Innovation, Germany*

**ABSTRACT**

The world is changing at an incredible rate, and different processes are using technology more and more every day. One of the most widely used applications of artificial intelligence today is to simplify employee tasks and office automation. In the future, robots can, like an author, produce articles or create conferences and instructional videos. The more intelligent AI becomes, the more advanced the new education system will be. In such days, the educational method for each person may be different depending on his/her situation. The speed of teaching and learning, interaction with the teacher, and reaching answers in the intelligent education system increases. Artificial intelligence provides a variety of facilities for students with different physical problems. An increasing need for the use of the latest technology advances in learning students and students will accelerate their growth and progress and gives them the ability to confront the challenges of the ever-competitive world. After the epidemic of the COVID-19 virus, both teachers and knowledge have been educated to a new understanding of technology use, which means that strategies for coping with real-world restrictions (such as what time limitations caused by this pandemic and quarantine have been witnessed) are more and more practical.

**KEYWORDS**

Artificial Intelligence, Meta, E-learning, Education, COVID-19.

## 1. INTRODUCTION

Artificial intelligence (AI) has been introduced as a branch of science that tries to simulate the methods that humans use to solve their problems. AI experts try to teach the machine to act like a human. The term intelligence is defined as the competence or ability to solve a problem, and artificial means any systematic human method that may accomplish problem-solving goals. Meta AI refers to an artificial intelligence system that can automatically learn from given data or adapt quickly to new environments with minimal supervision by human experts (Canhoto and Clear, 2020). Because meta-AI can be a great automation tool, the meta-AI system can be used in a variety of deep learning projects. In addition, in this highly connected and super-intelligent society, the demand for data processing is increasing. With this acceleration, meta-artificial intelligence will surely benefit many users in the near future.

In this article, first, the meta-artificial intelligence system will be introduced. Then, the opportunities and facilities that artificial intelligence provides to students are examined. Given the experience that the world has faced in recent years through the encounter with the COVID-19 pandemic, and virtual education has been used to an incredible extent in the world, the role of artificial intelligence in the future of virtual education is undeniable and necessary to study. The most challenging part of E-learning at the beginning of its widespread use in the world was related to exam security. In the following, the solutions provided by meta-artificial intelligence experts are discussed. In addition to the advantages that every new technology offered in the world has, it also has disadvantages and weaknesses that its use does not require the presence of human thought and ethics.

# 2. BODY OF PAPER

## 2.1 The Meta AI System

In the development of a meta AI system, three main parts must be considered: creating a meta artificial intelligence interface, developing core algorithms, and creating a cluster infrastructure(Arrieta et al., 2020). An interface must first be created to provide users with detailed information about the system process, as well as to receive data and other inputs from them. Also, design interfaces to test the models produced and their distribution. Second, implement two main types of algorithms to implement automation(Pappa et al., 2014).

One is the technology that automatically finds the most appropriate neural network structure for learning data sets. Online architecture view has been proposed, which allows efficient search of network architecture with optimization algorithms. In addition, try to implement a technique that can search not only predefined modules in networks but the entire structure of neural networks. Another is the automatic selection of meta-parameters used in machine learning. For example, before training, professionals must properly adjust meta-parameters - the parameters needed for deep learning - based on their experience and knowledge, taking into account the characteristics of the tasks assigned to them, but this requires considerable manpower and time(Bengio et al., 2021).

By automatically selecting meta-parameters, services are designed so that the proposed models can operate efficiently at the request of users, and at the same time the participation of experts and users is minimized (Wang et al., 2020). One of the important areas that AI will transform in the future is the field of modern education(Holmes et al., 2019). Computers today are able to learn and solve the most complex problems. One of the most important uses of AI today is to simplify the tasks of employees and office automation. Graduation books, registers, and anything on paper in modern education will be destroyed. In addition, teachers no longer have to spend long hours correcting exam papers and entering grades. AI lonely will play the role of an educational staff. The ranking of scientific articles, grades, and all scientific standards will be more accurate. In addition, teachers and professors will have more time to educate and communicate with students (Dwivedi et al., 2021). AI and education are growing in parallel. Smart content is one of the elements that will bring dramatic changes to modern education. In addition, artificial intelligence has been introduced in writing textbooks and schools will be equipped with digital books. Netex Learning is one of the companies active in the field of modern education. By visiting the company's website, people can receive a curriculum with the help of AI and find their strengths and weaknesses. The most interesting part is that they can receive audio and video files, which are made entirely by AI, according to their needs(Sethi et al., 2020).

## 2.2 AI Opportunities for Students

All students are more interested in some of the lessons. In some subjects, they score better and in others they are weak. In the traditional system, a single teaching method is used for all students. They are given similar assignments and all take the same exam. AI has solved this problem. In an AI-based education system, new education will be unique to each person and the student will be assessed before reading a book or entering the classroom. The strengths and weaknesses of each student are measured and the academic process is based on individual abilities. The smarter AI becomes, the more advanced the modern education system will be. In the not-too-distant future, the system may be able to assess students' conditions by scanning their faces. It is even possible for a student to change his or her teaching style completely if the student has a very difficult learning experience(Holmes et al., 2019). Fast feedback is one of the keys to successful training. AI can provide the conditions for students to receive answers from their teachers as soon as they ask a question. Some universities, for example, use a robot named Alexa for the day-to-day needs of the university. This robot can answer frequently asked questions of students. In addition, the use of such systems is very interesting and exciting for students and can motivate them to study(Ostrom et al., 2019).

## 2.3 AI Future Perspective in E-Learning

AI will help to remove borders in this area, and modern education will become a global thing. Technology increases the speed of knowledge transfer by facilitating new education and learning. In the future, the transfer of knowledge and learning around the world will accelerate dramatically. Artificial intelligence provides access to education for students with special needs: deaf and hard of hearing, visually impaired, people with special and severe diseases use artificial intelligence tools and teach them successfully (Valadão et al., 2011). Students always have access to learning with the help of online-based artificial intelligence. AI using IT technology can increase efficiency in many areas. The most important part of using artificial intelligence can be considered as helping humans to know their purpose. Students choose a job by realizing their purpose and talent. With the spread of COVID-19 pandemic and the holding of virtual education in all educational centers around the world, despite the educational concerns, the closer we get to the student exam season, the more we worry about holding the exam. But due to the restrictions, we had to use the online test. There are many virtual tools for conducting online exams, but artificial intelligence tools help to conduct online exams as well as possible to solve predictable problems during the exam.

## 2.4 Application of AI in Online Examinations

Artificial intelligence tools that can be used when taking an online test are: 1. Viewing pictures of students when taking an online test by the teacher. This tool makes it easy for the teacher and management to record students' performance and monitor their behavior during the test. 2. Using artificial intelligence (image vision) to identify students. 3. Use of students' position (GPS). With this tool, the teacher can observe the position of the students during the test, and if the students are holding the test in close positions, the system will notify the teacher of the status. 4. Use of response analysis. Using artificial intelligence, students with the same answer can be identified. 5. Use time tools in response. Even if the order of the questions in the online test is different, the AI detects which students are answering the same questions at the same time. 6. Analysis of answers for learning. Artificial intelligence helps the teacher to determine students 'understanding of the content according to the students' answers to the questions (hard/medium/easy). This tool helps the teacher to identify students' learning problems(Nigam et al., 2021).

## 2.5 Negative Aspects of Using AI in the Educational System

With all these details, the negative aspects of using robots in the educational system should not be overlooked. For example, a robot is not able to interact socially like a human. They cannot listen to students' social problems or solve their problems. This is especially true for first-year students, where the role of social and moral behaviors is more important than instruction(Marcinkowski et al., 2020). The main issue here is the stagnation or non-growth of Gross Domestic Product (GDP) at the expected unemployment rate. With such a situation, people do not acquire the skills in demand, and therefore we will see a deep gap between supply and demand(Wirtz et al., 2019).

# 3. CONCLUSION

The world is changing at an incredible rate, and different processes are using technology more and more every day. One of the applications of AI, which is still very effective today, is the simplification of tasks of employees and office automation. In the future, robots can, like a writer, produce articles or create conferences and instructional videos. The smarter AI becomes, the more advanced the new education system will be. AI provides a variety of possibilities for students with different physical problems. Because meta AI can be a great automation tool, the meta AI system can be used in a variety of deep learning projects. In addition, in this highly connected and super-intelligent society, the demand for data processing is increasing. With this acceleration, meta artificial intelligence will surely benefit many users in the near future. Finally, despite all the statistics and predictions, only time can show the real and amazing impact of artificial intelligence in education.

# REFERENCES


Arrieta, A. B. et al, 2020. Explainable Artificial Intelligence (XAI): Concepts, taxonomies, opportunities and challenges toward responsible AI. *Information fusion,* 58, 82-115.

Bengio, Y. et al, 2021. Machine learning for combinatorial optimization: a methodological tour d'horizon. *European Journal of Operational Research,* 290, 405-421.

Canhoto, A. I. & Clear, F. 2020. Artificial intelligence and machine learning as business tools: A framework for diagnosing value destruction potential. *Business Horizons,* 63, 183-193.

Dwivedi, Y. K. et al, 2021. Artificial Intelligence (AI): Multidisciplinary perspectives on emerging challenges, opportunities, and agenda for research, practice and policy. *International Journal of Information Management,* 57, 101994.

Holmes, W. et al, 2019. Artificial intelligence in education. *Boston: Center for Curriculum Redesign,* 2019, 1-35.

Marcinkowski, F. et al, 2020. Implications of AI (un-) fairness in higher education admissions: the effects of perceived AI (un-) fairness on exit, voice and organizational reputation. Proceedings of the 2020 conference on fairness, accountability, and transparency, 122-130.

Nigam, A. et al, 2021. A systematic review on ai-based proctoring systems: Past, present and future. *Education and Information Technologies,* 26, 6421-6445.

Ostrom, A. L. et al, 2019. Customer acceptance of AI in service encounters: understanding antecedents and consequences. *Handbook of Service Science, Volume II.* Springer.

Pappa, G. L. et al, 2014. Contrasting meta-learning and hyper-heuristic research: the role of evolutionary algorithms. *Genetic Programming and Evolvable Machines,* 15, 3-35.

Sethi, K. et al, 2020. Impact of social and cultural challenges in education using AI. *Revolutionizing Education in the Age of AI and Machine Learning.* IGI Global.

Valadão, C. et al, 2011.Educational robotics as a learning aid for disabled children. ISSNIP Biosignals and Biorobotics Conference 2011, IEEE, 1-6.

Wang, R. et al, 2020. Structured prediction for conditional meta-learning. *Advances in Neural Information Processing Systems,* 33, 2587-2598.

Wirtz, B. W. et al, 2019. Artificial intelligence and the public sector—applications and challenges. *International Journal of Public Administration,* 42, 596-615.